Contents

Summary

The federal budget deficit, which has fallen sharply during the past few years, is projected to hold steady relative to the size of the economy through 2018. Beyond that point, however, the gap between spending and revenues is projected to grow, further increasing federal debt relative to the size of the economy—which is already historically high.

Those projections by the Congressional Budget Office, based on the assumption that current laws governing taxes and spending will generally remain unchanged, are built upon the agency's economic forecast. According to that forecast, the economy will expand at a solid pace in 2015 and for the next few years—to the point that the gap between the nation's output and its potential (that is, maximum sustainable) output will be essentially eliminated by the end of 2017. As a result, the unemployment rate will fall a little further, and more people will be encouraged to enter or stay in the labor force. Beyond 2017, CBO projects, real (inflation-adjusted) gross domestic product (GDP) will grow at a rate that is notably less than the average growth during the 1980s and 1990s.

Rising Deficits After 2018 Are Projected to Gradually Boost Debt Relative to GDP

CBO estimates that the deficit for this fiscal year will amount to $468 billion, slightly less than the deficit in 2014 (see Summary Table 1). At 2.6 percent of GDP, this year's deficit is projected to be the smallest relative to the nation's output since 2007 but close to the 2.7 percent that deficits have averaged over the past 50 years.

Although the deficits in CBO's baseline projections remain roughly stable as a percentage of GDP through 2018, they rise after that. The deficit in 2025 is projected to be $1.1 trillion, or 4.0 percent of GDP, and cumulative deficits over the 2016–2025 period are projected to total $7.6 trillion. CBO expects that federal debt held by the public will amount to 74 percent of GDP at the end of this fiscal year—more than twice what it was at the end of 2007 and higher than in any year since 1950 (see Summary Figure 1). By 2025, in CBO's baseline projections, federal debt rises to nearly 79 percent of GDP.

Outlays

In CBO's projections, outlays rise from a little more than 20 percent of GDP this year (which is about what federal spending has averaged over the past 50 years) to a little more than 22 percent in 2025 (see Summary Figure 2 on page 4). Four key factors underlie that increase:

■ The retirement of the baby-boom generation,

■ The expansion of federal subsidies for health insurance,

■ Increasing health care costs per beneficiary, and

■ Rising interest rates on federal debt.

Consequently, under current law, spending will grow faster than the economy for Social Security; the major health care programs, including Medicare, Medicaid, and subsidies offered through insurance exchanges; and net interest costs. In contrast, mandatory spending other than that for Social Security and health care, as well as both defense and nondefense discretionary spending, will shrink relative to the size of the economy. By 2019, outlays in those three categories taken together will fall below the percentage of GDP they were from 1998 through 2001, when such spending was the lowest since at least 1940 (the earliest year for which comparable data have been reported).

Summary Table 1.

CBO's Baseline Budget Projections

	Actual, 2014	2015	2016	2017	2018	2019	2020	2021	2022	2023	2024	2025	Total 2016-2020	Total 2016-2025
						In Billions of Dollars								
Revenues	3,021	3,189	3,460	3,588	3,715	3,865	4,025	4,204	4,389	4,591	4,804	5,029	18,652	41,670
Outlays	3,504	3,656	3,926	4,076	4,255	4,517	4,765	5,018	5,337	5,544	5,754	6,117	21,540	49,310
Deficit	-483	-468	-467	-489	-540	-652	-739	-814	-948	-953	-951	-1,088	-2,887	-7,641
Debt Held by the Public at the End of the Year	12,779	13,359	13,905	14,466	15,068	15,782	16,580	17,451	18,453	19,458	20,463	21,605	n.a.	n.a.
					As a Percentage of Gross Domestic Product									
Revenues	17.5	17.7	18.4	18.2	18.1	18.1	18.0	18.1	18.1	18.2	18.2	18.3	18.1	18.2
Outlays	20.3	20.3	20.8	20.7	20.7	21.1	21.4	21.6	22.0	21.9	21.8	22.3	21.0	21.5
Deficit	-2.8	-2.6	-2.5	-2.5	-2.6	-3.0	-3.3	-3.5	-3.9	-3.8	-3.6	-4.0	-2.8	-3.3
Debt Held by the Public at the End of the Year	74.1	74.2	73.8	73.4	73.3	73.7	74.3	75.0	76.1	76.9	77.7	78.7	n.a.	n.a.

Source: Congressional Budget Office.

Note: GDP = gross domestic product; n.a. = not applicable.

Revenues

Revenues are projected to rise significantly by 2016, buoyed by the expiration of several provisions of law that reduced tax liabilities and by the ongoing economic expansion. In CBO's projections, based on current law, revenues equal about 18½ percent of GDP in 2016 and remain between 18 percent and 18½ percent through 2025. Revenues at that level would represent a greater share of the economy than their 50-year average of about 17½ percent of GDP but would still be less than outlays by growing amounts over the course of the decade. Revenues from the individual income tax are expected to rise relative to GDP—mostly because people's income will move into higher tax brackets as income gains outpace inflation, to which those brackets are indexed. But those increases are expected to be offset by reductions relative to GDP in revenues from the corporate income tax and other sources.

Changes From CBO's Previous Budget Projections

The deficit that CBO now estimates for 2015 is essentially the same as what the agency projected in August.[1] CBO's estimate of outlays this year has declined by $94 billion, or about 3 percent, from the August projection because of a number of developments, including higher-than-expected receipts from auctions of licenses to

use the electromagnetic spectrum for commercial purposes. But CBO's estimate of revenues has dropped almost as much—by $93 billion, also about 3 percent—mostly because of the enactment of legislation that retroactively extended a host of expired tax provisions through December 2014.

Over the 2015–2024 period, deficits are now projected to total about $175 billion less than CBO's August estimate for that period. The current projections of revenues and outlays for those years are both lower than previously estimated, outlays a little more so.

The Longer-Term Outlook

When CBO last issued long-term budget projections (in July 2014), it projected that, under current law, debt would exceed 100 percent of GDP 25 years from now and would continue on an upward trajectory thereafter—a trend that could not be sustained.[2] (The 10-year

1. See Congressional Budget Office, *An Update to the Budget and Economic Outlook: 2014 to 2024* (August 2014), www.cbo.gov/publication/45653.

2. See Congressional Budget Office, *The 2014 Long-Term Budget Outlook* (July 2014), www.cbo.gov/publication/45471.

Summary Figure 1.

Federal Debt Held by the Public

Percentage of Gross Domestic Product

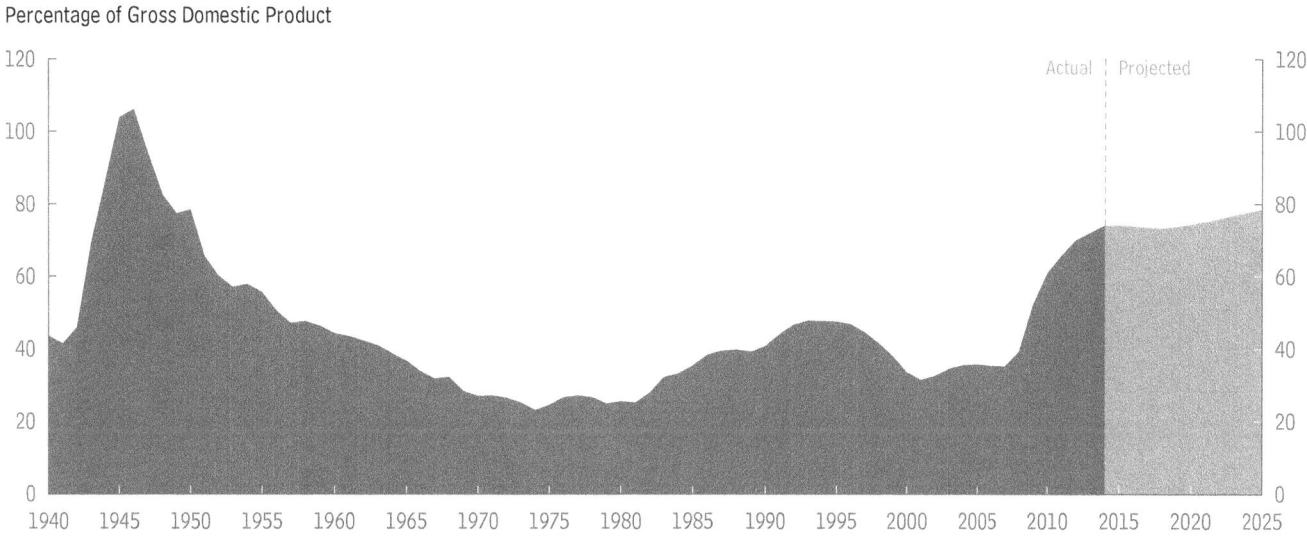

Source: Congressional Budget Office.

projections presented here do not materially change that outlook.)[3] Such large and growing federal debt would have serious negative consequences, including increasing federal spending for interest payments; restraining economic growth in the long term; giving policymakers less flexibility to respond to unexpected challenges; and eventually heightening the risk of a fiscal crisis.

The Economy Will Grow at a Solid Pace Over the Next Few Years

CBO anticipates that, under current law, economic activity will expand at a solid pace in 2015 and over the next few years—reducing the amount of underused resources, or "slack," in the economy.

Economic Growth Over the Next Few Years

In CBO's estimation, increases in consumer spending, business investment, and residential investment will drive the economic expansion this year and over the next few years. The growth in those categories of spending will derive mainly from increases in hourly compensation, rising wealth, the recent decline in crude oil prices, and a step-up in the rate of household formation (as people are more willing and able to set up new homes). As measured

3.   CBO's current projection of debt as a percentage of GDP in 2024 is quite close to that used as the starting point for the projections in *The 2014 Long-Term Budget Outlook*.

by the change from the fourth quarter of the previous year, real GDP will grow by about 3 percent in 2015 and 2016 and by 2½ percent in 2017, CBO expects (see Summary Figure 3).

The Degree of Slack in the Economy Over the Next Few Years

The difference between actual GDP and CBO's estimate of potential GDP—which is a measure of slack for the whole economy—was about 2 percent of potential GDP at the end of 2014. During the next few years, CBO expects, actual GDP will rise more rapidly than its potential, gradually eliminating that slack. For the labor market in particular, CBO anticipates that slack will dissipate by the end of 2017. By CBO's projections, increased hiring will reduce the unemployment rate from 5.7 percent in the fourth quarter of 2014 to 5.3 percent in the fourth quarter of 2017, which is close to the expected natural rate of unemployment (that is, the rate arising from all sources except fluctuations in the overall demand for goods and services). That increased hiring will also encourage more people to enter or stay in the labor force, boosting the labor force participation rate (which is the percentage of people who are working or actively looking for work).

Economic Growth in Later Years

The agency's projections beyond the next few years are not based on estimates of cyclical developments in the

Summary Figure 2.

Total Revenues and Outlays

Percentage of Gross Domestic Product

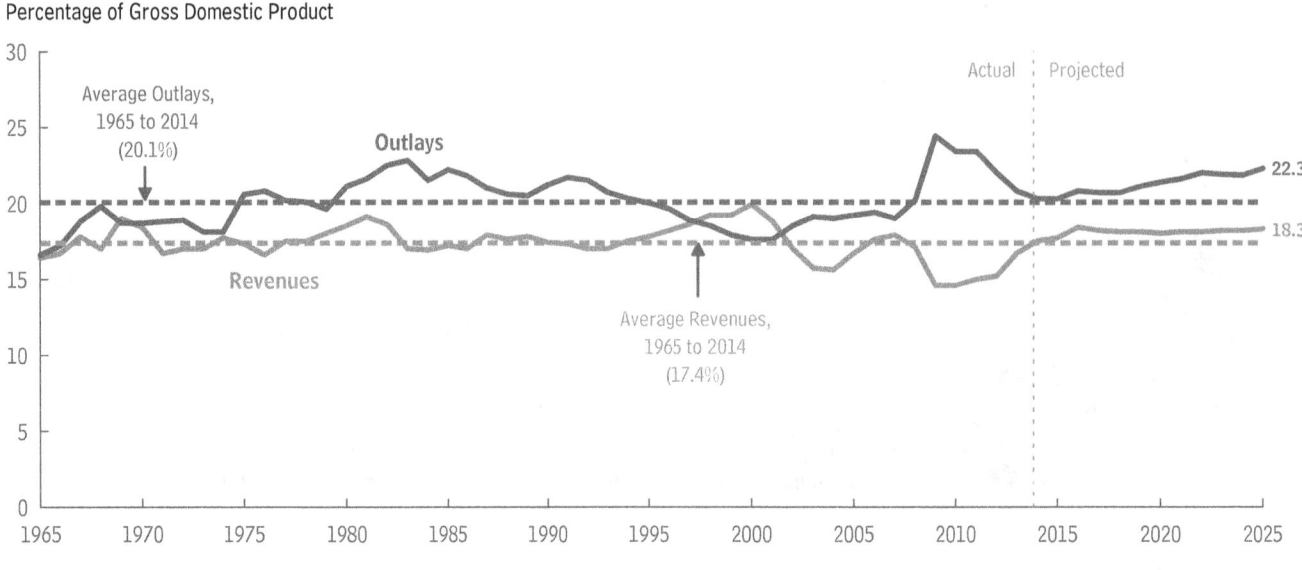

Source: Congressional Budget Office.

economy, because the agency does not attempt to predict economic fluctuations that far into the future; instead, those projections are based on estimates of underlying factors that affect the economy's productive capacity.

For 2020 through 2025, CBO projects that real GDP will grow by an average of 2.2 percent per year—a rate that matches the agency's estimate of the potential growth of the economy in those years. Potential output is expected to grow much more slowly than it did during the 1980s and 1990s primarily because the labor force is anticipated to expand more slowly than it did then. Growth in the potential labor force will be held down by the ongoing retirement of the baby boomers; by a relatively stable labor force participation rate among working-age women, after sharp increases from the 1960s to the mid-1990s; and by federal tax and spending policies set in current law.

Inflation and Interest Rates

The elimination of slack in the economy will eventually remove the downward pressure on the rate of inflation and on interest rates that has existed for the past several years. By CBO's estimates, the rate of inflation as measured by the price index for personal consumption

expenditures will move up gradually to the Federal Reserve's goal of 2 percent, hitting that mark in 2017 and beyond. Interest rates on Treasury securities, which have been exceptionally low since the recession, will rise considerably in the next few years, CBO expects, but remain lower than they were, on average, in previous decades. Between 2020 and 2025, the projected interest rates on 3-month Treasury bills and 10-year Treasury notes are 3.4 percent and 4.6 percent, respectively.

Changes From CBO's Previous Economic Projections

Last August, CBO projected real GDP growth averaging 2.7 percent per year for 2014 through 2018; CBO now anticipates that real GDP growth will average 2.5 percent annually over that period. The revision mainly reflects a reduction in CBO's estimate of potential output and therefore of the current amount of slack in the economy. On the basis of the current projection of potential output, CBO now forecasts that real GDP in 2024 will be roughly 1 percent lower than the level estimated in August. In addition, the sharper-than-anticipated drop in the unemployment rate in the second half of last year caused CBO to lower its projection of that rate for the next few years.

Summary Figure 3.

Actual Values and CBO's Projections of Key Economic Indicators

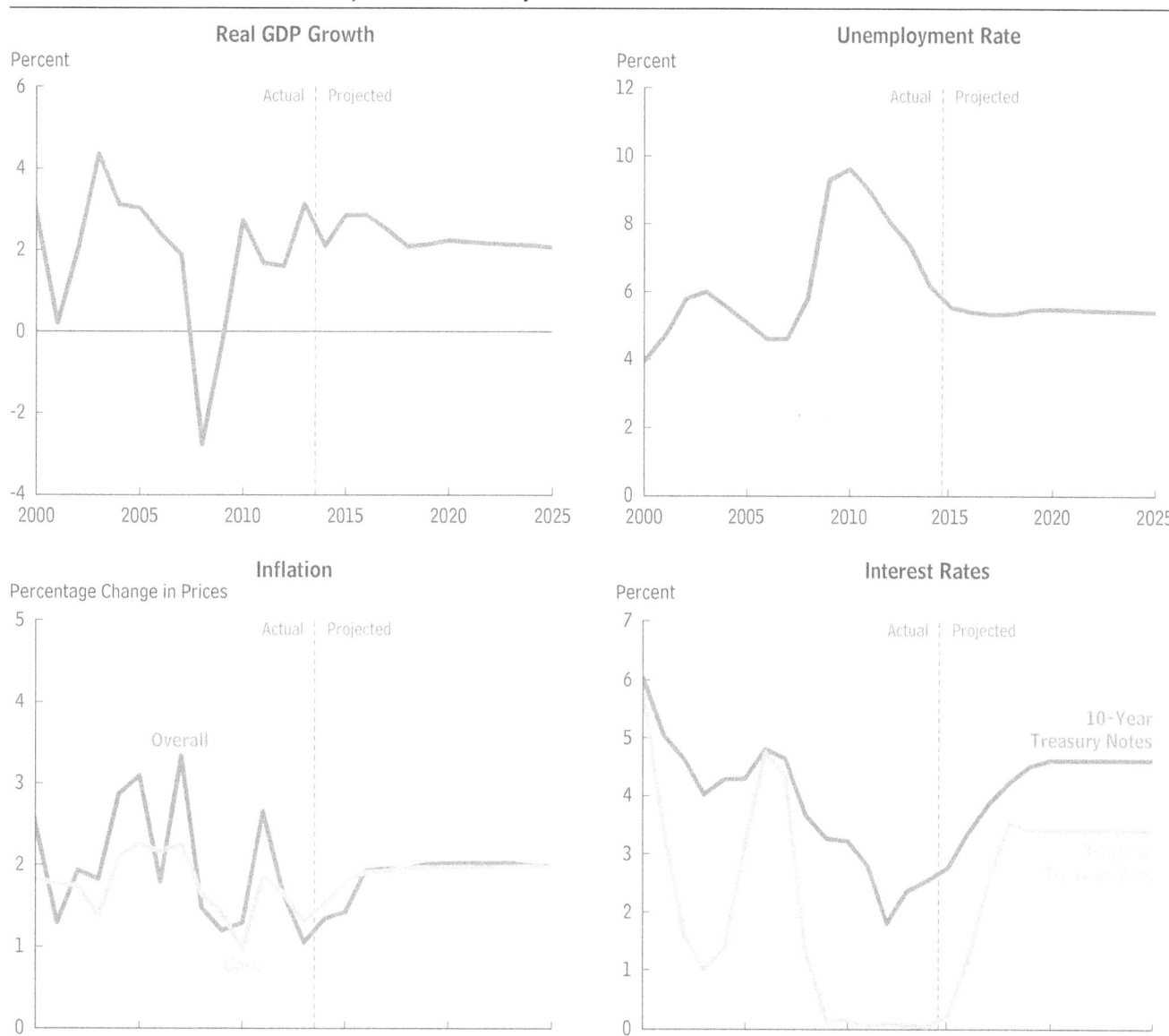

Sources: Congressional Budget Office; Bureau of Economic Analysis; Bureau of Labor Statistics; Federal Reserve.

Notes: Real gross domestic product is the output of the economy adjusted to remove the effects of inflation. The unemployment rate is a measure of the number of jobless people who are available for work and are actively seeking jobs, expressed as a percentage of the labor force. The overall inflation rate is based on the price index for personal consumption expenditures; the core rate excludes prices for food and energy.

Data are annual. For real GDP growth and inflation, actual data are plotted through 2013; the values for 2014 reflect CBO's estimates for the third and fourth quarters and do not incorporate data released by the Bureau of Economic Analysis since early December 2014. For the unemployment and interest rates, actual data are plotted through 2014.

For real GDP growth and inflation, percentage changes in GDP and prices are measured from the fourth quarter of one calendar year to the fourth quarter of the next.

GDP = gross domestic product.

The Budget Outlook

I f current laws remain in place, the federal budget deficit will total $468 billion in fiscal year 2015, the Congressional Budget Office estimates, slightly less than the deficit of $483 billion posted for fiscal year 2014. This will mark the sixth consecutive year in which the deficit—at 2.6 percent of gross domestic product (GDP)—has declined relative to the size of the economy since peaking at 9.8 percent in 2009 (see Figure 1-1). Nevertheless, debt held by the public will remain at 74 percent of GDP in 2015, CBO estimates, about the same as last year but higher than in any year between 1951 and 2013.

CBO constructs its 10-year baseline projections of federal revenues and spending under the assumption that current laws generally remain unchanged, following rules for those projections set in law.[1] That approach reflects the fact that CBO's baseline is not intended to be a forecast of budgetary outcomes; rather, it is meant to provide a neutral benchmark that policymakers can use to assess the potential effects of policy decisions.

Under that assumption:

■ Revenues as a share of GDP are projected to grow by two-thirds of one percentage point over the next year—from 17.7 percent in 2015 to 18.4 percent in 2016—and then remain near that level through 2025. The jump next year results primarily from the expiration of certain tax provisions that reduce tax liabilities; if all of those provisions were extended, as they have regularly been in recent years, the increase in revenues from 2015 to 2016 would be much smaller, and revenues throughout the projection period would be lower as a share of GDP.

■ Outlays as a share of GDP are projected to rise significantly more than revenues over the coming decade—by two percentage points, from 20.3 percent in 2015 to 22.3 percent in 2025. The increase in outlays reflects substantial growth in the cost of benefit programs that are targeted toward the elderly, related to health care, or both, as well as a sharp rise in payments of interest on the government's debt; those increases would more than offset a significant projected decline in discretionary spending relative to the size of the economy.

■ The projected deficit remains roughly stable as a percentage of GDP at about 2.5 percent through 2018 and then starts on an upward trajectory, growing from 3.0 percent of GDP in 2019 to 4.0 percent in 2025 (see Table 1-1). By the end of that period, CBO projects, annual deficits would be well above the average of 2.7 percent of GDP over the past 50 years.[2]

That pattern of initially stable deficits followed by higher deficits for the remainder of the projection period would cause debt held by the public to follow a similar trajectory. Relative to the nation's output, debt held by the

1. Section 257 of the Balanced Budget and Emergency Deficit Control Act of 1985 (the Deficit Control Act) specifies the rules for developing baseline projections.

2. In previous publications, CBO has generally cited a 40-year historical average for various categories of the federal budget. CBO has lengthened the period to cover the past 50 years in part because sufficient historical data are now available to allow for such calculations. (Data for certain categories of spending within the federal budget—such as for mandatory and discretionary outlays—are only available beginning in 1962.) In addition, the longer period captures years with both unusually high and unusually low values for most budget categories without giving excessive weight to any of those years. Using different historical periods would produce different averages, however. For example, the average deficit over the past 40 years was 3.2 percent of GDP, and the average for the 40 years ending in 2007—thus excluding the deficits recorded during the most recent recession and its aftermath—was noticeably lower at 2.3 percent of GDP.

Figure 1-1.

Total Deficits or Surpluses

As percentages of gross domestic product, projected deficits in CBO's baseline hold steady through 2018 but then grow as mandatory spending and interest payments rise and revenues remain essentially flat.

Percentage of Gross Domestic Product

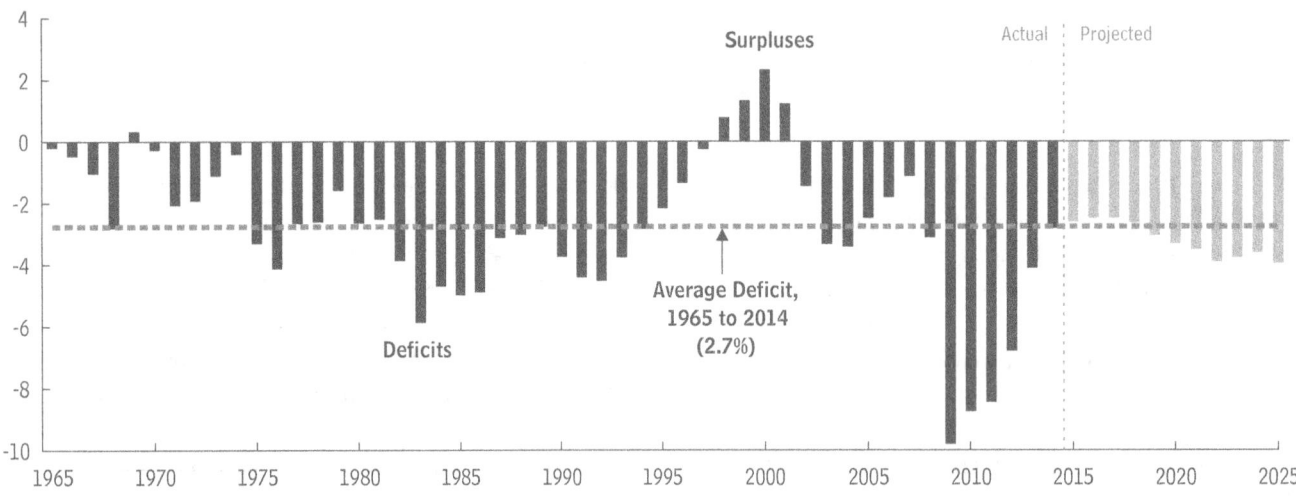

Source: Congressional Budget Office.

public is projected to be roughly constant between 2015 and 2020 but to rise thereafter, reaching 79 percent of GDP at the end of 2025.

Although federal debt relative to the size of the economy is projected to increase only modestly over the next decade, it is already high by historical standards: As recently as the end of 2007, debt held by the public was equal to just 35 percent of GDP, but by 2012 it had ballooned to 70 percent of GDP. Throughout the 10-year period that CBO's baseline projections span, federal debt remains greater relative to GDP than at any time since just after World War II. Such high and rising debt would have serious negative consequences for both the economy and the federal budget, including the following:

■ When interest rates rise to more typical levels, as CBO expects will happen in the next few years (see Chapter 2), federal spending on interest payments will increase considerably.

■ When the federal government borrows, it increases the overall demand for funds, which generally raises the cost of borrowing and reduces lending to businesses and other entities; the eventual result would be a smaller stock of capital and lower output and income than would otherwise be the case, all else being equal.

■ The large amount of debt might restrict policymakers' ability to use tax and spending policies to respond to unexpected future challenges, such as economic downturns or financial crises.

■ Continued growth in the debt might lead investors to doubt the government's willingness or ability to pay its obligations, which would require the government to pay much higher interest rates on its borrowing.[3]

Projected deficits and debt for the coming decade reflect some of the long-term budgetary challenges facing the nation. The aging of the population, the rising costs of health care, and the expansion in federal subsidies for health insurance that is now under way will substantially boost federal spending on Social Security and the government's major health care programs relative to GDP over the next 10 years. Moreover, the pressures of an aging population and rising costs of health care will continue to increase during the following decades. Unless the laws governing those programs are changed—or the increased spending is accompanied by corresponding reductions in

3. For a discussion of the consequences of elevated debt, see Congressional Budget Office, *Choices for Deficit Reduction: An Update* (December 2013), pp. 9–10, www.cbo.gov/publication/44967.

Table 1-1.

Deficits Projected in CBO's Baseline

Billions of Dollars

	Actual, 2014	2015	2016	2017	2018	2019	2020	2021	2022	2023	2024	2025	Total 2016-2020	Total 2016-2025
Revenues	3,021	3,189	3,460	3,588	3,715	3,865	4,025	4,204	4,389	4,591	4,804	5,029	18,652	41,670
Outlays	3,504	3,656	3,926	4,076	4,255	4,517	4,765	5,018	5,337	5,544	5,754	6,117	21,540	49,310
Total Deficit	**-483**	**-468**	**-467**	**-489**	**-540**	**-652**	**-739**	**-814**	**-948**	**-953**	**-951**	**-1,088**	**-2,887**	**-7,641**
Net Interest	229	227	276	332	410	480	548	606	664	722	777	827	2,046	5,643
Primary Deficit[a]	-254	-241	-191	-157	-130	-172	-191	-208	-283	-231	-173	-261	-841	-1,998
Memorandum (As a percentage of GDP):														
Total Deficit	-2.8	-2.6	-2.5	-2.5	-2.6	-3.0	-3.3	-3.5	-3.9	-3.8	-3.6	-4.0	-2.8	-3.3
Primary Deficit[a]	-1.5	-1.3	-1.0	-0.8	-0.6	-0.8	-0.9	-0.9	-1.2	-0.9	-0.7	-0.9	-0.8	-0.9
Debt Held by the Public at the End of the Year	74.1	74.2	73.8	73.4	73.3	73.7	74.3	75.0	76.1	76.9	77.7	78.7	n.a.	n.a.

Source: Congressional Budget Office.

Note: GDP = gross domestic product; n.a. = not applicable.

a.   Excludes net interest.

---

other spending relative to GDP, by sufficiently higher tax revenues, or by a combination of those changes—debt will rise sharply relative to GDP after 2025.[4]

In addition, holding discretionary spending within the limits required under current law—an assumption that underlies these projections—may be quite difficult. The caps on discretionary budget authority established by the Budget Control Act of 2011 (Public Law 112-25) and subsequently amended will reduce such spending to an unusually small amount relative to the size of the economy.[5] With those caps in place, CBO projects, discretionary spending will equal 5.1 percent of GDP in 2025; by comparison, the lowest share for discretionary spending in any year since 1962 (the earliest year for which such data have been reported) was 6.0 percent in 1999, and that share has averaged 8.8 percent over the past 50 years. (Nevertheless, total federal spending would constitute a

larger share of GDP than its average during the past 50 years because of higher spending on Social Security, Medicare, Medicaid, other health insurance subsidies for low-income people, and interest payments on the debt.) Because the allocation of discretionary spending is determined by annual appropriation acts, lawmakers have not yet decided which specific government services and benefits would be reduced or constrained to meet the overall limits.

The baseline budget outlook has changed little since August 2014, when CBO last published its 10-year projections.[6] At that time, deficits projected under current law totaled about 3 percent of GDP over the 2015–2024 period, or $7.2 trillion. In CBO's latest baseline, deficits are projected to be about $175 billion smaller over those 10 years but still total about 3 percent of GDP. The agency has reduced its projection of total revenues by 1.0 percent through 2024, but projected outlays have decreased by 1.2 percent. Revisions to the economic

---

4.   For a more detailed discussion of the long-term budget situation, see Congressional Budget Office, *The 2014 Long-Term Budget Outlook* (July 2014), www.cbo.gov/publication/45471.

5.   Budget authority is the authority provided by law to incur financial obligations that will result in immediate or future outlays of federal funds.

6.   For CBO's previous baseline budget projections, see Congressional Budget Office, *An Update to the Budget and Economic Outlook: 2014 to 2024* (August 2014), www.cbo.gov/publication/45653.

outlook account for roughly half of the change in both categories.

Although CBO's baseline does not incorporate potential changes in law, this chapter shows how some alternative policies would affect the budget over the next 10 years. For example, CBO has constructed a policy alternative under which funding for overseas contingency operations—that is, military operations and related activities in Afghanistan and other countries—would continue to decline through 2019 and then grow at the rate of inflation through 2025. Under that alternative, spending for such operations over the 2016–2025 period would be about $450 billion less than the amount projected in the baseline (which incorporates the assumption that funding grows at the rate of inflation throughout the projection period). Other alternative policies would result in larger deficits than those in the baseline. For example, continuing certain tax policies that were recently extended through 2014 but have since expired would lower revenues by about $900 billion over the 2016–2025 period. (For more details, see "Alternative Assumptions About Fiscal Policy" on page 23.)

A Review of 2014

In fiscal year 2014, the budget deficit dropped once again, to $483 billion—nearly 30 percent less than the $680 billion shortfall recorded in 2013. Revenues rose by $246 billion (or 9 percent) and outlays increased by $50 billion (or 1 percent). As a percentage of GDP, the deficit dropped from 4.1 percent in 2013 to 2.8 percent in 2014.

Revenues

Receipts from each of the major revenue sources—individual income taxes, payroll taxes, and corporate income taxes—and remittances from the Federal Reserve all rose relative to the size of the economy in 2014. Total revenues increased from 16.7 percent of GDP in 2013 to 17.5 percent in 2014, close to the average for the past 50 years of 17.4 percent.[7]

Individual income taxes, the largest revenue source, rose by $78 billion (or 6 percent), from 7.9 percent of GDP in 2013 to 8.1 percent in 2014. That percentage of GDP

is the highest since 2007 and is larger than the percentage recorded in any other year since 2001. The increase in receipts largely reflected gains in both 2013 and 2014 in wages and salaries as well as in nonwage income. The gains in wages also boosted payroll taxes, the second largest revenue source, which increased by $76 billion (or 8 percent), from 5.7 percent of GDP to 5.9 percent. Part of that increase occurred because the rate for employees' share of the Social Security payroll tax that was in effect during the first quarter of fiscal year 2014—that is, October 2013 through December 2013—was higher than that in effect during the same period the year before, following the expiration of the 2 percentage-point cut in that rate at the end of calendar year 2012.

Revenues from corporate income taxes and remittances from the Federal Reserve also rose relative to GDP. Corporate tax receipts increased by $47 billion (or 17 percent) in 2014, from 1.6 percent of GDP to 1.9 percent, reflecting growth in taxable profits. Remittances to the Treasury from the Federal Reserve rose by $23 billion (or 31 percent), from 0.5 percent of GDP to 0.6 percent, mostly because the central bank's portfolio of securities was larger and the yield on that portfolio was higher. Those remittances are the largest ever, both in dollars and as a share of GDP.

Outlays

After declining over the preceding two years, federal spending rose in 2014—by $50 billion—to $3.5 trillion. Nevertheless, at 20.3 percent of GDP, outlays were lower as a share of the nation's output than in any year since 2008. By comparison, outlays have averaged 20.1 percent of GDP over the past 50 years.[8]

Mandatory Spending. After remaining largely unchanged over the previous three years, outlays for mandatory programs (which include spending for benefit programs and certain other payments to people, businesses, nonprofit institutions, and state and local governments) rose by $65 billion (or 3.2 percent) in 2014. By comparison, mandatory outlays grew at an average annual rate of 5.6 percent during the preceding decade (between 2003 and 2013).

Major Health Care Programs. Federal spending for the major health care programs—Medicare (net of receipts

---

7. Looking at different historical periods, total revenues averaged 17.3 percent of GDP over the past 40 years and 17.7 percent over the 40 years ending in 2007.

8. Total outlays averaged 20.5 percent of GDP over the past 40 years and 19.9 percent over the 40 years ending in 2007.

from premiums and certain payments from states), Medicaid, the Children's Health Insurance Program, and subsidies offered through health insurance exchanges and related spending—equaled $831 billion in 2014, $63 billion (or 8.3 percent) more than the total for such spending in 2013. The largest increase was for Medicaid outlays, which grew by $36 billion (or 13.6 percent) last year, mostly because a little more than half the states expanded eligibility for Medicaid coverage under the provisions of the Affordable Care Act (ACA).[9] Similarly, subsidies for health insurance purchased through the exchanges that were established by the ACA first became available in January 2014. Outlays for those subsidies, along with related spending, totaled $15 billion last year; in 2013, related spending was only $1 billion (primarily for grants to states to establish exchanges).

In contrast, Medicare outlays continued to grow at a modest rate in 2014. In total, outlays for that program rose by $14 billion (or 2.8 percent) last year, slightly higher than the rate of growth in 2013 (after adjusting for a shift in the timing of certain payments) and less than the rate of growth in the number of Medicare beneficiaries. Over the past four years, Medicare spending has grown at an average annual rate of only 3.1 percent, compared with average annual growth of 3.6 percent in the number of beneficiaries.

Outlays for the Children's Health Insurance Program totaled $9 billion in both 2013 and 2014.

Social Security. Outlays for Social Security totaled $845 billion in 2014, $37 billion (or 4.6 percent) more than payments in 2013. Beneficiaries received a 1.5 percent cost-of-living adjustment in January (which applied to three-quarters of the fiscal year); the increase in the previous year was 1.7 percent. In addition, the number of people receiving benefits grew by 2.0 percent.

Fannie Mae and Freddie Mac. Payments to the Treasury from Fannie Mae and Freddie Mac dropped from $97 billion in 2013 to $74 billion in 2014. That reduction was primarily the result of differences in the timing and magnitude of revaluations of certain tax assets held by each entity. Those reassessments boosted the net worth of both entities and increased the size of the payments to the Treasury from Fannie Mae and

Freddie Mac. Fannie Mae's revaluation increased its fiscal 2013 payment to Treasury by about $50 billion; Freddie Mac's revaluation boosted its fiscal 2014 payment by about half that amount. Such payments are recorded as reductions in outlays.

Higher Education. Mandatory outlays for higher education include the net (negative) subsidies for direct student loans issued in the current year, revisions to the subsidy costs of loans made in previous years, and mandatory spending for the Federal Pell Grant Program. Last year, the Treasury recorded outlays of –$12 billion for those higher education programs, compared with outlays of -$26 billion recorded in 2013—thereby accounting for a net increase in outlays of $14 billion. Most of that net increase occurred because in 2014 there was a small upward revision to the subsidy costs of loans made in previous years while in 2013 there was a large downward revision.

Outlays were negative for direct student loans because, over the life of the loans made in 2014, the expected amounts received by the government are greater than the expected payments by the government, as measured on a discounted present-value basis—pursuant to the Federal Credit Reform Act.[10] In particular, the interest rates charged to borrowers of student loans are well above the interest rates the federal government pays to borrow money; therefore, even after accounting for anticipated loan defaults, the federal government is expected to receive more (on a present-value basis) in loan repayments and interest than it disburses for such loans.

Federal Housing Administration's Loan Guarantee Programs. In 2013, the Department of Housing and Urban Development recorded mandatory outlays of nearly $33 billion related to the Federal Housing Administration's loan guarantee programs. That outlay total for 2013 mostly reflects the revisions to the estimated costs

---

9. See Appendix B for more information about the provisions of the ACA that affect health insurance coverage.

10. Under that act, a program's subsidy costs are calculated by subtracting the discounted present value of the government's projected receipts from the discounted present value of its projected payments. The estimated subsidy costs can be increased or decreased in subsequent years to reflect updated assessments of the payments and receipts associated with the program. Present value is a single number that expresses a flow of current and future income (or payments) in terms of an equivalent lump sum received (or paid) today. The present value depends on the rate of interest (the discount rate) that is used to translate future cash flows into current dollars.

of guarantees provided in previous years. (Such revisions in the estimated costs of prior loan guarantees are recorded each year.) In 2014, the department recorded a much smaller increase in such costs, only $0.7 billion—a year-over-year reduction in mandatory outlays of $32 billion.

Unemployment Compensation. Spending for unemployment compensation dropped for the fourth consecutive year in 2014. The authority to pay emergency benefits expired at the end of December 2013, and the number of people receiving first-time payments of regular unemployment benefits fell to 7.2 million from 8.1 million the year before. As a result, outlays for unemployment compensation dropped by $25 billion last year, to $44 billion, equal to the program's spending in 2008.

Deposit Insurance. In 2014, the premium payments that insured financial institutions made to the Federal Deposit Insurance Corporation (FDIC) throughout the year exceeded the FDIC's spending by $14 billion (thereby reducing the government's net outlays by that amount). In contrast, net outlays for deposit insurance in 2013 totaled a positive $4 billion, in part because financial institutions prepaid in 2010 the premiums that would otherwise have been due during the first half of 2013. In addition, some excess premiums that had previously been paid by certain institutions were refunded in 2013; no such refunds were paid in 2014. As a result, net outlays for deposit insurance decreased by $18 billion in 2014.

Discretionary Spending. Discretionary outlays fell by $23 billion (or 2.0 percent) in 2014—the fourth consecutive year that such outlays have declined. Defense outlays dropped by $30 billion (or 4.8 percent), marking the third consecutive year of decline after increasing at an average annual rate of 6 percent over the previous five years. Spending was down across all major categories, and about 80 percent of the overall decline was attributable to reduced spending by the Army. Measured as a share of GDP, outlays for defense were 3.5 percent in 2014, down from 3.8 percent in 2013.

In contrast, nondefense discretionary outlays rose for the first time since 2010, increasing by $7 billion (or 1.1 percent) last year. A $7 billion decrease in the receipts credited to the Federal Housing Administration boosted net discretionary outlays by that amount. Spending for Pell grants and campus-based aid was also $7 billion higher than in the previous year. In the other direction, spending

from funds provided in the American Recovery and Reinvestment Act of 2009 (ARRA, P.L. 111-5) dropped by $8 billion in 2014. (By the end of 2014, roughly 95 percent of the discretionary funding provided by ARRA had been spent.)

Net Interest. Outlays for the budget category "net interest" consist of interest paid on Treasury securities and other interest that the government pays minus the interest that it collects from various sources. Such outlays rose from $221 billion in 2013 to $229 billion in 2014, an increase of nearly 4 percent. Because interest rates over the past few years have been very low by historical standards, those amounts are similar to the net interest outlays 15 to 20 years ago, when the government's debt was much smaller.

The Budget Outlook for 2015

If there are no changes in laws governing taxes and spending, the budget deficit will decline by $16 billion in fiscal year 2015, to $468 billion, CBO estimates (see Table 1-2). At 2.6 percent of GDP, this year's deficit will be close to the average recorded over the past 50 years.

Revenues

CBO projects that if current laws remain unchanged, revenues will increase by $168 billion (or 5.6 percent) in 2015, reaching $3.2 trillion. As a share of GDP, revenues are projected to edge up from 17.5 percent in 2014 to 17.7 percent in 2015, a little above the average recorded over the past 50 years.

The anticipated increase in revenues as a percentage of GDP in 2015 stems primarily from an expected increase in individual income tax receipts—to 8.3 percent of GDP, from 8.1 percent in 2014. That rise largely reflects two factors: an increase in average tax rates (total taxes as a percentage of total income) as economic growth increases people's income faster than the inflation-indexed tax brackets grow (the phenomenon called real bracket creep) and growth in distributions from tax-deferred retirement accounts, whose balances have been boosted in the past few years by strong stock market gains.

A number of provisions that reduce tax liabilities expired at the end of 2014, a development that would ordinarily increase corporate and individual income tax payments starting this year. But those provisions had previously

Table 1-2.

CBO's Baseline Budget Projections

	Actual, 2014	2015	2016	2017	2018	2019	2020	2021	2022	2023	2024	2025	Total 2016-2020	Total 2016-2025
						In Billions of Dollars								
Revenues														
Individual income taxes	1,395	1,503	1,644	1,746	1,832	1,919	2,017	2,124	2,235	2,352	2,477	2,606	9,158	20,952
Payroll taxes	1,024	1,056	1,095	1,136	1,179	1,227	1,281	1,337	1,391	1,449	1,508	1,573	5,917	13,175
Corporate income taxes	321	328	429	437	453	450	447	450	459	472	488	506	2,216	4,591
Other	282	302	292	269	251	269	280	293	305	318	330	345	1,361	2,952
Total	**3,021**	**3,189**	**3,460**	**3,588**	**3,715**	**3,865**	**4,025**	**4,204**	**4,389**	**4,591**	**4,804**	**5,029**	**18,652**	**41,670**
On-budget	2,285	2,426	2,667	2,763	2,858	2,974	3,099	3,242	3,389	3,550	3,722	3,906	14,362	32,171
Off-budget[a]	736	763	793	824	857	891	926	962	1,001	1,040	1,081	1,124	4,291	9,499
Outlays														
Mandatory	2,096	2,255	2,475	2,563	2,653	2,816	2,968	3,137	3,363	3,486	3,616	3,891	13,474	30,967
Discretionary	1,179	1,175	1,176	1,182	1,193	1,221	1,248	1,276	1,310	1,336	1,361	1,400	6,019	12,701
Net interest	229	227	276	332	410	480	548	606	664	722	777	827	2,046	5,643
Total	**3,504**	**3,656**	**3,926**	**4,076**	**4,255**	**4,517**	**4,765**	**5,018**	**5,337**	**5,544**	**5,754**	**6,117**	**21,540**	**49,310**
On-budget	2,798	2,914	3,143	3,244	3,366	3,570	3,752	3,938	4,185	4,314	4,441	4,715	17,075	38,667
Off-budget[a]	706	742	784	832	889	948	1,012	1,080	1,152	1,230	1,313	1,402	4,465	10,643
Deficit (-) or Surplus	**-483**	**-468**	**-467**	**-489**	**-540**	**-652**	**-739**	**-814**	**-948**	**-953**	**-951**	**-1,088**	**-2,887**	**-7,641**
On-budget	-513	-489	-476	-481	-508	-595	-653	-696	-796	-764	-719	-809	-2,713	-6,496
Off-budget[a]	30	21	9	-8	-32	-57	-87	-118	-152	-190	-232	-279	-174	-1,144
Debt Held by the Public	12,779	13,359	13,905	14,466	15,068	15,782	16,580	17,451	18,453	19,458	20,463	21,605	n.a.	n.a.
Memorandum:														
Gross Domestic Product	17,251	18,016	18,832	19,701	20,558	21,404	22,315	23,271	24,261	25,287	26,352	27,456	102,810	229,438
					As a Percentage of Gross Domestic Product									
Revenues														
Individual income taxes	8.1	8.3	8.7	8.9	8.9	9.0	9.0	9.1	9.2	9.3	9.4	9.5	8.9	9.1
Payroll taxes	5.9	5.9	5.8	5.8	5.7	5.7	5.7	5.7	5.7	5.7	5.7	5.7	5.8	5.7
Corporate income taxes	1.9	1.8	2.3	2.2	2.2	2.1	2.0	1.9	1.9	1.9	1.9	1.8	2.2	2.0
Other	1.6	1.7	1.5	1.4	1.2	1.3	1.3	1.3	1.3	1.3	1.3	1.3	1.3	1.3
Total	**17.5**	**17.7**	**18.4**	**18.2**	**18.1**	**18.1**	**18.0**	**18.1**	**18.1**	**18.2**	**18.2**	**18.3**	**18.1**	**18.2**
On-budget	13.2	13.5	14.2	14.0	13.9	13.9	13.9	13.9	14.0	14.0	14.1	14.2	14.0	14.0
Off-budget[a]	4.3	4.2	4.2	4.2	4.2	4.2	4.1	4.1	4.1	4.1	4.1	4.1	4.2	4.1
Outlays														
Mandatory	12.2	12.5	13.1	13.0	12.9	13.2	13.3	13.5	13.9	13.8	13.7	14.2	13.1	13.5
Discretionary	6.8	6.5	6.2	6.0	5.8	5.7	5.6	5.5	5.4	5.3	5.2	5.1	5.9	5.5
Net interest	1.3	1.3	1.5	1.7	2.0	2.2	2.5	2.6	2.7	2.9	3.0	3.0	2.0	2.5
Total	**20.3**	**20.3**	**20.8**	**20.7**	**20.7**	**21.1**	**21.4**	**21.6**	**22.0**	**21.9**	**21.8**	**22.3**	**21.0**	**21.5**
On-budget	16.2	16.2	16.7	16.5	16.4	16.7	16.8	16.9	17.2	17.1	16.9	17.2	16.6	16.9
Off-budget[a]	4.1	4.1	4.2	4.2	4.3	4.4	4.5	4.6	4.8	4.9	5.0	5.1	4.3	4.6
Deficit (-) or Surplus	**-2.8**	**-2.6**	**-2.5**	**-2.5**	**-2.6**	**-3.0**	**-3.3**	**-3.5**	**-3.9**	**-3.8**	**-3.6**	**-4.0**	**-2.8**	**-3.3**
On-budget	-3.0	-2.7	-2.5	-2.4	-2.5	-2.8	-2.9	-3.0	-3.3	-3.0	-2.7	-2.9	-2.6	-2.8
Off-budget[a]	0.2	0.1	*	*	-0.2	-0.3	-0.4	-0.5	-0.6	-0.8	-0.9	-1.0	-0.2	-0.5
Debt Held by the Public	74.1	74.2	73.8	73.4	73.3	73.7	74.3	75.0	76.1	76.9	77.7	78.7	n.a.	n.a.

Source: Congressional Budget Office.

Note: n.a. = not applicable; * = between -0.05 and 0.05 percent.

a.   The revenues and outlays of the Social Security trust funds and the net cash flow of the Postal Service are classified as off-budget.

been set to expire at the end of 2013 and were retro-actively extended for a year by the Tax Increase Prevention Act of 2014 (Division A of P.L. 113-295), which was enacted in December 2014. Because that extension occurred so late in the year, some corporate and, to a much lesser extent, individual taxpayers probably made tax payments in 2014 that will be refunded this year when they file tax returns.

Outlays

In the absence of changes to laws governing federal spending, outlays in 2015 will total $3.7 trillion, CBO estimates, $152 billion more than spending in 2014. That rise would represent an increase of 4.3 percent, about half a percentage point less than the average rate of growth experienced between 2003 and 2013. Outlays are projected to total 20.3 percent of GDP this year, the same percentage as in 2014.

Mandatory Spending. Under current law, spending for mandatory programs will rise by $158 billion (or 7.6 percent) in 2015, CBO estimates, amounting to 12.5 percent of GDP, up from the 12.2 percent recorded in 2014.

Major Health Care Programs. Outlays for the federal government's major health care programs will increase by $82 billion (or nearly 10 percent) this year, CBO estimates. Medicaid spending is expected to continue its recent trend of strong growth, primarily because of the optional expansion of coverage authorized by the ACA. CBO expects that more people in states that have already expanded Medicaid eligibility under the ACA will enroll in the program and that more states will expand Medicaid eligibility. All told, CBO projects that, under current law, enrollment in the program will increase by about 4 percent and outlays will climb by $34 billion (or about 11 percent) in 2015; the projected rate of growth in outlays is less than the 14 percent increase recorded in 2014 but well above the 6 percent rate of growth experienced in 2013.

Similarly, subsidies that help people who meet income and other eligibility criteria purchase health insurance through exchanges and meet their cost-sharing requirements, along with related spending, are expected to increase by $30 billion this year, reaching a total of $45 billion (see Appendix B). That growth largely reflects a significant increase in the number of people expected to purchase coverage through exchanges in 2015 and the

fact that subsidies for that coverage will be available for the entire fiscal year in 2015. (Last year the subsidies did not become available until January 2014.)

CBO estimates that Medicare's outlays will continue to grow slowly in 2015 under current law, increasing by $17 billion (or 3.4 percent). The projected growth rate is a little higher than last year's rate but about half the average annual increase of roughly 7 percent experienced between 2003 and 2013. That projection of spending for Medicare reflects the assumption that the fees that physicians receive for their services will be reduced by about 21 percent in April 2015 as required under current law. If lawmakers override those scheduled reductions—as they have routinely done in the past—and keep physician fees at their current levels instead, spending on Medicare in 2015 will be $6 billion more than the amount projected in CBO's baseline.

Fannie Mae and Freddie Mac. Transactions between the Treasury and Fannie Mae and Freddie Mac will again reduce federal outlays in 2015, CBO estimates, but by nearly $50 billion less than in 2014. The payments from those entities to the Treasury are projected to total $26 billion this year, compared with $74 billion last year. That drop is partly because Freddie Mac's payments were boosted by nearly $24 billion in fiscal year 2014 as a result of a onetime revaluation of certain tax assets. In addition, financial institutions are expected to make fewer payments to Fannie Mae and Freddie Mac in 2015 to settle allegations of fraud in connection with residential mortgages as well as certain other securities.

Social Security. CBO anticipates that, under current law, Social Security outlays will increase by $38 billion (or 4.5 percent) in 2015, a rate of increase similar to last year's growth. This January's cost-of-living adjustment was slightly higher (1.7 percent) than the increase in January 2014, whereas the projected growth in the number of beneficiaries (1.9 percent) is slightly lower.

Receipts From Spectrum Auctions. Under current law, the Federal Communications Commission (FCC) intermittently auctions licenses to use the electromagnetic spectrum for commercial purposes. CBO estimates that net offsetting receipts from such auctions will total $41 billion in 2015, compared with $1 billion for licenses auctioned last year. In 2014, the FCC auctioned a set of licenses that were primarily of value to a single firm. By contrast, the licenses auctioned in fiscal year

2015 covered more bandwidth and had more desirable characteristics than those offered in 2014, which spurred intense competition among several large telecommunications firms, driving up receipts to the government.

Discretionary Spending. Discretionary budget authority enacted for 2015 totals $1,120 billion, which is $13 billion (or 1 percent) less than such funding totaled in 2014. Although the limits set for budget authority for defense by the Bipartisan Budget Act of 2013 (P.L. 113-67) were about the same in 2015 as they were in 2014, overall funding for defense declined by $20 billion (or 3.3 percent) this year because of a reduction in appropriations for overseas contingency operations, which are not constrained by those caps. Funding for nondefense discretionary programs is $8 billion (or 1.5 percent) higher than in 2014.

If no additional appropriations are enacted for this year, discretionary outlays will fall by $4 billion (or 0.3 percent) from the 2014 amounts, CBO projects. Defense outlays will again decline in 2015, largely because spending for overseas contingency operations will drop. All told, defense spending is expected to fall by $13 billion (or 2.2 percent), about half the rate of decrease recorded in 2014. The largest reductions are for procurement, operation and maintenance, and personnel; outlays for each category are expected to decline by $4 billion. As a result, defense outlays will total $583 billion in 2015, CBO estimates.

Outlays for nondefense programs are expected to rise by $9 billion (or 1.5 percent) this year, to a total of $592 billion. That amount is the net result of a number of relatively small increases and decreases to various programs.

Net Interest. Outlays for net interest will be nearly unchanged in 2015, falling by $3 billion (or 1 percent), to $227 billion, CBO estimates, primarily because Treasury interest rates remain very low. At 1.3 percent of GDP, such outlays would be well below their 50-year average of 2.0 percent.

CBO's Baseline Budget Projections for 2016 to 2025

CBO constructs its baseline in accordance with provisions set forth in the Balanced Budget and Emergency Deficit Control Act of 1985 and the Congressional Budget and Impoundment Control Act of 1974. For the

most part, those laws require that the agency's baseline projections incorporate the assumption that current laws governing taxes and spending in future years remain in place.

Under that assumption, CBO projects that the budget deficit would remain near 2.5 percent of GDP through 2018. But beginning in 2019, the deficit is projected to increase in most years, both in dollar terms and as a share of the economy, reaching 4.0 percent of GDP by 2025.

The pattern of stable deficits over the next several years followed by generally rising deficits through 2025 is the result, in part, of shifts in the timing of certain payments from one fiscal year to another because scheduled payment dates will fall on a weekend; without those shifts, the deficit would reach a low of 2.3 percent of GDP in 2016 and then increase throughout the rest of the projection period.[11]

Revenues
If current laws remain unchanged, revenues are estimated to increase by 8.5 percent in 2016—in part because various tax provisions that had expired at the end of 2013 were recently extended through 2014 and have subsequently expired again (see Chapter 4 for more details on those changes). As a result, revenues are anticipated to rise to 18.4 percent of GDP in 2016, an increase of 0.7 percentage points.

From 2017 through 2025, revenues in CBO's baseline remain between 18.0 and 18.3 percent of GDP, largely reflecting offsetting movements in individual and corporate income taxes and remittances from the Federal Reserve. Individual income taxes are projected to generate increasing revenues relative to the size of the economy, growing from 8.7 percent of GDP in 2016 to 9.5 percent in 2025. The increase stems mostly from real bracket creep, a phenomenon in which growth in real, or inflation-adjusted, income of individuals pushes more income into higher tax brackets. In addition, taxable distributions from tax-deferred retirement accounts are expected to grow more rapidly than GDP as the population ages in coming years. Labor income is also projected to grow

---

11. Because October 1 will fall on a weekend in 2016, 2017, 2022, and 2023, certain payments that are due on those days will instead be made at the end of September, thus shifting them into the previous fiscal year.

Figure 1-2.

Spending and Revenues Projected in CBO's Baseline, Compared With Levels in 1965 and 1990

Percentage of Gross Domestic Product

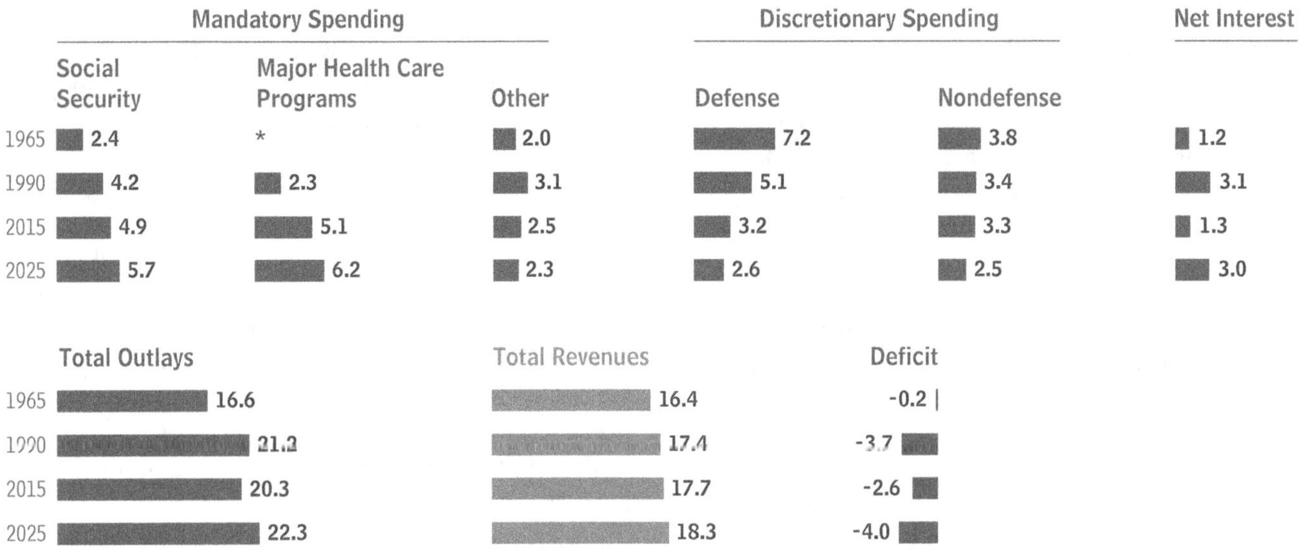

	Mandatory Spending			Discretionary Spending		Net Interest
	Social Security	Major Health Care Programs	Other	Defense	Nondefense	
1965	2.4	*	2.0	7.2	3.8	1.2
1990	4.2	2.3	3.1	5.1	3.4	3.1
2015	4.9	5.1	2.5	3.2	3.3	1.3
2025	5.7	6.2	2.3	2.6	2.5	3.0

	Total Outlays	Total Revenues	Deficit
1965	16.6	16.4	-0.2
1990	21.2	17.4	-3.7
2015	20.3	17.7	-2.6
2025	22.3	18.3	-4.0

Source: Congressional Budget Office.

Notes: Major health care programs consist of Medicare, Medicaid, the Children's Health Insurance Program, and subsidies for health insurance purchased through exchanges and related spending. (Medicare spending is net of premiums paid by beneficiaries and other offsetting receipts.)

  * = between zero and 0.05 percent.

faster than GDP over this period, further boosting income tax collections.

In contrast, corporate income tax receipts and remittances from the Federal Reserve are projected to decline relative to the size of the economy after this year or next. Corporate income tax receipts are projected to decline as a share of GDP after 2016 largely because of an anticipated drop in domestic economic profits relative to GDP, the result of growing labor costs and rising interest payments on businesses' debt. Remittances from the Federal Reserve, which have been very high by historical standards since 2010 because of changes in the size and composition of the central bank's portfolio of securities, decline to more typical levels in CBO's projections starting in 2016.

Outlays

Outlays in CBO's baseline grow to nearly 21 percent of GDP in 2016, remain roughly steady as a share of GDP through 2018, and then follow an upward trend, reaching 22.3 percent of GDP by 2025.[12] Although the 10-year baseline projections do not fully reflect the

long-term budgetary pressures facing the United States, those pressures are evident in the path of federal outlays over the next decade. Because of the aging of the population, rising health care costs, and a significant expansion in eligibility for federal subsidies for health insurance, outlays for Social Security and the federal government's major health care programs are projected to rise substantially relative to the size of the economy over the next 10 years (see Figure 1-2). In addition, growing debt and rising interest rates will boost net interest payments. Specifically, in CBO's baseline:

■ Outlays for Social Security are projected to remain at 4.9 percent of GDP in 2016 and 2017 but then climb to 5.7 percent of GDP by 2025.

■ Outlays for the major health care programs— Medicare (net of receipts from premiums and certain payments from states), Medicaid, the Children's

---

12. Without the shifts in the timing of certain payments, outlays would increase relative to GDP in each year of the projection period, CBO estimates.

Health Insurance Program, and subsidies offered through health insurance exchanges and related spending—soon exceed outlays for Social Security. Spending for those programs is estimated to total 5.3 percent of GDP in 2016 and to grow rapidly in coming years, reaching 6.2 percent of GDP in 2025.

■ Net interest equals 1.5 percent of GDP in 2016, but rising interest rates and mounting debt cause that total to double as a percentage of GDP by 2025.

Those three components of the budget account for nearly 85 percent of the total increase in outlays (in nominal terms) over the coming decade (see Figure 1-3). By the end of the projection period, they would be the largest categories of spending in the budget.

In contrast, under current law, all other spending will decrease from 9.2 percent of GDP in 2016 to 7.4 percent in 2025, CBO projects. That decline is projected to occur because spending for many of the other mandatory programs is expected to rise roughly with inflation (which is projected to be well below the rate of growth of nominal GDP) and because most discretionary funding is capped through 2021 at amounts that increase more slowly than GDP.

Mandatory Spending. The Deficit Control Act requires CBO's projections for most mandatory programs to be made in keeping with the assumption that current laws continue unchanged.[13] Thus, CBO's baseline projections for mandatory spending reflect expected changes in the economy, demographics, and other factors, as well as the across-the-board reductions in certain mandatory programs that are required under current law.

Mandatory spending (net of offsetting receipts, which reduce outlays) is projected to increase by close to 10 percent in 2016, reaching 13.1 percent of GDP. That growth is partially the result of a few unusual circumstances:

---

13. The Deficit Control Act specifies some exceptions. For example, spending programs whose authorizations are set to expire are assumed to continue if they have outlays of more than $50 million in the current year and were established at or before enactment of the Balanced Budget Act of 1997. Programs established after that law was enacted are not automatically assumed to continue but are considered individually by CBO in consultation with the House and Senate Budget Committees.

Figure 1-3.

Components of the Total Increase in Outlays in CBO's Baseline Between 2015 and 2025

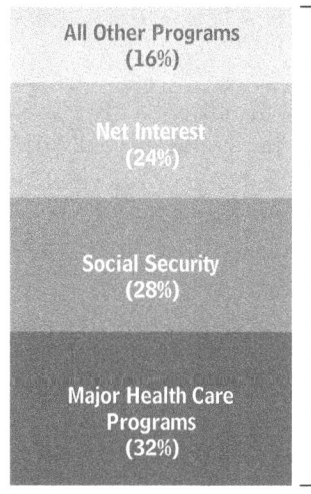

All Other Programs (16%)

Net Interest (24%)

Social Security (28%)

Major Health Care Programs (32%)

Total Increase in Outlays: $2.5 Trillion

Source: Congressional Budget Office.

Note: Major health care programs consist of Medicare, Medicaid, the Children's Health Insurance Program, and subsidies for health insurance purchased through exchanges and related spending. (Medicare spending is net of premiums paid by beneficiaries and other offsetting receipts.)

■ Receipts from the auctioning of licenses to use a portion of the electromagnetic spectrum—which are recorded as offsets to mandatory outlays—are anticipated to reduce such outlays by $41 billion in 2015. However, the net receipts associated with those auctions are expected to drop to near zero in 2016 because spending related to making the frequencies auctioned this year available for commercial uses will largely offset the receipts being collected. Beyond 2016, net receipts will total $18 billion over the remainder of the projection period.

■ October 1, 2016, falls on a weekend, so certain payments that are scheduled for the first of the month will be made in September, shifting about $37 billion in mandatory outlays from fiscal year 2017 to fiscal year 2016.

■ Cash payments from Fannie Mae and Freddie Mac to the Treasury will be recorded in the budget as reducing outlays by $26 billion in 2015, CBO estimates. However, the transactions of those two entities are not treated on a cash basis in CBO's baseline after the current year but are considered instead as credit programs of the government.[14] Reflecting that difference in treatment, outlays for Fannie Mae and Freddie Mac in 2016 are estimated to total $3 billion, a net increase in spending of $29 billion. (On a cash basis, outlays in 2016 would be similar to those in 2015.)

If not for those factors, mandatory outlays would increase by 5 percent in 2016. In the years beyond 2016, mandatory spending is projected to grow at an average rate of about 5 percent annually, reaching 14.2 percent of GDP in 2025 (compared with 12.2 percent in 2014).

Over the entire 10-year period, spending for Social Security is projected to rise at an average annual rate of 5.9 percent; for the major health care programs, 6.4 percent; and for all other programs and activities in the mandatory category, 3.2 percent.

Discretionary Spending. For discretionary spending, CBO's baseline incorporates the caps on such funding that are currently in place through 2021 and then reflects the assumption that funding keeps pace with inflation in later years; the elements of discretionary funding that are not constrained by the caps, such as appropriations for overseas contingency operations, are assumed to increase with inflation throughout the next decade.

Discretionary outlays are estimated to remain virtually unchanged from 2015 through 2017 and then to grow at an average annual rate of 2.1 percent after 2017; that rate is roughly half of the projected growth rate of nominal GDP. As a result, spending for both defense and nondefense discretionary programs is projected to fall

---

14. Because the government placed Fannie Mae and Freddie Mac into conservatorship in 2008 and now controls their operations, CBO considers the activities of those two entities to be governmental. Therefore, for the 10-year period that follows the current fiscal year, CBO projects the subsidy costs of the entities' new activities using procedures similar to those specified in the Federal Credit Reform Act of 1990 for determining the costs of federal credit programs but with adjustments to reflect the market risk associated with those activities. The Administration, by contrast, considers Fannie Mae and Freddie Mac to be outside of the federal government for budgetary purposes and records cash transactions between those entities and the Treasury as federal outlays or receipts. (In CBO's view, those transactions are intragovernmental.) To provide CBO's best estimate of what the Treasury will ultimately report as the federal deficit for 2015, CBO's current baseline includes an estimate of the cash receipts from the two entities to the Treasury for this year (while retaining its risk-adjusted projections of subsidy costs for later years).

relative to GDP under CBO's baseline assumptions. Outlays for defense are projected to drop from 3.1 percent of GDP in 2016 to 2.6 percent in 2025, 2.4 percentage points below the average share they represented from 1965 through 2014 and the lowest share in any year since before 1962 (which is the earliest year for which such data have been reported). For nondefense discretionary spending, outlays are projected to drop from 3.1 percent of GDP in 2016 to 2.5 percent in 2025, 1.3 percentage points below the average from 1965 through 2014 and also the lowest share in any year since before 1962.

Net interest. Under CBO's baseline assumptions, net interest payments increase from $227 billion, or 1.3 percent of GDP, in 2015 to $827 billion, or 3.0 percent of GDP, in 2025—the highest ratio since 1996. Two factors drive that sharp increase—rising interest rates and growing debt. The interest rate paid on 3-month Treasury bills will rise from 0.1 percent in 2015 to 3.4 percent in 2018 and subsequent years, and the rate on 10-year Treasury notes will increase from 2.6 percent in 2015 to 4.6 percent in 2020 and subsequent years. Meanwhile, debt held by the public will increase, according to CBO's projections, from 74.2 percent of GDP at the end of 2015 to 78.7 percent at the end of 2025.

Federal Debt

Federal debt held by the public consists mostly of securities that the Treasury issues to raise cash to fund the federal government's activities and to pay off its maturing liabilities.[15] The Treasury borrows money from the public by selling securities in the capital markets; that debt is purchased by various buyers in the United States, by private investors overseas, and by the central banks of other countries. Of the $12.8 trillion in federal debt held by the public at the end of 2014, 52 percent ($6.7 trillion) was held by domestic investors and 48 percent ($6.1 trillion) was held by foreign investors.[16] Other measures of federal debt are sometimes used for various purposes, such as to provide a more comprehensive picture of the

---

15. A small amount of debt held by the public is issued by other agencies, mainly the Tennessee Valley Authority.

16. The largest U.S. holders of Treasury debt are the Federal Reserve System (18 percent), individual households (6 percent), and mutual funds (6 percent); investors in China and Japan have the largest foreign holdings of Treasury securities, accounting for nearly 20 percent of U.S. public debt. For additional information, see Congressional Budget Office, *Federal Debt and Interest Costs* (December 2010), Chapter 1, www.cbo.gov/publication/21960.

Table 1-3.

Federal Debt Projected in CBO's Baseline

Billions of Dollars

	Actual, 2014	2015	2016	2017	2018	2019	2020	2021	2022	2023	2024	2025
Debt Held by the Public at the Beginning of the Year	11,983	12,779	13,359	13,905	14,466	15,068	15,782	16,580	17,451	18,453	19,458	20,463
Changes in Debt Held by the Public												
Deficit	483	468	467	489	540	652	739	814	948	953	951	1,088
Other means of financing	314	112	79	72	62	62	59	57	54	52	55	54
Total	797	580	546	561	602	714	798	870	1,002	1,005	1,006	1,142
Debt Held by the Public at the End of the Year	**12,779**	**13,359**	**13,905**	**14,466**	**15,068**	**15,782**	**16,580**	**17,451**	**18,453**	**19,458**	**20,463**	**21,605**
Debt Held by the Public at the End of the Year (As a percentage of GDP)	74.1	74.2	73.8	73.4	73.3	73.7	74.3	75.0	76.1	76.9	77.7	78.7
Memorandum:												
Debt Held by the Public Minus Financial Assets[a]												
In billions of dollars	11,544	12,011	12,450	12,909	13,420	14,044	14,754	15,540	16,458	17,382	18,303	19,360
As a percentage of GDP	66.9	66.7	66.1	65.5	65.3	65.6	66.1	66.8	67.8	68.7	69.5	70.5
Gross Federal Debt[b]	17,792	18,472	19,126	19,831	20,576	21,404	22,294	23,227	24,244	25,247	26,231	27,288
Debt Subject to Limit[c]	17,781	18,462	19,115	19,820	20,565	21,392	22,281	23,214	24,231	25,234	26,217	27,275
Average Interest Rate on Debt Held by the Public (Percent)[d]	1.8	1.7	2.0	2.3	2.7	3.0	3.3	3.5	3.6	3.7	3.8	3.8

Source: Congressional Budget Office.

Note: GDP = gross domestic product.

a. Debt held by the public minus the value of outstanding student loans and other credit transactions, cash balances, and other financial instruments.

b. Federal debt held by the public plus Treasury securities held by federal trust funds and other government accounts.

c. The amount of federal debt that is subject to the overall limit set in law. Debt subject to limit differs from gross federal debt mainly because most debt issued by agencies other than the Treasury and the Federal Financing Bank is excluded from the debt limit. That limit was most recently set at $17.2 trillion but has been suspended through March 15, 2015. On March 16, the debt limit will be raised to its previous level plus the amount of federal borrowing that occurred while the limit was suspended.

d. The average interest rate is calculated as net interest divided by debt held by the public.

government's financial condition or to account for debt held by federal trust funds.

Debt Held by the Public. Debt held by the public increased by about $800 billion in 2014, reaching 74 percent of GDP, higher than the amount recorded in 2013 (72 percent) or in any other year since 1950. As recently as 2007, such debt equaled 35 percent of GDP. Under the assumptions that govern CBO's baseline, the federal government is projected to borrow another $8.8 trillion from 2015 through 2025, pushing debt held by the

public up to 79 percent of GDP by the end of the projection period (see Table 1-3).

That amount of debt relative to the size of the economy would be the highest since 1950 and more than double the average of 38 percent experienced over the 1965–2014 period or the average of 34 percent experienced over the 40 years ending in 2007, before the recent sharp increase in debt. By historical standards, debt that high—and heading higher—would have significant consequences for the budget and the economy:

- The nation's net interest costs would be very high (after interest rates move up to more typical levels) and rising.

- National saving would be held down, leading to more borrowing from abroad and less domestic investment, which in turn would decrease income in the United States compared with what it would be otherwise.

- Policymakers' ability to use tax and spending policies to respond to unexpected challenges—such as economic downturns, financial crises, or natural disasters—would be constrained. As a result, such challenges could have worse effects on the economy and people's well-being than they would otherwise.

- The risk of a fiscal crisis would be higher. During such a crisis, investors would lose so much confidence in the government's ability to manage its budget that the government would be unable to borrow funds at affordable interest rates.

The amount of money the Treasury borrows by selling securities (net of the maturing securities it redeems) is determined primarily by the annual budget deficit. However, several factors—collectively labeled "other means of financing" and not directly included in budget totals—also affect the government's need to borrow from the public. Those factors include changes in the government's cash balance and investments in the Thrift Savings Plan's G fund, as well as the cash flows associated with federal credit programs (such as student loans) because only the subsidy costs of those programs (calculated on a present-value basis) are reflected in the budget deficit.

CBO projects that the increase in debt held by the public will exceed the deficit in 2015 by $112 billion, mainly because the government will need cash to finance new student loans and other credit programs. The same is true for each year from 2016 to 2025: CBO estimates that the government will need to borrow about $60 billion more per year, on average, during that period than the budget deficits would suggest.

Other Measures of Federal Debt. Three other measures are sometimes used in reference to federal debt:

Debt held by the public less financial assets subtracts from debt held by the public the value of the government's financial assets, such as student loans. That measure provides a more comprehensive picture of the govern-

ment's financial condition and its overall impact on credit markets than does debt held by the public. Calculating the measure is not straightforward, however, because neither the financial assets to be included nor the method for evaluating them is well defined. Under CBO's base-line assumptions, that measure is smaller than debt alone but varies roughly in line with it.

Gross federal debt consists of debt held by the public and debt issued to government accounts (for example, the Social Security trust funds). The latter type of debt does not directly affect the economy and has no net effect on the budget. In CBO's projections, debt held by the public is expected to increase by $8.8 trillion between the end of 2014 and the end of 2025, and debt held by government accounts is estimated to rise by $0.7 trillion. As a result, gross federal debt is projected to rise by $9.5 trillion over that period and to total $27.3 trillion at the end of 2025. About one-fifth of that sum would be debt held by government accounts.

Debt subject to limit is the amount of debt that is subject to the statutory limit on federal borrowing; it is virtually identical to gross federal debt. The amount of outstanding debt subject to limit is now about $18.0 trillion; under current law, it is projected to reach $27.3 trillion at the end of 2025.

Currently, there is no statutory limit on the issuance of new federal debt because the Temporary Debt Limit Suspension Act (P.L. 113-83) suspended the debt ceiling through March 15, 2015. Under the act, the debt limit after that date will equal the previous limit of $17.2 trillion plus the amount of borrowing accumulated during the suspension of the limit.

Therefore, if the current suspension is not extended and a higher debt limit is not specified in law before March 16, 2015, the Treasury will have no room to borrow under standard borrowing procedures beginning on that date. To avoid a breach in the debt ceiling, the Treasury would begin employing its well-established toolbox of so-called extraordinary measures to allow continued borrowing for a limited time. CBO anticipates that the Treasury would probably exhaust those measures in September or October of this year. If that occurred, the Treasury would soon run out of cash and be unable to fully pay its obligations, a development that would lead to delays of payments for government activities, a default on the government's debt obligations, or both. However, the government's cash flows cannot be predicted with certainty, and the actual cash flows during the coming months will affect the dates on which the Treasury would exhaust the extraordinary measures and the date on which it would run out of cash.[17]

Changes in CBO's Baseline Since August 2014

CBO completed its previous set of baseline projections in August 2014. Since then, the agency has reduced its estimate of the deficit in 2015 by $2 billion. The agency has also lowered its baseline projection of the cumulative deficit from 2015 through 2024 by $175 billion, from $7.2 trillion to $7.0 trillion (see Appendix A). Almost all of that reduction occurs in the projections for fiscal years 2016 through 2018; baseline deficits for other years are nearly unchanged. A number of different factors led to those changes: Legislation enacted since last August caused CBO to lower projected deficits through 2024 by $91 billion; a revised economic outlook reduced them by $38 billion; and other, technical changes decreased projected deficits by an additional $46 billion (see Table 1-4).

Those relatively small changes to the overall baseline totals reflect larger, but nearly offsetting, changes to baseline revenues and outlays, as both revenues and outlays are lower than CBO projected in August.

CBO has reduced its estimate of cumulative revenues through 2024 by $415 billion (or 1.0 percent) since last August:

■ More than half of that change ($234 billion) stems from changes to the economic outlook, primarily slightly lower projections of economic growth.

■ Technical changes, which reflect new information from tax returns, recent tax collections, new analysis of elements of the projections, and other factors, have reduced projected revenues by $137 billion over the period; the largest reductions were in projected receipts from corporate income taxes.

■ Legislation enacted since August has reduced projected revenues by $81 billion in 2015 and boosted

them by $38 billion between 2016 and 2024, a net reduction of $44 billion. Those legislative changes result almost entirely from the Tax Increase Prevention Act of 2014, which retroactively extended—through 2014—a host of tax provisions that reduce tax liabilities and that had expired at the end of 2013.

Projected outlays through 2024 have declined by $590 billion (or 1.2 percent) since August, more than offsetting the decrease in projected revenues:

■ The revised economic outlook accounted for $272 billion of that reduction. The largest reductions were in projected spending for Social Security (down by $110 billion) and net interest costs (reduced by $147 billion, excluding debt-service costs) because CBO now anticipates lower inflation this year and lower interest rates over much of the projection period.

■ A variety of technical changes, primarily to estimates for mandatory programs, further reduced outlays by $70 billion in 2015 and by $184 billion between 2015 and 2024.

■ Finally, legislation enacted since August lowered projected outlays through 2024 by $134 billion. Much of that decrease occurs because the current projections are based on 2015 appropriations, whereas the August baseline reflected 2014 appropriations. The amount of funding for overseas contingency operations in 2015 is less than the amount provided for 2014, and the projections throughout the 10-year period are extrapolated from that lower funding.

Uncertainty in Budget Projections

Even if federal laws remained unchanged for the next decade, actual budgetary outcomes would differ from CBO's baseline projections because of unanticipated changes in economic conditions and in a host of other factors that affect federal spending and revenues. The agency aims for its projections to be in the middle of the distribution of possible outcomes given the baseline assumptions about federal tax and spending policies, while recognizing that there will always be deviations from any such projections.

CBO's projections of outlays depend on the agency's economic projections for the coming decade, including forecasts for such variables as interest rates, inflation, and

---

17. For more information on the debt limit and extraordinary measures, see Congressional Budget Office, *Federal Debt and the Statutory Limit* (November 2013), www.cbo.gov/publication/44877.

Table 1-4.

Changes in CBO's Baseline Projections of the Deficit Since August 2014

Billions of Dollars

											Total 2015–2019	Total 2015–2024
	2015	2016	2017	2018	2019	2020	2021	2022	2023	2024		
Deficit in CBO's August 2014 Baseline	-469	-556	-530	-560	-661	-737	-820	-946	-957	-960	-2,777	-7,196
Changes												
Legislative												
Revenues	-81	18	11	7	5	1	*	-1	-2	-2	-40	-44
Outlays	1	-10	-9	-13	-12	-17	-17	-18	-19	-20	-44	-134
Subtotal[a]	-82	28	20	21	17	18	17	17	17	18	4	91
Economic												
Revenues	29	11	-17	-34	-36	-39	-43	-40	-36	-29	-47	-234
Outlays	-25	-26	-29	-22	-28	-31	-30	-28	-27	-26	-130	-272
Subtotal[a]	54	37	12	-12	-8	-8	-13	-12	-9	-3	83	38
Technical												
Revenues	-40	7	-11	-6	-11	-20	-9	-15	-16	-16	-61	-137
Outlays	-70	-16	-21	-17	-12	-8	-11	-7	-11	-9	-137	-184
Subtotal[a]	30	24	10	11	1	-12	2	-8	-5	-6	75	46
Total Effect on the Deficit[a]	2	89	41	20	9	-3	6	-2	4	9	161	175
Deficit in CBO's January 2015 Baseline	-468	-467	-489	-540	-652	-739	-814	-948	-953	-951	-2,615	-7,021
Memorandum:												
Total Effect on Revenues	-93	37	-17	-33	-43	-58	-52	-56	-53	-46	-149	-415
Total Effect on Outlays	-94	-52	-58	-53	-52	-55	-58	-54	-57	-55	-310	-590

Source: Congressional Budget Office.

Note: * = between -$500 million and zero.

a.   Negative numbers indicate an increase in the deficit; positive numbers indicate a decrease in the deficit.

the growth of real GDP. Discrepancies between those forecasts and actual economic outcomes can result in significant differences between baseline budgetary projections and budgetary outcomes. For instance, CBO's baseline economic forecast anticipates that interest rates on 3-month Treasury bills will increase from 0.9 percent in fiscal year 2016 to 3.4 percent in fiscal year 2018 and subsequent years and that interest rates on 10-year Treasury notes will rise from 3.2 percent to 4.6 percent in 2020 and subsequent years. If interest rates on all types of Treasury securities were 1 percentage point higher or lower each year from 2016 through 2025 and all other economic variables were unchanged, cumulative outlays projected for the 10-year period would be about $1.3 trillion higher or lower (excluding changes in the costs of servicing the federal debt) and revenues would be $0.1 trillion higher or lower. (For further discussion

of how some key economic projections affect budget projections, see Appendix C.)

Uncertainty also surrounds myriad technical factors that can substantially affect CBO's baseline projections of outlays. For example, spending per enrollee for Medicare and Medicaid is very difficult to predict. If per capita costs in those programs rose 1 percentage point faster or slower per year than CBO has projected for the next decade, total federal outlays for Medicare (net of receipts from premiums) and Medicaid would be roughly $900 billion higher or lower for that period. The effects of the Affordable Care Act are another source of significant uncertainty. To estimate the effects of the law's broad changes to the nation's health care and health insurance systems, CBO and the staff of the Joint Committee on Taxation (JCT) have made projections concerning an array of programs and institutions, some of which—such as the health insurance exchanges—have been in place only for a year.

Projections of revenues are quite sensitive to many economic and technical factors. Revenues depend on total amounts of wages and salaries, corporate profits, and other income, all of which are encompassed by CBO's economic projections. For example, if the growth of real GDP and taxable income was 0.1 percentage point higher or lower per year than in CBO's baseline projections, revenues would be roughly $290 billion higher or lower over the 2016–2025 period.

In addition, forecasting the amount of revenue that the government will collect from taxpayers for a given amount of total income requires technical estimates of the distribution of income and of many aspects of taxpayers' behavior. For example, estimates are required of the amounts of deductions and credits that people will receive and the amount of income in the form of capital gains they will realize from selling assets. Differences between CBO's judgments about such behavior and actual outcomes can lead to significant deviations from the agency's baseline projections of revenues.

Even relatively small deviations in revenues and outlays compared to CBO's projections could have a substantial effect on budget deficits. For example, if revenues projected for 2025 were too high by 5 percent (that is, if average annual growth in revenues during the coming decade was about 0.5 percentage points less than CBO estimated) and outlays projected for mandatory programs were too low by 5 percent, the deficit for that year would be about $450 billion greater than the $1.1 trillion in CBO's baseline; if GDP matched CBO's projection, that larger deficit would be 5.6 percent of GDP rather than the 4.0 percent in the baseline. Outcomes could differ by larger amounts and in the other direction as well.

Alternative Assumptions About Fiscal Policy

CBO's baseline budget projections—which are constructed in accordance with provisions of law—are intended to show what would happen to federal spending, revenues, and deficits if current laws generally remained unchanged. Future legislative action, however, could lead to markedly different budgetary outcomes.

To assist policymakers and analysts who may hold differing views about the most useful benchmark against which to consider possible changes to laws, CBO has estimated

the effects on budgetary projections of some alternative assumptions about future policies (see Table 1-5). The discussion below focuses on how those policy actions would directly affect revenues and outlays. Such changes would also influence the costs of servicing the federal debt (shown separately in the table).

Military and Diplomatic Operations in Afghanistan and Other War-Related Activities

One alternative path addresses spending for operations in Afghanistan and similar activities, sometimes called overseas contingency operations. The outlays projected in the baseline come from budget authority provided for those purposes in 2014 and prior years that has not been used, the $74 billion in budget authority provided for 2015, and the $822 billion that is projected to be appropriated over the 2016–2025 period (under the assumption that annual funding is set at $74 billion with adjustments for anticipated inflation, in accordance with the rules governing baseline projections).[18]

In coming years, the funding required for overseas contingency operations—in Afghanistan or other countries—might be smaller than the amounts projected in the baseline if the number of deployed troops and the pace of operations diminished. For that reason, CBO has formulated a budget scenario that anticipates a reduction in the number of U.S. military personnel deployed abroad for military actions and a concomitant reduction in diplomatic operations and foreign aid. Many other scenarios—some costing more and some less—are also possible.

In 2014, the number of U.S. active-duty, reserve, and National Guard personnel deployed for military and diplomatic operations that have been designated as overseas contingency operations averaged about 110,000, CBO estimates. In this alternative scenario, the average number of military personnel deployed for such purposes would decline over the next two years from roughly 90,000 in 2015 to 50,000 in 2016 and to 30,000 in 2017 and thereafter. (Those numbers could represent various allocations of forces around the world.) Under that scenario, and assuming that the extraordinary funding for diplomatic operations and foreign aid declines at a similar rate, total discretionary outlays over the 2016–2025

---

18. Funding for overseas contingency operations in 2015 includes $64 billion for military operations and indigenous security forces and $9 billion for diplomatic operations and foreign aid.

Table 1-5.

Budgetary Effects of Selected Policy Alternatives Not Included in CBO's Baseline

Billions of Dollars

	2015	2016	2017	2018	2019	2020	2021	2022	2023	2024	2025	Total 2016-2020	Total 2016-2025
Policy Alternatives That Affect Discretionary Outlays													
Reduce the Number of Troops Deployed for Overseas Contingency Operations to 30,000 by 2017[a]													
Effect on the deficit[b]	0	12	28	39	46	51	53	55	56	57	58	175	454
Debt service	0	*	1	2	4	6	8	11	14	16	19	13	81
Increase Discretionary Appropriations at the Rate of Inflation After 2015[c]													
Effect on the deficit[b]	0	-20	-30	-36	-41	-47	-52	-57	-62	-66	-69	-174	-480
Debt service	0	*	-1	-2	-4	-6	-8	-11	-14	-17	-20	-14	-83
Freeze Most Discretionary Appropriations at the 2015 Amount[d]													
Effect on the deficit[b]	0	-7	4	25	49	74	100	128	155	184	216	145	929
Debt service	0	*	*	*	2	5	8	13	20	27	35	7	111
Policy Alternative That Affects Mandatory Outlays													
Maintain Medicare's Payment Rates for Physicians at the Current Rate[e]													
Effect on the deficit[b]	-6	-9	-10	-10	-11	-13	-14	-15	-16	-16	-17	-54	-131
Debt service	*	*	*	-1	-2	-2	-3	-3	-4	-5	-6	-5	-27
Policy Alternative That Affects Both Discretionary and Mandatory Outlays													
Prevent the Automatic Spending Reductions Specified in the Budget Control Act[f]													
Effect on the deficit[b]	n.a.	-63	-91	-99	-103	-106	-106	-109	-115	-119	-99	-462	-1,010
Debt service	n.a.	-1	-3	-7	-12	-16	-21	-27	-32	-38	-43	-39	-200

Continued

period would be $454 billion less than the amount in the baseline, CBO estimates.[19]

Other Discretionary Spending

Policymakers could vary discretionary funding in many ways from the amounts projected in the baseline. For example, if appropriations grew each year through 2025 at the same rate as inflation after 2015 rather than being

---

19. The reduction in budget authority under this alternative is similar to those arising from some proposals to cap discretionary appropriations for overseas contingency operations. Such caps could result in reductions in CBO's baseline projections of discretionary spending. However, those reductions might simply reflect policy decisions that have already been made or would be made in the absence of caps. Moreover, if future policymakers believed that national security required appropriations above the capped levels, they would almost certainly provide emergency appropriations that would not, under current law, be counted against the caps.

constrained by the caps, discretionary spending would be $480 billion higher for that period than it is in the baseline. If, by contrast, lawmakers kept appropriations for 2016 through 2025 at the nominal 2015 amount, total discretionary outlays would be $929 billion lower over that period. Under that scenario (sometimes called a freeze in regular appropriations), total discretionary spending would fall from 6.5 percent of GDP in fiscal year 2015 to 4.3 percent in 2025. (Such spending is already projected to fall to 5.1 percent of GDP in 2025 under CBO's baseline, reflecting the caps on most new discretionary funding through 2021 and adjustments for inflation after 2021.)

Medicare's Payments to Physicians

Spending for Medicare is constrained by a rate-setting system—called the sustainable growth rate—for the fees that physicians receive for their services. If the system is allowed to operate as currently structured, physicians' fees

Table 1-5.   Continued

Budgetary Effects of Selected Policy Alternatives Not Included in CBO's Baseline

Billions of Dollars

	2015	2016	2017	2018	2019	2020	2021	2022	2023	2024	2025	Total 2016-2020	2016-2025
					Policy Alternative That Affects the Tax Code								
Extend Expiring Tax Provisions[g]													
Effect on the deficit[b]	-42	-109	-78	-73	-93	-88	-88	-89	-91	-94	-97	-440	-898
Debt service	*	-2	-5	-8	-13	-17	-21	-26	-31	-36	-41	-45	-200
Memorandum:													
Outlays for Overseas Contingency Operations in CBO's Baseline	83	78	75	75	76	78	79	81	83	84	86	382	797
Deficit in CBO's Baseline	-468	-467	-489	-540	-652	-739	-814	-948	-953	-951	-1,088	-2,887	-7,641

Sources: Congressional Budget Office; staff of the Joint Committee on Taxation.

Notes: Negative numbers indicate an increase in the deficit; positive numbers indicate a decrease in the deficit.

n.a. = not applicable; * = between -$500 million and $500 million.

a. For this alternative, CBO does not extrapolate the $74 billion in budget authority for military operations, diplomatic activities, and aid to Afghanistan and other countries provided for 2015. Rather, the alternative incorporates the assumption that funding for overseas contingency operations declines from $50 billion in 2016 to a low of $25 billion in 2019. Thereafter, such funding would slowly increase, reaching about $30 billion per year by the end of the projection period—for a total of $300 billion over the 2016–2025 period.

b. Excludes debt service.

c. These estimates reflect the assumption that appropriations will not be constrained by caps set by the Budget Control Act of 2011 as amended and will instead grow at the rate of inflation from their 2015 level. Discretionary funding related to federal personnel is inflated using the employment cost index for wages and salaries; other discretionary funding is inflated using the gross domestic product price index.

d. This option reflects the assumption that appropriations other than those for overseas contingency operations would generally be frozen at the 2015 level through 2025.

e. Medicare's payment rates for physicians' services are scheduled to drop by 21 percent on April 1, 2015, and to change by small amounts in subsequent years. In this alternative, payment rates are assumed to continue at their current levels through 2025.

f. The Budget Control Act of 2011 specified that if lawmakers did not enact legislation originating from the Joint Select Committee on Deficit Reduction that would reduce projected deficits by at least $1.2 trillion, automatic procedures would go into effect to reduce both discretionary and mandatory spending during the 2013–2021 period. Those procedures are now in effect and take the form of equal cuts (in dollar terms) in funding for defense and nondefense programs. For the 2016–2021 period, the automatic procedures lower the caps on discretionary budget authority specified in the Budget Control Act (caps for 2014 and 2015 were revised by the Bipartisan Budget Act of 2013); for the 2022–2025 period, CBO has extrapolated the reductions estimated for 2021. Nonexempt mandatory programs will be reduced through sequestration; those provisions have been extended through 2024. The budgetary effects of this option cannot be combined with those of any of the other alternatives that affect discretionary spending, except for the one to reduce the number of troops deployed for overseas contingency operations.

g. These estimates are mainly from the staff of the Joint Committee on Taxation and are preliminary. They reflect the impact of extending about 70 tax provisions that either expired on December 31, 2014, or are scheduled to expire by December 31, 2025. Nearly all of those provisions have been extended previously; some, such as the research and experimentation tax credit, have been extended multiple times.

will be reduced by about 21 percent in April 2015 and will both increase and decrease by small amounts in subsequent years, CBO projects. If, instead, lawmakers overrode those scheduled reductions—as they have every year since 2003—spending on Medicare might be greater than the amounts projected in CBO's baseline. For example, holding payment rates through 2025 at current levels would raise outlays for Medicare (net of premiums paid by beneficiaries) by $6 billion in 2015 and by $131 billion (or nearly 2 percent) between 2016 and 2025. The net effects of such a change in payment rates for physicians on spending for Medicare and on the deficit would depend on whether lawmakers offset the effects of the change, as they often have done in the past, with other changes to reduce deficits.

Automatic Spending Reductions

The Budget Control Act put in place automatic procedures to reduce discretionary and mandatory spending through 2021. Those procedures require equal reductions (in dollar terms) in defense and nondefense spending. Subsequent legislation extended the required reductions to mandatory spending (a process called sequestration) through 2024. If lawmakers chose to prevent those automatic cuts each year—starting in 2016—without making other changes that reduced spending, total outlays over the 2016–2025 period would be $1.0 trillion (or about 2 percent) higher than the amounts in CBO's baseline. Total discretionary outlays would be $845 billion (or 6.7 percent) higher, and outlays for mandatory programs—most of which are not subject to sequestration—would be $164 billion (or 0.5 percent) higher.[20]

Revenues

A host of tax provisions—many of which have been extended repeatedly—have recently expired or are scheduled to expire over the next decade. If all of those provisions were permanently extended, CBO and JCT estimate, revenues would be lower and, although a much smaller effect, outlays for refundable tax credits would be higher, by a total of $898 billion over the 2016–2025 period.

Most of those tax provisions were recently extended retroactively through 2014 and have subsequently expired. They include a provision allowing certain businesses to immediately deduct 50 percent of new investments in equipment, which JCT estimates accounts for $224 billion of the budgetary effects of extending all of the provisions over the next 10 years. The budgetary cost of extending all of the tax provisions would be higher in the latter part of the 10-year period than in the first few years because certain provisions affecting refundable tax credits are scheduled to expire at the end of 2017. Extending those provisions would boost outlays for refundable

credits and reduce revenues by a total of $200 billion over the 2019–2025 period. (Payments for refundable credits are typically made a year after the applicable tax year.)

The Long-Term Budget Outlook

Beyond the coming decade, the fiscal outlook is significantly more worrisome. In CBO's most recent long-term projections—which extend through 2039—budget deficits rise steadily under the extended baseline, which follows CBO's 10-year baseline projections for the first decade and then extends the baseline concept for subsequent years.[21] Although long-term budget projections are highly uncertain, the aging of the population, the growth in per capita spending on health care, and the ongoing expansion of federal subsidies for health insurance would almost certainly push up federal spending significantly relative to GDP after 2025 if current laws remained in effect. Federal revenues also would continue to increase relative to GDP under current law, but they would not keep pace with outlays. As a result, public debt would exceed 100 percent of GDP by 2039, CBO estimates, about equal to the percentage recorded just after World War II.

Such high and rising debt relative to the size of the economy would dampen economic growth and thus reduce people's income compared with what it would be otherwise. It would also increasingly restrict policymakers' ability to use tax and spending policies to respond to unexpected challenges and would boost the risk of a fiscal crisis, in which the government would lose its ability to borrow at affordable rates.

Moreover, debt would still be on an upward path relative to the size of the economy in 2039, a trend that would ultimately be unsustainable. To avoid the negative consequences of high and rising federal debt and to put debt on a sustainable path, lawmakers will have to make significant changes to tax and spending policies—letting revenues rise more than they would under current law, reducing spending for large benefit programs below the projected amounts, or adopting some combination of those approaches.

---

20. Because of interactions between the effects of different policy options, the estimated budgetary effects of this option cannot be added to the estimated budgetary effects of any of the other alternatives that affect discretionary spending except for the one to reduce the number of troops deployed for overseas contingency operations.

21. See Congressional Budget Office, *The 2014 Long-Term Budget Outlook* (July 2014), www.cbo.gov/publication/45471. Federal debt in 2024 under CBO's current baseline is a little lower than the amount the agency previously projected for that year, but the long-term outlook remains about the same.

The Economic Outlook

The Congressional Budget Office anticipates that, under the assumption that current laws governing federal taxes and spending generally remain in place, economic activity will expand at a solid pace in 2015 and the next few years. As measured by the change from the fourth quarter of the previous year, real (inflation-adjusted) gross domestic product (GDP) will grow by 2.9 percent this year, by another 2.9 percent in 2016, and by 2.5 percent in 2017, CBO expects. By comparison, the agency estimates that real GDP increased by 2.1 percent in 2014—the net result of a decline in the first quarter and brisk growth later in the year (see Box 2-1).

Economic expansion this year and over the next few years will be driven by increases in consumer spending, business investment, and residential investment, CBO expects. In addition, government purchases of goods and services are expected to contribute slightly to growth in 2016 and 2017. By contrast, net exports are projected to impose a drag on growth in 2015 and 2016 but to contribute to growth thereafter.

CBO expects the pace of output growth to reduce the quantity of underused resources, or "slack," in the economy over the next few years. The difference between actual GDP and CBO's estimate of potential (that is, maximum sustainable) GDP—which is a measure of slack for the whole economy—was about 2 percent of potential GDP at the end of 2014, but the agency expects that gap to be essentially eliminated by the second half of 2017. CBO also expects slack in the labor market—which is indicated by such factors as the elevated unemployment rate and a relatively low rate of labor force participation—to dissipate over the next few years. In particular, the agency projects that increased hiring will reduce the unemployment rate from 5.7 percent in the fourth quarter of 2014 to 5.3 percent in the fourth quarter of 2017. Also, the increased hiring will encourage

some people to enter or stay in the labor force, in CBO's estimation. That will slow the decline in labor force participation, which arises from underlying demographic trends and federal policies, but it will also slow the fall of the unemployment rate.

Over the next few years, reduced slack in the economy will diminish the downward pressure on inflation and interest rates. Nevertheless, because slack is expected to dissipate only slowly—and because of a strengthening dollar, broadly held expectations for low inflation, and a recent sharp decline in oil prices (which put downward pressure on energy costs)—CBO expects the rate of inflation, as measured by the price index for personal consumption expenditures (PCE), to stay below the Federal Reserve's goal of 2 percent during the next few years. CBO anticipates that the interest rate on 3-month Treasury bills will remain near zero until the second half of 2015 and then rise to 3½ percent by 2018. The agency further expects that the rate on 10-year Treasury notes will rise from an average of 2½ percent last year to 4½ percent by 2019.

CBO's projections for the period from 2020 through 2025 exclude possible cyclical developments in the economy, because the agency does not attempt to predict the timing or magnitude of such developments so far in the future. CBO projects that real GDP will grow by an average of 2.2 percent per year from 2020 through 2025—a rate that matches the agency's estimate of the growth of potential output in those years. CBO anticipates that output will grow much more slowly than it did during the 1980s and 1990s, primarily because the labor force is expected to grow more slowly than it did then. The lingering effects of the recent recession and of the ensuing slow recovery are also expected to cause GDP to be lower from 2020 through 2025 than it would otherwise have

---

Box 2-1.

Data Released Since Early December

In this chapter, the Congressional Budget Office's estimates of economic output in 2014 and economic projections for this year and future years are based on data available in early December 2014. Since then, revised and newly released data indicate that the growth of real (inflation-adjusted) gross domestic product (GDP) was stronger during the second half of 2014 than CBO had estimated. In addition, interest rates on long-term Treasury securities have been lower and oil prices have declined further since mid-December than CBO had anticipated.

The unexpected strength in economic activity in the second half of last year and the continued decline in oil prices suggest that output may grow more this year than CBO forecast. Lower interest rates, taken alone, have the same implication; however, lower rates may reflect a worsening in the outlook for global growth among some observers, and diminished prospects for growth in other countries would weigh on growth in the United States. Providing a

small offset to the positive effects, a larger-than-expected increase in the exchange value of the dollar since mid-December points to slightly weaker net exports this year than CBO forecast. Moreover, labor market developments in December were mixed: The decline in the unemployment rate and the increase in payroll employment were larger than CBO had expected, but there was a surprisingly low rate of labor force participation and unexpectedly weak growth of average hourly earnings.

All told, the newly available data suggest that slack in the economy may dissipate a little more quickly than CBO had anticipated. A preliminary assessment of that new information does not significantly alter CBO's view of potential (or maximum sustainable) GDP, but it does suggest that the difference between GDP and potential GDP at the end of 2014 was roughly one-quarter of one percentage point smaller than the estimate that CBO made for the forecast presented here.

---

been. CBO projects that the unemployment rate between 2020 and 2025 will average 5.4 percent and that inflation (as measured by the PCE price index) will be 2.0 percent. Over the same period, the projected interest rates on 3-month Treasury bills and 10-year Treasury notes are 3.4 percent and 4.6 percent, respectively.

Recognizing that economic forecasts are always uncertain, CBO constructs its forecasts to be in the middle of the distribution of possible outcomes for the economy, given the federal fiscal policies that are embodied in current law. Nevertheless, even if fiscal policies remain as they are projected under current law, many developments—such as unforeseen changes in the housing and labor markets, in business confidence, and in international conditions—could cause economic outcomes to differ substantially from those that CBO has projected.

CBO's current economic projections differ in a number of ways from its most recent previous ones, which it

published in August 2014. For instance, for the period from 2014 through 2018, CBO now projects real GDP growth averaging 2.5 percent annually, a rate roughly 0.2 percentage points lower than the rate projected in August. The principal reason for that difference is that CBO has revised downward its estimates of potential output and consequently its estimate of the current amount of slack in the economy. Also as a result of the downward revision to estimated potential output, CBO currently forecasts that real GDP will be roughly 1 percent lower in 2024 than it did in August. In addition, CBO now projects lower rates of unemployment for the next several years than it did in August.

CBO's current economic projections do not differ much from the projections of other forecasters. They are generally very similar to those of the *Blue Chip* consensus, which is based on the forecasts of about 50 private-sector economists. CBO's projections also differ only slightly from the forecasts made by the Federal Reserve that were

Figure 2-1.

Projected Growth in Real GDP

Economic activity will expand at a solid pace in 2015 and over the next few years, CBO projects.

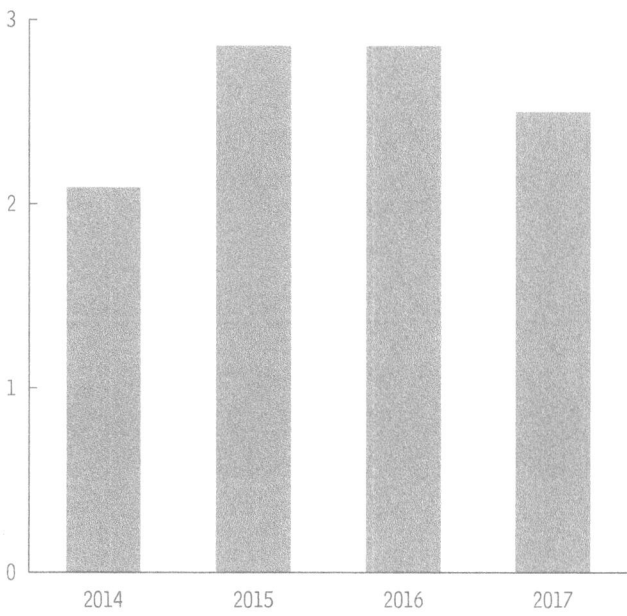

Percent

Source: Congressional Budget Office.

Notes: Real gross domestic product is the output of the economy adjusted to remove the effects of inflation.

Data are annual. The percentage change in real GDP is measured from the fourth quarter of one calendar year to the fourth quarter of the next year.

The value for 2014 does not incorporate data released by the Bureau of Economic Analysis since early December 2014.

GDP = gross domestic product.

presented at the December 2014 meeting of the Federal Open Market Committee.

The Economic Outlook for 2015 Through 2019

CBO expects output to grow faster in the next few years than it has in the past few years—at an annual rate of 2.9 percent over the next two years and then by 2.5 percent in 2017 (see Figure 2-1 and Table 2-1). By comparison, the agency estimates that annual GDP growth averaged about 2¼ percent over the past three years. CBO anticipates that consumer spending and

investment will be the primary contributors to the growth of output over the next few years. In CBO's projections, the changes in fiscal policy that will occur under current law have little effect on growth in the near term; monetary policy supports growth this year and over the next few years, but by smaller degrees over time. The agency also expects that output growth will be boosted this year by the steep decline in crude oil prices in the second half of 2014 (see Box 2-2).

CBO expects slack in the labor market to keep diminishing from 2015 through 2017. In the agency's projections, the greater demand for workers lowers the unemployment rate through 2017 and contributes to faster growth in hourly labor compensation; those developments are expected to encourage more people to enter, reenter, or remain in the labor force. CBO anticipates that the rate of inflation will remain low this year but rise over the next few years as the economy strengthens and as shifts in the supply of and demand for crude oil—as expected in oil futures markets—begin to push oil prices up. However, CBO expects the rate of inflation to remain below the Federal Reserve's longer-term goal of 2 percent until 2017.

Those projections for 2015 through 2017 are based on CBO's forecasts of cyclical developments in the economy. In contrast, the agency's projections for the 2020–2025 period are based primarily on average historical relationships—for example, the average historical relationship of output to potential output and of the unemployment rate to the natural rate of unemployment (the rate arising from all sources except fluctuations in the overall demand for goods and services). The projections of output and of the unemployment rate for the intervening years, 2018 and 2019, represent transition paths toward those average historical relationships.

Federal Fiscal Policy

Changes in federal fiscal policy (that is, the government's tax and spending policies) that result from current law will have little effect on the growth of the economy this year, because of three small and largely offsetting effects:

■ The dollar value of federal purchases, relative to the size of the economy, will be lower this year than in 2014, slowing GDP growth slightly, CBO estimates.

Table 2-1.

CBO's Economic Projections for Calendar Years 2015 to 2025

	Estimated, 2014	Forecast 2015	Forecast 2016	Forecast 2017	Projected Annual Average 2018–2019	Projected Annual Average 2020–2025
		Percentage Change From Fourth Quarter to Fourth Quarter				

	Estimated, 2014	2015	2016	2017	2018–2019	2020–2025
Percentage Change From Fourth Quarter to Fourth Quarter						
Gross Domestic Product						
Real (Inflation-adjusted)	2.1	2.9	2.9	2.5	2.1	2.1
Nominal	4.0	4.2	4.6	4.5	4.2	4.2
Inflation						
PCE price index	1.3	1.4	1.9	2.0	2.0	2.0
Core PCE price index[a]	1.5	1.8	1.9	1.9	2.0	2.0
Consumer price index[b]	1.2 [c]	1.5	2.3	2.3	2.4	2.4
Core consumer price index[a]	1.7 [c]	2.1	2.2	2.3	2.3	2.3
GDP price index	1.8	1.3	1.7	1.9	2.0	2.0
Employment Cost Index[d]	2.3	2.7	3.2	3.6	3.6	3.4
Fourth-Quarter Level (Percent)						
Unemployment Rate	5.7 [c]	5.5	5.4	5.3	5.5 [e]	5.4 [f]
Percentage Change From Year to Year						
Gross Domestic Product						
Real	2.2	2.8	3.0	2.7	2.1	2.2
Nominal	3.9	4.5	4.6	4.6	4.2	4.2
Inflation						
PCE price index	1.4	1.1	1.9	1.9	2.0	2.0
Core PCE price index[a]	1.4	1.7	1.9	1.9	2.0	2.0
Consumer price index[b]	1.6 [c]	1.1	2.2	2.3	2.4	2.4
Core consumer price index[a]	1.7 [c]	2.0	2.2	2.3	2.3	2.3
GDP price index	1.6	1.6	1.6	1.9	2.0	2.0
Employment Cost Index[d]	2.0	2.7	3.0	3.5	3.6	3.4
Calendar Year Average						
Unemployment Rate (Percent)	6.2 [c]	5.5	5.4	5.3	5.4	5.4
Payroll Employment (Monthly change, in thousands)[g]	234 [c]	184	148	111	69	78
Interest Rates (Percent)						
Three-month Treasury bills	* [c]	0.2	1.2	2.6	3.5	3.4
Ten-year Treasury notes	2.5 [c]	2.8	3.4	3.9	4.4	4.6
Tax Bases (Percentage of GDP)						
Wages and salaries	42.7	42.6	42.6	42.7	42.8	43.0
Domestic economic profits	9.9	10.0	9.7	9.4	8.8	8.0

Sources: Congressional Budget Office; Bureau of Labor Statistics; Federal Reserve.

Notes: Estimated values for 2014 do not reflect the values for GDP and related series released by the Bureau of Economic Analysis since early December 2014.

Economic projections for each year from 2015 to 2025 appear in Appendix F.

GDP = gross domestic product; PCE = personal consumption expenditures; * = between zero and 0.05 percent.

a. Excludes prices for food and energy.

b. The consumer price index for all urban consumers.

c. Actual value for 2014.

d. The employment cost index for wages and salaries of workers in private industries.

e. Value for 2019.

f. Value for 2025.

g. Calculated as the monthly average of the fourth-quarter-to-fourth-quarter change in payroll employment.

Box 2-2.

The Effect of the Recent Drop in Oil Prices on U.S. Output

Oil prices have fallen markedly since the Congressional Budget Office completed its previous forecast in August 2014. The prices of two major varieties of crude oil, West Texas Intermediate and Brent, stood at $60 and $65 per barrel, respectively, in early December 2014, when CBO finalized its economic forecast. Those prices were roughly $40 per barrel lower than when CBO finalized its projection in the summer, and the lowest in nearly six years.[1] Prices for crude oil in futures markets in early December signaled an end to the decline in prices in early 2015; prices were then expected to return to a modest upward trajectory. Still, futures markets suggested that crude oil deliverable in 2020 would cost about $20 per barrel less than those markets suggested when the summer forecast was completed. On the basis of those readings, CBO incorporated into its current forecast an estimate that the reduction in oil prices since August 2014 would raise real (inflation-adjusted) gross domestic product (GDP) in the United States slightly this year and have a very small positive effect on GDP in the longer term.

Since early December, crude oil prices have declined by a further $15 per barrel, and crude oil futures market prices for 2020 have declined by a further $7 per barrel. That further reduction in oil prices, taken by itself, suggests that output may grow faster this year than CBO forecast.

The Near Term

CBO estimates that the declines in oil prices for immediate and future delivery that occurred between August and December 2014 will raise real GDP in the United States by 0.3 percent at the end of 2015. The decline in expected future oil prices will also raise GDP during the 2016–2019 period, but by less than in 2015 because of the anticipated partial rebound in those prices.

The boost to GDP over the next five years will be the net effect of two partly offsetting sets of factors. On the one hand, the drop in oil prices has several positive effects. It has lowered the prices of petroleum products, including gasoline. As a result, U.S. households will have savings on purchases of petroleum products that they can spend on other goods and services, raising GDP. Also, when businesses that use petroleum

products pass some of their lower costs on to consumers in the form of lower prices, U.S. households can similarly use their savings on those items to increase consumption. Furthermore, the large and sudden decline in gasoline prices appears to have raised consumer confidence, which provides an additional boost to household spending. Some of the additional consumer spending will result in higher imports, boosting output in other countries rather than in the United States; but most of the additional spending will be on U.S. goods and services, which will boost U.S. GDP, as will greater domestic investment by firms responding to the increase in demand for goods and services.

On the other hand, U.S. GDP will be reduced because lower oil prices reduce the incentive for domestic oil producers to explore and develop additional resources. That reduced incentive will dampen the oil producers' investment in 2015; indeed, CBO projects that such investment will decline this year after rapid growth in recent years. Lower oil prices also reduce the wealth of U.S. households that own stock in oil producers or otherwise own oil-related assets, which reduces spending by those households (although that response is estimated to be much smaller than the increase in spending by other U.S. households mentioned above).

The Longer Term

In CBO's projection, lower oil prices have a very small positive effect on GDP between 2020 and 2025, when real GDP is projected to depend on the quantity of labor and capital supplied to the U.S. economy and on the productivity of that labor and capital. In particular, lower oil prices are expected to have a small positive impact on the productivity of labor and capital. That increase also will be the result of two partly offsetting effects. The lower price of one input into production, energy, will lead firms to use more of that input and thus make other inputs more productive. However, lower oil prices will reduce investment in the development of shale resources—that is, crude oil trapped in shale and certain other dense rock formations. In CBO's view, the development of shale resources boosts the productivity of labor and capital in the mining sector, so less development means a smaller boost.[2] However, CBO estimates that the shale projects that are abandoned or are not undertaken because of lower oil prices will be the least productive ones, so their abandonment will have little effect on GDP.

---

1. The decline in prices resulted from a mismatch between changes in consumption and production. In particular, European and Chinese consumption slowed; Libyan supplies increased, following significant declines that resulted from a civil war; and the growth of U.S. oil production outpaced expectations. In addition, OPEC (Organization of the Petroleum Exporting Countries) decided in November 2014 not to cut production.

2. For a discussion of the impact of shale resources on GDP, see Congressional Budget Office, *The Economic and Budgetary Effects of Producing Oil and Natural Gas From Shale* (December 2014), www.cbo.gov/publication/49815.

- However, the growing number of people who will receive Medicaid coverage or subsidies through health insurance exchanges because of the Affordable Care Act (ACA)—along with the resulting rise in health insurance coverage—will both stimulate greater demand for health care and allow lower-income households that gain subsidized coverage to increase their spending on other goods and services, slightly boosting GDP growth.[1]

- In addition, the recent retroactive extension through 2014 of various tax provisions that had expired at the end of 2013 is projected to make businesses' tax payments in 2015 smaller than they would otherwise have been and, as a result, to provide a small boost to output growth this year. (Those provisions, which reduced the tax liabilities of individuals and corporations, include bonus depreciation allowances, which permit certain businesses to deduct the cost of new investments from taxable income more rapidly than they could otherwise.)

By contrast, changes in federal fiscal policy restrained output growth in the past several years. For example, in 2013, they reduced growth by roughly 1½ percentage points, according to CBO's estimates, primarily because tax rates on some income increased when certain tax provisions expired and because the federal government cut its purchases of goods and services (relative to the size of the economy) as sequestration under the Budget Control Act of 2011 (Public Law 112-25) took effect. In 2014, changes in fiscal policy reduced output growth by an estimated one-quarter of one percentage point. The main reason was that extended unemployment insurance expired at the end of 2013. Also, the temporary expiration of bonus depreciation at the end of 2013 increased tax payments and may have discouraged investment by firms that did not expect bonus depreciation to be retroactively extended through 2014. In addition, continued reductions in federal purchases (relative to the size of the economy) restrained the demand for goods and services.

From 2016 through 2019, changes in federal fiscal policy that result from current law will affect the economy in different ways.[2] The stimulus provided by the automatic stabilizers in the federal budget (that is, provisions of law that automatically decrease revenues or increase outlays when the economy weakens) will continue to wane as the

economy improves and will therefore provide a smaller boost to the demand for goods and services.[3] Collections of corporate and individual income taxes will rise because of the expiration at the end of 2014 of bonus depreciation and other tax provisions, reducing GDP. In addition, rising income will push some taxpayers into higher tax brackets over time, which will reduce their incentive to work and thus reduce labor supply and GDP.

The ACA will also affect the labor market in coming years and therefore affect output.[4] The largest impact of the ACA on the labor market, especially as slack diminishes, will be that some provisions of the act raise effective tax rates on earnings and thus reduce the amount of labor that some workers choose to supply. That effect occurs partly because the health insurance subsidies that the act provides through the Medicaid expansion and the exchanges are phased out for people with higher income, creating an implicit tax on additional earnings by some people, and partly because the act directly imposes higher taxes on the labor income of other people.

Monetary Policy and Interest Rates

CBO expects that, over the next few years, the Federal Reserve will gradually reduce the extent to which monetary policy supports economic growth. In CBO's forecast, the federal funds rate—the interest rate that financial institutions charge each other for overnight loans of their monetary reserves—rises from 0.1 percent at the end of 2014 to 0.6 percent by the end of 2015 and then settles at 3.7 percent in 2019. CBO expects the Federal Reserve to achieve that increase by raising the interest rate that it pays banks on their deposits at the Federal Reserve (the interest rate on overnight reserves) and by selling and repurchasing some securities on a temporary basis (in what are known as reverse repurchase agreements).

---

1. For CBO's current estimates of how the ACA will affect health insurance coverage, see Appendix B.

2. The effects described in this paragraph and the following one are incorporated into CBO's projections; however, the agency has not separately quantified the impact that each would have.

3. All else being equal, automatic stabilizers affect the demand for goods and services by changing the amount of taxes that households and businesses pay and the transfer payments that households receive. The change in demand, in turn, affects businesses' decisions to gear up production and hire workers, changing income and demand further. For CBO's current estimates of the automatic stabilizers' effects on the federal budget, see Appendix D.

4. For more information, see Congressional Budget Office, *The Budget and Economic Outlook: 2014 to 2024* (February 2014), Appendix C, www.cbo.gov/publication/45010.

Figure 2-2.

Interest Rates on Treasury Securities

Percent

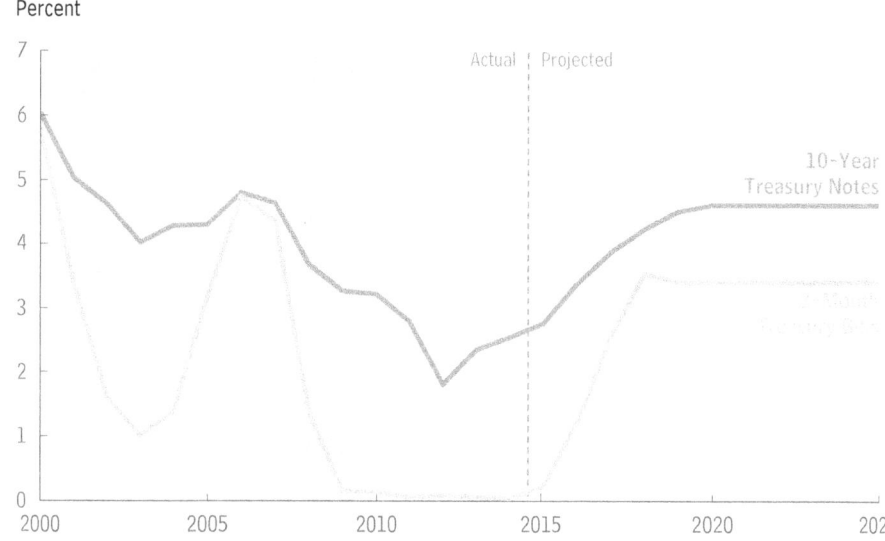

Over the next several years, interest rates are projected to be pushed up by a tightening of monetary policy by the Federal Reserve and by market participants' expectations of an improving economy.

Sources: Congressional Budget Office; Federal Reserve.

Note: Data are annual. Actual data are plotted through 2014.

CBO projects the interest rate on three-month Treasury bills to remain near zero until mid-2015, to increase to 2.6 percent in 2017, and to be 3.4 percent in 2019 (see Figure 2-2). CBO's projections for short-term interest rates were broadly consistent with the expectations of participants in the financial markets when the agency's forecast was completed in early December, although those expectations now suggest somewhat lower interest rates over the next few years.

According to CBO's projections, the interest rate on 10-year Treasury notes will rise from 2.4 percent in the second half of 2014 to 3.9 percent in 2017 and then settle at 4.6 percent by the end of 2019. That rise will reflect continued improvement in economic conditions and the expected rise in short-term interest rates. However, CBO expects that those long-term rates will reach 4.6 percent somewhat later than the interest rate on three-month Treasury bills reaches 3.4 percent. The main reason for the difference in timing is that the long-term rates will probably be held down by the Federal Reserve's large portfolio of long-term assets. The Federal Reserve has indicated that it will begin to gradually reduce its holdings of long-term assets at some point after it starts raising the federal funds rate, depending on economic and financial conditions and the economic outlook; CBO projects that those holdings will start to decline in 2016, but that they will take many years to fall to historical levels.

Contributions to the Growth of Real GDP

CBO expects the growth of real GDP from 2015 through 2019 to be driven largely by consumer spending and investment, both business and residential. Government purchases are projected to have a small positive effect on GDP growth in 2016 and 2017. In contrast, net exports will restrain growth in 2015 and 2016, although they will contribute to growth thereafter, CBO projects.

Consumer Spending. After growing by an estimated 2.2 percent from the fourth quarter of 2013 to the fourth quarter of 2014, real spending on consumer goods and services will grow by 3.3 percent in 2015, CBO expects. Because consumer spending accounts for about two-thirds of GDP, that projection means that consumer spending will contribute 2.3 percentage points to the projected growth of GDP this year (see Figure 2-3). CBO estimates that consumer spending will grow more slowly in later years and contribute an average of about 1½ percentage points to the growth of output from 2016 through 2019, which would be close to its average contribution over the past five years.

The same factors that spurred the growth of consumer spending in 2014—solid gains in real disposable (after-tax) personal income and household wealth—will continue to do so over the next few years, in CBO's assessment. The agency expects that real disposable personal income will again grow solidly in 2015, driven

Figure 2-3.

Projected Contributions to the Growth of Real GDP

Consumer spending and investment will drive the growth of real GDP over the next few years, CBO expects.

Percentage Points

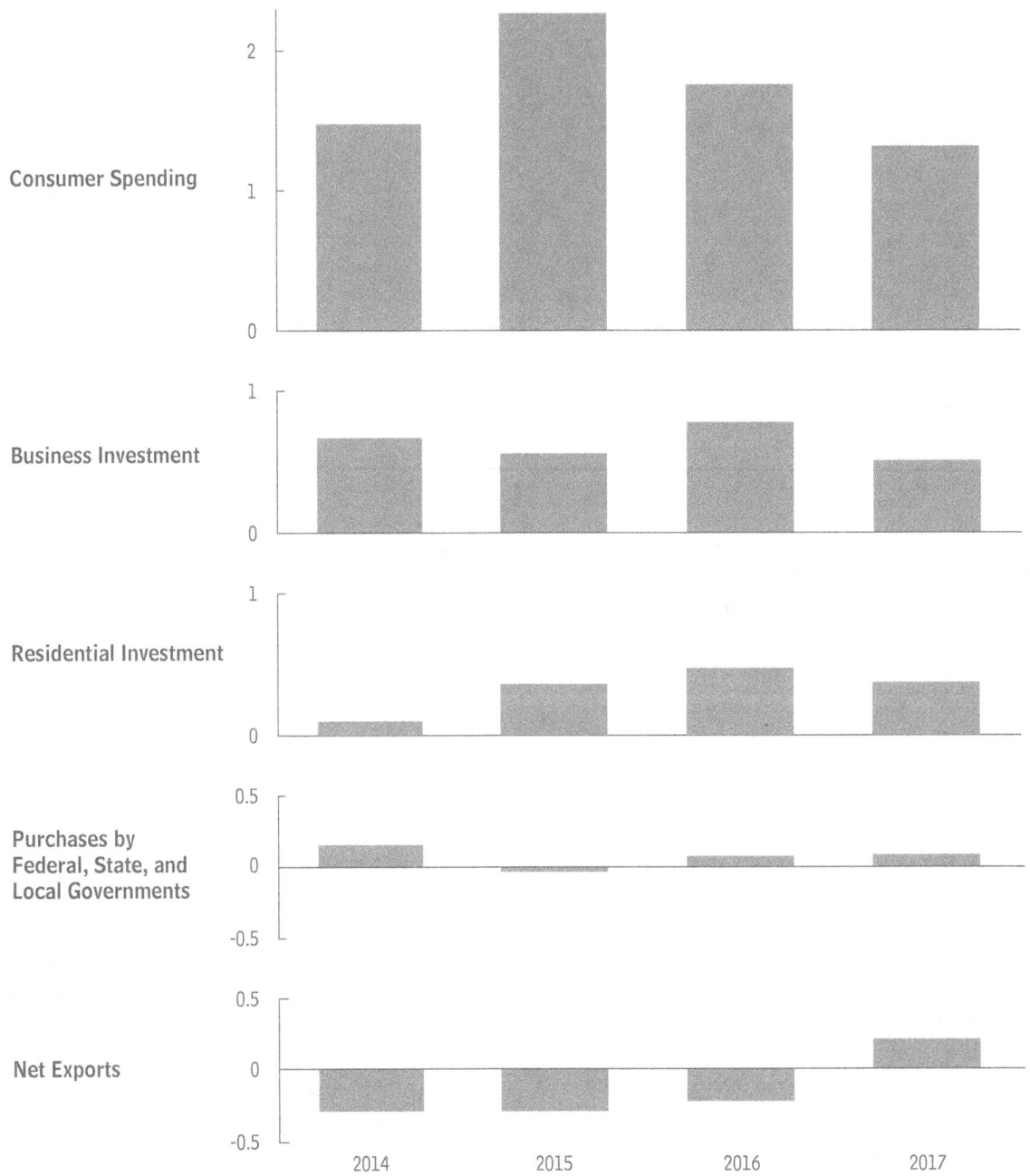

Source: Congressional Budget Office.

Notes: Data are annual. The values show the percentage-point contribution of the major components of GDP to the fourth-quarter-to-fourth-quarter growth rate of real GDP (output adjusted to remove the effects of inflation). Consumer spending is personal consumption expenditures. Business investment includes purchases of equipment, nonresidential structures, and intellectual property products and the change in inventories. Residential investment includes the construction of single-family and multifamily structures, manufactured homes, and dormitories; spending on home improvements; and brokers' commissions and other ownership-transfer costs. The measure of purchases by federal, state, and local governments is taken from the national income and product accounts. Net exports are exports minus imports. The values for 2014 do not incorporate data released by the Bureau of Economic Analysis since early December 2014.

GDP = gross domestic product.

primarily by growth in the compensation of employees (see Figure 2-4). Moreover, energy prices are expected to keep falling in the first part of this year, boosting households' purchasing power, just as they did in the second half of last year. Household wealth increased sharply in 2014, largely because of gains in stock prices, and it is projected to rise again this year—though more slowly—mostly because of rising house prices. In addition, significant improvements in consumer confidence last year are expected to continue to boost spending.

Continued improvements in consumers' creditworthiness and in the availability of credit will also support increases in consumer spending over the next few years, CBO projects. Delinquency rates on consumer loans and home mortgage loans continued to fall last year, and banks have become more willing to make consumer loans. The ratio of household debt to disposable personal income, which had fallen markedly from 2010 through 2012, declined much more slowly in 2013 and 2014, suggesting that households are becoming more willing to borrow, that financial institutions are becoming more willing to lend, or both.

Business Investment. CBO expects investment by businesses—which consists of fixed investment (investment in equipment, nonresidential structures, and intellectual property products) and investment in inventories—to be a key contributor to the growth of real GDP over the next few years. CBO anticipates that real business investment will increase by 4.3 percent between the fourth quarter of 2014 and the fourth quarter of 2015, by 5.9 percent the following year, and by smaller amounts in subsequent years. That projection means that real business investment will contribute 0.6 percentage points to the growth of real GDP in 2015, 0.8 percentage points in 2016, and somewhat less in later years (see Figure 2-3).

The components of fixed investment that have historically been the most sensitive to the business cycle—investment in equipment and nonmining structures—will contribute the most to the growth of investment in 2015, in CBO's estimation.[5] Growth in those

components will be strong enough to offset a decline in investment in mining structures, which will result from lower oil prices. The decline in mining investment is projected to abate in 2016 as oil prices stabilize, further boosting the overall growth of fixed investment. Inventory investment will be somewhat smaller in 2015 than in 2014, CBO estimates, but have little impact on GDP growth in subsequent years.

Stronger projected growth in the demand for goods and services is a major reason for CBO's expectation of rising business investment. As the effects of very weak growth in demand during and immediately after the recession have faded, businesses have had a greater incentive to increase productive capacity and thus capital services (the flow of services available for production from the stock of capital; see Figure 2-4). As a result, business investment has expanded rapidly in recent years, growing at an average annual rate of 8 percent since 2009. Over the next few years, in response to increasing demand for their products, businesses will keep boosting investment at a pace faster than output growth, CBO projects.

Residential Investment. CBO expects rapid growth in real residential investment over the next few years, but the small size of the sector will limit its contribution to the growth of real GDP. Real residential investment is expected to grow by 11 percent this year on a fourth-quarter-to-fourth-quarter basis, and by more than 13 percent next year, before moderating in subsequent years. That projection implies a contribution to output growth of roughly one-half of one percentage point over each of the next few years (see Figure 2-3).

Housing starts—new, privately owned housing units on which construction begins in a given period—account for a large share of residential investment, and CBO expects them to post very strong growth, from an estimated 1.0 million units in 2014 to roughly 1.7 million units in 2019. The number of housing starts has been low in recent years because of weak household formation and a high vacancy rate (that is, the percentage of homes that are vacant). Household formation has been weaker since 2012 than one would expect, given the size of the increases in employment since then and the historical relationship between employment and household formation (see Figure 2-4). That weakness has probably resulted partly from the fact that lending standards for mortgages have remained fairly tight; household formation may also have been weak because households'

5. The term "business cycle" describes fluctuations in overall economic activity accompanied by fluctuations in the unemployment rate, interest rates, income, and other variables. Over the course of a business cycle, real activity rises to a peak and then falls until it reaches a trough; then it starts to rise again, beginning a new cycle. Business cycles are irregular, varying in frequency, magnitude, and duration.

Figure 2-4.

Factors Underlying the Projected Contributions to the Growth of Real GDP

Solid **growth in the inflation-adjusted compensation of employees** is projected to support faster growth in consumer spending in the next two years.

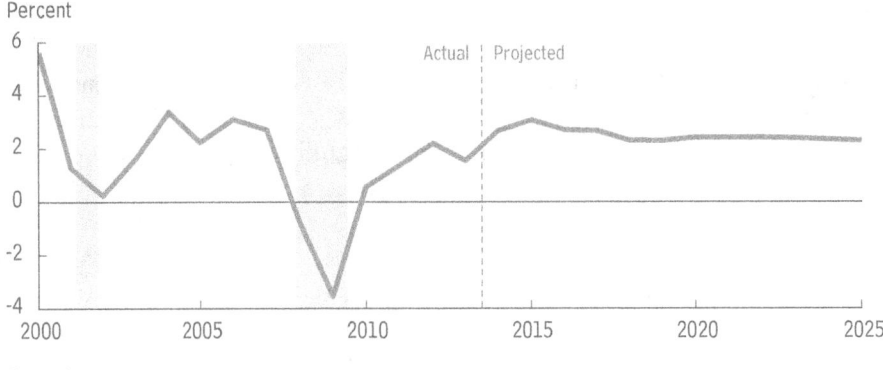

The **growth of capital services** is projected to rise over the next few years because increases in the demand for goods and services will spur business investment.

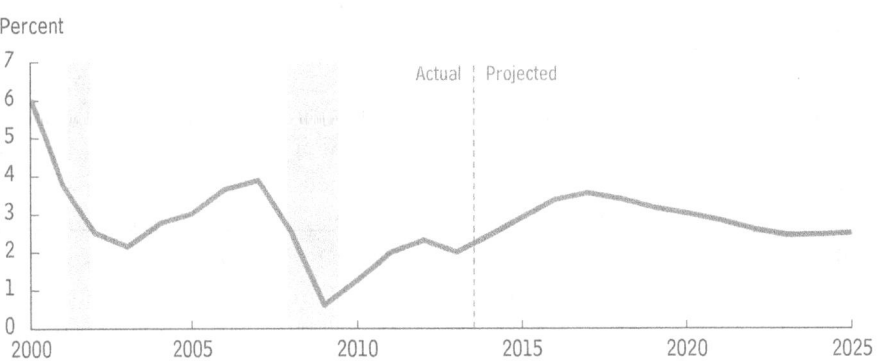

Sources: Congressional Budget Office; Bureau of Economic Analysis; Bureau of the Census; Consensus Economics.

Notes: Data are annual. Actual data are plotted through 2013. Values for 2014 are CBO's estimates.

In the top panel, inflation-adjusted compensation of employees is total wages, salaries, and supplements divided by the price index for personal consumption expenditures. Percentage changes are measured from the average of one calendar year to the next.

In the bottom panel, capital services are a measure of the flow of services available for production from the real (inflation-adjusted) stock of capital (equipment, structures, intellectual property products, inventories, and land). Percentage changes are measured from the average of one calendar year to the next.

- -

Continued

expectations for income growth have been slow to improve since the recession and because student loans have rendered some young adults unable or unwilling to obtain a mortgage. Better prospects for jobs and wages, as well as greater access to mortgage credit, will encourage more household formation and raise the demand for housing, in CBO's view, despite the negative effects of an expected rise in interest rates for mortgage loans. The greater demand for housing will help to reduce the vacancy rate, which will further encourage home building.

CBO anticipates that the stronger growth in demand for housing will put upward pressure on house prices. That upward pressure will be offset to some degree by the projected increase in the supply of housing units. On balance, CBO projects, house prices—as measured by the

Federal Housing Finance Agency's (FHFA's) price index for home purchases—will increase by almost 3 percent in 2015 and by about 2½ percent per year, on average, over the 2016–2019 period. According to CBO's forecast, FHFA's index will surpass its prerecession peak (without being adjusted for overall inflation) in 2017.

Government Purchases. CBO projects that purchases of goods and services by governments at the federal, state, and local levels—which make up the portion of government spending directly included in GDP—will have little direct effect on the growth of output this year and contribute slightly in later years (see Figure 2-3 on page 34). In 2014, real government purchases increased by nearly 1 percent on a fourth-quarter-to-fourth-quarter basis, providing a mild positive contribution to real GDP growth. (During the previous four years, real government

Figure 2-4.   Continued

Factors Underlying the Projected Contributions to the Growth of Real GDP

A rise in **household formation** is projected to boost the demand for housing and spur residential investment for the next few years.

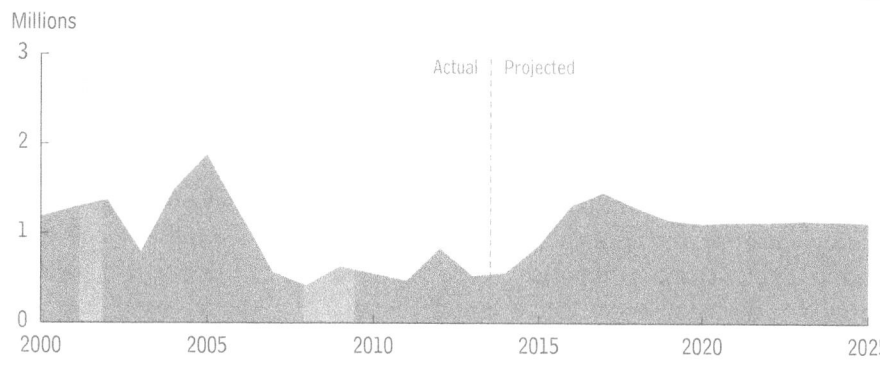

The rise in the **growth of real GDP in the United States relative to that among its leading trading partners** is projected to contribute to lower net exports this year.

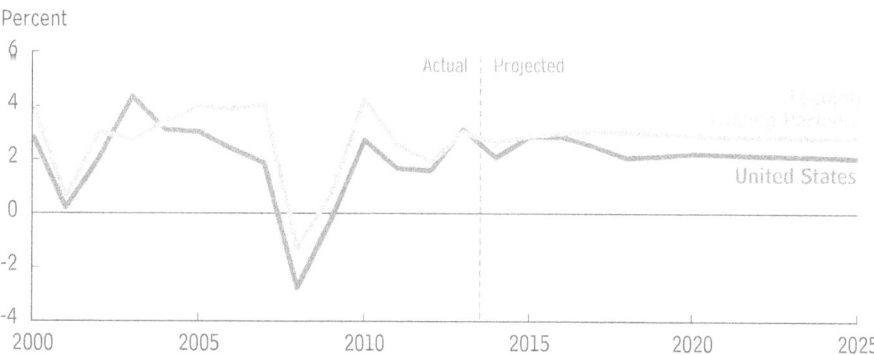

Notes: In the top panel, household formation is the change in the number of households from one calendar year to the next.

In the bottom panel, the percentage change in real (inflation-adjusted) gross domestic product among the United States' leading trading partners is calculated using an average of the rates of growth of their real GDPs, weighted by their shares of U.S. exports. The trading partners included in the average are Australia, Brazil, Canada, China, Hong Kong, Japan, Mexico, Singapore, South Korea, Switzerland, Taiwan, the United Kingdom, and the countries of the euro zone. Percentage changes are measured from the fourth quarter of one calendar year to the fourth quarter of the next.

GDP = gross domestic product.

purchases had dampened real GDP growth.) This year, CBO expects an increase in real purchases by state and local governments to roughly offset a decline in real purchases by the federal government; in later years, growth in purchases by the former are expected to more than offset continued contractions in purchases by the latter.

CBO's projections of real purchases by state and local governments reflect the agency's expectation that those governments' finances will continue to improve. The recession and weak subsequent recovery, combined with a sharp drop in house prices between 2007 and 2011, significantly reduced those governments' tax revenues and strained their finances. In the past two years, however, the stronger economy and increases in house prices have improved state and local governments' finances, which has allowed them to purchase more. CBO expects real purchases by state and local governments to increase by

about 1 percent per year from 2015 through 2019. In contrast, under current law, real purchases by the federal government—mostly stemming from discretionary appropriations—are projected to fall by 2 percent this year and by an annual average of 0.7 percent over the 2015–2019 period.

Net Exports. CBO expects that net exports (that is, exports minus imports) will impose a drag on GDP growth in 2015 and 2016, just as they did last year. In real terms, net exports are projected to be about $50 billion lower in the fourth quarter of 2015 than they were in the fourth quarter of 2014, dampening GDP growth by about 0.3 percentage points (see Figure 2-3 on page 34). Real net exports are projected to decline further in 2016, but by a smaller amount—about $40 billion. In each of the following three years, however, CBO projects that net exports will rise and add slightly to GDP growth.

CBO's projection of net exports is based partly on important differences in the expected pace of economic activity in the United States and among the nation's leading trading partners (see Figure 2-4 on page 36). CBO expects growth in the United States this year to improve relative to the growth of the leading trading partners; consequently, U.S. spending on imports will rise more than the trading partners' spending on U.S. exports will, reducing net exports.[6] For example, the economies of the euro zone are expected to grow unevenly and sluggishly in 2015 and 2016, and China's economy is projected to grow more modestly over the next few years than in previous years. Over time, though, CBO expects U.S. growth to slow slightly relative to growth among the nation's trading partners and particularly the countries in the euro zone; that will provide a small boost to net exports. Another factor affecting CBO's forecast of net exports is growing domestic energy production, which is expected to reduce demand for imported energy products.

CBO's projection of net exports is also based on the increase in the exchange value of the dollar last year and on the agency's forecast of a slight further increase in the exchange value this year. The increase last year was partly caused by a decline in long-term interest rates among leading U.S. trading partners, particularly in Europe and Asia, and by a deterioration in the outlook for foreign growth. Those developments increased the exchange value of the dollar by boosting the relative demand for dollar-denominated assets. This year, CBO expects the rise in economic growth in the United States relative to growth among the nation's trading partners to continue to contribute to rising interest rates in the United States relative to those abroad. That widening divergence in interest rates is projected to provide an additional boost to the relative demand for dollar-denominated assets and to further increase the exchange value of the dollar. The higher exchange value for the dollar will make imports for U.S. consumers cheaper and U.S. exports to foreign buyers more expensive, dampening net exports in the near term. As growth in foreign economies strengthens over time, however, CBO expects foreign central banks to tighten their monetary policies gradually, which will

lower the exchange value of the dollar and contribute to stronger net exports later in the projection period.

The Labor Market

Employment climbed briskly in 2014, marking more than four years of gains. An average of 234,000 nonfarm jobs were added per month in 2014, significantly more than the monthly average of about 185,000 jobs in the previous three years. Nearly all employment growth since the end of the recession in 2009 has occurred in the private sector, where employment in 2014 surpassed its prerecession peak; employment in the public sector remains well below its prerecession peak (see Figure 2-5).

Although conditions in the labor market improved notably in 2014, CBO estimates that a significant amount of slack remains. But CBO anticipates that the strengthening economy will lead to continued gains in employment, largely eliminating that slack by 2017.

Figure 2-5.

Changes in Private and Public Employment Since the End of 2007

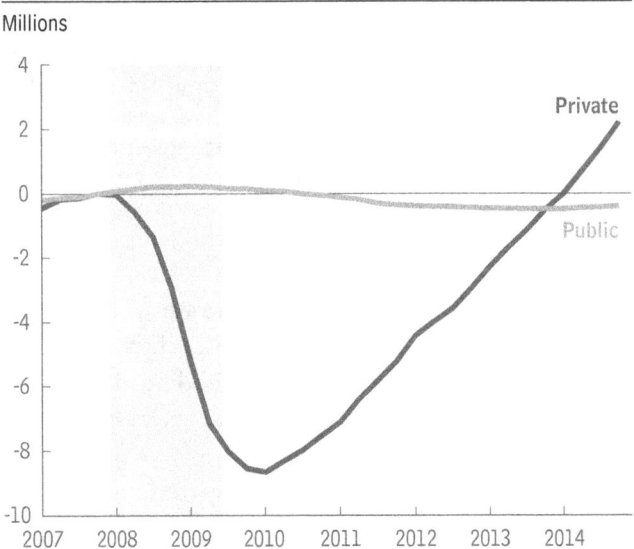

Millions

Sources: Congressional Budget Office; Bureau of Labor Statistics.

Notes: Private employment consists of all employees on the payrolls of nonfarm private industries. Public employment consists of all employees on government payrolls, excluding temporary and intermittent workers hired by the federal government for the decennial census.

Changes are measured from the beginning of the recession in the fourth quarter of 2007.

Data are quarterly and are plotted through the fourth quarter of 2014.

---

6. CBO calculates the growth of leading U.S. trading partners using a weighted average of their growth rates. That measure uses shares of U.S. exports as weights. Similarly, CBO's measure of the exchange value of the dollar is an export-weighted average of the exchange rates between the dollar and the currencies of leading U.S. trading partners.

Current Slack in the Labor Market. Slack in the labor market includes the degree to which people who are not working would work if employment prospects were better, as well as the degree to which people who are employed would work longer hours if they could. Measuring slack is difficult, especially in light of the unusual developments that have taken place in the labor market since the recent recession. But in CBO's view, the key components of slack in the labor market are the following:

- The number of people working or actively looking for work is smaller than would be expected if the demand for workers was stronger. Specifically, the labor force participation rate—the percentage of people in the civilian noninstitutionalized population who are at least 16 years old and are either working or actively seeking work—is well below CBO's estimate of the *potential* labor force participation rate, which is the rate that would exist if not for the temporary effects of fluctuations in the overall demand for goods and services attributable to the business cycle.

- The unemployment rate is higher than CBO's estimate of the current natural rate of unemployment.

- The share of part-time workers who would prefer full-time work is unusually high.

Several indicators provide additional evidence that significant slack remains in the labor market. Most important is hourly labor compensation, which continues to grow more slowly than it did before the recession. Other indicators are the rate at which job seekers are hired and the rate at which workers are quitting their jobs, both of which remain lower than they were before the last recession.

If the unemployment rate had returned to its level in December 2007, and if the labor force participation rate had equaled its potential rate, there would have been more people employed in 2014—about 2¾ million more in the fourth quarter, according to CBO's estimates. The elevated unemployment rate and the depressed labor force participation rate account for that shortfall in roughly equal proportions. The equivalent shortfall in employment in the fourth quarter of 2013 was about 5¼ million people, largely reflecting the elevated unemployment rate, CBO estimates; at its peak in 2009, the shortfall was 8½ million people. Those estimates of

shortfalls in employment use a measure that does not include the number of people who have left the labor force permanently in response to the recession and slow recovery. However, the measure includes unemployed workers who would have difficulty finding jobs even if demand for workers were higher. Different measures of shortfalls in employment might be appropriate for some purposes.

Labor Force Participation. The labor force participation rate fell from 65.9 percent in the fourth quarter of 2007, at the beginning of the recession, to 62.8 percent in the second quarter of 2014; it has since stabilized. About 1¾ percentage points of that roughly 3 percentage-point decline in participation, CBO estimates, stems from long-term trends (especially the aging of the population), but the rest of the decline is attributable to the weakness of the economy during the past several years. Specifically, about three-quarters of one percentage point represents the extent to which actual participation is lower than potential participation because of the recent cyclical weakness in employment prospects and wages; that gap is one component of slack in the labor market, and it will close over time as more people enter or reenter the labor force (as this chapter discusses below in "The Labor Market Outlook Through 2019" on page 42). And about one-half of one percentage point of the decline represents workers who became discouraged by the persistent weakness in the labor market and permanently dropped out of the labor force.[7]

Unemployment. The unemployment rate was 5.7 percent in the fourth quarter of 2014, roughly three-quarters of one percentage point above its level at the end of 2007. CBO estimates that roughly one-quarter of one percentage point of the difference between the rate in the fourth quarter and the rate before the recession is a temporary effect of cyclical weakness in the economy and thus is another component of slack in the labor market. (At its peak, in late 2009, the temporary effect of cyclical weakness on the unemployment rate was about 4¼ percentage points, CBO estimates.) CBO estimates that structural

---

7. Since publishing its most recent previous projections in *An Update to the Budget and Economic Outlook: 2014 to 2024* (August 2014), www.cbo.gov/publication/45653, CBO has revised downward its estimate of the degree to which the persistent weakness in the labor market led some workers to become discouraged and permanently drop out of the labor force. See "Comparison With CBO's August 2014 Projections" on page 52.

Figure 2-6.

Rates of Short- and Long-Term Unemployment

Percent

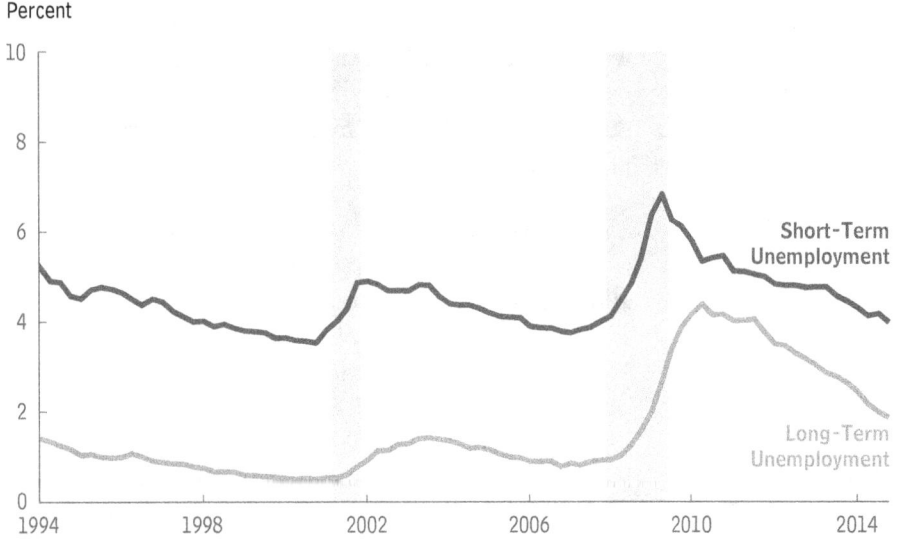

The overall unemployment rate remains elevated partly because of weakness in the demand for goods and services and partly because of the stigma and erosion of skills that can stem from long-term unemployment.

Sources: Congressional Budget Office; Bureau of Labor Statistics.

Notes: The rate of short-term unemployment is the percentage of the labor force that has been out of work for 26 weeks or less. The rate of long-term unemployment is the percentage of the labor force that has been out of work for at least 27 consecutive weeks.

Data are quarterly and are plotted through the fourth quarter of 2014.

factors account for the remainder of the difference (and an equivalent increase in CBO's estimate of the natural rate of unemployment).[8] In particular, the stigma and erosion of skills that can stem from long-term unemployment (that is, unemployment that lasts for at least 27 consecutive weeks), which have remained higher than they were before the recent recession, are continuing to push up the unemployment rate.[9]

The difference between the unemployment rate in the fourth quarter and the unemployment rate before the recession can be explained entirely by an increase in long-term unemployment. Though the rate of short-term unemployment (the number of people unemployed for 26 weeks or less as a percentage of the labor force) in the fourth quarter of 2014 nearly matched the rate in the

8. CBO has revised that estimate of the effect of the structural factors downward since publishing its most recent previous projections in August. See "Comparison With CBO's August 2014 Projections" on page 52.

9. Another structural factor that raised the unemployment rate until recently, in CBO's view, was a decrease in the efficiency with which employers filled vacancies. CBO estimates that that effect dissipated by late 2014.

fourth quarter of 2007, the rate of long-term unemployment was still nearly 1 percentage point above the earlier rate of 0.9 percent (see Figure 2-6). The elevated rate of long-term unemployment in part reflects an increase in the natural rate of unemployment, but in CBO's view, that elevated rate also reflects slack in the labor market. CBO expects that many of the long-term unemployed who are not near retirement age will be employed again in the next few years. Indeed, much of the decline in the rate of long-term unemployment last year appears to have happened because people found work, not because they left the labor force.

Part-Time Employment. Another component of labor market slack is the number of people employed but not working as many hours as they would like. The incidence of part-time employment for economic reasons (that is, part-time employment among workers who would prefer full-time employment) remains significantly higher than it was before the recession (see Figure 2-7). The continued large share of part-time workers is one reason that the Bureau of Labor Statistics' U-6 measure of underused labor stood at 11.4 percent in the fourth quarter of 2014, down from a peak of 17.1 percent in the fourth quarter

Figure 2-7.

Underuse of Labor

Percentage of the Labor Force Plus Marginally Attached Workers

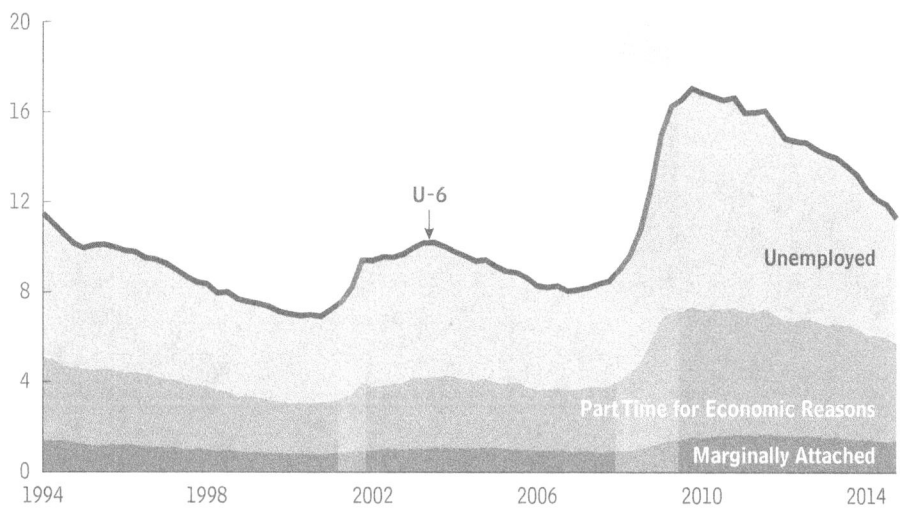

The **U-6 measure of the underuse of labor** has fallen since the end of the recession but remains quite high: The percentage of people who are unemployed, the percentage of people who are employed **part time for economic reasons**, and the percentage of people who are **marginally attached** to the labor force are all greater than they were before the recession began.

Sources: Congressional Budget Office; Bureau of Labor Statistics.

Notes: Part-time employment for economic reasons refers to part-time employment among workers who would prefer full-time employment. People who are marginally attached to the labor force are those who are not currently looking for work but have looked for work in the past 12 months.

Data are quarterly and are plotted through the fourth quarter of 2014.

of 2009 but still nearly 3 percentage points above its level before the recession.[10]

Indicators of Labor Market Slack. Continued weak growth in hourly rates of labor compensation (that is, wages, salaries, and benefits) is an important signal that significant slack remains in the labor market. The reason is that when slack exists—that is, when labor resources are underused and many workers are unemployed or working fewer hours than they would like—firms can hire from a large pool of underemployed workers. Hence, the firms have a smaller incentive to increase compensation in order to attract workers.

---

10. The U-6 measure combines the number of unemployed people, the number of people who are employed part-time for economic reasons, and the number of people who are "marginally attached" to the labor force (that is, who are not currently looking for work but have looked for work in the past 12 months). It divides the total by the number of people in the labor force plus the number of marginally attached workers. The number of workers who are marginally attached to the labor force is also larger than it was before the recession—about 2.1 million people in the fourth quarter of 2014, up from about 1.4 million in the fourth quarter of 2007.

Labor compensation continues to grow considerably more slowly than it did before the recession, although it sped up a bit in 2014, according to some measures. Hourly rates of compensation, as measured by the employment cost index (ECI) for workers in private industry, grew by 2.0 percent in 2013; during the year ending in the third quarter of 2014, such compensation rose at an annual rate of 2.3 percent (see Figure 2-8). Similarly, the ECI for wages and salaries alone rose slightly faster last year than in the previous year—at an annual rate of 2.2 percent during the year ending in the third quarter of 2014, as opposed to 2.0 percent in 2013. Another measure—the average hourly earnings of production and nonsupervisory workers on private non-farm payrolls, which measures only wages—grew a bit more slowly in 2014 than in 2013. However, all of those compensation measures were growing faster before the recession.

Two other indicators of slack in the labor market, the rate at which job seekers are hired and the rate at which workers are quitting their jobs (as a fraction of total employment), also have not fully recovered. Those rates have improved since reaching low points in the second quarter

Figure 2-8.

Measures of Compensation Paid to Employees

Percentage Change

When labor is underused—as is currently the case—firms can hire from a relatively large pool of underemployed workers and thus have less incentive to increase compensation to attract workers.

Accordingly, compensation has been growing considerably more slowly than it did before the recession.

Sources: Congressional Budget Office; Bureau of Labor Statistics.

Notes: Average hourly earnings are earnings of production and nonsupervisory workers on private nonfarm payrolls. Compensation is measured by the employment cost index for workers in private industry.

Data are quarterly. Average hourly earnings are plotted through the fourth quarter of 2014; the employment cost index is plotted through the third quarter of 2014. Percentage changes are measured from the same quarter one year earlier.

of 2009, suggesting that employers are gaining confidence in the strength of the economy and that workers are more confident about finding new jobs after quitting. However, each rate has recovered only about two-thirds of the decline from its 2001–2007 average.

Difficulties in Measuring Slack in the Labor Market. Considerable difficulties arise in measuring slack in the labor market, especially under current circumstances. For example, in assessing potential labor force participation, CBO estimated how many people permanently dropped out of the labor force because of such factors as long-term unemployment. However, CBO may have underestimated or overestimated that number, and therefore potential labor force participation could be lower or higher, respectively, than the agency thinks. Similarly, CBO's estimate of the increase in the natural rate of unemployment since before the recession incorporates the agency's estimate of the decrease in the efficiency with which employers fill vacancies. That decrease in efficiency has dissipated over the past year, in CBO's judgment, as workers have acquired new skills, shifted to faster-growing industries and occupations, and relocated to take

advantage of new opportunities. But if such adjustments in the labor market have occurred more slowly than CBO has estimated, the natural rate of unemployment would currently be higher than CBO has estimated. A higher natural rate would suggest more upward pressure on wages for any given unemployment rate.

The Labor Market Outlook Through 2019. The growth of output this year will increase the demand for labor, leading to solid employment gains and a further reduction in labor market slack, according to CBO's estimates. Those developments are expected to continue at a more moderate pace over the following two years. The unemployment rate is projected to fall to 5.5 percent in the fourth quarter of 2015 and to edge down to 5.3 percent by the fourth quarter of 2017 (see Table 2-1 on page 30). CBO expects the decline in the unemployment rate to be tempered by the fact that labor force participation, because of the stronger labor market, will decline less than would be expected on the basis of demographics and certain other factors. CBO also expects the diminished slack in the labor market to raise the growth of hourly labor compensation modestly.

Figure 2-9.

The Labor Force, Employment, and Unemployment

The percentage of the population that is employed is projected to fall over the next 10 years because of declining participation in the labor force, mainly by baby boomers as they age and move into retirement.

Percentage of the Population

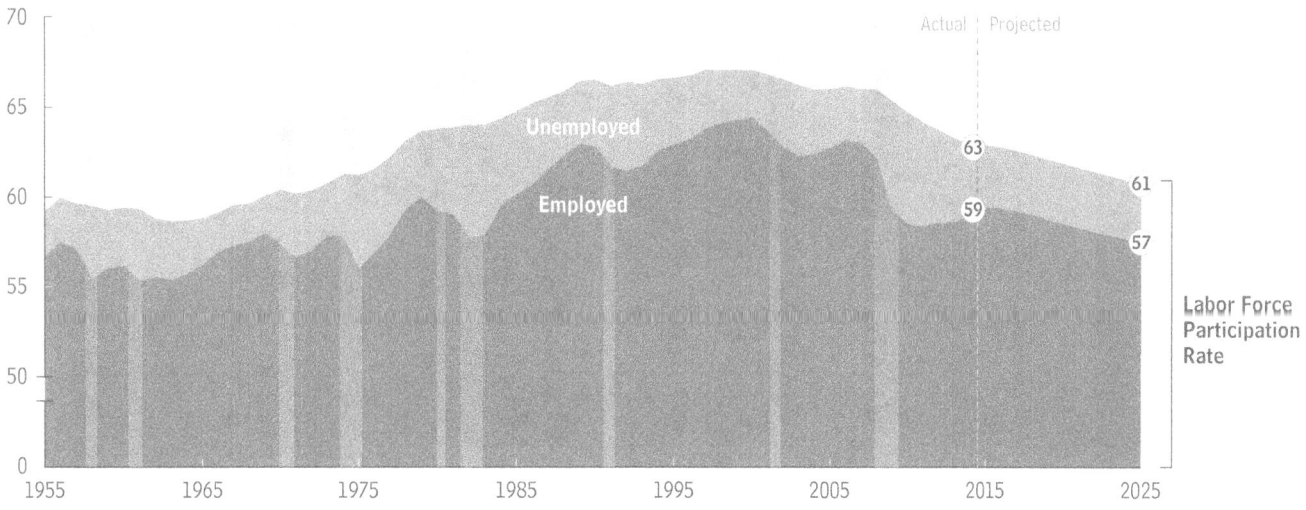

Sources: Congressional Budget Office; Bureau of Labor Statistics.

Notes: The labor force consists of people who are employed and people who are unemployed but who are available for work and are actively seeking jobs. Unemployment as a percentage of the population is not the same as the official unemployment rate, which is expressed as a percentage of the labor force. The population is the civilian noninstitutionalized population age 16 or older.

Data are annual. Actual data are plotted through 2014.

CBO's labor market projections for 2018 and 2019 are largely based on a transition to the agency's projections for later years, when the relationship between the unemployment rate and the natural rate of unemployment is expected to match its historical average. Therefore, CBO projects slightly higher unemployment rates in 2018 and 2019—5.4 percent and 5.5 percent, respectively.

Employment. CBO expects nonfarm payroll employment to rise by an average of about 180,000 jobs per month in 2015. In 2016 and 2017, the average projected increase is about 130,000 per month, a number that is consistent with the expected moderation of output growth as output converges on its potential. That projection is also consistent with the expected improvement in productivity growth. Growth in employment and in total hours worked in the past two years was faster than what the modest growth in GDP during that period would have suggested, which meant that labor productivity grew unusually slowly. This year, CBO expects that labor productivity will grow at close to its average rate over the most recent business cycle, which means that output can grow more rapidly than it did last year even though

employment is projected to grow a little more slowly than it did last year.

Despite the diminishing slack in the labor market, the number of people employed as a percentage of the population is projected to remain close to its current level—about 59 percent—through 2019 (see Figure 2-9). That percentage is well below the levels seen in the two decades before the recent recession, a difference that primarily reflects the long-term trends pushing down labor force participation, above all the aging of the baby boomers and their move into retirement.

Labor Force Participation. The rate of labor force participation has dropped noticeably in recent years, and CBO expects the rate to continue to decline—by about one-half of one percentage point (to 62.5 percent) by the end of 2017 and by an additional one-half of one percentage point (to 62 percent) by 2019. A number of factors will dampen participation. The most important is the ongoing movement of the baby-boom generation into retirement. Federal tax and spending policies—in particular, certain aspects of the ACA, and also the structure of

Figure 2-10.

Overall and Natural Rates of Unemployment

Percent

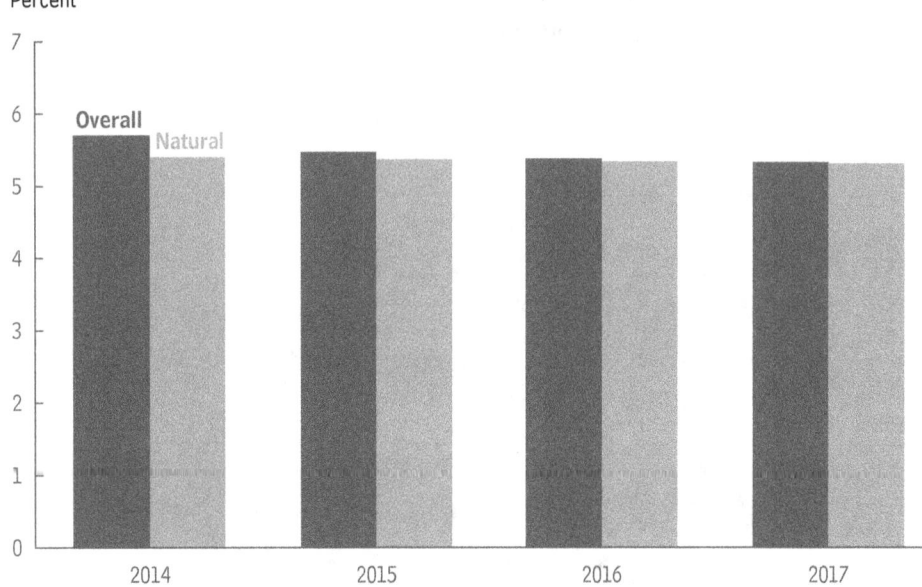

Stronger demand for labor will close the gap between the overall rate of unemployment and CBO's estimate of the natural rate.

CBO also expects the natural rate to fall, as the effects of stigma and erosion of skills among the long-term unemployed fade.

Sources: Congressional Budget Office; Bureau of Labor Statistics.

Notes: The overall unemployment rate is a measure of the number of jobless people who are available for work and are actively seeking jobs, expressed as a percentage of the labor force. The natural rate is CBO's estimate of the rate arising from all sources except fluctuations in the overall demand for goods and services.

Data are fourth-quarter values. The value for the overall rate in 2014 is actual; values in other years are projected.

the tax code, whereby rising income pushes some people into higher tax brackets—will also tend to lower the participation rate in the next several years.[11]

But another factor is projected to offset some of those effects. Increasing demand for labor as the economy improves is expected to boost participation in the next few years: Some workers who left the labor force temporarily, or who stayed out of the labor force because of weak employment prospects, will enter the labor force, and other workers will choose to stay in the labor force rather than drop out. Those factors will push the labor force participation rate back toward its potential rate. Therefore, the projected decline in the labor force participation rate over the next few years is slower than what would result from demographic changes and the effects of fiscal policy alone.

The Unemployment Rate. For two reasons, CBO expects the unemployment rate to decline from an average of 6.2 percent in 2014 to 5.3 percent in 2017 (see Figure 2-10). First, stronger demand for labor will close the gap between the unemployment rate and the natural rate. Second, CBO expects the natural rate to fall as the effects of stigma and erosion of skills among the long-term unemployed fade.

However, the unemployment rate is projected to decline much less than it has in recent years, because CBO expects growth in employment and the drop in the labor force participation rate to be slower during the next few years, on balance, than they have been in the past few years.

Labor Compensation. CBO projects stronger growth in hourly labor compensation over the next several years than in 2014. That pickup is consistent with the agency's projection of firms' stronger demand for workers. To some degree, firms can attract unemployed or underemployed workers without increasing compensation growth. However, as slack in the labor market diminishes

---

11. For more information about the ACA's effects on labor force participation, see Congressional Budget Office, *The Budget and Economic Outlook: 2014 to 2024* (February 2014), Appendix C, www.cbo.gov/publication/45010.

Figure 2-11.

Inflation

Percentage Change in Prices

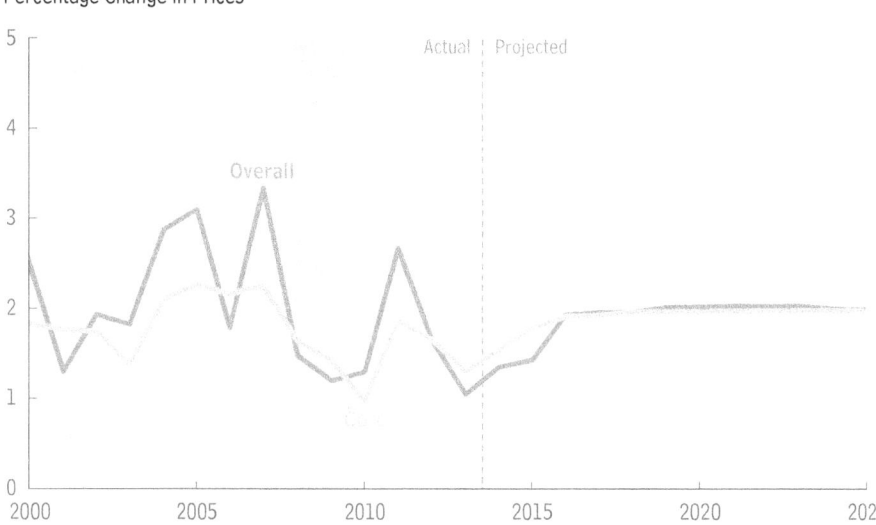

CBO anticipates that prices will rise modestly over the next several years, reflecting the remaining slack in the economy and widely held expectations for low and stable inflation.

Sources: Congressional Budget Office; Bureau of Economic Analysis.

Notes: The overall inflation rate is based on the price index for personal consumption expenditures; the core rate excludes prices for food and energy.

Data are annual. Percentage changes are measured from the fourth quarter of one calendar year to the fourth quarter of the next. Actual data are plotted through 2013; the values for 2014 are CBO's estimates and do not incorporate data released by the Bureau of Economic Analysis since early December 2014.

and firms must increasingly compete for workers, CBO projects that growth in hourly compensation will pick up. That increase in compensation will boost labor force participation and the number of available workers, thereby moderating the overall increase in compensation growth. CBO expects the ECI for total compensation of workers in private industry to increase at an average annual rate of 3.6 percent from 2015 through 2019, compared with an average of about 2 percent during the past several years. The growth of other measures of hourly labor compensation, such as the average hourly earnings of production and nonsupervisory workers in private industries, is similarly expected to increase.

Inflation

CBO projects that the rate of inflation in 2015—as measured by the percentage change in the PCE price index from the fourth quarter of 2014 to the fourth quarter of 2015—will remain subdued (see Table 2-1 on page 30 and Figure 2-11). CBO expects less downward pressure on inflation this year and in the next few years because of the diminishing amount of slack in the economy. In 2015, however, CBO expects significant downward pressure on inflation to result from two recent developments: the increase in the exchange value of the dollar, which

will reduce inflation by lowering import prices, and lower prices for crude oil, which will reduce energy prices (see Box 2-2 on page 31). In CBO's projections, inflation in the PCE price index will be 1.4 percent this year, very slightly above last year's estimated 1.3 percent. By contrast, CBO expects the *core* PCE price index—which excludes prices for food and energy—to rise at a faster 1.8 percent rate this year after an estimated 1.5 percent increase last year.

In 2016 and 2017, CBO projects the rate of overall PCE inflation to be close to the rate of core PCE inflation because of a partial rebound—consistent with prices in oil futures markets—in the price of crude oil. Given expectations for inflation and the anticipated reduction in slack, the projected rate of inflation for both measures rises to 1.9 percent in 2016 and stabilizes at 2.0 percent by the end of 2017. That rate is equal to the Federal Reserve's longer-term goal, reflecting CBO's judgment that consumers and businesses expect inflation to occur at about that rate and that the Federal Reserve will make changes in monetary policy to prevent inflation from exceeding or falling short of its goal for a prolonged period.

Figure 2-12.

GDP and Potential GDP

Trillions of 2009 Dollars

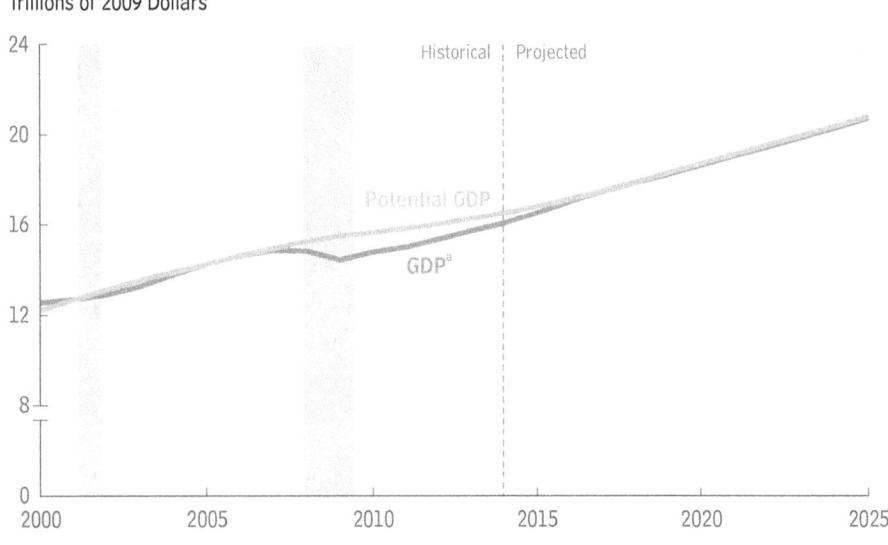

The gap between GDP and potential GDP—a measure of underused resources, or slack—will essentially be eliminated by the end of 2017, CBO expects.

Sources: Congressional Budget Office; Bureau of Economic Analysis.

Notes: Potential gross domestic product is CBO's estimate of the maximum sustainable output of the economy.

Data are annual. Actual data are plotted through 2013; projections are plotted through 2025 and are based on data available through early December 2014.

GDP = gross domestic product.

a.   From 2020 to 2025, the projection for actual GDP falls short of that for potential GDP by one-half of one percent of potential GDP.

The consumer price index for all urban consumers (CPI-U) and its core version are expected to increase a little more rapidly than their PCE counterparts, because of the different methods used to calculate them and also because housing rents play a larger role in the consumer price indexes. CBO projects that the difference between inflation as measured by the CPI-U and inflation as measured by the PCE price index after this year will generally be about 0.4 percentage points per year, which is close to the average difference over the past several decades.

The Economic Outlook for 2020 Through 2025

CBO's economic projections for 2020 through 2025 are not based on forecasts of cyclical developments in the economy, as its projections for the next several years are. Rather, they are based on projections of underlying growth factors—such as the growth of the labor force, of hours worked, and of productivity—that exclude cyclical movements. Actual outcomes will no doubt deviate from what the underlying growth factors suggest, so CBO's economic projections are intended to reflect average

outcomes. The projections take into account several factors: historical patterns for the nonfarm business sector and for the rest of the economy; projected changes in demographics; the response of investment to those and other long-term trends; CBO's estimates of the persistent effects of the 2007–2009 recession and of the slow economic recovery that followed it; and federal tax and spending policies under current law.

CBO projects that real GDP will be about one-half of one percent below real potential GDP, on average, during the 2020–2025 period (see Figure 2-12). That gap is based on CBO's estimate that output has been roughly that much lower than potential output, on average, over the period from 1961 to 2009, a period that included seven complete business cycles (measured from trough to trough). Indeed, over the course of each of the five complete business cycles that have occurred since 1975, output has been lower than potential output, on average: CBO estimates that over each of those cycles, the shortfall in output relative to potential output during and after that cycle's economic downturn has been larger and has lasted longer than the excess of output over potential output during that cycle's economic boom.[12]

In CBO's projections for the 2020–2025 period:

- The growth of real GDP averages 2.2 percent per year, as does the growth of real potential GDP.

- The unemployment rate edges down from 5.5 percent in 2020 to 5.4 percent in 2022 and subsequent years; during that period, it slightly exceeds CBO's estimate of the natural rate of unemployment, which is consistent with CBO's projection that output will fall short of potential output.

- Both inflation and core inflation, as measured by the PCE price index, average 2.0 percent a year. Inflation as measured by the CPI-U is somewhat higher.

- The interest rates on 3-month Treasury bills and 10-year Treasury notes are 3.4 percent and 4.6 percent, respectively.

Potential Output

The growth in real potential output that CBO projects for the 2020–2025 period (2.2 percent per year, on average) is substantially slower than CBO's estimate of the growth in real potential output during the business cycles, as measured from peak to peak, that occurred between 1982 and 2007 (3.1 percent per year, on average) but substantially faster than the growth in potential output during the current business cycle so far—that is, between 2008 and 2014 (1.4 percent per year, on average). Those differences reflect changes in the growth of potential hours worked, the growth of capital services, and the growth of potential productivity—primarily in the nonfarm business sector, which represents roughly three-quarters of total output. In addition, CBO's projection for potential output in the 2020–2025 period is lower than it would have been if the 2007–2009 recession had not occurred. According to CBO's estimates, the recession and the ensuing slow recovery have weakened the factors that determine potential output—labor supply, capital services, and productivity—for an extended period.

---

12. Further discussion will be provided in Congressional Budget Office, *Why CBO Projects Average Output Will Be Below Potential Output* (forthcoming).

Overall Output Growth. The main reason that potential output is projected to grow more slowly than it did in the earlier business cycles is that CBO expects growth in the potential labor force (the labor force adjusted for variations caused by the business cycle) to be much slower than it was earlier (see Table 2-2). Growth in the potential labor force will be held down by the ongoing retirement of the baby boomers; by a relatively stable labor force participation rate among working-age women, after sharp increases from the 1960s to the mid-1990s; and by federal tax and spending policies set in current law, which will reduce some people's incentives to work (as this chapter discusses below, in "The Labor Market" on page 50).

The main reason that CBO expects potential output to grow more quickly than it has over the past half-dozen years is that the agency expects the potential productivity of the labor force to grow more quickly. In CBO's projections, potential productivity grows at an annual rate of 1.6 percent from 2020 through 2025, which would be close to its average rate of growth during the business cycles between 1982 and 2007 and substantially higher than the 0.9 percent average rate that CBO estimates for 2008 through 2014. That projected increase, in turn, mostly reflects CBO's assessment of potential total factor productivity, or TFP—which is the average real output per unit of combined labor and capital services—in the nonfarm business sector. That measure has grown unusually slowly since the onset of the recession in 2007, but CBO estimates that it will accelerate during the next few years, returning to its average rate of growth during the years before the recession.

The Nonfarm Business Sector. In the nonfarm business sector, CBO projects that potential output will grow at an average rate of 2.6 percent per year over the 2020–2025 period. Like the projected growth rate of *overall* potential output, that growth rate would be lower than it was during the business cycles from 1982 through 2007 but higher than it has been since 2007.

Potential hours worked in the nonfarm business sector are projected to grow at an average annual rate of 0.6 percent from 2020 through 2025—more slowly than they did in earlier periods (particularly from 1982 through 2001) but more quickly than they did from 2008 through 2014. The reason that growth in hours in that sector is expected to be faster than it was during that most recent period, despite the projected slow growth of the

Table 2-2.

Key Inputs in CBO's Projections of Potential GDP

Percent, by Calendar Year

	Average Annual Growth							Projected Average Annual Growth		
	1950–1973	1974–1981	1982–1990	1991–2001	2002–2007	2008–2014	Total, 1950–2014	2015–2019	2020–2025	Total, 2015–2025
	Overall Economy									
Potential GDP	4.0	3.3	3.2	3.2	2.8	1.4	3.3	2.1	2.2	2.1
Potential Labor Force	1.6	2.5	1.6	1.3	0.9	0.5	1.5	0.5	0.6	0.5
Potential Labor Force Productivity[a]	2.4	0.8	1.6	1.9	1.9	0.9	1.8	1.6	1.6	1.6
	Nonfarm Business Sector									
Potential Output	4.1	3.7	3.3	3.6	3.2	1.6	3.5	2.5	2.6	2.5
Potential Hours Worked	1.4	2.4	1.6	1.2	0.7	0.2	1.3	0.5	0.6	0.6
Capital Services	3.9	4.1	4.0	4.3	3.0	2.1	3.7	3.1	2.8	2.9
Potential TFP	1.9	0.8	1.0	1.4	1.8	0.9	1.4	1.2	1.3	1.3
Potential TFP excluding adjustments	1.9	0.8	1.0	1.3	1.3	0.9	1.4	1.2	1.3	1.3
Adjustments to TFP (Percentage points)[b]	0	0	0	0.1	0.5	*	0.1	*	*	*
Contributions to the Growth of Potential Output (Percentage points)										
Potential hours worked	1.0	1.7	1.1	0.9	0.5	0.1	0.9	0.3	0.5	0.4
Capital input	1.2	1.2	1.2	1.3	0.9	0.6	1.1	0.9	0.8	0.9
Potential TFP	1.9	0.8	1.0	1.4	1.8	0.9	1.4	1.2	1.3	1.3
Total Contributions	4.0	3.6	3.3	3.6	3.1	1.6	3.5	2.5	2.6	2.5
Potential Labor Productivity[c]	2.7	1.3	1.7	2.3	2.5	1.5	2.2	2.0	1.9	2.0

Source: Congressional Budget Office.

Notes: Potential GDP is CBO's estimate of the maximum sustainable output of the economy.

    GDP = gross domestic product; TFP = total factor productivity; * = between -0.05 percentage points and zero.

a. The ratio of potential GDP to the potential labor force.

b. The adjustments reflect CBO's estimate of the unusually rapid growth of TFP between 2001 and 2003 and changes in the average level of education and experience of the labor force.

c. The ratio of potential output to potential hours worked in the nonfarm business sector.

overall potential labor force, is that other sectors—including owner-occupied housing, nonprofit institutions serving households, and state and local governments—are expected to become a smaller share of the economy.[13]

Capital services in the nonfarm business sector are also projected to grow more slowly from 2020 through 2025 than they did during the business cycles from 1982 through 2007, primarily because of the slower growth of potential hours worked. But the projected growth of

capital services from 2020 through 2025 is somewhat faster than such growth has been since 2007, reflecting projected increases in investment. The growth of capital

---

13. The output of the state and local government sector includes only the compensation of state and local employees and the depreciation of equipment, structures, and intellectual property products owned by state and local governments. Other purchases by state and local governments—such as new capital investments, goods that are not capital investments, and contracted services—are part of the output of other sectors of the economy, primarily the nonfarm business sector.

services has been restrained since 2007 because of weak investment, which itself was a response to the cyclical weakness of demand; in the long run, however, the growth of capital services depends mostly on the growth of hours worked and on the rate of increase in productivity.

CBO projects that potential TFP growth in the nonfarm business sector between 2020 and 2025 will equal its average between 2002 and 2007 (after the effects of a temporary surge in the early 2000s are excluded) of 1.3 percent. That is, CBO projects the growth rate of potential TFP to be essentially what recent history, before the recession, would have suggested. That approach is similar to the one that CBO uses to project trends in other factors that determine the growth of potential output. The projected growth rate is also close to the average observed during the business cycles from 1982 through 2007, a longer period that witnessed marked swings in the growth of TFP.[14] However, the projected rate is more rapid than the estimated average annual rate of growth of 0.9 percent from 2008 to 2014, as this chapter discusses below.

Lingering Effects of the Recession and Slow Recovery.
Incorporated into the projection of overall potential output growth is CBO's expectation that each of the factors that determine potential output—potential labor hours, capital services, and potential TFP—will be lower through 2025 than it would have been if not for the recession and slow recovery. In most cases, it is difficult to quantify the effects of the recession and slow recovery on those factors. For example, there is significant uncertainty in estimating how much of the recent weakness in TFP can be traced to the effect of the recession and slow recovery on potential TFP, and how much reflects other developments in the economy. In addition, the effects of the recession and slow recovery on the labor force, capital services, and productivity are interrelated; for example, a smaller potential labor force implies a smaller need for firms to invest in capital services.

In CBO's assessment, the recession and weak recovery have led to a reduction in potential labor hours. Persistently weak demand for workers has led some people to leave the labor force permanently, and persistently high long-term unemployment has generated some stigma and erosion of skills for some workers, pushing the natural rate of unemployment above its prerecession level. CBO estimates that the lasting effects of the recession and slow recovery will, in 2025, boost the unemployment rate by about 0.2 percentage points and depress the labor force participation rate by about 0.3 percentage points.

CBO projects that, by 2025, the primary effect of the recession and the weak recovery on capital services will occur through the number of workers and TFP: Fewer workers require proportionately less capital, all else being equal, and lower TFP tends to reduce investment as well. The economic weakness has also affected capital services because of the plunge in investment during the recession, although CBO expects that effect to dissipate by 2025. In addition, the sharp increase in federal debt—which resulted from changes in fiscal policies that were made in response to the weak economy, as well as from the automatic stabilizers—is estimated to crowd out additional capital investment in the long term. CBO has not quantified the effect of each of those factors in its current projection.

Finally, CBO estimates that the recession and slow recovery contributed to the significant slowdown in the growth of potential TFP from 2008 to 2014 compared with the previous business cycles since 1982—and that slowdown will result in a lower level of potential TFP throughout the next decade even if growth in potential TFP picks up, as CBO expects it to. In CBO's judgment, the protracted weakness in demand for goods and services and the large amount of slack in the labor market lowered potential TFP growth by reducing the speed with which resources were reallocated to their most productive uses, slowing the rate at which workers gained new skills, and restraining businesses' spending on research and development. However, quantifying the role of the recession and weak recovery in the slowdown in potential TFP growth is difficult because factors unrelated to the weak economy may also have slowed such growth. For example, there appears to have been a slowdown in advances in information technology beginning in the few years prior to the

---

14. During that period, potential TFP grew at an average annual rate of 1.4 percent if the surge in the early 2000s is included and at a rate of 1.2 percent if it is excluded, CBO estimates.

recession.[15] (For more discussion, see "Comparison With CBO's August 2014 Projections" on page 52.)

The Labor Market

CBO projects that the unemployment rate will edge down from 5.5 percent at the beginning of 2020 to 5.4 percent in 2025, and the agency's estimate of the natural rate of unemployment falls from 5.3 percent to 5.2 percent over the same period. The labor force participation rate is expected to fall as well, from about 62 percent in 2020 to about 61 percent in 2025.

The decline in the estimated natural rate of unemployment over the 2020–2025 period reflects the diminishing effect of structural factors associated with the extraordinary increase in long-term unemployment—namely, the stigma of being unemployed for a long time and the erosion of skills that can occur. After contributing 0.5 percentage points to the natural rate in 2014, those factors are projected to contribute 0.3 percentage points at the beginning of 2020 and 0.2 percentage points in 2025.

The projected difference of roughly one-quarter of one percentage point between the unemployment rate and the natural rate during the 2020–2025 period is not based on a forecast of particular cyclical movements in the economy. Rather, it is based on CBO's estimate that the unemployment rate has been roughly that much higher than the natural rate, on average, over the 50-year period ending in 2009.[16] The difference between the projections of the unemployment rate and the natural rate over the 2020–2025 period corresponds to the projected gap between output and potential output that was discussed above.

CBO's projection of the labor force participation rate in 2025—approximately 61 percent—is about 1 percentage point lower than the rate that it projects for 2020 and 5¼ percentage points lower than that rate at the end of

2007. Most of the projected decline between 2007 and 2025 can be attributed to long-term trends, especially the aging of the population, CBO estimates. The remainder stems from the reduction in some people's incentive to work resulting from the ACA and the structure of the tax code and from the permanent withdrawal of some workers from the labor force in response to the recession and slow recovery.

Inflation

In CBO's projections, inflation as measured by the PCE price index and the core PCE price index averages 2.0 percent annually during the 2020–2025 period; that rate is consistent with the Federal Reserve's longer-term goal. As measured by the CPI-U and the core CPI-U, projected inflation is higher during that period, at 2.4 percent and 2.3 percent, respectively. (Differences in the ways that the two price indexes are calculated make the CPI-U grow faster than the PCE price index, on average.)

Interest Rates

CBO projects that the interest rates on 3-month Treasury bills and 10-year Treasury notes will be 3.4 percent and 4.6 percent, respectively, from 2020 through 2025. CBO expects the federal funds rate to be 3.7 percent during that period.

After being adjusted for inflation as measured by the CPI-U, the projected real interest rate on 10-year Treasury notes equals 2.2 percent between 2020 and 2025. That would be well above the current real rate, but roughly three-quarters of a percentage point below the average real rate between 1990 and 2007, a period that CBO uses for comparison because it featured fairly stable expectations for inflation and no significant financial crises or severe economic downturns. According to CBO's analysis, a number of factors will act to push down real interest rates on Treasury securities relative to their earlier average: slower growth of the labor force (which reduces the return on capital), slightly slower growth of productivity (which also reduces the return on capital), a greater share of total income going to high-income households (which tends to increase saving), and a higher risk premium on risky assets (which increases the relative demand for risk-free Treasury securities, boosting their prices and thereby lowering their interest rates). Other factors will act to raise real interest rates relative to their earlier average: a larger amount of federal debt as a percentage of GDP (which increases the relative supply of

---

15. See John Fernald, *Productivity and Potential Output Before, During, and After the Great Recession*, Working Paper 20248 (National Bureau of Economic Research, June 2014), www.nber.org/papers/w20248.

16. Specifically, that has been the average difference between the unemployment rate and CBO's estimate of the natural rate between 1961 and 2009. The average difference was larger during more recent periods: about three-quarters of one percentage point between 1973 and 2009 and about 1 percentage point between 1973 and 2014.

Treasury securities), smaller net inflows of capital from other countries as a percentage of GDP (which reduces the supply of funds available for borrowing), a smaller number of workers in their prime saving years relative to the number of older people drawing down their savings (which tends to decrease saving and thus also reduces the supply of funds available for borrowing), and a higher share of income going to capital (which increases the return on capital assets with which Treasury securities compete). CBO expects that, on balance, those factors will result in real interest rates on Treasury securities that are lower than those between 1990 and 2007.[17]

Projections of Income

Economic activity and federal tax revenues depend not only on the amount of total income in the economy but also on how that income is divided among its constituent parts: labor income, domestic economic profits, proprietors' income, interest and dividend income, and other categories.[18] CBO projects various categories of income by estimating their shares of gross domestic income (GDI).[19] Of the categories of income, the most important components of the tax base are labor income, especially wage and salary payments, and domestic corporate profits.

In CBO's projections, labor income grows faster than the other components of GDI over the next decade, increasing its share from an estimated 56.8 percent in 2014 to 58.3 percent in 2025 (see Figure 2-13).[20] The projected increase in labor income's share of GDI stems

Figure 2-13.

Labor Income

Percentage of Gross Domestic Income

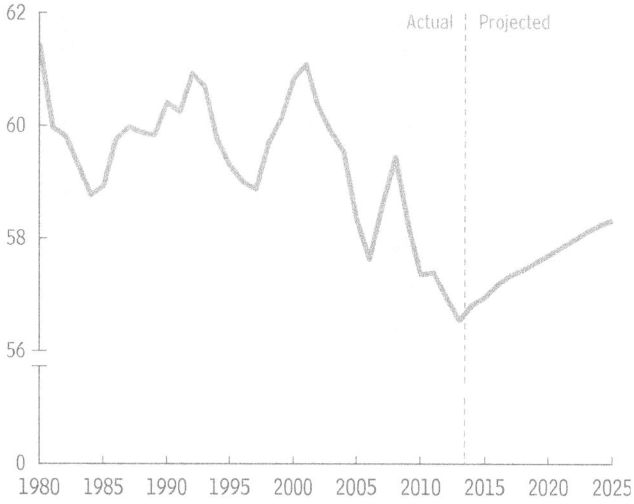

Sources: Congressional Budget Office; Bureau of Economic Analysis.

Notes: Labor income is defined as the sum of employees' compensation and CBO's estimate of the share of proprietors' income that is attributable to labor. Gross domestic income is all income earned in the production of gross domestic product. For further discussion of the labor share of income, see Congressional Budget Office, *How CBO Projects Income* (July 2013), www.cbo.gov/publication/44433.

Data are annual. Actual data are plotted through 2013; the value for 2014 is CBO's estimate and does not incorporate data released by the Bureau of Economic Analysis since early December 2014.

primarily from an expected pickup in the growth of real hourly labor compensation, which will result from strengthening demand for labor. However, CBO expects some factors that have depressed labor income's share of GDI in recent years to continue during the coming decade, preventing that share from reaching its 1980–2007 average of nearly 60 percent. In particular, globalization has tended to move the production of labor-intensive goods and services to locations where labor costs

---

17. For a more detailed discussion of the factors affecting interest rates in the future, see Congressional Budget Office, *The 2014 Long-Term Budget Outlook* (July 2014), pp. 108–109, www.cbo.gov/publication/45471.

18. Domestic economic profits are corporations' domestic profits adjusted to remove distortions in depreciation allowances caused by tax rules and to exclude the effects of inflation on the value of inventories. Domestic economic profits exclude certain income of U.S.-based multinational corporations that is derived from foreign sources, most of which does not generate corporate income tax receipts in the United States.

19. In principle, GDI equals GDP, because each dollar of production yields a dollar of income; in practice, they differ because of difficulties in measuring both quantities. GDP was about 1 percent smaller than GDI in 2014, but CBO projects that GDP will grow slightly faster than GDI over the next decade, which will leave the gap between the two in 2025 equal to its long-run historical average.

20. CBO defines labor income as the sum of employees' compensation and a percentage of proprietors' income. That percentage is employees' compensation as a share of the difference between GDI and proprietors' income. For further discussion of labor income's share of GDI, see Congressional Budget Office, *How CBO Projects Income* (July 2013), www.cbo.gov/publication/44433.

are lower, and technological change appears to have made it easier for employers to substitute capital for labor.

In CBO's projections, domestic economic profits fall from 9.8 percent of GDI in 2014 to 7.8 percent in 2025. That decline occurs largely because of two factors: the pickup in the growth of labor compensation and a projected increase in corporate interest payments, the result of rising interest rates.

Some Uncertainties in the Economic Outlook

Significant uncertainty surrounds CBO's economic forecast—which the agency constructed to be in the middle of the distribution of possible outcomes, given the federal fiscal policies embodied in current law. But even if no significant changes are made to those policies, economic outcomes will undoubtedly differ from CBO's projections. Many developments—such as unforeseen changes in the housing market, the labor market, business confidence, and international conditions—could cause economic growth and other variables to differ substantially from what CBO has projected.[21]

The agency's current forecast of employment and output from 2015 through 2019 may be too pessimistic. For example, if firms responded to the expected increase in overall demand for goods and services with more robust hiring than CBO anticipates, the unemployment rate could fall more sharply than CBO projects. In addition, a greater-than-expected easing of borrowing constraints in mortgage markets could support stronger residential investment, accelerating the housing market's recovery and further boosting house prices. Households' increased wealth could then buttress consumer spending, raising GDP.

Alternatively, CBO's forecast for the next five years may be too optimistic. For instance, if investment by businesses rose less than CBO projects, production would

also rise more slowly, and hiring would probably be weaker as well. That outcome could restrain consumer spending, which would reinforce the weakness in business investment. An unexpected worsening in international political or economic conditions could likewise weaken the U.S. economy by disrupting the international financial system, interfering with international trade, and reducing business and consumer confidence. In addition, because oil prices are set in international markets, disruptions to foreign oil production could affect U.S. energy prices.

A number of factors that will determine the economy's output later in the coming decade are also uncertain. For example, the economy could grow considerably faster than CBO forecasts if the labor force grew more quickly than expected (say, because older workers chose to stay in the labor force longer than expected), business investment was stronger, or productivity grew more rapidly. Similarly, lower-than-expected growth would occur if the stigma and erosion of skills that stem from elevated long-term unemployment dissipate more slowly than CBO projects, because then growth in the number of hours worked would be smaller (if all other factors were held equal), which would in turn lead to less business investment.

Comparison With CBO's August 2014 Projections

CBO's current economic projections differ somewhat from the projections that it issued in August 2014 (see Table 2-3). For the period from 2014 through 2018—the first period examined in that report—real GDP is now expected to grow by 2.5 percent annually, on average, which is about 0.2 percentage points less than CBO projected at the time. Because projected growth from 2019 through 2024 is almost unchanged, on average, the change in the earlier period means that real GDP is now projected to be roughly 1 percent lower in 2024 than the agency projected in August. The projected unemployment rate is also slightly lower in CBO's current forecast than it was in its August forecast, as are interest rates after 2018. CBO's projection of inflation in 2015 is currently lower than it was in August, but its projection of inflation in later years is roughly unchanged.

Output
Although real GDP grew faster than expected in 2014 and was about one-half of one percent higher at the end

21. The inherent uncertainty underlying economic forecasts will be discussed in Congressional Budget Office, *CBO's Economic Forecasting Record: 2015 Update* (forthcoming). CBO regularly evaluates the quality of its economic forecasts by comparing them with the economy's actual performance and with forecasts by the Administration and the *Blue Chip* consensus. Such comparisons indicate the extent to which imperfect information and analysis—factors that affect all forecasters—might have caused CBO to misread patterns and turning points in the economy.

Table 2-3.

Comparison of CBO's Current and Previous Economic Projections for Calendar Years 2014 to 2024

	Estimated, 2014	Forecast			Projected Annual Average	
		2015	2016	2017	2018–2024	2014–2024
		Percentage Change From Fourth Quarter to Fourth Quarter				
Real (Inflation-adjusted) GDP						
January 2015	2.1	2.9	2.9	2.5	2.1	2.3
August 2014	1.5	3.4	3.4	2.7	2.2	2.4
Nominal GDP						
January 2015	4.0	4.2	4.6	4.5	4.2	4.3
August 2014	3.2	5.2	5.3	4.7	4.2	4.3
PCE Price Index						
January 2015	1.3	1.4	1.9	2.0	2.0	1.9
August 2014	1.9	1.7	1.8	1.9	2.0	1.9
Core PCE Price Index[a]						
January 2015	1.5	1.8	1.9	1.9	2.0	1.9
August 2014	1.6	1.9	1.9	1.9	2.0	1.9
Consumer Price Index[b]						
January 2015	1.2 [c]	1.5	2.3	2.3	2.4	2.2
August 2014	2.5	1.9	2.0	2.2	2.4	2.3
Core Consumer Price Index[a]						
January 2015	1.7 [c]	2.1	2.2	2.3	2.3	2.2
August 2014	1.9	2.2	2.2	2.3	2.3	2.2
GDP Price Index						
January 2015	1.8	1.3	1.7	1.9	2.0	1.9
August 2014	1.8	1.7	1.8	1.9	2.0	1.9
Employment Cost Index[d]						
January 2015	2.3	2.7	3.2	3.6	3.5	3.3
August 2014	1.9	3.0	3.5	3.7	3.4	3.3
Real Potential GDP						
January 2015	1.6	1.8	2.1	2.2	2.2	2.1
August 2014	1.7	1.9	2.1	2.2	2.2	2.1
		Calendar Year Average				
Unemployment Rate (Percent)						
January 2015	6.2 [c]	5.5	5.4	5.3	5.4	5.5
August 2014	6.2	5.9	5.7	5.7	5.6	5.7
Interest Rates (Percent)						
Three-month Treasury bills						
January 2015	* [c]	0.2	1.2	2.6	3.4	2.5
August 2014	0.1	0.3	1.1	2.1	3.4	2.5
Ten-year Treasury notes						
January 2015	2.5 [c]	2.8	3.4	3.9	4.5	4.0
August 2014	2.8	3.3	3.8	4.2	4.7	4.3
Tax Bases (Percentage of GDP)						
Wages and salaries						
January 2015	42.7	42.6	42.6	42.7	42.9	42.8
August 2014	42.8	42.7	42.5	42.6	43.0	42.9
Domestic economic profits						
January 2015	9.9	10.0	9.7	9.4	8.2	8.7
August 2014	9.2	9.3	9.4	9.3	7.9	8.3

Notes: Estimated values for 2014 do not reflect the values for GDP and related series released by the Bureau of Economic Analysis since early December 2014.

GDP = gross domestic product; PCE = personal consumption expenditures; * = between zero and 0.05 percent.

a. Excludes prices for food and energy.

b. The consumer price index for all urban consumers.

c. Actual value for 2014.

d. The employment cost index for wages and salaries of workers in private industries.

of the year than CBO anticipated in August, CBO has revised downward its projection of real GDP after 2015. Specifically, the agency projected in August that real GDP would increase at an average annual pace of 2.7 percent in 2014 through 2018; it now projects an average 2.5 percent rate. The primary reason for that change is that the agency has reduced its estimate of potential output.

The revision to potential output mainly results from CBO's reassessment of the growth in potential TFP in the nonfarm business sector since 2007. In CBO's previous projection, that measure of productivity grew by 1.2 percent per year, on average, from 2007 through 2014—one-tenth of a percentage point below the pace that CBO estimated for the 2002–2007 trend (excluding the effects of a temporary surge in the early 2000s) because of a small estimated effect of the recession. However, CBO now estimates that potential TFP slowed more significantly after 2007, growing by only 0.9 percent per year from 2008 to 2014. That revision to CBO's estimate of potential TFP growth reduces the estimated growth of potential GDP between 2007 and 2014, and it lowers CBO's estimate of the level of potential GDP in the fourth quarter of 2014 by about 1 percent.

What prompted that change? In previous periods of cyclical weakness, actual TFP has generally been lower than potential TFP, and CBO's August projection followed that pattern. But the growth of actual TFP in the past few years has persistently been lower than CBO anticipated, so the gap between actual TFP and CBO's previous estimate of potential TFP was widening even as other economic measures, such as the gap between the unemployment rate and the natural rate of unemployment, were improving.

Consequently, CBO now interprets more of the persistent weakness in *actual* TFP in the nonfarm business sector as reflecting weakness in *potential* TFP for the sector—concluding that potential TFP grew more slowly from 2008 to 2014 than the agency had previously estimated.[22] That slowdown may have resulted from larger-than-anticipated effects of the factors that CBO has repeatedly attributed to the economy's prolonged weakness: delayed reallocation of resources to their most productive uses, slower adoption of new skills and technologies, and curtailed spending on research and development. The slowdown may also reflect factors unrelated to

the recession and weak recovery—such as a reduction in the pace of innovation in industries that produce and use information technology, which may have begun before the recession.[23]

Because the growth of potential TFP in the nonfarm business sector has been revised downward for the past six years and is nearly unrevised for the next decade, the estimated *level* of TFP in that sector is lower throughout the coming decade than it was in CBO's August projections—and therefore the estimated level of potential nonfarm business sector output is lower as well. As a result, CBO has revised its projection of potential output in 2024 (the last year of the agency's August projection) downward by 1 percent, a revision similar to the one that the agency made for 2014.[24]

---

22. In the current projection, CBO uses one trend in TFP for the 2001–2007 business cycle and another for the following years through 2014. (In both cases, CBO estimated trends after accounting for business cycle effects.) The agency's current approach yields a gap between actual TFP and estimated potential TFP that is roughly constant in recent years. CBO views that gap as resulting largely from ongoing cyclical weakness in the economy.

23. See John Fernald, *Productivity and Potential Output Before, During, and After the Great Recession*, Working Paper 20248 (National Bureau of Economic Research, June 2014), www.nber.org/papers/w20248.

24. Since 2007, CBO has lowered its projection of potential output in 2017—the end of the projection period for the estimates made in 2007—by about 9 percent. (That comparison excludes the effects of changes that the Bureau of Economic Analysis made to the definition of GDP during its comprehensive revision of the national income and product accounts in 2013.) Calculating the degree to which different factors have contributed to that revision is very difficult and subject to considerable uncertainty. Nonetheless, CBO estimates that reassessments of economic trends that had started before the recession began account for about one-half of the revision. For example, CBO has concluded that rates of growth in potential labor hours in the 2000s were generally lower than they were in the 1990s and lower than the agency had estimated in its 2007 projection. The remainder of the revision to potential output is attributable to a number of factors that have each had a smaller effect. Those factors include the recession and weak recovery, revisions of historical data, changes in CBO's methods for estimating potential output, revisions to estimated net flows of immigration based on analysis of recently released data, and the effect of higher federal debt in crowding out capital investment in the long term. For further discussion, see Congressional Budget Office, *Revisions to CBO's Projection of Potential Output Since 2007* (February 2014), pp. 8–11, www.cbo.gov/publication/45150.

CBO has also revised downward its projection of average real GDP growth from 2014 through 2018—a revision that reflects primarily the downward revision to CBO's estimate of potential GDP but also some recent economic developments, including the appreciation in the exchange value of the dollar. For the end of 2014, real GDP is revised upward by one-half of one percent, relative to CBO's August projections. Coupling that upward revision with CBO's 1 percent downward revision to potential output, CBO estimates that the gap between actual and potential GDP at the end of 2014—currently estimated to be 2¼ percent—is 1½ percentage points narrower than the agency projected in August. A narrower output gap suggests that there is less room for a strengthening economy to keep output growth above the growth rate of potential output without inducing a tightening of monetary policy to keep inflation from rising above the Federal Reserve's longer-term goal. As a result, CBO now projects that output growth over the next few years will be modestly slower than in its previous projection (and that short-term interest rates will rise more rapidly).

The Labor Market

During the second half of 2014, employment rose (and the unemployment rate fell) more than CBO anticipated, which led the agency to reduce its projection of the unemployment rate from 5.9 percent to 5.5 percent in 2015 and by smaller amounts in subsequent years. In addition, CBO now expects the growth of nonfarm payroll employment to be about 50,000 jobs (per month, on average) greater this year, and about 30,000 jobs greater next year, than the agency projected in August. Recent evidence suggests better employment prospects for those currently outside the labor force than CBO previously anticipated. Moreover, the stronger labor market in CBO's current forecast suggests greater incentives for people to enter or remain in the labor force than in CBO's previous forecast. As a result, the expected rate of labor force participation has been revised upward from 62.7 percent to 62.9 percent in 2015 and from 62.5 percent to 62.8 percent in 2016.

CBO also revised downward its projection of the natural rate of unemployment over the next decade—by about one-quarter of a percentage point each year over the next few years and by about one-tenth of a percentage point in later years—for two reasons. First, recent evidence about employment and wages suggests that reductions in the efficiency with which employers fill vacancies have been

causing a smaller disruption to the labor market than CBO previously estimated; thus, that effect is estimated to have dissipated by the end of 2014, more quickly than CBO previously thought. Second, evidence about the propensity of the long-term unemployed to find jobs suggests that they experience somewhat less stigma and erosion of skills than CBO previously estimated.[25] In particular, although the long-term unemployed tend to have considerably worse labor market outcomes than the short-term unemployed have, the difference now appears to be a little smaller than CBO previously estimated.

Further, CBO revised upward its projection of the potential labor force participation rate over the next decade—by 0.1 percentage point each year, on average. CBO estimates that unusual aspects of the slow recovery of the labor market that have led workers to become discouraged and permanently drop out of the labor force are having a slightly smaller effect than the agency projected in August. CBO now expects that fewer of the long-term unemployed will leave the labor force permanently, in light of the evidence that their labor market outcomes seem to differ less from those of the short-term unemployed than the agency previously estimated. In addition, evidence since 2013 shows a surprising uptick in the number of people moving directly from outside the labor force into employment, which suggests better employment prospects for those outside the labor force than CBO anticipated.

For the period from 2020 through 2025, CBO revised its projections of the actual unemployment rate and the actual labor force participation rate to be consistent with its revisions to the natural rate of unemployment and the potential participation rate. The agency has done so because it projects (just as it did in August) that the unemployment rate and the participation rate will return to their historical relationships with the natural rate of unemployment and the potential participation rate.

Interest Rates

CBO currently projects generally higher short-term interest rates and lower long-term interest rates during the

---

25. For examples, see Rob Dent and others, *How Attached to the Labor Market Are the Long-Term Unemployed?* (Federal Reserve Bank of New York, November 2014), http://tinyurl.com/kt772t8; and Rob Valletta, *Long-Term Unemployment: What Do We Know?* Economic Letter 2013-03 (Federal Reserve Bank of San Francisco, February 2013), http://tinyurl.com/mxqty5j.

2015–2019 period than it projected in August. Short-term rates are projected to be higher, on average, because CBO now estimates that there is less slack in the economy than the agency previously estimated, and therefore expects that the Federal Reserve will provide slightly less support for growth through its conduct of monetary policy over the next few years. The lower projection for long-term interest rates reflects CBO's estimate that factors that have led to an unexpected decline in long-term rates (as the next paragraph explains) will persist over the next decade.

CBO's projections of short- and long-term interest rates between 2020 and 2025 are 0.1 percentage point lower than they were in August. Over the past six months, the outlook for growth among leading U.S. trading partners has unexpectedly deteriorated, which implies poorer investment opportunities in those countries and lower rates of return on assets in those countries. In addition, CBO anticipates that foreign central banks will respond to slower-than-expected growth by maintaining slightly looser monetary policy than CBO expected, which also lowers rates of return abroad. As a result of those factors, U.S. Treasury securities have become relatively more attractive to investors, a development that has put downward pressure on U.S. interest rates.

Comparison With Other Economic Projections

CBO's projections of the growth of real GDP, the unemployment rate, inflation, and interest rates in 2015 and 2016 are generally very similar to the projections of the *Blue Chip* consensus published in January 2015 (see Figure 2-14). CBO's forecast of the growth of real GDP matches that of the *Blue Chip* consensus for this year and is 0.1 percentage point faster for next year. CBO's forecast of inflation, as measured by the CPI-U, is 0.1 percentage point higher than the *Blue Chip* consensus this year but

does not differ from it next year. CBO's projection for the unemployment rate is close to that of the *Blue Chip* consensus this year but is modestly higher next year. Finally, relative to the *Blue Chip* consensus for 2015 and 2016, CBO's forecast for short-term interest rates is somewhat lower, while the forecast for long-term interest rates is similar.

Similarly, CBO's projections differ only slightly from the forecasts made by the Federal Reserve that were presented at the December 2014 meeting of the Federal Open Market Committee (see Figure 2-15). The Federal Reserve reports two sets of forecasts: a range (which reflects the highest and lowest forecasts of the members of the Board of Governors of the Federal Reserve System and of the presidents of the Federal Reserve Banks) and a central tendency (which excludes the range's three highest and three lowest projections). CBO's projections of the growth of real GDP and inflation in 2015 and beyond are within the Federal Reserve's central tendencies. CBO's projections of the unemployment rate in 2015 and beyond fall within the Federal Reserve's ranges but are at the high end of the central tendencies or slightly above them.

CBO's projections probably differ from those of the other forecasters at least partly because of varying assumptions about the government's future tax and spending policies. For example, CBO's projections, which are based on current law, incorporate the effects of the recent retroactive extension through 2014 of certain provisions that reduce the tax liabilities of individuals and firms, but also reflect an assumption that those cuts will not be subsequently extended. Other forecasters might assume extensions of those tax cuts beyond 2014. Also, CBO's projections might differ from those of the other forecasters because of differences in the economic news available when the forecasts were completed and differences in the economic and statistical models used.

Figure 2-14.

Comparison of Economic Projections by CBO and the *Blue Chip* Consensus

Percent

2015   2016

Growth of Real GDP

CBO

Blue Chip

Consumer Price Index Inflation[a]

CBO

Blue Chip

GDP Price Index Inflation

CBO

Blue Chip

Unemployment Rate[b]

CBO

Blue Chip

Interest Rate on Three-Month Treasury Bills[b]

CBO

Blue Chip

Interest Rate on Ten-Year Treasury Notes[b]

CBO

Blue Chip

   0   1   2   3   4   5   6   0   1   2   3   4   5   6

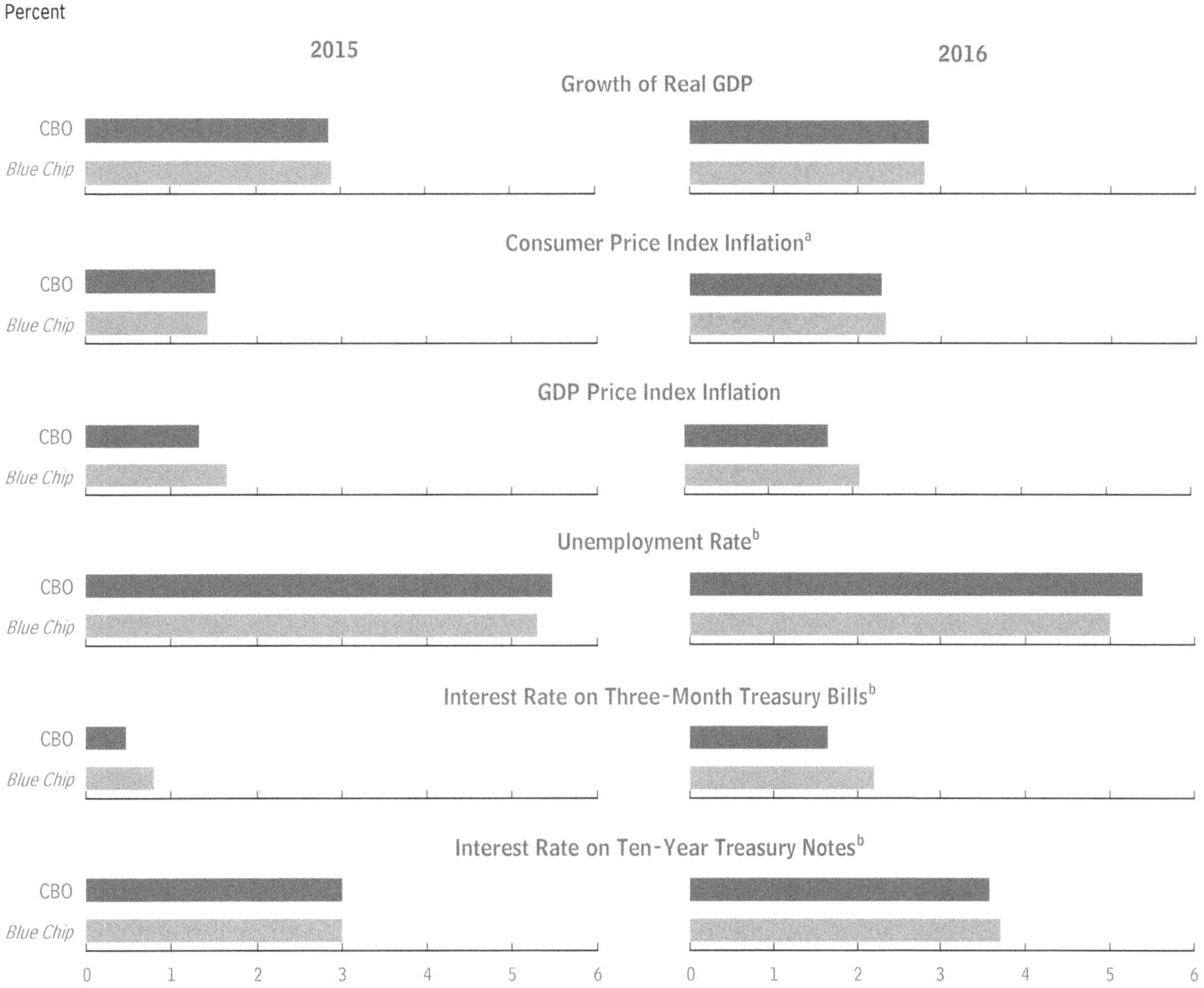

Sources: Congressional Budget Office; Aspen Publishers, *Blue Chip Economic Indicators* (January 10, 2015).

Notes: The *Blue Chip* consensus is the average of about 50 forecasts by private-sector economists.

Real gross domestic product is the output of the economy adjusted to remove the effects of inflation.

Growth of real GDP and inflation rates are measured from the fourth quarter of one calendar year to the fourth quarter of the next year.

The unemployment rate is a measure of the number of jobless people who are available for work and are actively seeking jobs, expressed as a percentage of the labor force.

GDP = gross domestic product.

a. The consumer price index for all urban consumers.

b. Rate in the fourth quarter.

Figure 2-15.

Comparison of Economic Projections by CBO and the Federal Reserve

CBO's projections of the growth of real GDP and of inflation are within the Federal Reserve's central tendencies, and CBO's projections of the unemployment rate are at the high end of or slightly above the central tendencies.

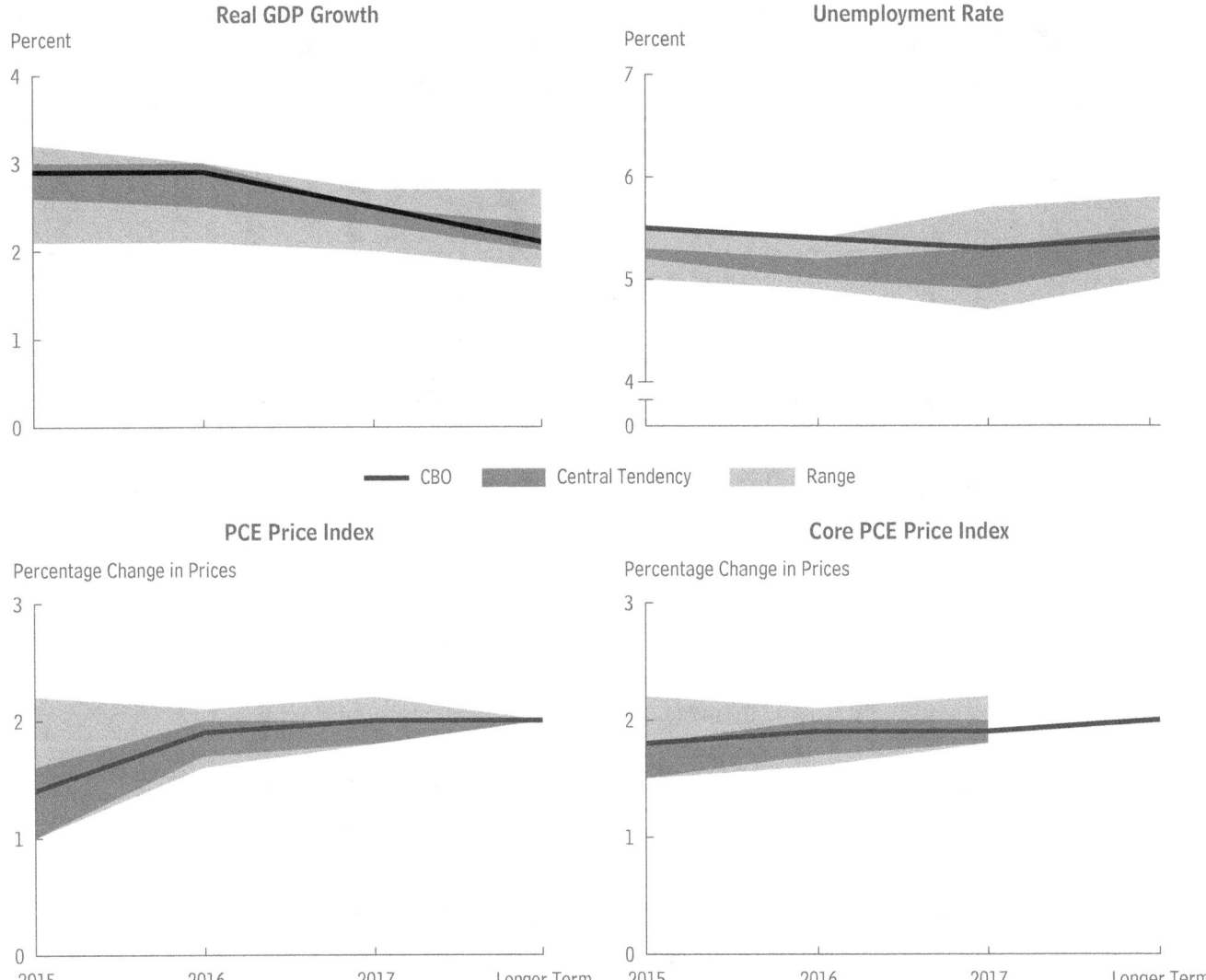

Sources: Congressional Budget Office; Board of Governors of the Federal Reserve System, "Economic Projections of Federal Reserve Board Members and Federal Reserve Bank Presidents, December 2014" (December 17, 2014).

Notes: The range of estimates from the Federal Reserve reflects the projections of each member of the Board of Governors and the president of each Federal Reserve Bank. The central tendency is that range without the three highest and three lowest projections.

For CBO, longer-term projections are values for 2025. For the Federal Reserve, longer-term projections are described as the value at which each variable would settle under appropriate monetary policy and in the absence of further shocks to the economy.

Real gross domestic product is the output of the economy adjusted to remove the effects of inflation.

The unemployment rate is a measure of the number of jobless people who are available for work and are actively seeking jobs, expressed as a percentage of the labor force.

The core PCE price index excludes prices for food and energy.

Data are annual.

GDP = gross domestic product; PCE = personal consumption expenditures.

The Spending Outlook

Under the provisions of current law, federal outlays in 2015 will total $3.7 trillion, the Congressional Budget Office estimates, roughly $150 billion (or 4.3 percent) more than the amount spent in 2014. They are projected to grow faster over the coming decade—at an average annual rate of more than 5 percent—and reach $6.1 trillion in 2025.

All of the projected growth for 2015 is attributable to mandatory spending, which makes up about 60 percent of the federal budget and is projected to rise by nearly $160 billion, from $2.1 trillion last year to $2.3 trillion this year (see Table 3-1). In contrast, discretionary spending and the government's net interest payments are expected to change very little. Discretionary spending, which totaled $1.2 trillion in 2014, is projected to edge down by $4 billion in 2015. Net outlays for interest are expected to dip by $3 billion this year to $227 billion. (See Box 3-1 for descriptions of the three major types of federal spending.)

All told, federal outlays in 2015 will equal 20.3 percent of gross domestic product (GDP), CBO estimates, which is the same as last year's percentage and only slightly higher than the 20.1 percent that such spending has averaged over the past 50 years. But the mix of that spending has changed noticeably over time. Mandatory spending (net of the offsetting receipts credited against such spending) is expected to equal 12.5 percent of GDP in 2015, whereas over the 1965–2014 period, it averaged 9.3 percent. Meanwhile, the other major components of federal spending have declined relative to GDP: Discretionary spending is anticipated to equal 6.5 percent of GDP this year, down from its 8.8 percent average over the past 50 years, and net outlays for interest are expected to be 1.3 percent of GDP, down from the 50-year average of 2.0 percent (see Figure 3-1 on page 62).

In CBO's baseline projections, outlays rise over the coming decade, reaching 22.3 percent of GDP in 2025, an increase of 2.0 percentage points. Mandatory spending is projected to contribute 1.7 percentage points to that increase—a combination of rapid growth in spending for Social Security and the major health care programs and a drop, relative to GDP, in outlays for other mandatory programs. As interest rates return to more typical levels and debt continues to mount, net outlays for interest are also projected to increase significantly, contributing another 1.7 percentage points to the growth in outlays. However, discretionary spending, measured as a percentage of GDP, falls by 1.4 percentage points in CBO's baseline projections.

Specifically, CBO's baseline for federal spending includes the following projections:

- Outlays for the largest federal program, Social Security, are expected to rise from 4.9 percent of GDP in 2015 to 5.7 percent in 2025.

- Federal outlays for major health care programs—including Medicare, Medicaid, subsidies for health insurance purchased through exchanges and related spending, and the Children's Health Insurance Program (CHIP)—are projected to increase more rapidly than outlays for Social Security, growing from 5.1 percent of GDP (net of premium payments and other offsetting receipts for Medicare) in 2015 to 6.2 percent in 2025.

- Outlays for all other mandatory programs (net of other offsetting receipts) are expected to decline from 2.5 percent of GDP in 2015 to 2.3 percent in 2025.

- Discretionary spending relative to the size of the economy is projected to fall by more than 20 percent over the next 10 years, from 6.5 percent of GDP in 2015 to 5.1 percent in 2025.

- Net interest payments are projected to more than double, rising from 1.3 percent of GDP in 2015 to 3.0 percent in 2025.

Table 3-1.

Outlays Projected in CBO's Baseline

	Actual, 2014	2015	2016	2017	2018	2019	2020	2021	2022	2023	2024	2025	Total 2016-2020	2016-2025
							In Billions of Dollars							
Mandatory														
Social Security	845	883	921	971	1,032	1,096	1,165	1,237	1,313	1,392	1,476	1,564	5,185	12,167
Medicare	600	622	668	681	699	772	826	886	986	1,021	1,052	1,175	3,645	8,765
Medicaid	301	335	360	384	405	428	452	477	503	530	558	588	2,029	4,686
Other spending	626	690	741	764	770	783	797	824	863	864	866	910	3,855	8,184
Offsetting receipts	-276	-275	-216	-237	-253	-263	-273	-288	-303	-321	-336	-346	-1,241	-2,835
Subtotal	2,096	2,255	2,475	2,563	2,653	2,816	2,968	3,137	3,363	3,486	3,616	3,891	13,474	30,967
Discretionary														
Defense	596	583	587	592	599	616	631	646	666	677	689	711	3,025	6,413
Nondefense	583	592	589	590	594	605	617	630	644	658	672	689	2,995	6,288
Subtotal	1,179	1,175	1,176	1,182	1,193	1,221	1,248	1,276	1,310	1,336	1,361	1,400	6,019	12,701
Net interest	229	227	276	332	410	480	548	606	664	722	777	827	2,046	5,643
Total Outlays	3,504	3,656	3,926	4,076	4,255	4,517	4,765	5,018	5,337	5,544	5,754	6,117	21,540	49,310
On-budget	2,798	2,914	3,143	3,244	3,366	3,570	3,752	3,938	4,185	4,314	4,441	4,715	17,075	38,667
Off-budget[a]	706	742	784	832	889	948	1,012	1,080	1,152	1,230	1,313	1,402	4,465	10,643
Memorandum:														
Gross Domestic Product	17,251	18,016	18,832	19,701	20,558	21,404	22,315	23,271	24,261	25,287	26,352	27,456	102,810	229,438
						As a Percentage of Gross Domestic Product								
Mandatory														
Social Security	4.9	4.9	4.9	4.9	5.0	5.1	5.2	5.3	5.4	5.5	5.6	5.7	5.0	5.3
Medicare	3.5	3.5	3.5	3.5	3.4	3.6	3.7	3.8	4.1	4.0	4.0	4.3	3.5	3.8
Medicaid	1.7	1.9	1.9	1.9	2.0	2.0	2.0	2.1	2.1	2.1	2.1	2.1	2.0	2.0
Other spending	3.6	3.8	3.9	3.9	3.7	3.7	3.6	3.5	3.6	3.4	3.3	3.3	3.8	3.6
Offsetting receipts	-1.6	-1.5	-1.1	-1.2	-1.2	-1.2	-1.2	-1.2	-1.2	-1.3	-1.3	-1.3	-1.2	-1.2
Subtotal	12.2	12.5	13.1	13.0	12.9	13.2	13.3	13.5	13.9	13.8	13.7	14.2	13.1	13.5
Discretionary														
Defense	3.5	3.2	3.1	3.0	2.9	2.9	2.8	2.8	2.7	2.7	2.6	2.6	2.9	2.8
Nondefense	3.4	3.3	3.1	3.0	2.9	2.8	2.8	2.7	2.7	2.6	2.6	2.5	2.9	2.7
Subtotal	6.8	6.5	6.2	6.0	5.8	5.7	5.6	5.5	5.4	5.3	5.2	5.1	5.9	5.5
Net interest	1.3	1.3	1.5	1.7	2.0	2.2	2.5	2.6	2.7	2.9	3.0	3.0	2.0	2.5
Total Outlays	20.3	20.3	20.8	20.7	20.7	21.1	21.4	21.6	22.0	21.9	21.8	22.3	21.0	21.5
On-budget	16.2	16.2	16.7	16.5	16.4	16.7	16.8	16.9	17.2	17.1	16.9	17.2	16.6	16.9
Off-budget[a]	4.1	4.1	4.2	4.2	4.3	4.4	4.5	4.6	4.8	4.9	5.0	5.1	4.3	4.6

Source: Congressional Budget Office.

a. Off-budget outlays stem from transactions related to the Social Security trust funds and the net cash flow of the Postal Service.

Box 3-1.

Categories of Federal Spending

On the basis of its treatment in the budget process, federal spending can be divided into three broad categories: mandatory spending, discretionary spending, and net interest.

Mandatory spending consists primarily of spending for benefit programs, such as Social Security, Medicare, and Medicaid. The Congress generally determines funding for those programs by setting rules for eligibility, benefit formulas, and other parameters rather than by appropriating specific amounts each year. In making baseline projections, the Congressional Budget Office generally assumes that the existing laws and policies governing those programs will remain unchanged. Mandatory spending also includes offsetting receipts—fees and other charges that are recorded as negative budget authority and outlays. Offsetting receipts differ from revenues in that revenues are collected in the exercise of the government's sovereign powers (income taxes, for example), whereas offsetting receipts are generally collected from other government accounts or from members of the public for businesslike transactions (premiums for Medicare or rental payments and royalties for the drilling of oil or gas on public lands, for example).

Discretionary spending is controlled by annual appropriation acts in which policymakers stipulate how much money will be provided for certain government programs in specific years. Appropriations fund a broad array of items and activities, including defense, law enforcement, transportation, the national park system, disaster relief, and foreign aid. Some of the fees and charges triggered by appropriation acts are classified as offsetting collections and are credited against discretionary spending for the particular accounts affected.

CBO's baseline depicts the path of spending for individual discretionary accounts as directed by the provisions of the Balanced Budget and Emergency Deficit Control Act of 1985. That act stated that current appropriations should be assumed to grow with inflation in the future.[1] However, the Budget Control

Act of 2011 (Public Law 112-25) imposed caps on discretionary appropriations through 2021 (and subsequent legislation modified those limits), so the baseline also incorporates the assumption that discretionary funding will not exceed the current caps.

The caps can, however, be adjusted upward for appropriations for certain activities, including war-related activities known as overseas contingency operations, certain disaster assistance efforts, specified program integrity initiatives, or designated emergencies. In CBO's baseline, the most recent appropriations for those categories, with increases for inflation, are used to project future adjustments to the caps.

In addition to outlays from appropriations subject to caps, the baseline also includes discretionary spending for highway and airport infrastructure programs and public transit programs, all of which receive mandatory budget authority from authorizing legislation. Each year, however, appropriation acts control spending for those programs by limiting how much of the budget authority the Department of Transportation can obligate. For that reason, those obligation limitations are often treated as a measure of discretionary resources, and the resulting outlays are considered discretionary spending.

Net interest includes interest paid on Treasury securities and other interest that the government pays (for example, that paid on late refunds issued by the Internal Revenue Service) minus the interest that it collects from various sources (for example, from states that pay the federal unemployment trust fund interest on advances they received when the balances of their state unemployment accounts were insufficient to pay benefits in a timely fashion). Net interest is determined by the size and composition of the government's debt and by market interest rates.

---

1. In CBO's baseline, discretionary funding related to federal personnel is inflated using the employment cost index for wages and salaries; other discretionary funding is adjusted using the gross domestic product price index.

Figure 3-1.

Outlays, by Type of Spending

Percentage of Gross Domestic Product

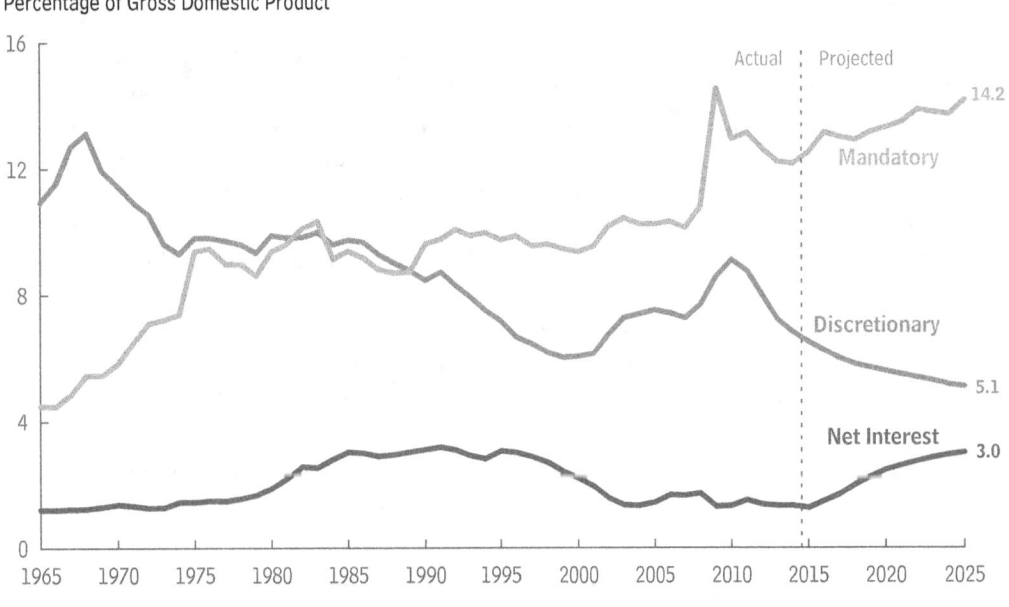

Under current law, rising spending for Social Security and the major health care programs will boost mandatory outlays.

Total discretionary spending is projected to fall relative to GDP as funding grows modestly in nominal terms.

At the same time, higher interest rates and growing debt will push up net interest payments.

Source: Congressional Budget Office.

In developing its baseline projections, CBO generally assumes, in accordance with the rules established by the Balanced Budget and Emergency Deficit Control Act of 1985, that the provisions of current law governing federal taxes and spending will remain unchanged. Therefore, when projecting spending for mandatory programs, CBO assumes that existing laws will not be altered and that future outlays will depend on changes in caseloads, benefit costs, economic variables, and other factors. When projecting spending for discretionary programs, CBO assumes that most discretionary appropriations provided between 2016 and 2021 will be constrained by the statutory caps and other provisions of the Budget Control Act of 2011 (Public Law 112-25) and that thereafter appropriations in a given year will equal those in the prior year with an adjustment for inflation.[1]

Mandatory Spending

Mandatory—or direct—spending includes spending for benefit programs and certain other payments to people, businesses, nonprofit institutions, and state and local governments. It is generally governed by statutory criteria and is not normally constrained by the annual appropriation process.[2] Certain types of payments that federal agencies receive from the public and from other government agencies are classified as offsetting receipts and reduce gross mandatory spending.

Total mandatory spending amounted to 12.2 percent of GDP in 2014. That figure is lower than the 13.1 percent such spending averaged over the previous five years but higher than the 10.3 percent of GDP it averaged in the five years before the most recent recession. Over the next 10 years, however, the aging of the population, the expansion of health insurance subsidies, and the rising per-beneficiary cost of health care will boost spending for

---

1. Appropriations for certain activities—overseas contingency operations, activities designated as emergency requirements, disaster relief, and initiatives designed to enhance program integrity by reducing overpayments in certain benefit programs— are not constrained by the caps and are assumed to grow with inflation from the amounts provided in 2015. (Overseas contingency operations refer to military operations and related activities in Afghanistan and elsewhere.)

2. Each year, some mandatory programs are modified by provisions contained in annual appropriation acts. Such changes may decrease or increase spending for the affected programs for either a single year or multiple years. Provisions of the Deficit Control Act and the Balanced Budget Act of 1997 govern how CBO projects spending for mandatory programs whose authorizations are scheduled to expire under current law, some of which are assumed to continue.

federal programs that serve the elderly and subsidize health care. As a result, mandatory spending will be higher as a share of GDP throughout the coming decade than it was in 2014, CBO projects.

Mandatory spending will jump by nearly 8 percent in 2015, to $2.3 trillion (or 12.5 percent of GDP), CBO estimates, if no additional laws are enacted that affect such spending this year. The major contributors to that growth include outlays for Medicaid, subsidies for health insurance purchased through exchanges, and the government's transactions with Fannie Mae and Freddie Mac. Some of that growth in spending will be offset by receipts from auctions of portions of the electromagnetic spectrum, which are expected to bring in more than $40 billion to the federal government this year. Over the next 10 years, mandatory spending is projected to rise at an average rate of close to 6 percent per year, reaching $3.9 trillion, or 14.2 percent of GDP, in 2025 (see Table 3-2). By comparison, mandatory spending has averaged 11.9 percent of GDP over the past 10 years and 9.3 percent over the past 50 years.

At $1.8 trillion in 2015, federal outlays for Social Security combined with those for Medicare, Medicaid, and other major health care programs will make up roughly half of all federal outlays and 80 percent of mandatory spending (net of offsetting receipts). Under current law, CBO projects, spending for those programs will increase at an average annual rate of 6 percent over the 2015–2025 period and will total $3.3 trillion in 2025. By that year, spending for Social Security and the major health care programs will have risen from 10.0 percent of GDP in 2015 to 11.9 percent of GDP. In contrast, other mandatory spending relative to GDP is projected to decline slightly.

After Social Security and the major health care programs, the next largest set of mandatory programs consists of several that are designed to provide income security. Those programs—including certain refundable tax credits, the Supplemental Nutrition Assistance Program (SNAP), Supplemental Security Income (SSI), and unemployment compensation—will account for $307 billion, or 1.7 percent of GDP, in 2015, by CBO's estimate.[3] Those programs, in total, are projected to grow by an average of only 1.5 percent per year; declining outlays for refundable tax credits and for SNAP contribute to that slow rate of growth. As a result, by 2025 outlays for

mandatory income security programs are projected to shrink to 1.3 percent of GDP.

Other mandatory spending programs include retirement benefits for federal civilian and military employees, certain benefits for veterans, student loans, and support for agriculture. Under current law, CBO projects, outlays for all of those other programs will grow at an average annual rate of 2.5 percent from 2015 through 2025, causing such spending to slide from 1.8 percent of GDP in 2015 to 1.5 percent of GDP in 2025. (Civilian and military retirement benefits account for roughly half of those amounts.)

CBO estimates that offsetting receipts (other than those for Medicare) will reduce mandatory outlays by 1.0 percent of GDP in 2015 and by an average of about 0.5 percent of GDP in ensuing years. Receipts from auctioning a portion of the electromagnetic spectrum have substantially boosted that total this year but are expected to have much smaller effects, on average, in later years. In addition, because of the way CBO treats the activities of Fannie Mae and Freddie Mac in its baseline projections, offsetting receipts from those entities are not reflected beyond the current year.

Social Security

Social Security, which is the largest federal spending program, provides cash benefits to the elderly, to people with disabilities, and to their dependents and survivors. Social Security comprises two main parts: Old-Age and Survivors Insurance (OASI) and Disability Insurance (DI). Social Security outlays grew by about 5 percent in 2014 because of increases in caseloads and average benefits.

CBO estimates that, under current law, outlays for Social Security will total $883 billion, or 4.9 percent of GDP, in 2015 and will climb steadily (by an average of about 6 percent per year) over the next decade as the nation's elderly population grows and as average benefits rise. By 2025, CBO estimates, Social Security outlays will total $1.6 trillion, or 5.7 percent of GDP, if current laws remain unchanged (see Figure 3-2 on page 66).

---

3. Tax credits reduce a taxpayer's overall income tax liability; if a refundable credit exceeds a taxpayer's other income tax liabilities, all or a portion of the excess (depending on the particular credit) is refunded to the taxpayer, and that payment is recorded as an outlay in the budget.

Table 3-2.

Mandatory Outlays Projected in CBO's Baseline

Billions of Dollars

	Actual, 2014	2015	2016	2017	2018	2019	2020	2021	2022	2023	2024	2025	Total 2016-2020	Total 2016-2025
Social Security														
Old-Age and Survivors Insurance	703	738	772	817	873	931	994	1,058	1,124	1,195	1,269	1,347	4,387	10,379
Disability Insurance	142	145	149	154	159	165	171	180	189	198	208	216	798	1,788
Subtotal	845	883	921	971	1,032	1,096	1,165	1,237	1,313	1,392	1,476	1,564	5,185	12,167
Major Health Care Programs														
Medicare[a]	600	622	668	681	699	772	826	886	986	1,021	1,052	1,175	3,645	8,765
Medicaid	301	335	360	384	405	428	452	477	503	530	558	588	2,029	4,686
Exchange subsidies and related spending[b]	15	45	71	93	101	106	110	116	122	125	128	131	482	1,104
Children's Health Insurance Program	9	10	11	6	6	6	6	6	6	6	6	6	34	62
Subtotal[a]	926	1,012	1,111	1,163	1,210	1,312	1,394	1,485	1,617	1,682	1,744	1,900	6,190	14,617
Income Security Programs														
Earned income, child, and other tax credits[c]	86	87	89	90	91	75	76	77	78	79	80	82	420	816
Supplemental Nutrition Assistance Program	76	78	78	76	75	74	74	74	73	74	74	75	378	747
Supplemental Security Income	54	55	60	57	54	61	63	64	71	68	65	72	295	636
Unemployment compensation	44	35	36	37	39	42	46	49	51	54	57	60	200	472
Family support and foster care[d]	31	31	32	32	32	33	33	33	34	34	34	35	162	331
Child nutrition	20	21	22	23	24	25	26	27	28	29	31	32	120	268
Subtotal	311	307	317	316	316	310	316	324	336	338	341	355	1,575	3,269
Federal Civilian and Military Retirement														
Civilian[e]	100	97	99	102	105	108	112	116	120	124	128	132	526	1,145
Military	55	57	62	59	56	62	64	66	73	70	67	74	303	653
Other	8	7	6	6	7	7	8	9	9	9	9	9	34	79
Subtotal	164	160	167	167	168	178	184	191	202	203	204	215	863	1,878
Veterans' Programs[f]														
Income security	71	74	82	79	74	83	84	85	93	87	81	91	402	840
Other	16	25	20	16	16	18	18	19	21	21	21	23	88	195
Subtotal	87	99	102	95	91	100	103	105	114	109	103	114	490	1,035
Other Programs														
Agriculture	19	11	16	19	17	16	15	15	15	15	15	15	83	159
MERHCF	9	10	10	10	11	11	12	13	14	15	16	17	55	128
Deposit insurance	-14	-10	-10	-10	-9	-14	-16	-10	-12	-13	-14	-15	-59	-124
Fannie Mae and Freddie Mac[g]	0	0	3	3	3	2	1	1	2	2	2	2	13	21
Higher education	-12	-3	-7	-4	-1	0	2	2	1	1	1	1	-10	-4
Other	38	61	62	69	68	68	64	64	64	64	65	69	329	655
Subtotal	40	69	73	87	89	83	78	84	84	84	84	89	411	835

Continued

Old-Age and Survivors Insurance. OASI, the larger of Social Security's two components, pays full benefits to workers who start collecting them at a specified full retirement age that depends on a worker's year of birth. (Full retirement age is defined as age 66 for those born before 1955 and increases incrementally for those born in 1955 and later years, reaching age 67 for those born in 1960 or later.) Workers can, however, choose to start collecting reduced benefits as early as age 62. The program also makes payments to eligible spouses and children of deceased workers. OASI spending totaled $703 billion in 2014, accounting for more than 80 percent of Social Security's outlays.

Table 3-2.

Continued

Mandatory Outlays Projected in CBO's Baseline

Billions of Dollars

	Actual, 2014	2015	2016	2017	2018	2019	2020	2021	2022	2023	2024	2025	2016-2020	2016-2025
Offsetting Receipts														
Medicare[h]	-95	-99	-106	-113	-121	-130	-139	-149	-163	-178	-189	-199	-609	-1,487
Federal share of federal employees' retirement														
Social Security	-16	-16	-17	-17	-18	-18	-19	-20	-20	-21	-22	-23	-89	-195
Military retirement	-21	-20	-19	-20	-20	-21	-22	-23	-23	-24	-25	-26	-102	-223
Civil service retirement and other	-29	-32	-32	-34	-35	-36	-37	-38	-39	-40	-41	-42	-174	-373
Subtotal	-65	-68	-68	-71	-73	-75	-78	-80	-83	-85	-88	-90	-365	-791
Receipts related to natural resources	-14	-13	-13	-13	-17	-16	-17	-18	-17	-18	-19	-19	-75	-165
MERHCF	-8	-7	-7	-8	-8	-9	-9	-10	-10	-11	-11	-12	-41	-94
Fannie Mae and Freddie Mac[g]	-74	-26	0	0	0	0	0	0	0	0	0	0	0	0
Other	-20	-62	-22	-32	-34	-32	-31	-32	-30	-30	-29	-26	-151	-298
Subtotal	-276	-275	-216	-237	-253	-263	-273	-288	-303	-321	-336	-346	-1,241	-2,835
Total Mandatory Outlays	2,096	2,255	2,475	2,563	2,653	2,816	2,968	3,137	3,363	3,486	3,616	3,891	13,474	30,967
Memorandum:														
Mandatory Spending Excluding the Effects of Offsetting Receipts	2,373	2,530	2,691	2,799	2,905	3,079	3,241	3,425	3,666	3,808	3,952	4,237	14,715	33,802
Spending for Medicare Net of Offsetting Receipts	505	523	562	568	577	641	687	737	823	843	863	976	3,036	7,278
Spending for Major Health Care Programs Net of Offsetting Receipts[i]	831	913	1,005	1,051	1,089	1,182	1,255	1,336	1,454	1,504	1,555	1,701	5,581	13,130

Source: Congressional Budget Office.

Notes: Data on spending for benefit programs in this table generally exclude administrative costs, which are discretionary.

MERHCF = Department of Defense Medicare-Eligible Retiree Health Care Fund (including TRICARE for Life).

a. Gross spending, excluding the effects of Medicare premiums and other offsetting receipts. (Net Medicare spending is included in the memorandum section of the table.)

b. Subsidies for health insurance purchased through exchanges established under the Affordable Care Act.

c. Includes outlays for the American Opportunity Tax Credit and other credits.

d. Includes the Temporary Assistance for Needy Families program, the Child Support Enforcement program, the Child Care Entitlement program, and other programs that benefit children.

e. Includes Civil Service, Foreign Service, Coast Guard, and other, smaller retirement programs as well as annuitants' health care benefits.

f. Income security programs include veterans' compensation, pensions, and life insurance programs. Other benefits are primarily education subsidies. Most of the costs of veterans' health care are classified as discretionary spending and thus are not shown in this table.

g. The cash payments from Fannie Mae and Freddie Mac to the Treasury are recorded as offsetting receipts in 2014 and 2015. Beginning in 2016, CBO's estimates reflect the net lifetime costs—that is, the subsidy costs adjusted for market risk—of the guarantees that those entities will issue and of the loans that they will hold, counted as federal outlays in the year of issuance.

h. Includes premium payments, recoveries of overpayments made to providers, and amounts paid by states from savings on Medicaid's prescription drug costs.

i. Consists of outlays for Medicare (net of offsetting receipts), Medicaid, the Children's Health Insurance Program, and subsidies for health insurance purchased through exchanges and related spending.

Figure 3-2.

Projected Outlays in Major Budget Categories

Percentage of Gross Domestic Product

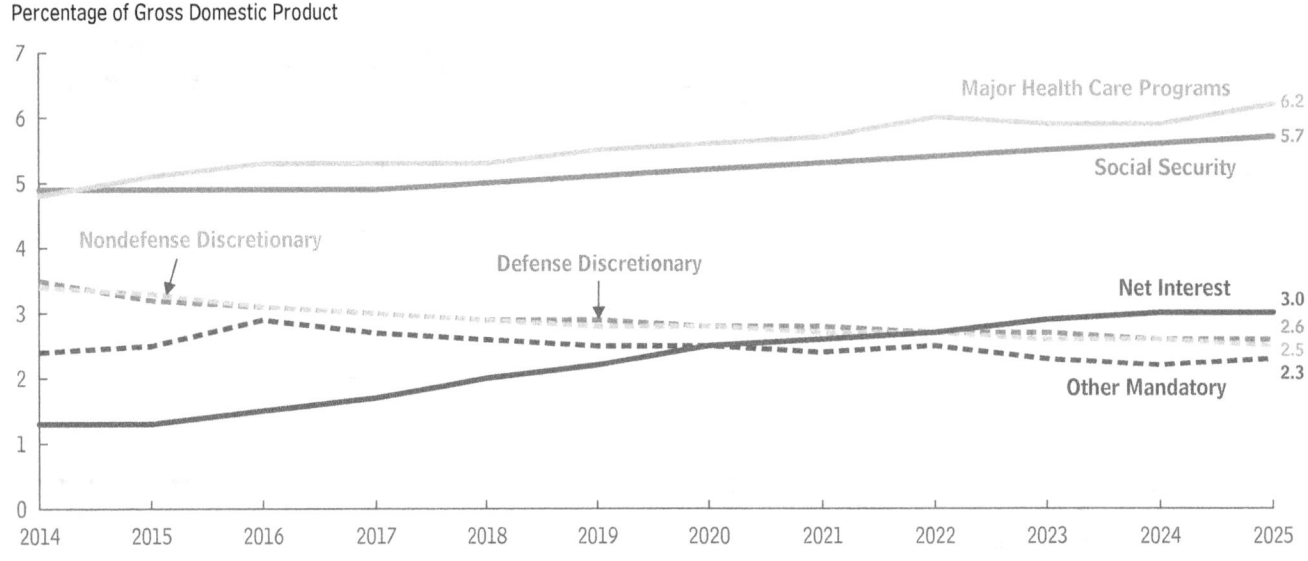

Source: Congressional Budget Office.

Note: Major health care programs consist of Medicare, Medicaid, the Children's Health Insurance Program, and subsidies for health
insurance purchased through exchanges and related spending. (Medicare spending is net of offsetting receipts.) Other mandatory
spending is all mandatory spending other than that for major health care programs and Social Security.

About 47 million people received OASI benefits in 2014. Over the 2015–2025 period, as more baby boomers (people born between 1946 and 1964) become eligible to receive benefits under the program, the number of people collecting those benefits will increase by an average of about 3 percent per year, CBO estimates. By 2025, nearly 65 million people will be receiving OASI benefits— 37 percent more than the number of recipients in 2014 and 59 percent more than the number in 2007, the last year before the first baby boomers became eligible for benefits under the program.

Average benefits will also rise in the future because beneficiaries generally receive annual cost-of-living adjustments (COLAs) and because initial benefits are based on people's lifetime earnings, which tend to increase over time. OASI beneficiaries received a COLA of 1.7 percent in January 2015; CBO anticipates that beneficiaries will receive a COLA of 0.9 percent in 2016 and that COLAs will average 2.4 percent annually from 2017 through 2025. (Each year's COLA is determined by the annual increase in the consumer price index for urban wage earners.) All told, the average benefit will rise by about 3 percent per year over the 2015–2025 period, according to CBO's estimates. The increasing average benefit, in

combination with the growing number of beneficiaries, is projected to boost outlays for OASI by an average of about 6 percent per year over that period.

Disability Insurance. Social Security's disability benefits are paid to workers who suffer debilitating health conditions before they reach OASI's full retirement age. Payments are also made to the eligible spouses and children of those recipients. In 2014, federal spending for DI totaled $142 billion.

The number of people receiving those benefits rose by about 0.5 percent in 2014, to 11 million—a much slower rate of growth than the program had experienced during the previous several years. The growth in the DI caseload is expected to remain modest as the economy continues to improve, leading fewer people to seek disability benefits, and as more Americans reach the age at which they qualify for benefits under OASI. Like OASI beneficiaries, those receiving benefits under DI received a COLA of 1.7 percent for 2015. Including COLAs that will be paid in future years, average DI benefits under current law will grow by about 3 percent per year, on average, from 2015 through 2025, and the program's outlays will rise by an average of about 4 percent annually during those years, CBO estimates.

CBO projects that the balance of the DI trust fund will be exhausted during fiscal year 2017. After that time, additional revenues will continue to be credited to the DI trust fund, but, in CBO's estimation, the amounts will be insufficient to pay all of the benefits due. However, in keeping with the rules in section 257 of the Deficit Control Act, CBO's baseline incorporates the assumption that full benefits will continue to be paid after the balance of the trust fund has been exhausted, although there will be no legal authority to make such payments in the absence of legislative action.

Medicare, Medicaid, and Other Major Health Care Programs

At $926 billion in 2014, gross federal outlays for Medicare, Medicaid, and other major programs related to health care accounted for 39 percent of gross mandatory spending and equaled 5.4 percent of GDP. (Those amounts do not reflect the income received by the government from premiums paid by Medicare beneficiaries or from other offsetting receipts.) Under current law, CBO estimates, gross federal outlays for those programs will jump to $1.0 trillion, or 5.6 percent of GDP, in 2015. In CBO's baseline projections, that spending grows robustly—at an average rate of nearly 7 percent per year—and thus nearly doubles between 2015 and 2025, reaching $1.9 trillion, or 6.8 percent of GDP, by the end of that period.

Medicare. Medicare provides subsidized medical insurance to the elderly and to some people with disabilities. The program has three principal components: Part A (Hospital Insurance), Part B (Medical Insurance, which covers doctors' services, outpatient care, home health services, and other medical services), and Part D (which covers outpatient prescription drugs).[4] People generally become eligible for Medicare at age 65 or two years after they qualify for Social Security disability benefits.

Gross spending for Medicare will total $622 billion in 2015, CBO estimates, or 3.5 percent of GDP, the same

share as in 2014. By 2025, the program's spending will reach nearly $1.2 trillion, or 4.3 percent of GDP, if current laws remain in place. Medicare also collects substantial offsetting receipts—mostly in the form of premiums paid by beneficiaries—which, in CBO's baseline projections, rise from $99 billion in 2015 to $199 billion in 2025. (See "Offsetting Receipts" on page 74.) Under current law, spending for Medicare net of those offsetting receipts will be 2.9 percent of GDP in 2015 and 3.6 percent in 2025, CBO estimates.

Spending for Medicare (not including offsetting receipts) is expected to grow by an average of nearly 7 percent per year over the next 10 years under current law. About 60 percent of that growth results from higher costs per beneficiary; the rest stems from an increasing number of beneficiaries. CBO projects that Medicare caseloads will expand at an average rate of 3 percent per year as growing numbers of baby boomers turn 65 and become eligible for benefits. In 2014, Medicare had about 54 million beneficiaries; that number is expected to climb to 73 million in 2025.

CBO projects that, under current law, nominal spending per beneficiary will grow at an average rate of 4 percent per year over the coming decade—much more slowly than it has grown historically. After adjusting for inflation (as measured by the price index for personal consumption expenditures), Medicare spending per beneficiary is expected to increase at an average annual rate of 1.2 percent between 2015 and 2025, whereas it averaged real annual growth of 4 percent between 1985 and 2007 (excluding the jump in spending that occurred in 2006 with the implementation of Part D).

The comparatively slow growth in per-beneficiary spending that CBO projects for the next decade results from a combination of factors. One of those factors is the anticipated influx of new beneficiaries, which will bring down the average age of Medicare beneficiaries and therefore, holding all else equal, reduce average health care costs per beneficiary because younger beneficiaries tend to use fewer health care services.

A second factor is the slowdown in the growth of Medicare spending across all types of services, beneficiaries, and major geographic regions in recent years. Although the reasons for that slower growth are not yet

---

4. Medicare Part C (known as Medicare Advantage) specifies the rules under which private health care plans can assume responsibility for, and be compensated for, providing benefits covered under Parts A, B, and D.

entirely clear, CBO projects that the slowdown will persist for some years to come.[5] For example, since March 2010, CBO has reduced its projection of Medicare outlays in 2020 (the last year included in the March 2010 projection) by $122 billion, or about 14 percent, based on subsequent analysis by its staff and other analysts of data on Medicare spending. (CBO has also made revisions to its projections for Medicare spending in response to legislative action and revisions to the economic outlook.)

A third factor that contributes to the slow projected growth in Medicare spending per beneficiary over the next decade is the constraints on service payment rates that are built into current law:

■ Payment rates for physicians' services are set according to the sustainable growth rate mechanism (SGR).[6] Under current law, payment rates for those services will be reduced by 21 percent in April 2015 and raised or lowered by small amounts in subsequent years, so CBO incorporates those changes into its projections. If, however, future legislation overrides the scheduled reductions (as has happened in every year since 2003), spending for Medicare will be greater than the amount that is projected in CBO's baseline. For example, if payment rates for physicians' services remained at the current level from April 2015 through 2025, CBO estimates that net Medicare outlays through 2025 would be $137 billion (or roughly 2 percent) higher than in its baseline projections. If those payment rates were increased over time, the effect on Medicare outlays would be even greater.

■ Payments to other types of providers are limited by provisions of the Affordable Care Act (ACA) that

hold annual increases in payment rates for Medicare services (apart from those provided by physicians) to about 1 percentage point less than inflation. Under CBO's economic projections, those payment rates are expected to increase by about 1 percent per year on average.

■ Payments to Medicare providers will also be affected—especially later in the coming decade—by a provision originally enacted in the Budget Control Act of 2011 and extended by subsequent laws that reduces payment rates for most Medicare services by 2.0 percent through March 2023 and then by varying amounts over the next year and a half: by 2.9 percent through September 2023, then by 1.1 percent through March 2024, and then by 4.0 percent through September 2024.

Despite the relatively slow growth in per-beneficiary Medicare spending projected over the next 10 years, net federal spending per beneficiary for Parts A and B is projected to grow by 38 percent. Net federal spending per beneficiary for Part D, which accounts for a small share of total Medicare spending, is projected to grow much more—by 77 percent—largely because of rising drug costs combined with provisions in the ACA that expand the extent of coverage for some prescription drugs.

Medicaid. Medicaid is a joint federal and state program that funds medical care for certain low-income, elderly, and disabled people. The federal government shares costs for approved services, as well as administrative costs, with states; the federal share varies from state to state but averaged about 57 percent in most years prior to 2014. (During some economic downturns, the federal government's share has temporarily increased.)

Beginning in January 2014, the ACA gave states the option of expanding eligibility for their Medicaid programs to people with income at or below 138 percent of the federal poverty guidelines. In 2014, 27 states and the District of Columbia expanded their programs. The federal government pays a greater share of the costs incurred by enrollees who were made eligible for Medicaid in those states than it does for traditional enrollees: The federal share for those newly eligible enrollees is 100 percent from 2014 through 2016 and declines thereafter, falling

---

5. See Michael Levine and Melinda Buntin, *Why Has Growth in Spending for Medicare Fee-for-Service Slowed?* Working Paper 2013-06 (Congressional Budget Office, August 2013), www.cbo.gov/publication/44513. That analysis reviews the observed slowdown in growth in Medicare spending between the 2000–2005 and 2007–2010 periods. It suggests that demand for health care by Medicare beneficiaries was not measurably diminished by the financial turmoil and recession and that, instead, much of the slowdown in spending growth was caused by other factors affecting beneficiaries' demand for care and by changes in providers' behavior.

6. The SGR was enacted as part of the Balanced Budget Act of 1997 as a method for controlling spending by Medicare on physicians' services.

to 90 percent in 2020.[7] (See Appendix B for more information on the insurance coverage provisions of the ACA.)

Federal outlays for Medicaid totaled $301 billion in 2014, 14 percent more than 2013 spending for the program. CBO estimates that slightly more than half of that increase resulted from enrollment of people who were newly eligible because of the ACA and from the greater share of costs paid by the federal government for those new enrollees. Provisions of the ACA also led to increased enrollment of individuals who were previously eligible for Medicaid. CBO cannot, however, precisely determine the total share of growth between 2013 and 2014 resulting from the ACA because there is no way to know whether new enrollees who would have been eligible in the absence of the ACA would have signed up had it not been enacted.

CBO projects that, under current law, federal spending for Medicaid will jump by an additional 11 percent this year as more people in states that have already expanded Medicaid eligibility enroll in the program and as more states expand eligibility. The number of people enrolled in Medicaid on an average monthly basis is expected to rise from 63 million in 2014 to 66 million in 2015. CBO anticipates that, by 2020, 80 percent of the people who meet the new eligibility criteria will live in states that have extended Medicaid coverage and that enrollment in Medicaid will be 75 million.

From 2016 to 2025, growth in federal spending for Medicaid is projected to increase at about the same rate of growth that such spending averaged over the past 10 years—about 6 percent annually. By 2025, about 78 million people will be enrolled in Medicaid on an average monthly basis, CBO projects. In that year, federal outlays for Medicaid are, under current law, projected to total $588 billion, or about 2.1 percent of GDP, up from 1.9 percent of GDP in 2015.

Exchange Subsidies and Related Spending. Individuals and families can now purchase private health insurance coverage through marketplaces known as exchanges that are operated by the federal government, by state

governments, or through a partnership between federal and state governments. (See Appendix B for more information on the insurance coverage provisions of the ACA.) Subsidies of purchases made through those exchanges fall into two categories: subsidies to cover a portion of participants' health insurance premiums, and subsidies to reduce their cost-sharing amounts (out-of-pocket payments required under insurance policies). Related spending consists of grants to states for establishing health insurance exchanges and outlays for risk adjustment and reinsurance.[8] Outlays for those exchange subsidies and related spending are expected to rise from $15 billion last year to $45 billion in 2015, to $71 billion in 2016, and to $131 billion by 2025.

Exchange subsidies make up the largest portion of that spending: Outlays are projected to total $28 billion in 2015 (up from $13 billion in 2014) and to reach $112 billion by 2025. (A portion of the subsidies for health insurance premiums will be provided in the form of reductions in recipients' tax payments.)[9] In 2014, CBO estimates, an average of 5 million people per month received subsidies through the exchanges. CBO and the staff of the Joint Committee on Taxation project that about 9 million people will receive such subsidies in 2015 and that the number will grow to roughly 16 million in 2016 and to between 17 million and 19 million in each year from 2017 to 2025. (Other people who will not be eligible for subsidies are also expected to purchase health insurance coverage through the exchanges.)

---

8. CBO previously anticipated that the transactions of the risk corridor program created by the ACA, which reduces risk for health insurers by partially offsetting high losses and sharing large profits, would be recorded in the budget as mandatory spending and revenues. However, the Administration plans to record the program's outflows as discretionary spending and inflows as offsetting collections to such spending, and CBO will follow that treatment. That difference in classification reduces both mandatory spending and revenues in CBO's baseline by the same amounts. In addition, because CBO expects that the additional discretionary spending and offsetting collections will be of equal amounts in each year, the reclassification will have no net impact on discretionary spending. Consequently, it has no net effect on CBO and the Joint Committee on Taxation's estimates of the effects of the ACA's insurance coverage provisions.

9. The subsidies for health insurance premiums are structured as refundable tax credits; the portions of such credits that exceed taxpayers' other income tax liabilities are refunded to the taxpayer and classified as outlays, whereas the portions that reduce tax payments appear in the budget as reductions in revenues.

---

7. Taking into account the enhanced federal matching rates for populations made eligible under the ACA, the average federal share of spending for Medicaid is expected to be between 60 percent and 62 percent in 2015 and later years.

CBO estimates that outlays for grants to states for exchange operations will be about $1 billion in 2015. Because funds for new grants needed to be obligated by the end of 2014, spending of such grants is winding down. In CBO's baseline, outlays associated with grants for operating state exchanges decline to zero by 2018.

In accordance with the ACA, new programs requiring the federal government to make payments to health insurance plans for risk adjustment (amounts paid to plans that attract less healthy enrollees) and for reinsurance (amounts paid to plans that enroll individuals who end up with high costs) became effective in 2014. The two programs are intended to spread more widely—either to other insurance plans or to the federal government—some of the risk that health insurers face when selling health insurance through the new exchanges or in other individual or small group markets. Outlays for the two programs are expected to begin in 2015 and to total $16 billion in that year; over the 2016–2025 period, CBO projects, outlays for those programs will total $181 billion. Those payments will be offset by associated revenues. Under current law, the reinsurance program is authorized only for insurance issued through 2016 (although spending associated with the programs is expected to continue for an additional year), but the risk-adjustment program is permanent.

Children's Health Insurance Program. The Children's Health Insurance Program provides health insurance coverage to children in families whose income, although modest, is too high for them to qualify for Medicaid. The program is jointly financed by the federal government and the states and is administered by the states within broad federal guidelines. Total federal spending for CHIP was approximately $9 billion in 2014 and is expected to rise to $10 billion in 2015—the last year for which funding is provided in law. Funding for CHIP in 2015 consists of two semiannual allotments of $2.85 billion—much smaller amounts than were allotted in the four preceding years—and $15.4 billion in onetime funding for the program, which will supplement the first allotment.

Following the rules governing baseline projections, CBO assumes in its baseline that funding for CHIP after 2015 is set at about $6 billion a year (that is, at the annualized rate of the second of the semiannual allotments for 2015).[10] Nevertheless, annual spending for CHIP is projected to reach $11 billion in 2016 because some of the funds allocated to states in previous years will be spent in

that year; outlays are projected to fall to about $6 billion in 2017 and remain there in subsequent years. Nearly 6 million people will be enrolled in CHIP on an average monthly basis in 2015, CBO estimates. Enrollment drops later in the decade in CBO's baseline projections, mostly because funding is assumed to decline after 2015.

Income-Security Programs

The federal government makes various payments to people and government entities in order to assist the poor, the unemployed, and others in need. Federal spending for the refundable portions of the earned income tax credit (EITC), the child tax credit, certain other tax credits, SNAP, SSI, unemployment compensation, family support, foster care, and other services increased rapidly during the most recent recession, peaking in 2010 at $437 billion, or 3.0 percent of GDP. By 2014, such spending had dropped to $311 billion, or 1.8 percent of GDP. Under current law, spending on mandatory income-security programs is projected to decline slightly in 2015 and then to grow modestly. By 2025, outlays for those programs are anticipated to be $355 billion, or 1.3 percent of GDP.

Earned Income, Child, and Other Tax Credits. Refundable tax credits reduce a filer's overall income tax liability; if the credit exceeds the rest of the filer's income tax liability, the government pays all or some portion of that excess to the taxpayer. Those payments—including the ones made for the refundable portions of the EITC, the child tax credit, and the American Opportunity Tax Credit (AOTC)—are categorized as outlays. The EITC is a fully refundable credit available primarily to people with earnings and income that fall below established maximums. The child tax credit is a partially refundable credit (limited to 15 percent of earnings over a predetermined threshold) available to qualifying families with dependent children. The AOTC allows certain individuals (including those who owe no taxes) to claim a credit for college expenses. Outlays for those credits totaled $86 billion in 2014.

Such outlays are projected to reach $91 billion in 2018 before dropping to $75 billion in 2019, following the expiration, under current law, of the AOTC and of the temporary expansions in the child tax credit and EITC

---

10. Although CBO's projections assume that $6 billion in funding will be provided for 2016 and subsequent years, if lawmakers provide no such funding, state programs will terminate in 2016.

that were first enacted in 2009 and most recently extended in January 2013. Under current law, by 2025 outlays for refundable tax credits will total $82 billion, CBO projects. Those tax credits also affect the budget, to a lesser extent, by reducing tax revenues. However, the portion of the refundable tax credit that reduces revenues is not reported separately in the federal budget.

Supplemental Nutrition Assistance Program. Outlays for SNAP fell by 8 percent in 2014 to $76 billion after having risen each year since 2008, when the most recent recession began. CBO estimates that the program's spending will rise modestly this year, to $78 billion, and that 46 million people will receive those benefits. CBO expects that the number of people collecting SNAP benefits, which increased dramatically in the wake of the most recent recession, will gradually decline over the coming years. Average per-person benefits, however, will increase each year because of adjustments for inflation in prices for food. Based on the assumption that the program will be extended after it expires at the end of fiscal year 2018 (as provided in the rules governing baseline projections), CBO projects that by 2025, 33 million people will be enrolled in SNAP and the program's outlays will total $75 billion.

Supplemental Security Income. SSI provides cash benefits to people with low incomes who are elderly or disabled. Outlays for SSI rose by about 2 percent in 2014 to $54 billion. According to CBO's estimates, spending for that program will increase at an average annual rate of close to 3 percent over the coming decade. In CBO's projections, the number of beneficiaries for SSI edges up at an average annual rate of less than half a percent; most of the anticipated growth in spending for that program through 2025 stems from COLA increases. Under current law, spending for SSI benefits will be $72 billion in 2025, CBO estimates.

Unemployment Compensation. In 2014, outlays for unemployment compensation were $44 billion, about two-thirds of the amount spent in 2013. Such spending peaked at $159 billion in 2010, in part because of the exceptionally high unemployment rate and in part because of legislation that significantly expanded benefits for individuals who had been unemployed for long periods. The improving economy and the expiration of those temporary provisions at the end of December 2013 have reduced outlays considerably. If there are no changes to

current law, outlays will drop again in 2015, CBO estimates, to $35 billion, close to the amount spent in 2007.

Over the next 10 years, outlays for unemployment compensation are projected to rise gradually, pushed up by growth in the labor force and wages (which serve as the basis for benefits). By 2025, CBO projects, outlays for the program will, under current law, amount to $60 billion, or 0.2 percent of GDP.

Family Support and Foster Care. Spending for family support programs—grants to states that help fund welfare programs, foster care, child support enforcement, and the Child Care Entitlement—is expected to remain close to last year's level, about $31 billion, in 2015. Spending for those programs is projected to rise only gradually through 2025, at an average annual rate of 1 percent.

Funding for two major components of family support is capped: The regular Temporary Assistance to Needy Families (TANF) program is limited to roughly $17 billion annually (although some additional funding is available if states' unemployment rates or SNAP caseloads exceed certain thresholds), and funding for the Child Care Entitlement is capped at just under $3 billion per year. Under current law, the regular TANF program and the Child Care Entitlement are funded only through the end of this fiscal year, but CBO's baseline reflects the assumption (as specified in the Deficit Control Act) that such funding will continue throughout the projection period.

Outlays for federal grants to states for foster care and adoption assistance and for child support enforcement are expected to remain near the 2014 amounts—about $7 billion and $4 billion, respectively—in 2015. CBO estimates that, under current law, spending for the two programs will increase modestly over the coming decade and amount to $9 billion and $5 billion, respectively, in 2025.

Child Nutrition. CBO projects that federal spending for child nutrition—which provides cash and commodities for meals and snacks in schools, day care settings, and summer programs—will rise by 5 percent in 2015, to $21 billion. Much of that increase stems from higher per-meal reimbursement rates, which are adjusted automatically each school year to account for inflation. CBO anticipates that growth in the number of meals provided and in reimbursement rates will lead to spending increases averaging 4 percent per year from 2016 through 2025, for a total of $32 billion in 2025.[11]

Civilian and Military Retirement

Retirement and survivors' benefits for federal civilian employees (along with benefits provided through several smaller retirement programs for employees of various government agencies and for retired railroad workers) amounted to $108 billion in 2014. Under current law, such outlays will grow by about 3 percent annually over the next 10 years, CBO projects, reaching $141 billion in 2025.

Growth in federal civil service retirement benefits is attributable primarily to cost-of-living adjustments for retirees and to increases in federal salaries, which boost benefits for people entering retirement. (CBO's projections reflect the assumption that federal salaries will rise in accordance with the employment cost index for wages and salaries of workers in private industry.) One factor that is restraining growth in spending for retirement benefits is the ongoing, gradual replacement of the Civil Service Retirement System (CSRS) with the Federal Employees Retirement System (FERS). FERS covers employees hired after 1983 and provides a smaller benefit than that provided by CSRS. FERS recipients are, however, eligible for Social Security benefits on the basis of their federal employment, whereas CSRS employees are not. In addition, under FERS, employees' contributions to the federal Thrift Savings Plan are matched in part by their employing agencies (but those matching funds are categorized as discretionary—not mandatory—costs because they come out of annual appropriations to the agencies).

The federal government also provides annuities to personnel who retire from the military and their survivors. Outlays for those annuities totaled $55 billion in 2014. Most of the annual growth in those outlays results from COLAs and increases in military basic pay. Outlays for military retirement annuities are projected to grow over the next 10 years by an average of about 3 percent per year, rising to $74 billion in 2025.

---

11. Spending for child nutrition includes roughly $1 billion in outlays each year related to the Funds for Strengthening Markets program (also known as Section 32), which, among other things, provides funds to purchase commodities that are distributed to schools as part of child nutrition programs.

Veterans' Benefits

Mandatory spending for veterans' benefits includes disability compensation, readjustment benefits, pensions, insurance, housing assistance, and burial benefits. Outlays for those benefits totaled $87 billion in 2014, of which roughly 75 percent represented disability compensation. That amount does not include most federal spending for veterans' health care, which is funded by discretionary appropriations.

Spending for mandatory veterans' benefits is projected to rise by 14 percent, to $99 billion, in 2015. The growth projected for 2015 largely reflects new mandatory spending for medical services and facilities resulting from the Veterans Access, Choice, and Accountability Act of 2014 (P.L. 113-146). That law provided onetime funding of $5 billion to expand health care hiring and infrastructure of the Department of Veterans Affairs and $10 billion to temporarily cover the costs of contracted medical care for veterans. (That funding was an exception to the usual approach of funding veterans' health care through discretionary appropriations.) Other growth, though less substantial, stems from an expected increase in the average benefit for veterans' disability compensation.

CBO expects that, under current law, moderate growth in mandatory spending for veterans' benefits (averaging about 1.4 percent a year between 2015 and 2025) will cause outlays to rise to $114 billion in 2025.

Other Mandatory Spending

Other mandatory spending includes outlays for agricultural support, some smaller health care programs, net outlays for deposit insurance, subsidy costs for student loans, and other payments. Outlays in some of those categories fluctuate markedly from year to year and may be either positive or negative.

Agricultural Support. Mandatory spending for agricultural programs totaled $19 billion in 2014. The relatively high spending last year included significant payments for livestock disaster assistance for drought-related losses since 2012 and crop insurance payments for crop losses in 2013. Spending for agricultural support is projected to average $15 billion per year between 2015 and 2025 based on the assumption (specified in the Deficit Control Act) that the current programs that are scheduled to expire during that period will be extended.

Deposit Insurance. Net outlays for deposit insurance were negative last year: The program's collections (premiums paid by financial institutions) exceeded its disbursements (the cost of resolving failed institutions) by $14 billion. Premium payments will continue to exceed amounts spent on failed institutions, CBO projects, and net outlays for deposit insurance will range from –$9 billion to –$16 billion annually over the coming decade.

Medicare-Eligible Retiree Health Care Fund. The Department of Defense's Medicare-Eligible Retiree Health Care Fund (MERHCF) provides health care benefits, mainly through the TRICARE for Life program, to retirees of the uniformed services (and to their dependents and surviving spouses) who are eligible for Medicare. Outlays for those benefits totaled $9 billion in 2014. Over the coming decade, spending from the MERHCF is projected to rise at an average annual rate of roughly 6 percent, reaching $17 billion in 2025.

Fannie Mae and Freddie Mac. In September 2008, the government placed Fannie Mae and Freddie Mac, two institutions that facilitate the flow of funding for home loans nationwide, into conservatorship.[12] Because the Administration considers Fannie Mae and Freddie Mac to be nongovernmental entities for federal budgeting purposes, it recorded the Treasury's payments to those entities as outlays in the budget and reports payments by those entities to the Treasury, such as those made in 2014 and expected in 2015, as offsetting receipts. (For further details, see page 75.)

In contrast to the Administration, CBO projects the budgetary impact of the two entities' operations in future years as if they were being conducted by a federal agency because of the degree of management and financial control that the government exercises over them.[13] Therefore, CBO estimates the net lifetime costs—that is, the subsidy costs adjusted for market risk—of the guarantees that those entities will issue and of the loans that they will hold and shows those costs as federal outlays in the year of issuance. CBO estimates that those outlays will amount to $21 billion from 2016 through 2025.

Higher Education. Mandatory outlays for higher education fall into three categories: the net costs (on a present-value basis) of student loans originated in a given year, which are frequently estimated to be negative; a portion of the costs of Pell grants provided in that year; and spending for some smaller programs.[14] In 2014, total mandatory outlays for higher education were –$12 billion. That amount included the following: the budgetary effects of student loans originated last year, which amounted to –$22 billion (on a present-value basis); a slight increase in the estimated cost of direct and guaranteed loans originated in previous years, which amounted to $1 billion (also on a present-value basis); and mandatory spending for Pell grants, which totaled $8 billion.[15]

In 2015, the net costs for new student loans will be –$15 billion, mandatory spending for the Federal Pell Grant Program will be $11 billion, and other spending will be $0.4 billion, resulting in net mandatory outlays for higher education of –$3 billion, CBO estimates. In later years, projected mandatory outlays for higher

---

12. Conservatorship is the legal process in which an entity, in this case the federal government, is appointed to establish control and oversight of a company to put it in a sound and solvent condition.

13. See Congressional Budget Office, *CBO's Budgetary Treatment of Fannie Mae and Freddie Mac* (January 2010), www.cbo.gov/publication/41887.

14. CBO calculates subsidy costs for student loans following the procedures specified in the Federal Credit Reform Act of 1990 (FCRA). Under FCRA accounting, the discounted present value of expected income from federal student loans made during the 2015–2025 period is projected to exceed the discounted present value of the government's costs. (Present value is a single number that expresses a flow of current and future income or payments in terms of an equivalent lump sum received or paid today; the present value depends on the rate of interest—known as the discount rate—that is used to translate future cash flows into current dollars.) Credit programs that produce net income rather than net outlays are said to have negative subsidy rates, which result in negative outlays. The original subsidy calculation for a set of loans or loan guarantees may be increased or decreased in subsequent years by a credit subsidy reestimate based on an updated assessment of the present value of the cash flows associated with the outstanding loans or loan guarantees.

FCRA accounting does not, however, consider all costs borne by the government. In particular, it omits market risk—the risk taxpayers face because federal receipts from payments on student loans tend to be low when economic and financial conditions are poor and resources are therefore more valuable. Fair-value accounting methods account for such risk, so the program's savings are less (or its costs are greater) under fair-value accounting than they are under FCRA accounting.

15. Under current law, the Pell grant program also receives funding from discretionary appropriations. For 2014, those appropriations totaled $23 billion.

education trend from modestly negative to slightly positive. That switch occurs primarily because rising interest rates will, in CBO's estimation, increase the subsidy cost of student loans (making it less negative) to the point that the negative outlays for new student loans will no longer fully offset the cost of mandatory spending for Pell grants and other higher education programs under current law. (Those projected outlays do not include any potential revision to the estimated subsidy costs of loans or guarantees made before 2015.)

Additional Mandatory Spending. Other mandatory spending includes outlays for a number of different programs; some of those outlays are associated with significant offsetting receipts or revenues collected by the federal government. For example, $138 billion in mandatory outlays over the 2016–2025 period is related to the administration of justice, including some activities of the Department of Homeland Security. Most of that spending is offset by revenues and by fees, penalties, fines, and forfeited assets that are credited in the budget as offsetting receipts. An additional $115 billion in outlays over the 2016–2025 period stems from the Universal Service Fund and is offset in the federal budget by revenues of similar amounts. Other mandatory spending over the 2016–2025 period includes the following outlays:

- $59 billion for conservation activities on private lands;

- $57 billion for grants to states for social services, such as vocational rehabilitation;

- $40 billion in subsidy payments to state and local governments related to the Build America Bonds program for infrastructure improvements; and

- $32 billion in payments to states and territories, primarily from funds generated from mineral production on federal land.

Offsetting Receipts

Offsetting receipts are funds collected by federal agencies from other government accounts or from the public in businesslike or market-oriented transactions that are recorded as negative outlays (that is, as credits against direct spending). Such receipts include beneficiaries' premiums for Medicare, intragovernmental payments made by federal agencies for their employees' retirement benefits, royalties and other charges for the production of oil

and natural gas on federal lands, proceeds from sales of timber harvested and minerals extracted from federal lands, payments by Fannie Mae and Freddie Mac, and various fees paid by users of public property and services.

In 2014, offsetting receipts totaled $276 billion. The total for this year will be nearly unchanged at $275 billion, CBO estimates. That amount reflects a decrease in receipts from Fannie Mae and Freddie Mac, which is mostly offset by an increase in proceeds from the Federal Communications Commission's auctions of licenses to use a portion of the electromagnetic spectrum. Over the coming decade, offsetting receipts are projected to increase by just over 2 percent per year, on average, rising to $346 billion by 2025 (see Table 3-2 on page 64).

Medicare. Offsetting receipts for Medicare are composed primarily of premiums paid by Medicare beneficiaries, but they also include recoveries of overpayments made to providers and payments made by states to cover a portion of the prescription drug costs for low-income beneficiaries. In 2014, those receipts totaled $95 billion, constituting one-third of all offsetting receipts and covering about 16 percent of gross Medicare spending. Over the coming years, those receipts are projected to rise at about the same rate as spending for Medicare, totaling $199 billion in 2025.

Federal Retirement. In 2014, $65 billion in offsetting receipts consisted of intragovernmental transfers from federal agencies to the federal funds from which employees' retirement benefits are paid (mostly trust funds for Social Security and for military and civilian retirement). Those payments from agencies' operating accounts to the funds have no net effect on federal outlays. Such payments will grow by nearly 3 percent per year, on average, CBO estimates, reaching $90 billion in 2025.

Natural Resources. Receipts stemming from the extraction of natural resources—particularly oil, natural gas, and minerals—from federally owned lands totaled $14 billion in 2014. By 2025, CBO estimates, those receipts will be $19 billion. The royalty payments included in that category fluctuate depending on the price of the commodity extracted.

Medicare-Eligible Retiree Health Care Fund. Intragovernmental transfers are also made to the Department of Defense's MERHCF (discussed above). Contributions to the fund are made on an accrual basis: Each year, the services contribute an amount sufficient to cover the increase in the estimated future costs of retirement benefits for their currently active service members. Such payments totaled $8 billion in 2014 and, because of rising health care costs, are projected to grow to $12 billion by 2025.

Fannie Mae and Freddie Mac. In the first few years after they were placed into conservatorship, the Treasury made payments to Fannie Mae and Freddie Mac; however, over the past couple of years, those entities have been making payments to the government. The Administration has recorded the payments by the government as outlays and the payments to the government from those two entities as offsetting receipts. To match the reporting for the current year in the *Monthly Treasury Statements*, CBO adopts the Administration's presentation for 2015, but for later years, because of the extent of government control over the two entities, CBO considers them to be part of the government and their transactions with the Treasury to be intragovernmental.

In 2014, the Treasury made no payments to those entities and received payments from them totaling $74 billion. CBO estimates that net payments from those entities to the Treasury will amount to $26 billion in 2015. That drop occurs partly because in fiscal year 2014 Freddie Mac's payments to the Treasury were boosted by a nearly $24 billion payment following a onetime revaluation of certain tax assets. In addition, financial institutions are expected to make fewer settlement payments to Fannie Mae and Freddie Mac in 2015 for allegations of fraud in connection with residential mortgages and certain other securities.

Legislation Assumed in the Baseline for Expiring Programs

In keeping with the rules established by the Deficit Control Act, CBO's baseline projections incorporate the assumption that some mandatory programs will be extended when their authorization expires, although the assumptions apply differently to programs created before and after the Balanced Budget Act of 1997. All direct spending programs that predate that act and have current-year outlays greater than $50 million are assumed to continue in CBO's baseline projections. For programs established after 1997, continuation is assessed program

by program in consultation with the House and Senate Budget Committees.

CBO's baseline projections therefore incorporate the assumption that the following programs, whose authorization expires within the current projection period, will continue: SNAP, TANF, CHIP, rehabilitation services, the Child Care Entitlement, trade adjustment assistance for workers, child nutrition, promoting safe and stable families, most farm subsidies, certain transportation programs, and some recreation fees. In addition, the Deficit Control Act directs CBO to assume that a cost-of-living adjustment for veterans' compensation will be granted each year. In CBO's projections, the assumption that expiring programs will continue accounts for less than $1 billion in mandatory outlays for 2015 and about $940 billion between 2016 and 2025, mostly for SNAP and TANF (see Table 3-3).

Discretionary Spending

Roughly one-third of federal outlays stem from budget authority provided in annual appropriation acts.[16] That funding—referred to as discretionary—translates into outlays when the money is spent. Although some appropriations (for example, those designated for employees' salaries) are spent quickly, others (such as those intended for major construction projects) are disbursed over several years. In any given year, discretionary outlays include spending from new budget authority and from budget authority provided in previous appropriations.

Several transportation programs have an unusual budgetary treatment: Their budget authority is provided in authorizing legislation, rather than in appropriation acts, but their spending is constrained by *obligation limitations* imposed by appropriation bills. Consequently, their budget authority is considered mandatory, but their outlays are discretionary. (The largest of those programs is the Federal-Aid Highway Program, which is funded from the

---

16. Budget authority is the authority provided by law to incur financial obligations that will result in immediate or future outlays of federal funds. Budget authority may be provided in an appropriation act or an authorization act and may take the form of a direct appropriation of funds from the Treasury, borrowing authority, contract authority, entitlement authority, or authority to obligate and expend offsetting collections or receipts. Offsetting collections and receipts are shown as negative budget authority and outlays.

Table 3-3.

Costs for Mandatory Programs That Continue Beyond Their Current Expiration Date in CBO's Baseline

Billions of Dollars

	2015	2016	2017	2018	2019	2020	2021	2022	2023	2024	2025	Total 2016-2020	2016-2025
Supplemental Nutrition Assistance Program													
Budget authority	0	0	0	0	74	74	74	73	74	74	75	148	518
Outlays	0	0	0	0	72	74	74	73	74	74	75	146	515
Temporary Assistance for Needy Families													
Budget authority	0	17	17	17	17	17	17	17	17	17	17	86	173
Outlays	0	13	16	17	17	17	17	17	17	17	17	81	167
Commodity Credit Corporation[a]													
Budget authority	0	0	0	0	2	3	8	8	9	9	10	5	50
Outlays	0	0	0	0	1	2	8	8	9	9	10	2	45
Children's Health Insurance Program													
Budget authority	0	6	6	6	6	6	6	6	6	6	6	29	57
Outlays	0	5	6	6	6	6	6	6	6	6	6	28	57
Veterans' Compensation COLAs													
Budget authority	0	2	4	5	7	8	10	13	13	14	15	26	92
Outlays	0	2	4	5	7	8	10	13	13	14	15	26	91
Rehabilitation Services													
Budget authority	0	0	0	0	0	0	0	0	4	4	4	0	12
Outlays	0	0	0	0	0	0	0	0	2	4	4	0	10
Child Care Entitlements to States													
Budget authority	0	3	3	3	3	3	3	3	3	3	3	15	29
Outlays	0	2	3	3	3	3	3	3	3	3	3	14	28
Trade Adjustment Assistance for Workers[b]													
Budget authority	0	1	1	1	1	1	1	1	1	1	1	4	9
Outlays	0	*	1	1	1	1	1	1	1	1	1	4	9
Child Nutrition[c]													
Budget authority	0	1	1	1	1	1	1	1	1	1	1	4	9
Outlays	0	1	1	1	1	1	1	1	1	1	1	4	9

Continued

Highway Trust Fund.) As a result, total discretionary outlays in the budget are greater than total discretionary budget authority. In some cases, the amounts of those obligation limitations are added to discretionary budget authority to produce a measure of the total *funding* provided for discretionary programs.

In CBO's baseline projections, most appropriations for the 2015–2021 period are assumed to be constrained by the caps set by the Budget Control Act of 2011 and modified in subsequent legislation, including the automatic reductions required by that act. For the period from 2022

Table 3-3.   Continued

Costs for Mandatory Programs That Continue Beyond Their Current Expiration Date in CBO's Baseline

Billions of Dollars

	2015	2016	2017	2018	2019	2020	2021	2022	2023	2024	2025	Total 2016-2020	2016-2025
Promoting Safe and Stable Families													
Budget authority	0	0	*	*	*	*	*	*	*	*	*	1	3
Outlays	0	0	*	*	*	*	*	*	*	*	*	1	3
Ground Transportation Programs Not Subject to Annual Obligation Limitations													
Budget authority	*	1	1	1	1	1	1	1	1	1	1	3	6
Outlays	*	*	*	1	1	1	1	1	1	1	1	2	6
Ground Transportation Programs Controlled by Obligation Limitations[d]													
Budget authority	17	50	50	50	50	50	50	50	50	50	50	251	501
Outlays	0	0	0	0	0	0	0	0	0	0	0	0	0
Air Transportation Programs Controlled by Obligation Limitations[d]													
Budget authority	0	3	3	3	3	3	3	3	3	3	3	16	32
Outlays	0	0	0	0	0	0	0	0	0	0	0	0	0
Natural Resources													
Budget authority	0	0	0	0	0	0	0	0	0	0	0	0	0
Outlays	0	*	*	*	*	*	*	*	*	*	*	*	*
Total													
Budget authority	17	83	85	87	165	167	174	177	182	183	186	588	1,491
Outlays	*	24	30	33	108	113	120	123	126	129	133	307	939

Source: Congressional Budget Office.

Note: COLAs = cost-of-living adjustments; * = between -$500 million and $500 million.

a.   Agricultural commodity price and income supports and conservation programs under the Agricultural Act of 2014 generally expire after 2018. Although permanent price support authority under the Agricultural Adjustment Act of 1938 and the Agricultural Act of 1949 would then become effective, CBO continues to adhere to the rule in section 257(b)(2)(ii) of the Deficit Control Act that indicates that the baseline should assume that the Agricultural Act's provisions remain in effect.

b.   Does not include the cost of extending Reemployment Trade Adjustment Assistance, which, if extended through 2025, would increase mandatory outlays by $0.4 billion, CBO estimates.

c.   Includes the Summer Food Service program and states' administrative expenses.

d.   Authorizing legislation for those programs provides contract authority, which is counted as mandatory budget authority. However, because the programs' spending is subject to obligation limitations specified in annual appropriation acts, outlays are considered discretionary.

Figure 3-3.

Discretionary Outlays, by Category

Percentage of Gross Domestic Product

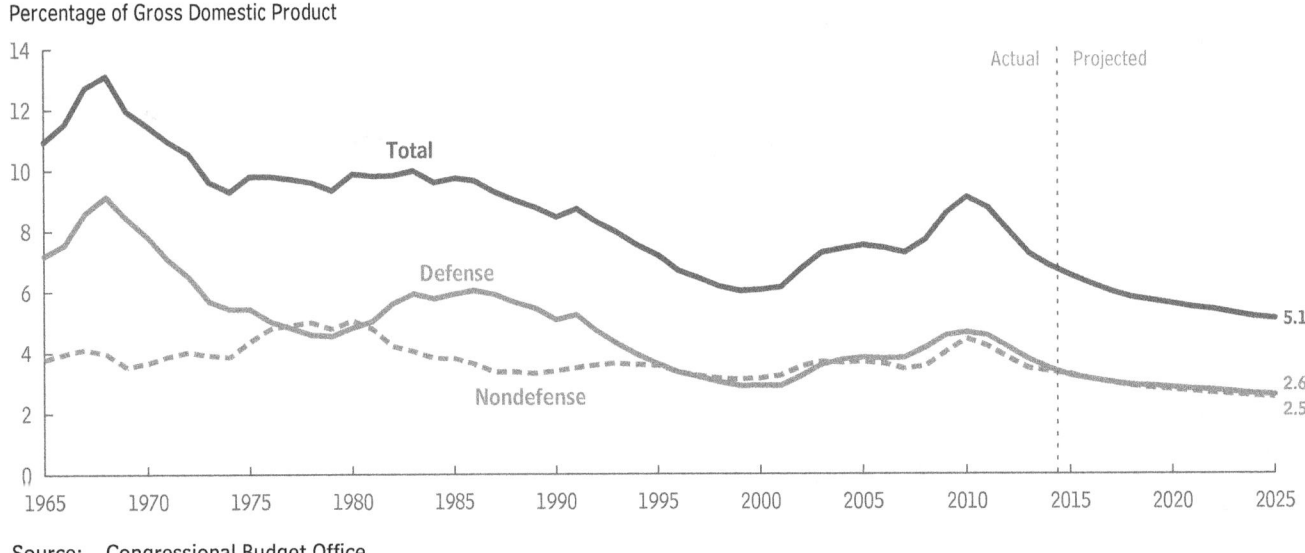

Source: Congressional Budget Office.

through 2025, CBO assumes that those appropriations will grow at the rate of inflation from the amounts estimated for 2021.[17]

Funding for certain purposes is not constrained by the caps: Military and diplomatic operations in Afghanistan and elsewhere that have been designated as overseas contingency operations (OCO), responses to events designated as emergencies, disaster relief, and initiatives designed to enhance program integrity by reducing over-payments in some benefit programs are all exempt activities. CBO developed projections for such funding by assuming that it would grow at the rate of inflation from the amounts appropriated for 2015.

Under those assumptions, discretionary outlays in CBO's baseline grow by an average of less than 2 percent a year from 2015 through 2025. Because that pace is less than the projected growth rate of nominal GDP, discretionary outlays in CBO's baseline projections fall from 6.5 percent of GDP in 2015 to 5.1 percent of GDP in 2025, a

smaller share than in any year since before 1962 (the first year for which comparable data are available).

Trends in Discretionary Outlays

Since the 1960s, the share of federal spending that is governed by the annual appropriation process has dropped by about half—from 67 percent of total spending in 1962 to 34 percent in 2014. Discretionary outlays averaged 12 percent of GDP over the 1962–1969 period, fell to about 10 percent during much of the 1970s and 1980s, and gradually declined to 6.0 percent in 1999 (see Figure 3-3). They then began to increase relative to the size of the economy, reaching 7.7 percent of GDP in 2008. That rise occurred in part because of actions taken in response to the terrorist attacks of September 11, 2001, and the subsequent military operations in Afghanistan and Iraq. (Funding for those operations from 2001 to 2015 is examined in Box 3-2.)

By 2010, discretionary outlays reached a recent peak of 9.1 percent of GDP, largely because of $281 billion in discretionary funding provided by the American Recovery and Reinvestment Act of 2009 (ARRA; P.L. 111-5). Since then, discretionary outlays have again declined as a share of GDP, falling to 6.8 percent in 2014, mostly because of the constraints put in place by the Budget Control Act and because of declines in spending for OCO and for activities funded by ARRA.

---

17. CBO develops projections of discretionary spending by first inflating the appropriations provided for specific activities in 2015 and then reducing total projected defense and nondefense funding by the amounts necessary to bring them in line with the caps. In CBO's baseline, discretionary funding related to federal personnel is inflated using the employment cost index for wages and salaries; other discretionary funding is adjusted using the gross domestic product price index.

During the 1990s, declines in discretionary outlays relative to the size of the economy largely reflected reductions in defense spending, which reached a low of 2.9 percent of GDP from 1999 through 2001. In part boosted by funding for operations in Afghanistan and Iraq, outlays for defense began to rise in 2002, reaching 4.7 percent of GDP in 2010 when funding for defense-related activities peaked. Since then, defense spending has fallen again relative to GDP, to 3.5 percent in 2014, owing mostly to a reduction in funding for OCO. As a whole, between 2010 and 2014, funding for defense declined by 15 percent in nominal terms, or nearly 21 percent in constant 2010 dollars. That change was heavily influenced by reductions in funding for OCO. Excluding those amounts, funding for defense fell by roughly 6 percent in nominal terms, or 12 percent in real terms, over that period.

Nondefense discretionary programs encompass such activities as transportation, education grants, housing assistance, health-related research, veterans' health care, most homeland security activities, the federal justice system, foreign aid, and environmental protection. Historically, nondefense discretionary outlays represented a fairly stable share of GDP, averaging 3.8 percent over the 1962–2008 period and rarely exceeding 5.0 percent or falling below 3.2 percent. Funding from ARRA, enacted in 2009, helped push that share to a recent high of 4.5 percent in 2010, but by 2012 agencies had spent roughly 85 percent of that funding, and nondefense discretionary outlays fell back to the historical average of 3.8 percent of GDP. Between 2010 and 2014, funding for nondefense discretionary programs declined by 4.4 percent in nominal terms, or 10.7 percent in constant 2010 dollars. Outlays for those programs have followed the downward trend in funding and have fallen notably relative to GDP, reaching 3.4 percent in 2014.

Discretionary Appropriations and Outlays in 2015
The Consolidated and Further Continuing Appropriations Act, 2015 (P.L. 113-235) provided discretionary budget authority totaling $1,120 billion.[18] (That amount includes, on an annualized basis, appropriations for the Department of Homeland Security that are available only through February 27, 2015.) In total, discretionary budget authority for fiscal year 2015 is roughly 1 percent less than the $1,133 billion for fiscal year 2014 (see Table 3-4 on page 82).

The caps on budget authority for 2015 had been set at $521.3 billion for defense programs and at $492.4 billion for nondefense programs, for a total of $1,013.6 billion. Those limits are adjusted, however, when appropriations are provided for certain purposes. Budget authority designated as an emergency requirement or provided for OCO leads to an increase in the caps, as does budget authority provided for some types of disaster relief or for certain program integrity initiatives.[19] To date, such adjustments to the caps on discretionary budget authority for 2015 have totaled $86 billion; most of that amount, $74 billion, resulted from funding for OCO. Those adjustments raise the caps to a total of $1,100 billion.

The amount of discretionary budget authority in CBO's baseline, however, is about $20 billion more than the adjusted caps, mostly because changes to mandatory programs included in P.L. 113-235 resulted in reductions to budget authority for such programs in 2015 that were credited against discretionary funding levels when the legislation was enacted. In CBO's baseline, those reductions are reflected in the relevant mandatory accounts, and the full amount of discretionary budget authority is shown in the discretionary accounts.

Assuming that funding for the Department of Homeland Security remains at the annualized levels specified in P.L. 113-235 and that no additional appropriations are made, CBO estimates that discretionary outlays will edge down in 2015 to $1,175 billion, slightly below the $1,179 billion of such outlays in 2014 and equal to 6.5 percent of GDP. That sum represents the lowest amount of discretionary outlays since 2008. Since their recent peak in 2010, discretionary outlays have declined by 13 percent in nominal terms and 18 percent in real terms (adjusted for inflation using the price index for personal consumption expenditures).

Defense Discretionary Funding and Outlays. Budget authority provided for defense discretionary programs in 2015 totals $586 billion—3.3 percent less than the 2014 amount of $606 billion. (Almost all defense spending is

---

18. Obligation limitations for transportation programs in 2015 total an additional $53 billion, which is the same amount legislated for 2014.

19. Such initiatives identify and reduce improper payments for benefit programs such as DI, SSI, Medicare, Medicaid, and CHIP.

Box 3-2.

Funding for Operations in Afghanistan and Iraq and Related Activities

Since September 2001, lawmakers have provided $1.6 trillion in budget authority for operations in Afghanistan and Iraq and related activities (see the table). That amount includes funding for military and diplomatic operations in Afghanistan, Iraq, and elsewhere related to the fight against terrorism; for some defense activities that are designated as related to those overseas operations; for some veterans' benefits and services; and for related activities of the Department of Justice. Appropriations specifically designated for those purposes averaged about $85 billion a year from 2001 through 2007 and peaked at $187 billion in 2008. Funding declined to an average of $150 billion over the 2009–2012 period and to an average of $93 billion in 2013 and 2014. Lawmakers have appropriated $74 billion for such activities in 2015.

Funding to date for military operations and other defense activities has totaled almost $1.5 trillion, most of which has gone to the Department of Defense (DoD), including about $910 billion for operation and maintenance costs, $310 billion for procurement, and $200 billion for military personnel costs. Lawmakers have also provided $91 billion to train and equip indigenous security forces in Afghanistan and Iraq.[1] In addition, $90 billion has been provided for diplomatic operations and aid to Afghanistan, Iraq, and other countries that are assisting the United States in its fight against terrorism.

---

1. That $91 billion includes $5 billion provided for Iraqi security forces in 2004 in an appropriation for the State Department's Iraq Relief and Reconstruction Fund.

The majority of those funds have gone to the Economic Support Fund ($24 billion), to diplomatic and consular programs ($20 billion), and to the Iraq Relief and Reconstruction Fund ($16 billion).

DoD reports that in fiscal year 2014, obligations for operations in Afghanistan and Iraq and related activities averaged $5 billion per month. That monthly average is about $1.8 billion less than the amount reported for 2013. Operation Enduring Freedom (in and around Afghanistan) accounted for almost all of those obligations in 2014.

Because most appropriations for operations in Afghanistan and Iraq and related activities appear in the same budget accounts as appropriations for DoD's other functions, it is impossible to determine precisely how much has been spent on those activities alone. The Congressional Budget Office estimates that the $1.5 trillion appropriated between 2001 and 2015 for military operations and other defense activities in Afghanistan and Iraq and for indigenous security forces in those two countries has resulted in outlays of about $1.4 trillion through 2014; about $95 billion of that was spent in 2014. Of the $90 billion appropriated for international affairs activities related to the war efforts over the 2001–2015 period, about $68 billion was spent by the end of 2014, CBO estimates, with $8 billion of that spending occurring in 2014. In total, outlays for all activities related to the operations in Afghanistan and Iraq amounted to about $103 billion last year. On the basis of sums appropriated for 2015, CBO estimates that outlays will total about $80 billion this year.

Continued

categorized as discretionary.) The decline in funding is attributable to a $21 billion reduction in defense appropriations for OCO, which total $64 billion in 2015; excluding the amounts for OCO, funding for defense programs in 2015 is $1 billion (or 0.2 percent) higher than last year. The latest drop in OCO-related appropriations continues a marked decline in such funding, which has fallen by 60 percent (in nominal terms) since 2011. As a whole, reductions in defense appropriations over the past several years have caused outlays to fall to an

estimated $583 billion in 2015—2.2 percent less than the 2014 amount. CBO projects that, as a share of GDP, defense outlays will decline from 3.5 percent in 2014 to 3.2 percent in 2015, the lowest level since 2002.

Three major categories of Department of Defense funding account for most of the defense appropriation for 2015 (as they have in preceding years): operation and maintenance ($246 billion), military personnel ($140 billion), and procurement ($101 billion). Appropriations

Box 3-2.   Continued

Funding for Operations in Afghanistan and Iraq and Related Activities

Estimated Budget Authority Provided for U.S. Operations in Afghanistan and Iraq and Related Activities for Fiscal Years 2001 to 2015

Billions of Dollars

	2001–2007	2008	2009	2010	2011	2012	2013[a]	2014	2015	Total, 2001–2015
Military Operations and Other Defense Activities[b]										
Iraq[c]	369	133	90	59	42	10	3	1	4	710
Afghanistan	80	29	38	87	98	89	65	74	51	611
Other[d]	81	13	13	5	6	6	10	6	4	143
Subtotal	530	175	140	151	146	104	78	81	59	1,465
Indigenous Security Forces[e]										
Iraq	19	3	1	1	2	0	0	0	2	27
Afghanistan	11	3	6	9	12	11	4	5	3	64
Subtotal	30	6	7	10	13	11	4	5	5	91
Diplomatic Operations and Foreign Aid[f]										
Iraq	25	3	2	2	0	4	4	2	1	43
Afghanistan	5	1	5	2	0	5	5	1	3	27
Other	7	*	1	*	0	2	2	3	5	20
Subtotal	37	5	7	4	0	11	11	7	9	90
Other Services and Activities[g]										
Iraq	1	1	*	0	0	0	0	0	0	2
Afghanistan	*	*	*	0	0	0	0	0	0	*
Other	*	*	*	0	0	0	0	0	0	1
Subtotal	1	2	*	0	0	0	0	0	0	3
Total	**598**	**187**	**154**	**165**	**159**	**127**	**93**	**92**	**74**	**1,649**

Source: Congressional Budget Office.

Note: * = between zero and $500 million.

a. Amounts for 2013 are net of reductions implemented in response to the Administration's sequestration order of March 1, 2013.

b. CBO estimated the funding provided for operations in Afghanistan and Iraq using information in budget justification materials from the Department of Defense and in the department's monthly reports on its obligations. Some allocations for prior years have been adjusted to reflect more recent information.

c. Includes funding for military operations against the Islamic State in Iraq and Syria.

d. Includes Operation Noble Eagle (homeland security missions, such as combat air patrols, in the United States), additional personnel and restructuring efforts for Army and Marine Corps units, classified activities not funded by appropriations for the Iraq Freedom Fund, the European Reassurance Initiative, and improvements to military readiness. (From 2005 through 2015, funding for Operation Noble Eagle has been intermingled with regular appropriations for the Department of Defense; that funding is not included in this table.)

e. Funding for indigenous security forces is used to train and equip military and police units in Afghanistan and Iraq. That funding was appropriated in accounts for diplomatic operations and foreign aid (budget function 150) in 2004 and in accounts for defense (budget function 050) starting in 2005.

f. In 2010 and 2011, most funding for diplomatic operations in, and foreign aid to, countries helping the United States fight terrorism was provided in regular appropriations and cannot be isolated.

g. Includes funding for some veterans' benefits and services and for certain activities of the Department of Justice. Excludes about $34 billion in spending by the Department of Veterans Affairs for the incremental costs of medical care, disability compensation, and survivors' benefits for veterans of operations in Afghanistan and Iraq and of the war on terrorism. That amount is based on CBO's estimates of spending from regular appropriations for the Department of Veterans Affairs and was not explicitly appropriated for war-related expenses.

Table 3-4.

Changes in Discretionary Budget Authority From 2014 to 2015

Billions of Dollars

	Actual, 2014	Estimated, 2015	Percentage Change
Defense			
Funding constrained by caps	520	521	0.2
Overseas contingency operations	85	64	-24.5
Other cap adjustments	*	*	-50.2
Subtotal	606	586	-3.3
Nondefense			
Funding constrained by caps	514	513	-0.2
Overseas contingency operations	7	9	42.0
Other cap adjustments	7	12	90.7
Subtotal	527	534	1.5
Total Discretionary Budget Authority			
Funding constrained by caps	1,034	1,034	**
Overseas contingency operations	92	74	-19.8
Other cap adjustments	7	13	86.1
Total	1,133	1,120	-1.1

Source: Congressional Budget Office.

Notes: Excludes budgetary resources provided by obligation limitations for certain ground and air transportation programs.

   Budget authority designated as an emergency requirement or provided for overseas contingency operations leads to an increase in the caps, as does budget authority provided for some types of disaster relief or for certain program integrity initiatives.

   n.a. = not applicable; * = between zero and $500 million; ** = between -0.05 percent and zero.

for research and development ($64 billion) account for an additional 11 percent of total funding for defense. The rest of the appropriation, about 6 percent, comprises funding for military construction, family housing, and other Department of Defense programs ($9 billion); funding for atomic energy activities, primarily within the Department of Energy ($18 billion); and funding for various defense-related programs in other departments and agencies ($8 billion).

Nondefense Discretionary Funding and Outlays. To date, funding for nondefense programs in 2015 totals $588 billion. That amount represents $534 billion in appropriations (including, on an annualized basis, the appropriations for the Department of Homeland Security that are available for only part of the year) and $53 billion in obligation limitations for several ground and air transportation programs. The 2015 amount is $8 billion more than the funding provided in 2014, in part because of $5 billion in emergency funding appropriated in response to the Ebola outbreak in West Africa. CBO anticipates that nondefense discretionary outlays will rise from

$583 billion in 2014 to $592 billion in 2015—an increase of 1.5 percent; however, as a share of GDP, discretionary outlays will fall from 3.4 percent in 2014 to 3.3 percent in 2015 because the economy is projected to grow faster than those outlays.

Seven broad budget categories (referred to as budget functions) account for about 80 percent of the $588 billion in resources provided in 2015 for nondefense discretionary activities (see Table 3-5). Activities related to education, training, employment, and social services received $92 billion, claiming 16 percent of total nondefense discretionary funding.[20] Transportation programs received $85 billion (including appropriations and obligation limitations), or 14 percent of the total. Income-security programs and veterans' benefits and services each received $65 billion, or 11 percent of total

---

20. Spending for student loans and for several other federal programs in the category of education, training, employment, and social services is not included in that total because funding for those programs is considered mandatory.

Table 3-5.

Changes in Nondefense Discretionary Funding From 2014 to 2015

Billions of Dollars

Budget Function	Actual, 2014	Estimated, 2015	Change
Education, Training, Employment, and Social Services	92	92	*
Transportation[a]	85	85	*
Income Security	65	65	*
Veterans' Benefits and Services	64	65	2
Health	56	59	3
Administration of Justice	52	51	-1
International Affairs	50	54	3
Natural Resources and Environment	34	34	*
General Science, Space, and Technology	29	30	*
Community and Regional Development	17	17	*
General Government	19	16	-2
Medicare	6	7	*
Agriculture	6	6	*
Social Security	6	6	*
Energy	5	5	*
Commerce and Housing Credit	-6	-4	3
Total	**580**	**588**	**8**

Source: Congressional Budget Office.

Note: * = between -$500 million and $500 million.

a.   Includes budgetary resources provided by obligation limitations for certain ground and air transportation programs.

nondefense funding. Health programs account for $59 billion, or 10 percent of such funding, while the shares of total funding allocated for international affairs ($54 billion) and administration of justice ($51 billion), are each about 9 percent.[21]

Projections for 2016 Through 2025

For 2016, the caps on discretionary appropriations are set at $523 billion for defense and $493 billion for non-defense activities, for a total of $1,016 billion—$2 billion more than the 2015 caps (prior to adjustments for appropriations for OCO and other activities not constrained by the caps). In CBO's baseline, the amounts projected for activities that result in cap adjustments in 2016 total $88 billion (equal to the 2015 amounts adjusted for inflation)—bringing total 2016 appropriations projected in the baseline to $1,104 billion, the lowest amount of discretionary appropriations since 2007. That amount is 1.5 percent less than the 2015 appropriations, mostly

because the budget authority enacted for 2015 includes about $20 billion that was offset by reductions in mandatory programs; similar actions are not assumed in the baseline for subsequent years.

CBO estimates that achieving compliance with the 2016 cap on nondefense appropriations without using any offsets from changes to mandatory programs would require a 3.8 percent reduction in budget authority relative to 2015 appropriations. With such a reduction, non-defense outlays would fall, CBO estimates, but only by 0.5 percent because residual outlays of earlier onetime appropriations—including funds provided under ARRA for high-speed rail projects and appropriations enacted in response to Hurricane Sandy—would help offset the reduction in spending attributable to the drop in 2016 appropriations. Funding equal to the 2016 cap on defense appropriations would generate increases in defense-related appropriations and outlays in 2016 of an estimated 0.5 percent and 0.7 percent, respectively. In total, discretionary outlays are projected to total $1,176 billion in 2016—0.1 percent more than spending in 2015—and to equal 6.2 percent of GDP.

---

21. Some significant income-security programs, such as SNAP, unemployment compensation, and TANF, are not reflected in that total because they are included in mandatory spending.

From 2017 through 2021, caps on discretionary appropriations and the corresponding projected amounts of discretionary funding in CBO's baseline grow at an average annual rate of 2.4 percent; after 2021, when there are no caps, appropriations are projected (based on the methods described above) to grow by about 2.5 percent annually. Discretionary outlays are also projected to grow over those years, although at rates of less than 1 percent annually through 2018, largely reflecting the tapering of expenditures of earlier funding provided for OCO and in response to Hurricane Sandy. Starting in 2019, discretionary outlays in CBO's baseline grow at an average rate of 2.3 percent per year, following the projected growth in funding. Because that pace is well below the expected growth of nominal GDP, discretionary outlays are projected to fall steadily relative to the size of the economy, from 6.5 percent of GDP in 2015 to 5.1 percent in 2025.

Alternative Paths for Discretionary Spending

Total funding for discretionary activities in 2015 will amount to about $1,173 billion on an annualized basis, CBO estimates—$1,120 billion in budget authority and $53 billion in transportation-related obligation limitations. In CBO's baseline projections, discretionary funding is projected for subsequent years on the basis of the amounts and procedures prescribed in the Budget Control Act and related laws. However, if the policies governing discretionary appropriations changed, funding could differ greatly from the baseline projections. To illustrate such potential differences, CBO has estimated the budgetary consequences of several alternative paths for discretionary funding (see Table 3-6).

The first alternative path addresses spending for war-related activities that are designated as overseas contingency operations. The outlays projected in the baseline stem from budget authority provided for those purposes in 2014 and prior years, from the $74 billion in budget authority provided for 2015, and from the $822 billion that is assumed to be appropriated over the 2016–2025 period (under the assumption that annual funding is set at $74 billion plus adjustments for anticipated inflation, in accordance with the rules governing baseline projections).[22]

In coming years, the funding required for overseas contingency operations—in Afghanistan or other countries—might be smaller than the amounts projected in the baseline if the number of deployed troops and the

pace of operations diminished over time. For that reason, CBO has formulated a budget scenario that encompasses a reduction in the deployment of U.S. forces abroad for military actions and a concomitant reduction in diplomatic operations and foreign aid. Many other scenarios—some costing more and some less—are also possible.

In 2014, the number of U.S. active-duty, reserve, and National Guard personnel deployed for war-related activities averaged about 110,000, CBO estimates. In this alternative scenario, the average number of military personnel deployed for war-related purposes would decline over the next two years from roughly 90,000 in 2015 to 50,000 in 2016 and to 30,000 in 2017 and thereafter. (Those levels could represent various allocations of forces among Afghanistan and other regions.) Under that scenario, and assuming that the extraordinary funding for diplomatic operations and foreign aid declines at a similar rate, total discretionary outlays over the 2016–2025 period would be $454 billion less than the amount in the baseline.[23]

For the second policy alternative, CBO assumed that discretionary funding would grow at the rate of inflation after 2015. If that occurred, discretionary outlays would surpass CBO's baseline projections by $480 billion over the 2016–2025 period. In that scenario, discretionary outlays would increase by an average of 2.3 percent a year over the next decade.

The third scenario reflects the assumption that most discretionary budget authority and obligation limitations will be frozen at the 2015 level for the entire projection

---

22. Funding for overseas contingency operations in 2015 includes $64 billion for military operations and for indigenous security forces in Afghanistan and Iraq and $9 billion for diplomatic operations and foreign aid.

23. The reduction in budget authority under this alternative is similar to the reductions arising from some proposals to cap discretionary appropriations for overseas contingency operations. Such caps could result in reductions in CBO's baseline projections of discretionary spending. However, those reductions might simply reflect policy decisions that have already been made or would be made in the absence of caps. Moreover, if future policymakers believed that national security required appropriations above the capped levels, they would almost certainly provide emergency appropriations that would not, under current law, be counted against the caps.

period.[24] In that case, total discretionary outlays for the 10-year period would be $929 billion lower than those projected in the baseline, and total discretionary spending would fall to 4.3 percent of GDP by 2025.

For the final alternative scenario, CBO projected what would occur if lawmakers canceled the automatic reductions in the discretionary caps required by the Budget Control Act. Those automatic procedures will reduce discretionary spending over the 2016–2021 period (and mandatory spending through 2024). If, instead, lawmakers chose to set total discretionary funding equal to the caps originally specified under the Budget Control Act and prevent further automatic cuts to discretionary funding each year, outlays would be $845 billion (or about 7 percent) higher over the 2016–2025 period than the amount projected in CBO's baseline.

Net Interest

In 2014, net outlays for interest were $229 billion, about $8 billion more than the amount spent in 2013. As a percentage of GDP, net interest was 1.3 percent in 2014 and is expected to remain at that level in 2015.

Net interest outlays are dominated by the interest paid to holders of the debt that the Department of the Treasury issues to the public. The Treasury also pays interest on debt issued to trust funds and other government accounts, but such payments are intragovernmental transactions that have no effect on the budget deficit. Other federal accounts also pay and receive interest for various reasons.[25]

The federal government's interest payments depend primarily on market interest rates and the amount of debt held by the public; however, other factors, such as the rate of inflation and the maturity structure of outstanding securities, also affect interest costs. (For example, longer-term securities generally pay higher interest than do shorter-term securities.) Interest rates are determined by a combination of market forces and the policies of the Federal Reserve System. Debt held by the public is

determined mostly by cumulative budget deficits, which depend on policy choices about noninterest spending and revenues as well as on economic conditions and other factors. At the end of 2014, debt held by the public reached $12.8 trillion, and in CBO's baseline it is projected to total $21.6 trillion in 2025. (For detailed projections of debt held by the public, see Table 1-3 on page 19.)

Although debt held by the public surged in the past few years to its highest levels relative to GDP since the early 1950s, the government's interest costs have remained low relative to GDP because interest rates on Treasury securities have been remarkably low. Average rates on 3-month Treasury bills plummeted from nearly 5 percent in 2007 to 0.1 percent in 2010; those rates fell further to 0.04 percent in 2014. Similarly, average rates on 10-year Treasury notes dropped from nearly 5 percent in 2007 to a low of 1.9 percent in 2012; those rates, however, increased in 2014 to 2.7 percent. As a result of such low rates, even though debt held by the public more than doubled from the end of 2007 to the end of 2014, outlays for net interest fell from 1.7 percent of GDP to 1.3 percent over that period. By comparison, such outlays averaged about 3 percent of GDP in the 1980s and 1990s.

Baseline Projections of Net Interest

Under CBO's baseline assumptions, net interest costs are projected to nearly quadruple from $227 billion in 2015 to $827 billion in 2025. One reason for that increase is that debt held by the public is projected to rise by nearly 70 percent (in nominal terms) over the next 10 years (see Figure 3-4 on page 88).[26] More significantly, CBO estimates, the interest rate paid on 3-month Treasury bills will rise from 0.1 percent in 2015 to 3.4 percent in 2018 and subsequent years, and the rate on 10-year Treasury notes will increase from 2.6 percent in 2015 to 4.6 percent in 2020 and subsequent years. As a result, under current law, net interest outlays are projected to reach 3.0 percent of GDP in 2025.

Net interest costs consist of gross interest (the amounts paid on all of the Treasury's debt issuances) minus interest received by trust funds (which are intragovernmental

---

24. Some items, such as offsetting collections and payments made by the Treasury on behalf of the Department of Defense's TRICARE for Life program, would not be held constant.

25. See Congressional Budget Office, *Federal Debt and Interest Costs* (December 2010), www.cbo.gov/publication/21960.

26. Debt held by the public does not include securities issued by the Treasury to federal trust funds and other government accounts. Those securities are included as part of the measure of gross debt. (For further details, see Chapter 1.)

Table 3-6.

CBO's Projections of Discretionary Spending Under Selected Policy Alternatives

Billions of Dollars

	Actual, 2014	2015	2016	2017	2018	2019	2020	2021	2022	2023	2024	2025	Total 2016-2020	Total 2016-2025
CBO's January 2015 Baseline (Spending caps in effect through 2021)														
Budget Authority														
Defense	606	586	589	603	617	632	647	663	679	696	713	730	3,087	6,568
Nondefense	527	534	515	526	539	553	567	580	594	609	624	640	2,701	5,748
Total	1,133	1,120	1,104	1,129	1,156	1,185	1,214	1,243	1,273	1,305	1,337	1,370	5,788	12,316
Outlays														
Defense	596	583	587	592	599	616	631	646	666	677	689	711	3,025	6,413
Nondefense	583	592	589	590	594	605	617	630	644	658	672	689	2,995	6,288
Total	1,179	1,175	1,176	1,182	1,193	1,221	1,248	1,276	1,310	1,336	1,361	1,400	6,019	12,701
Reduce the Number of Troops Deployed for Overseas Contingency Operations to 30,000 by 2017[a]														
Budget Authority														
Defense	606	586	565	564	573	585	599	614	629	645	661	677	2,887	6,113
Nondefense	527	534	513	521	532	546	560	572	587	601	616	632	2,672	5,681
Total	1,133	1,120	1,079	1,085	1,105	1,131	1,159	1,186	1,216	1,246	1,277	1,309	5,559	11,794
Outlays														
Defense	596	583	576	566	564	575	586	599	618	629	639	660	2,867	6,011
Nondefense	583	592	589	588	590	600	612	624	637	651	665	681	2,978	6,236
Total	1,179	1,175	1,164	1,154	1,154	1,175	1,198	1,223	1,255	1,280	1,304	1,341	5,845	12,247
Increase Discretionary Appropriations at the Rate of Inflation After 2015[b]														
Budget Authority														
Defense	606	586	598	612	628	645	662	679	697	715	733	752	3,144	6,720
Nondefense	527	534	543	553	569	585	603	620	638	656	673	691	2,853	6,132
Total	1,133	1,120	1,141	1,165	1,197	1,230	1,265	1,299	1,335	1,371	1,406	1,443	5,997	12,852
Outlays														
Defense	596	583	593	600	608	628	644	661	683	695	708	732	3,072	6,551
Nondefense	583	592	604	612	620	634	651	667	684	702	719	737	3,121	6,630
Total	1,179	1,175	1,196	1,212	1,229	1,262	1,295	1,328	1,367	1,398	1,427	1,469	6,193	13,181

Continued

payments) and from other sources. In 2015, for example, estimated net outlays for interest ($227 billion) consist of $405 billion in gross interest, minus $139 billion received by the trust funds and $39 billion in other net interest receipts.

Gross Interest

In 2014, interest paid by the Treasury on all of its debt issuances totaled $431 billion (see Table 3-7 on page 89). More than one-third of that total, $158 billion, represents payments to other entities (such as trust funds) within the federal government; the remainder is paid to owners of Treasury debt issued to the public. In CBO's baseline, gross interest payments from 2016 through 2025 total $8.0 trillion. About 70 percent of that amount reflects interest paid on debt held by the public.

Interest Received by Trust Funds

The Treasury has issued more than $5.0 trillion in securities to federal trust funds and other government accounts. Trust funds are the dominant holders of such securities, owning more than 90 percent of them. The interest paid on those securities has no net effect on federal spending because it is credited to accounts elsewhere in the budget.

Table 3-6.   Continued

CBO's Projections of Discretionary Spending Under Selected Policy Alternatives

Billions of Dollars

	Actual, 2014	2015	2016	2017	2018	2019	2020	2021	2022	2023	2024	2025	Total 2016-2020	Total 2016-2025
Freeze Most Discretionary Appropriations at the 2015 Amount[c]														
Budget Authority														
Defense	606	586	587	589	590	592	594	596	598	600	603	605	2,952	5,955
Nondefense	527	534	534	531	532	533	536	537	539	540	540	540	2,666	5,362
Total	1,133	1,120	1,121	1,120	1,122	1,126	1,130	1,133	1,137	1,140	1,142	1,145	5,618	11,316
Outlays														
Defense	596	583	585	582	578	583	585	587	593	591	589	595	2,914	5,869
Nondefense	583	592	598	596	589	588	589	589	589	589	588	588	2,960	5,903
Total	1,179	1,175	1,183	1,177	1,168	1,171	1,174	1,176	1,182	1,180	1,177	1,183	5,874	11,772
Prevent the Automatic Spending Reductions Specified in the Budget Control Act[d]														
Budget Authority														
Defense	606	586	643	657	671	686	701	717	734	752	771	790	3,357	7,121
Nondefense	527	534	552	564	576	590	602	615	630	646	662	678	2,884	6,114
Total	1,133	1,120	1,195	1,220	1,247	1,275	1,303	1,331	1,364	1,398	1,433	1,468	6,241	13,235
Outlays														
Defense	596	583	621	637	649	668	684	699	720	733	745	769	3,259	6,925
Nondefense	583	592	608	621	628	640	653	665	679	694	709	726	3,150	6,621
Total	1,179	1,175	1,230	1,258	1,277	1,308	1,337	1,364	1,399	1,426	1,454	1,495	6,409	13,546

Source: Congressional Budget Office.

Note: Nondefense discretionary outlays are usually higher than budget authority because of spending from the Highway Trust Fund and the Airport and Airway Trust Fund that is subject to obligation limitations set in appropriation acts. The budget authority for such programs is provided in authorizing legislation and is not considered discretionary.

a.   For this alternative, CBO does not extrapolate the $74 billion in budget authority for military operations, diplomatic activities, and aid to Afghanistan and other countries provided for 2015. Rather, the alternative incorporates the assumption that, as the number of troops falls to about 30,000 by 2017, funding for overseas contingency operations declines as well, to $50 billion in 2016, $32 billion in 2017, and then an average of about $27 billion a year from 2018 on, for a total of $300 billion over the 2016–2025 period.

b.   These estimates reflect the assumption that appropriations will not be constrained by caps and will instead grow at the rate of inflation from their 2015 level. Discretionary funding related to federal personnel is inflated using the employment cost index for wages and salaries; other discretionary funding is adjusted using the gross domestic product price index.

c.   This option reflects the assumption that appropriations other than those for overseas contingency operations would generally be frozen at the 2015 level through 2025. Some items, such as offsetting collections and payments made by the Treasury on behalf of the Department of Defense's TRICARE for Life program, would not be held constant.

d.   The Budget Control Act of 2011 specified that if lawmakers did not enact legislation originating from the Joint Select Committee on Deficit Reduction that would reduce projected deficits by at least $1.2 trillion, automatic procedures would go into effect to reduce both discretionary and mandatory spending during the 2013–2021 period. Those procedures are now in effect and take the form of equal cuts (in dollar terms) in funding for defense and nondefense programs. For the 2016–2021 period, the automatic procedures lower the caps on discretionary budget authority specified in the Budget Control Act (caps for 2014 and 2015 were revised by the Bipartisan Budget Act of 2013); for the 2022–2025 period, CBO has extrapolated the reductions estimated for 2021.

Figure 3-4.

Projected Debt Held by the Public and Net Interest

Billions of Dollars

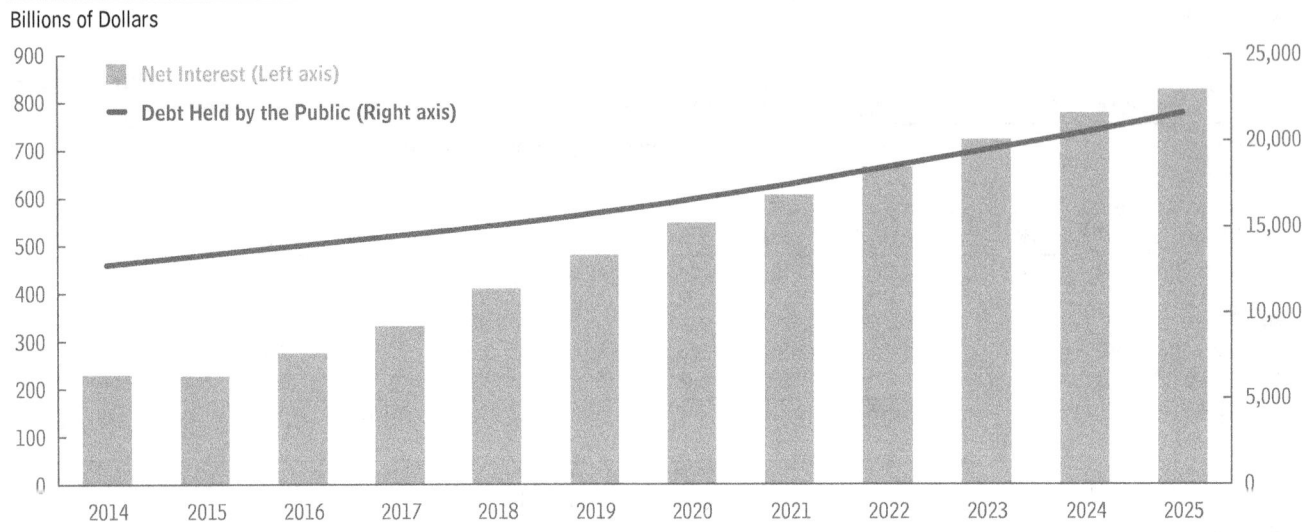

Source: Congressional Budget Office.

In 2015, trust funds will be credited with $139 billion of such intragovernmental interest, CBO estimates, mostly for the Social Security, Military Retirement, and Civil Service Retirement and Disability trust funds. Over the 2016–2025 period, the intragovernmental interest received by trust funds is projected to total $1.7 trillion.

Other Interest

CBO anticipates that the government will record net payments of $39 billion in other interest in 2015, representing the net result of many transactions, including both interest collections and interest payments.

The largest interest collections come from the government's credit financing accounts, which have been established to record the cash transactions related to federal direct loan and loan guarantee programs. For those programs, net subsidy costs are recorded in the budget, but the cash flows that move through the credit financing accounts are not. Credit financing accounts pay interest to and receive interest from Treasury accounts that appear in the budget, but, on net, they pay more interest to the Treasury than they receive from it. CBO estimates that net receipts from the credit financing accounts will total $31 billion in 2015 and steadily increase to $62 billion in 2025. Interest payments associated with the direct student loan program dominate those totals.

Table 3-7.

Federal Interest Outlays Projected in CBO's Baseline

Billions of Dollars

	Actual, 2014	2015	2016	2017	2018	2019	2020	2021	2022	2023	2024	2025	Total 2016-2020	Total 2016-2025
Interest on Treasury Debt Securities (Gross interest)[a]	431	405	472	541	631	713	790	857	919	981	1,040	1,092	3,148	8,036
Interest Received by Trust Funds														
Social Security	-100	-97	-92	-91	-92	-94	-94	-95	-94	-91	-87	-81	-464	-912
Other[b]	-58	-42	-60	-67	-74	-79	-83	-86	-87	-88	-91	-95	-364	-811
Subtotal	-158	-139	-152	-159	-166	-173	-178	-181	-180	-179	-179	-176	-828	-1,723
Other Interest[c]	-39	-39	-44	-50	-54	-58	-63	-69	-74	-78	-83	-88	-270	-662
NRRIT Investment Income (Non-Treasury holdings)[d]	-4	*	-1	-1	-1	-1	-1	-1	-1	-1	-1	-1	-4	-9
Net Interest Outlays	**229**	**227**	**276**	**332**	**410**	**480**	**548**	**606**	**664**	**722**	**777**	**827**	**2,046**	**5,643**

Source: Congressional Budget Office.

Note: NRRIT = National Railroad Retirement Investment Trust; * = between -$500 million and zero.

a. Excludes interest costs on debt issued by agencies other than the Treasury (primarily the Tennessee Valley Authority).

b. Mainly the Civil Service Retirement, Military Retirement, Medicare, and Unemployment Insurance Trust Funds.

c. Primarily interest on loans to the public.

d. Earnings on investments by the NRRIT, an entity created to manage and invest assets of the Railroad Retirement program.

The Revenue Outlook

The Congressional Budget Office projects that revenues will edge up from 17.5 percent of gross domestic product (GDP) in fiscal year 2014 to 17.7 percent in 2015, slightly above the 50-year average of 17.4 percent (see Figure 4-1). In 2016, CBO projects, if current laws generally do not change, federal revenues will rise significantly—to 18.4 percent of GDP—because of the expiration of certain provisions of law that reduce tax liabilities. After that, revenues as a share of GDP are projected to fall slightly and then remain relatively stable, near 18 percent of GDP, through 2025.

In 2015, federal revenues will total about $3.2 trillion, CBO estimates—$168 billion, or 5.6 percent, more than the amount collected in 2014. That increase, at a faster pace than GDP, stems largely from an anticipated rise in individual income tax receipts—up from 8.1 percent of GDP in 2014 to 8.3 percent this year, in part because of an increase in average tax rates (total taxes as a percentage of total income). As the economy grows, people's incomes rise faster than tax brackets increase because tax brackets are indexed only to inflation; that phenomenon is known as real bracket creep. In addition, CBO expects an increase in distributions from tax-deferred retirement accounts whose balances have been boosted in the past few years by strong stock market gains.

CBO projects that revenues will rise more rapidly in 2016, by 8.5 percent. Most of that increase results from the expiration, at the end of calendar year 2014, of several provisions that reduced the income tax liabilities of corporations and individuals—including one provision that allowed businesses to immediately deduct significant portions of their investments in equipment. Those provisions have been extended routinely in the past for limited periods, but CBO's baseline follows current law. Under current law, the expiration of those provisions will boost corporate and individual income tax payments somewhat in fiscal year 2015 but much more in 2016 and later years

because payments in 2015 will still reflect much of the effects of those provisions before expiration.

In CBO's baseline projections, revenues remain between 18.0 percent and 18.3 percent of GDP from 2017 through 2025, largely because of offsetting movements in three sources of revenue:

- Individual income tax receipts, which are projected to increase relative to GDP, mostly as a result of rising average tax rates from real bracket creep;

- Corporate income tax receipts, which are projected to decline relative to GDP, largely because of an expected drop in domestic economic profits relative to the size of the economy, the result of growing labor costs and rising interest payments on businesses' debt; and

- Remittances to the U.S. Treasury from the Federal Reserve System, which have been very large since 2010 because of substantial changes in the size and composition of the central bank's portfolio but which are projected to decline to more typical amounts relative to GDP.

CBO's projections of revenues for the 2015–2024 period are slightly below those it published in August 2014. At that time, CBO published revenue projections for the period from 2014 to 2024; the projections in this report cover the 2015–2025 period. For the overlapping years—2015 through 2024—the current projections are below the previous ones by $415 billion (or 1.0 percent), and they are lower in every year except 2016. Those revisions reflect the downward revision to CBO's forecast of GDP growth, the recent one-year extension of expired tax provisions, and other factors. (For more information on changes since August to the revenue projections, see Appendix A.)

Figure 4-1.

Total Revenues

Percentage of Gross Domestic Product

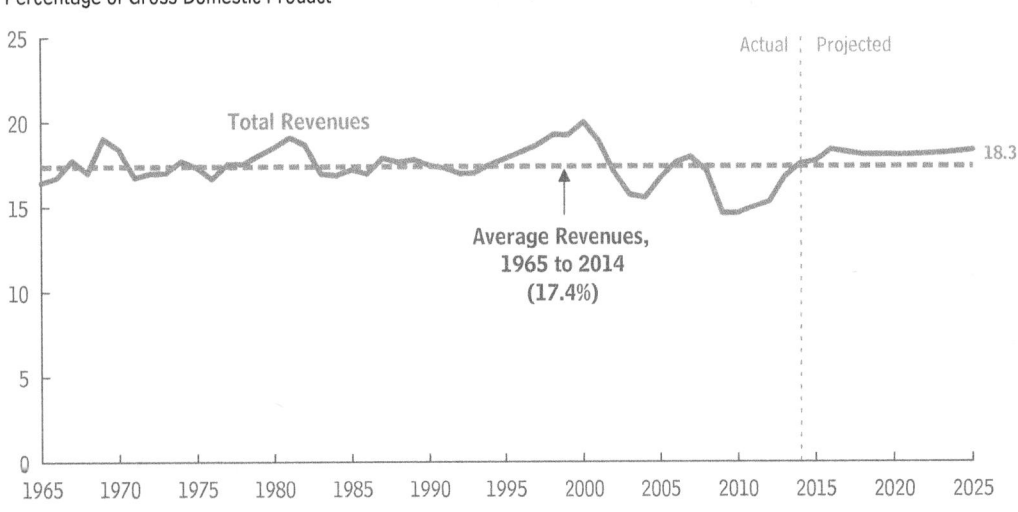

Source: Congressional Budget Office.

The tax rules that form the basis of CBO's projections include an array of exclusions, deductions, preferential rates, and credits that reduce revenues for any given level of tax rates, in both the individual and corporate income tax systems. Some of those provisions are called tax expenditures because, like government spending programs, they provide financial assistance to particular activities, entities, or groups of people. The tax expenditures with the largest effects on revenues are the following:

■ The exclusion from workers' taxable income of employers' contributions for health care, health insurance premiums, and long-term-care insurance premiums;

■ The exclusion of contributions to and earnings of pension funds (minus pension benefits that are included in taxable income);

■ Preferential tax rates on dividends and long-term capital gains; and

■ The deductions for state and local taxes (on nonbusiness income, sales, real estate, and personal property).

On the basis of estimates prepared by the staff of the Joint Committee on Taxation (JCT), CBO expects that under current law, those and other tax expenditures will total

almost $1.5 trillion in 2015—an amount equal to 8.1 percent of GDP, or equivalent to nearly half of the revenues projected for the year.[1] Most of that amount arises from the 11 largest tax expenditures, which CBO estimates will total 5.9 percent of GDP in 2015 and 6.6 percent of GDP from 2016 to 2025.

The Evolving Composition of Revenues

Federal revenues come from various sources: individual income taxes; payroll taxes, which are dedicated to certain social insurance programs; corporate income taxes; excise taxes; earnings of the Federal Reserve System, which are remitted to the Treasury; customs duties; estate and gift taxes; and miscellaneous fees and fines. Individual income taxes constitute the largest source of federal revenues, having contributed, on average, about 45 percent of total revenues (equal to 7.9 percent of GDP) over the past 50 years. Payroll taxes—mainly for Social Security and Medicare Part A (the Hospital Insurance program)— are the second-largest source of revenues, averaging about one-third of total revenues (equal to 5.7 percent of GDP) over the same period. Corporate income taxes contributed 12 percent of revenues (or 2.1 percent of GDP) over

1.   See Joint Committee on Taxation, *Estimates of Federal Tax Expenditures for Fiscal Years 2014–2018,* JCX-97-14 (August 2014), http://go.usa.gov/zDb5. CBO used its economic forecast to extrapolate the estimates beyond 2018 and included projected effects on payroll taxes.

Figure 4-2.

Revenues, by Major Source

Over the next decade, individual income taxes will grow at a faster rate than other taxes primarily because of "real bracket creep," which occurs when income grows faster than inflation and more income is pushed into higher tax brackets.

Percentage of Gross Domestic Product

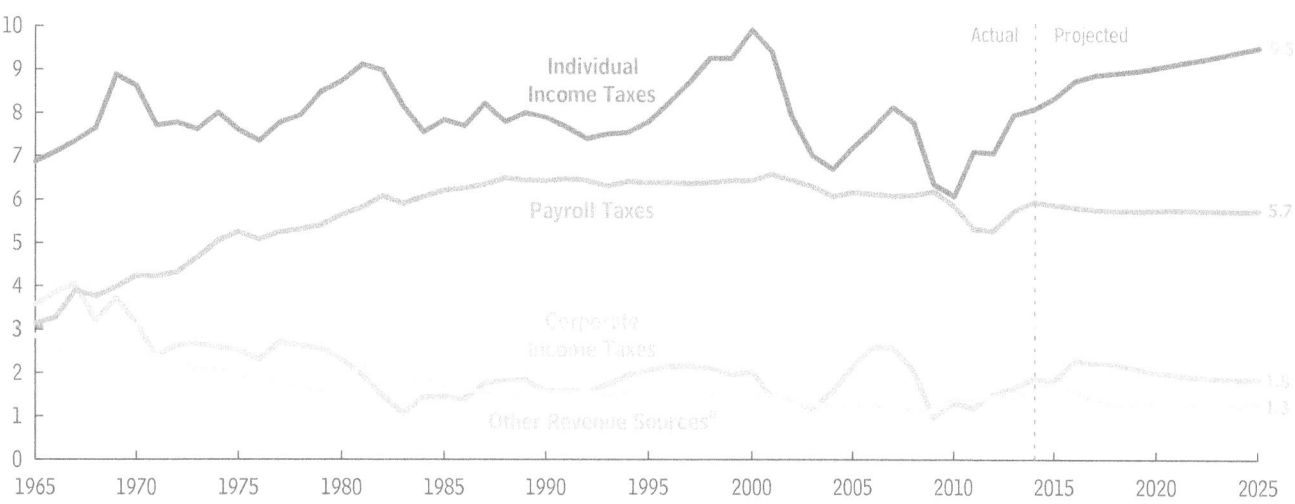

Source: Congressional Budget Office.

a.   Excise taxes, remittances from the Federal Reserve to the Treasury, customs duties, estate and gift taxes, and miscellaneous fees and fines.

the past 50 years, and all other sources combined contributed about 10 percent of revenues (or 1.7 percent of GDP).

Although that broad picture has remained roughly the same over the past several decades, the details have varied:

■ Receipts from individual income taxes have fluctuated more than the other major types of revenues, ranging from 41 percent to 50 percent of total revenues (and from 6.1 percent to 9.9 percent of GDP) between 1965 and 2014, but showing no clear trend over that period (see Figure 4-2).

■ Receipts from payroll taxes rose as a share of revenues from the mid-1960s through the 1980s—largely because of an expansion of payroll taxes to finance the new Medicare program and because of legislated increases in payroll tax rates for Social Security and in the amount of income to which those taxes applied. Those receipts reached about 37 percent of total revenues (and about 6.5 percent of GDP) by the late 1980s. Since 2001, payroll tax receipts have fallen slightly relative to GDP, accounting for 6.0 percent of the economy, on average; over the period from 2001

to 2014. Those receipts were unusually low in 2011 and 2012 because of a two-year cut in the employees' share of the Social Security payroll tax.

■ Revenues from corporate income taxes declined as a share of total revenues and GDP from the 1960s to the mid-1980s, mainly because of declining profits relative to the size of the economy. Those revenues have fluctuated widely since then, with no particular trend.

■ Revenues from the remaining sources together have slowly fallen relative to total revenues and GDP, largely because of declining receipts from excise taxes. However, that downward trend has reversed in the past several years because of the increase in remittances from the Federal Reserve System.

Under current law, CBO projects, individual income taxes will generate a growing share of revenues over the next decade. By 2020, they will account for more than half of total revenues, and by 2025, they will reach 9.5 percent of GDP, well above the historical average. Receipts from payroll taxes are projected to decline slightly relative to GDP, from 5.9 percent in 2014 to

5.7 percent for the period from 2018 to 2025. Corporate income taxes are expected to make roughly the same contribution that they have made on average for the past 50 years, supplying just over 10 percent of total revenues and averaging about 2 percent of GDP. Taken together, the remaining sources of revenue are expected to diminish somewhat relative to total revenues and GDP, largely because of a decline in Federal Reserve remittances to more typical amounts; those sources are projected to average a bit more than 1 percent of GDP from 2018 through 2025.

Individual Income Taxes

If current laws do not change, individual income taxes are expected to rise markedly relative to GDP over the next 10 years, the result of structural features of the tax system (such as real bracket creep), recent changes in tax provisions, and other factors. CBO projects that individual income tax receipts will increase from 8.1 percent of GDP in 2014 to 8.7 percent in 2016; they will then rise by about 0.1 percentage point of GDP per year, on average, through 2025 (see Table 4-1).

Significant Growth in Receipts Relative to GDP From 2014 to 2016

After declining by 23 percent between 2007 and 2010, receipts from individual income taxes have risen in each of the past four years. That trend continues in CBO's projection, with such receipts increasing by 8 percent in 2015 and by 9 percent in 2016. In 2016 they are projected to total more than $1.6 trillion; at 8.7 percent of GDP, they will equal the highest percentage since 2001 and be well above the 50-year average of 7.9 percent of GDP.

Part of the projected increase in individual income tax receipts in 2015 and 2016 results from projected growth in taxable personal income, as measured in the national income and product accounts (NIPAs) produced by the Bureau of Economic Analysis. That measure includes wages, salaries, dividends, interest, rental income, and proprietors' income; its expected growth in 2015 and 2016 of 4 percent to 4½ percent corresponds roughly to expected growth in nominal GDP. However, projected receipts from individual income taxes rise faster than projected taxable personal income—boosting receipts relative to GDP by 0.6 percentage points from 2014 to 2016—because of real bracket creep, recent changes in tax provisions, and other factors.

Real Bracket Creep. The most significant factor pushing up taxes relative to income is real bracket creep. That phenomenon occurs because the income tax brackets and exemptions under both the regular income tax and the alternative minimum tax (AMT) are indexed only to inflation.[2] If incomes grow faster than inflation, as generally occurs when the economy is growing, more income is pushed into higher tax brackets. In CBO's estimates, real bracket creep raises revenues relative to GDP by 0.2 percentage points between 2014 and 2016.

Recent Changes in Tax Provisions. The Tax Increase Prevention Act of 2014 (Division A of Public Law 113-295), which was enacted in December 2014, retroactively extended many tax provisions that reduced tax liabilities and had been extended routinely in previous years. However, those provisions were extended only through December 2014. Their expiration generates a marked increase in tax revenues next year in CBO's current-law projections. The largest effect will come from the expiration of rules allowing certain businesses to immediately deduct a portion of their equipment investments. That expiration will increase receipts from both the corporate income tax and the individual income tax, because the rules apply both to C corporations, whose income is subject to the corporate tax, and to S corporations and noncorporate businesses, whose income is subject to the individual tax. Other significant expiring tax provisions included the option to deduct state and local sales taxes rather than income taxes and the ability to exclude forgiven mortgage debt from taxable income. If the expired provisions are not extended again, those expirations will increase individual income tax liabilities starting in calendar year 2015, thus affecting income tax payments starting in fiscal year 2016, by CBO's estimates.[3]

---

2. The AMT is a parallel income tax system with fewer exemptions, deductions, and rates than the regular income tax. Households must calculate the amount that they owe under both the alternative minimum tax and the regular income tax, and then pay the larger of the two amounts.

3. CBO estimates that the effect of higher tax liabilities on tax payments in fiscal year 2015 will be offset by refunds that will be owed to taxpayers as a result of the retroactive nature of the recent extension. Some individual taxpayers probably increased their estimated payments in 2014 because of the previous expiration of the provisions at the end of 2013; because of the retroactive extension, those taxpayers will receive refunds (or make smaller payments than otherwise) when they file their tax returns in 2015. Such refunds will probably be more significant for corporations, which are required to adjust their estimated payments more than individual taxpayers are in response to changes in expected tax liabilities.

Table 4-1.

Revenues Projected in CBO's Baseline

	Actual, 2014	2015	2016	2017	2018	2019	2020	2021	2022	2023	2024	2025	Total 2016-2020	2016-2025
							In Billions of Dollars							
Individual Income Taxes	1,395	1,503	1,644	1,746	1,832	1,919	2,017	2,124	2,235	2,352	2,477	2,606	9,158	20,952
Payroll Taxes	1,024	1,056	1,095	1,136	1,179	1,227	1,281	1,337	1,391	1,449	1,508	1,573	5,917	13,175
Corporate Income Taxes	321	328	429	437	453	450	447	450	459	472	488	506	2,216	4,591
Other														
Excise taxes	93	96	98	102	105	107	108	111	113	115	117	119	520	1,094
Federal Reserve remittances	99	102	76	40	17	27	31	34	37	42	47	52	191	404
Customs duties	34	36	39	41	43	45	48	50	53	56	59	63	216	497
Estate and gift taxes	19	20	21	22	22	23	24	25	26	27	27	28	113	246
Miscellaneous fees and fines	36	48	57	63	63	67	69	73	76	78	81	82	320	710
Subtotal	282	302	292	269	251	269	280	293	305	318	330	345	1,361	2,952
Total	**3,021**	**3,189**	**3,460**	**3,588**	**3,715**	**3,865**	**4,025**	**4,204**	**4,389**	**4,591**	**4,804**	**5,029**	**18,652**	**41,670**
On-budget	2,285	2,426	2,667	2,763	2,858	2,974	3,099	3,242	3,389	3,550	3,722	3,906	14,362	32,171
Off-budget[a]	736	763	793	824	857	891	926	962	1,001	1,040	1,081	1,124	4,291	9,499
Memorandum:														
Gross Domestic Product	17,251	18,016	18,832	19,701	20,558	21,404	22,315	23,271	24,261	25,287	26,352	27,456	102,810	229,438
						As a Percentage of Gross Domestic Product								
Individual Income Taxes	8.1	8.3	8.7	8.9	8.9	9.0	9.0	9.1	9.2	9.3	9.4	9.5	8.9	9.1
Payroll Taxes	5.9	5.9	5.8	5.8	5.7	5.7	5.7	5.7	5.7	5.7	5.7	5.7	5.8	5.7
Corporate Income Taxes	1.9	1.8	2.3	2.2	2.2	2.1	2.0	1.9	1.9	1.9	1.9	1.8	2.2	2.0
Other														
Excise taxes	0.5	0.5	0.5	0.5	0.5	0.5	0.5	0.5	0.5	0.5	0.4	0.4	0.5	0.5
Federal Reserve remittances	0.6	0.6	0.4	0.2	0.1	0.1	0.1	0.1	0.2	0.2	0.2	0.2	0.2	0.2
Customs duties	0.2	0.2	0.2	0.2	0.2	0.2	0.2	0.2	0.2	0.2	0.2	0.2	0.2	0.2
Estate and gift taxes	0.1	0.1	0.1	0.1	0.1	0.1	0.1	0.1	0.1	0.1	0.1	0.1	0.1	0.1
Miscellaneous fees and fines	0.2	0.3	0.3	0.3	0.3	0.3	0.3	0.3	0.3	0.3	0.3	0.3	0.3	0.3
Subtotal	1.6	1.7	1.5	1.4	1.2	1.3	1.3	1.3	1.3	1.3	1.3	1.3	1.3	1.3
Total	**17.5**	**17.7**	**18.4**	**18.2**	**18.1**	**18.1**	**18.0**	**18.1**	**18.1**	**18.2**	**18.2**	**18.3**	**18.1**	**18.2**
On-budget	13.2	13.5	14.2	14.0	13.9	13.9	13.9	13.9	14.0	14.0	14.1	14.2	14.0	14.0
Off-budget[a]	4.3	4.2	4.2	4.2	4.2	4.2	4.1	4.1	4.1	4.1	4.1	4.1	4.2	4.1

Source: Congressional Budget Office.

a.   Receipts from Social Security payroll taxes.

Including other recently enacted legislation—which will have smaller effects—CBO estimates that changes in tax provisions will generate little net change in revenues in 2015 and will boost revenues relative to GDP by about 0.2 percentage points in 2016.

Other Factors. CBO anticipates that individual income tax revenues will also increase relative to GDP this year and next for a number of other reasons. The most significant one is that taxable distributions from tax-deferred retirement accounts, such as individual retirement accounts and 401(k) plans, are estimated to have risen substantially in 2014 and are expected to do so again in 2015 and 2016. Those larger projected distributions are the result of an increase in asset values (mainly because of rising equity prices over the past few years) that has raised the balances in people's retirement accounts. That factor and others are expected to boost revenues relative to GDP by about 0.3 percentage points between 2014 and 2016.

Table 4-2.

Payroll Tax Revenues Projected in CBO's Baseline

Billions of Dollars

	Actual, 2014	2015	2016	2017	2018	2019	2020	2021	2022	2023	2024	2025	Total 2016- 2020	Total 2016- 2025
Social Security	736	763	793	824	857	891	926	962	1,001	1,040	1,081	1,124	4,291	9,499
Medicare	224	234	245	258	270	282	295	309	323	338	354	370	1,351	3,045
Unemployment Insurance	55	51	48	44	42	44	50	55	56	58	60	65	229	523
Railroad Retirement	5	5	5	5	5	5	5	6	6	6	6	7	26	56
Other Retirement[a]	3	4	4	4	4	4	5	5	6	6	7	7	21	52
Total	1,024	1,056	1,095	1,136	1,179	1,227	1,281	1,337	1,391	1,449	1,508	1,573	5,917	13,175

Source: Congressional Budget Office.

a.   Consists primarily of federal employees' contributions to the Federal Employees Retirement System and the Civil Service Retirement System.

Steady Growth in Receipts Relative to GDP After 2016

CBO projects that, under current law, individual income tax receipts will rise from about $1.6 trillion in 2016 to about $2.6 trillion in 2025, for an average annual increase of roughly 5 percent; as a result, those receipts will climb from 8.7 percent of GDP in 2016 to 9.5 percent in 2025. Real bracket creep and several other factors will generate that increase, CBO projects.

Real Bracket Creep. Real bracket creep will raise individual income tax receipts relative to GDP by 0.4 percentage points between 2016 and 2025, CBO projects. That increase accounts for just over half of the total increase in individual income tax receipts as a percentage of GDP for the period.

Other Factors. CBO anticipates that individual income tax receipts will rise relative to GDP by 0.3 percentage points between 2016 and 2025 for other reasons. As the population ages, for example, taxable distributions from tax-deferred retirement accounts will tend to grow more rapidly than GDP. Earnings also are expected to grow faster for higher-income people than for others during the next decade—as they have for the past several decades—causing a larger share of income to be taxed at higher income tax rates. Furthermore, total earnings are projected to rise slightly relative to GDP from 2016 to 2025, reflecting a small increase in the labor share of national income (see Chapter 2 for a more detailed discussion).

Payroll Taxes

Receipts from payroll taxes, which fund social insurance programs, totaled about $1.0 trillion in 2014, or 5.9 percent of GDP. Under current law, CBO projects, those receipts will fall to 5.7 percent of GDP by 2018 and then roughly stabilize relative to GDP through 2025.

Sources of Payroll Tax Receipts

The two largest sources of payroll tax receipts are the taxes that are dedicated to Social Security and Part A of Medicare. Much smaller amounts are collected in the form of unemployment insurance taxes (most imposed by states but classified as federal revenues); employers' and employees' contributions to the Railroad Retirement System; and other contributions to federal retirement programs, mainly those made by federal employees (see Table 4-2). The premiums that Medicare enrollees pay for Part B (the Medical Insurance program) and Part D (prescription drug benefits) are voluntary and thus are not counted as tax revenues; rather, they are considered offsets to spending and appear on the spending side of the budget as offsetting receipts.

Payroll taxes for Social Security and Medicare are calculated as percentages of people's earnings. The Social Security tax is usually 12.4 percent of earnings, with the employer and employee each paying half. The tax applies only up to a certain amount of a worker's annual earnings (called the taxable maximum, currently $118,500) that is indexed to grow over time at the same pace as average earnings for all workers. The Medicare tax applies to all earnings (with no taxable maximum) and is levied at a rate of 2.9 percent, with the employer and employee each paying half. Starting in 2013, an additional Medicare tax of 0.9 percent has been assessed on the amount of an individual's earnings over $200,000 (or $250,000 for married couples filing joint income tax returns), bringing the total Medicare tax on such earnings to 3.8 percent.

Slight Decline in Projected Receipts Relative to GDP

Although wages and salaries, the main tax bases for payroll taxes, are projected to be fairly stable relative to GDP over the next several years, CBO estimates that payroll tax receipts will decline slightly relative to GDP through 2018 for two main reasons. First, payroll taxes are expected to decrease relative to wages and salaries—and hence GDP—because a growing share of earnings is anticipated to be above the taxable maximum amount for Social Security taxes.[4] Second, between 2014 and 2018, receipts from unemployment insurance taxes are projected to decline relative to wages and salaries. Those receipts grew rapidly from 2010 through 2012 as states raised their tax rates and tax bases to replenish unemployment insurance trust funds that had been depleted because of high unemployment; CBO expects unemployment insurance receipts to fall to more typical levels in the coming years.

For the rest of the projection period, from 2019 to 2025, CBO projects that offsetting factors will cause payroll tax receipts to be roughly stable relative to GDP. The share of earnings above the taxable maximum for Social Security taxes is expected to continue to increase, lowering payroll tax revenues relative to wages and salaries. However, that effect is largely offset by small projected increases in wages and salaries as a share of GDP.

Corporate Income Taxes

In 2014, receipts from corporate income taxes totaled $321 billion, or 1.9 percent of GDP—near the 50-year average. CBO expects corporate tax receipts to rise a little in nominal terms in 2015 and then to increase sharply in 2016 because of the expiration of several tax provisions. As a result, estimated receipts fall slightly as a share of GDP in 2015 and then jump to 2.3 percent of GDP in

2016. Thereafter through 2025, CBO projects, those receipts will fall relative to GDP—down to 1.8 percent—largely because profits are projected to decline relative to GDP.

Little Growth in Receipts in 2015

CBO expects income tax payments by corporations, net of refunds, to increase by about 2 percent this year, to $328 billion, even though the agency projects that domestic economic profits will grow by 8.5 percent. Because revenue growth is projected to rise at less than half the pace of GDP growth, projected revenues as a share of GDP decline slightly to 1.8 percent.

That projected slow growth in corporate income tax receipts results mostly from the retroactive one-year extension—enacted in December 2014 in the Tax Increase Prevention Act of 2014—of various provisions that reduce tax liabilities. The largest revenue impact will stem from the extension of rules that allowed businesses with large amounts of investment to expense—that is, to immediately deduct—50 percent of their investments in equipment.[5]

Because the more favorable rules for investment deductions and other tax-reducing provisions were not initially extended when they expired at the end of calendar year 2013, many companies paid more in estimated taxes during calendar year 2014. Because those provisions were extended retroactively late in the year, those businesses will receive refunds or make smaller final payments when they file their 2014 tax returns in 2015. The effect will be to slow growth in receipts this year.

Sharp Increase in Receipts in 2016

Under current law, CBO projects, corporate income tax revenues will rise to $429 billion in 2016, an increase of roughly $100 billion, or 31 percent, from the amount projected for 2015. As a result, corporate income tax revenues are projected to climb from 1.8 percent of GDP in 2015 to 2.3 percent in 2016, which would be the highest percentage since 2007. Of that 0.5 percentage-point increase, 0.4 percentage points stems from the retroactively enacted extension of the more favorable rules for

---

4. Because the income tax has a progressive rate structure, the increase in the share of earnings above the Social Security taxable maximum is projected to produce an increase in individual income tax receipts that will more than offset the decrease in payroll tax receipts.

5. By contrast, since 1982 businesses with relatively small amounts of investment in new equipment have been allowed to fully deduct those costs in the year in which the equipment is placed in service. Although that provision remains in effect today, the maximum amount of those deductions has changed over time.

depreciation and other tax-reducing provisions. That one-year extension lowers projected receipts in 2015 but not in 2016, thereby boosting growth between those years.

Most of the remaining increase in corporate tax revenues relative to GDP in 2016 results from an expected reversion in the average tax rate on domestic economic profits—that is, corporate taxes divided by domestic economic profits as measured in the NIPAs—toward more typical levels. That measure of the average tax rate fell sharply during the latest recession because of a combination of a sharp drop in capital gains realizations by corporations, a sharp increase in deductions of bad debts from corporate income, and changes in tax law. Since the recession ended in June 2009, that measure has recovered only partially, and the reasons for the slow recovery in that measure will not be known with certainty until additional information from tax returns becomes available in the future. Nevertheless, CBO expects that whatever factors have been at work will gradually dissipate over the next few years, and the average tax rate will return closer to its prerecession level.

Decline in Receipts Relative to GDP After 2016
In CBO's projections, corporate income tax receipts fall from 2.3 percent of GDP in 2016 to 1.8 percent in 2025. That decline occurs mostly because of a concurrent drop projected for domestic economic profits—from 9.8 percent of GDP in 2016 to 7.8 percent in 2025—primarily because of increases in labor costs and interest payments on businesses' debt relative to GDP.

CBO incorporated three other factors into its projection of a decline in corporate tax revenue as a percentage of GDP after 2016. First is the above-noted expiration of more favorable rules for deducting the cost of investment in business equipment. Under those rules, deductions were larger when investments were first made and smaller thereafter. Under the less favorable rules in effect under current law for calendar year 2015 and subsequent years, deductions are smaller when investments are made and larger thereafter. Projected receipts in fiscal year 2016 (the first fiscal year that fully reflects the less favorable rules) thus are higher because of the smaller initial deductions for new investments. Over time, however, that effect diminishes as larger deductions are taken for investments made under the less favorable rules.

Another factor contributing to the projected decline in corporate tax revenues relative to GDP is a pair of strategies that CBO expects corporations will follow to reduce their tax liabilities. One strategy is to continue decreasing the share of business activity that occurs in C corporations (which are taxed under the corporate income tax) while increasing the share that occurs in pass-through entities such as S corporations (which are taxed under the individual income tax rather than the corporate tax).[6] Another strategy is to increase the amount of corporate income that is shifted out of the United States through a combination of more aggressive transfer-pricing methods and intercompany loans, additional corporate inversions, and other techniques.[7] CBO expects that increasing adoption of such strategies will result in progressively larger reductions in corporate receipts over the 2015–2025 projection period. By 2025, in CBO's baseline, corporate income tax receipts are roughly 5 percent lower than they would be without that further erosion of the corporate tax base; slightly more than half of that difference is attributable to the shifting of additional income out of the United States.

A final factor that partially offsets the effects of the others—pushing corporate tax revenue up as a percentage of GDP—is the agency's expectation that, by 2019, the average tax rate on domestic economic profits will be closer to its historical average.

Smaller Sources of Revenues
The remaining sources of federal revenues are excise taxes, remittances from the Federal Reserve System to the Treasury, customs duties, estate and gift taxes, and miscellaneous fees and fines. Revenues from those sources totaled $282 billion in 2014, or 1.6 percent of GDP (see Table 4-3). CBO's baseline projection shows such revenues increasing to $302 billion in 2015, or 1.7 percent of GDP, and then falling to 1.2 percent or 1.3 percent

---

6. For a detailed analysis of the taxation of business income through the individual income tax, see Congressional Budget Office, *Taxing Businesses Through the Individual Income Tax* (December 2012), www.cbo.gov/publication/43750.

7. Under a corporate inversion, a U.S. corporation can change its country of tax residence, often by merging with a foreign company. Inversions reduce U.S. corporate tax revenue both because the inverted U.S. corporation no longer must pay U.S. taxes on earnings in other countries and because a corporation can shift additional income out of the United States through the use of intercompany loans and the resulting interest expenses.

Table 4-3.

Smaller Sources of Revenues Projected in CBO's Baseline

Billions of Dollars

	Actual, 2014	2015	2016	2017	2018	2019	2020	2021	2022	2023	2024	2025	Total 2016- 2020	2016- 2025
Excise Taxes														
Highway	37	38	39	39	39	39	39	39	39	38	38	38	195	388
Tobacco	15	14	14	14	13	13	13	13	12	12	12	12	67	128
Aviation	13	14	15	15	16	16	17	18	18	19	20	20	78	173
Alcohol	10	10	10	10	11	11	11	11	11	11	12	12	53	110
Health insurance providers	7	11	11	13	14	15	15	16	17	18	19	20	68	159
Other	10	9	10	11	12	13	13	14	15	16	17	18	58	137
Subtotal	93	96	98	102	105	107	108	111	113	115	117	119	520	1,094
Federal Reserve Remittances	99	102	76	40	17	27	31	34	37	42	47	52	191	494
Customs Duties	34	36	39	41	43	45	48	50	53	56	59	63	216	497
Estate and Gift Taxes	19	20	21	22	22	23	24	25	26	27	27	28	113	246
Miscellaneous Fees and Fines														
Universal Service Fund fees	10	10	11	12	12	12	12	12	13	13	13	13	59	123
Other fees and fines	26	38	46	52	51	55	57	60	63	66	68	69	261	587
Subtotal	36	48	57	63	63	67	69	73	76	78	81	82	320	710
Total	**282**	**302**	**292**	**269**	**251**	**269**	**280**	**293**	**305**	**318**	**330**	**345**	**1,361**	**2,952**

Source: Congressional Budget Office.

Note: This table shows all sources of revenues other than individual and corporate income taxes and payroll taxes.

of GDP each year from 2018 to 2025. The projected decline in those revenues relative to GDP stems largely from an expected drop in Federal Reserve remittances as the size and composition of the central bank's portfolio return to more typical conditions.

Excise Taxes

Unlike taxes on income, excise taxes are levied on the production or purchase of a particular type of good or service. Under the assumptions that govern CBO's baseline, almost 90 percent of excise tax receipts over the coming decade are projected to come from taxes related to highways, tobacco and alcohol, aviation, and health insurance. Receipts from excise taxes are expected to decrease slightly relative to GDP over the next decade, from 0.5 percent in 2015 to 0.4 percent in 2025. That decrease occurs largely because gasoline and tobacco taxes will decline in nominal dollars, which implies significant reductions relative to the size of the economy.

Highway Taxes. About 40 percent of excise tax receipts currently comes from highway taxes, primarily on the

consumption of gasoline, diesel fuel, and blends of those fuels with ethanol, as well as on the retail sale of trucks. Annual receipts from highway taxes, which are largely dedicated to the Highway Trust Fund, are projected to stay at $38 billion or $39 billion each year between 2015 and 2025 and therefore to shrink as a percentage of GDP.

That pattern is the net effect of generally declining receipts from taxes on gasoline and rising receipts from taxes on diesel fuel and trucks. CBO expects that gasoline consumption will decline over time, as improvements in vehicles' fuel economy resulting from tighter federal standards for fuel economy more than offset increases in the number of miles that people drive stemming from both population increases and real income gains per person. For 2015, however, the recent decline in gasoline prices will also boost miles driven, so CBO projects that gasoline use and tax revenues will be roughly in line with last year's figures; with prices of crude oil expected to rise again later this year, further price-induced increases in miles driven are not anticipated (see Box 2-2 on page 31).[8] Increasing fuel economy will likewise reduce the consumption of diesel fuel per miles driven—but not by enough over the next decade, according to CBO's projections, to offset an increase in the total number of miles driven in diesel-powered trucks.

Under current law, most of the federal excise taxes used to fund highways are scheduled to expire on September 30, 2016. In general, CBO's baseline incorporates the assumption that expiring tax provisions will follow the schedules set forth in current law. However, the Balanced Budget and Emergency Deficit Control Act of 1985 specifies that CBO's baseline should incorporate the assumption that expiring excise taxes dedicated to trust funds (including most of the highway taxes) will be extended.

Tobacco and Alcohol Taxes. Taxes on tobacco products will generate $14 billion in revenues in 2015, CBO projects. That amount is expected to decrease by about 2 percent per year over the next decade, as the decline in tobacco use that has been occurring for many years continues. By contrast, receipts from taxes on alcoholic beverages, which are expected to total $10 billion in 2015, are projected to rise at an average rate of 1.5 percent a year through 2025, the result of expected increases in consumption.

Aviation Taxes. CBO projects that receipts from taxes on airline tickets, aviation fuels, and other aviation-related items will increase from $14 billion in 2015 to $20 billion in 2025, yielding an average annual rate of growth of about 4 percent. That growth is close to the projected increase of GDP over the period, in part because the largest component of aviation excise taxes (a passenger ticket tax) is levied not on the number of units transacted (as gasoline taxes are, for example) but as a percentage of the dollar value of transactions—which causes receipts to increase as prices and real economic activity increase. Under current law, most aviation-related taxes are scheduled to expire on September 30, 2015, but CBO's baseline projections are required to incorporate the assumption that they, like the highway taxes described above, will be extended.

Tax on Health Insurance Providers. Under the Affordable Care Act (ACA), health insurers are subject to an excise tax. The amount is specified in law and must be divided among insurers according to their share of total premiums charged. However, several categories of health insurers—such as self-insured plans, federal and state governments, and tax-exempt providers—are fully or partially exempt from the tax. CBO estimates that revenues from the tax totaled $7 billion in 2014 and will rise to $11 billion in 2015 and to $20 billion by 2025.

Other Excise Taxes. Other excise taxes are projected to generate $9 billion in revenues in 2015 and $137 billion over the next decade. Of that 10-year amount, $96 billion stems from three charges instituted by the ACA, each estimated to yield revenue of between $31 billion and $33 billion over the 2016–2025 period: an annual fee charged on manufacturers and importers of brand-name drugs; a 2.3 percent tax on manufacturers and importers of certain medical devices; and a tax, beginning in 2018, on certain high-cost employment-based health insurance plans.[9]

Remittances From the Federal Reserve System

The income produced by the various activities of the Federal Reserve System, minus the cost of generating that income and the cost of the system's operations, is remitted to the Treasury and counted as revenues. The largest component of such income is what the Federal Reserve earns as interest on its holdings of securities. Over the past seven years, the central bank has quintupled the size of its asset holdings through purchases of Treasury securities and mortgage-backed securities issued by Fannie Mae, Freddie Mac, and the Government National Mortgage Association (known as Ginnie Mae). Those purchases raised remittances of the Federal Reserve from $34 billion (0.2 percent of GDP) in 2008 to $99 billion (0.6 percent of GDP) in 2014.

CBO expects remittances to remain around $100 billion in 2015 and then to decline sharply in subsequent years, falling to $17 billion (less than 0.1 percent of GDP) in 2018. That drop largely reflects a projected increase in

---

8. The recent decline in gasoline prices also has shifted the composition of vehicle purchases toward vehicles with lower fuel economy. Despite that change, the new vehicles still have higher fuel economy than those they are replacing, so overall fuel economy continues to improve.

9. The excise tax on high-cost health insurance plans also increases the amounts CBO projects for revenues from individual income and payroll taxes because businesses are expected to respond to the tax by shifting to lower-cost insurance plans—thereby reducing nontaxable labor compensation and increasing taxable compensation.

the rate at which the Federal Reserve pays interest to the financial institutions that hold deposits on reserve with it, thus increasing its interest expenses. CBO also projects an increase in interest rates on Treasury securities in the next several years, which will boost earnings for the Federal Reserve—but only gradually as it purchases new securities earning higher yields. (See Chapter 2 for a discussion of CBO's forecasts of monetary policy and interest rates in the coming decade.)

After 2018, CBO anticipates, the size and composition of the Federal Reserve's portfolio, along with its remittances to the Treasury, will gradually return to conditions more in line with historical experience. According to CBO's projections, remittances over the 2022–2025 period will average 0.2 percent of GDP, roughly matching the 2000–2009 average.

Customs Duties, Estate and Gift Taxes, and Miscellaneous Fees and Fines

Customs duties, which are assessed on certain imports, have totaled 0.2 percent of GDP in recent years, amounting to $34 billion in 2014. CBO projects that, under current law, those receipts will continue at that level relative to GDP throughout the next decade.

Receipts from estate and gift taxes in 2014 totaled $19 billion, or 0.1 percent of GDP. CBO projects that, under current law, those receipts will remain at that same percentage of GDP through 2025.

Miscellaneous fees and fines totaled $36 billion in 2014 (0.2 percent of GDP) and under current law will total $48 billion in 2015 (0.3 percent of GDP), CBO projects. The increase stems largely from provisions of the ACA, including the risk-adjustment process for which collections and payments begin this year. Under risk adjustment, health insurance plans whose enrollees are expected to have below-average health care costs must make payments to the government, which will distribute those sums to plans whose enrollees are expected to have above-average health care costs.[10] Miscellaneous fees and fines will continue to average 0.3 percent of GDP from 2016 through 2025, CBO projects.

Tax Expenditures

Many exclusions, deductions, preferential rates, and credits in the individual income tax, payroll tax, and corporate income tax systems cause revenues to be much lower than they would otherwise be for any underlying structure of tax rates. Some of those provisions, called tax expenditures, resemble federal spending in that they provide financial assistance to particular activities, entities, or groups of people.

Like conventional federal spending, tax expenditures contribute to the federal budget deficit. They also influence people's choices about working, saving, and investing, and they affect the distribution of income. The Congressional Budget and Impoundment Control Act of 1974 defines tax expenditures as "those revenue losses attributable to provisions of the Federal tax laws which allow a special exclusion, exemption, or deduction from gross income or which provide a special credit, a preferential rate of tax, or a deferral of tax liability."[11] That law requires the federal budget to list tax expenditures, and each year JCT and the Treasury's Office of Tax Analysis publish estimates of individual and corporate income tax expenditures.[12]

Tax expenditures are more similar to the largest benefit programs than they are to discretionary spending programs: Tax expenditures are not subject to annual appropriations, and any person or entity that meets the legal

---

10. Miscellaneous receipts related to the ACA also include collections for the reinsurance program, which will expire after 2016 and generate receipts through 2017. See Appendix B for more information.

11. Section 3(3) of the Congressional Budget and Impoundment Control Act of 1974, P.L. 93-344 (codified at 2 U.S.C. §622(3) (2006)).

12. For this analysis, CBO follows JCT's definition of tax expenditures as deviations from a "normal" income tax structure. For the individual income tax, that structure incorporates existing regular tax rates, the standard deduction, personal exemptions, and deductions of business expenses. For the corporate income tax, that structure includes the top statutory tax rate, defines income on an accrual basis, and allows for cost recovery according to a specified depreciation system. For more information, see Joint Committee on Taxation, *Estimates of Federal Tax Expenditures for Fiscal Years 2014–2018*, JCX-97-14 (August 2014), http://go.usa.gov/zDb5. Unlike JCT, CBO includes estimates of the largest payroll tax expenditures. CBO defines a normal payroll tax structure to include the existing payroll tax rates as applied to a broad definition of compensation—which consists of cash wages and fringe benefits. The Office of Management and Budget's definition of tax expenditures is broadly similar to JCT's. See Office of Management and Budget, *Budget of the U.S. Government, Fiscal Year 2015: Analytical Perspectives* (March 2014), pp. 203–239, http://go.usa.gov/zNQ5.

Figure 4-3.

Revenues, Tax Expenditures, and Selected Components of Spending in 2015

Tax expenditures, projected to total $1.5 trillion in 2015, cause revenues to be lower than they would be otherwise and, like spending programs, contribute to the federal deficit.

Percentage of Gross Domestic Product

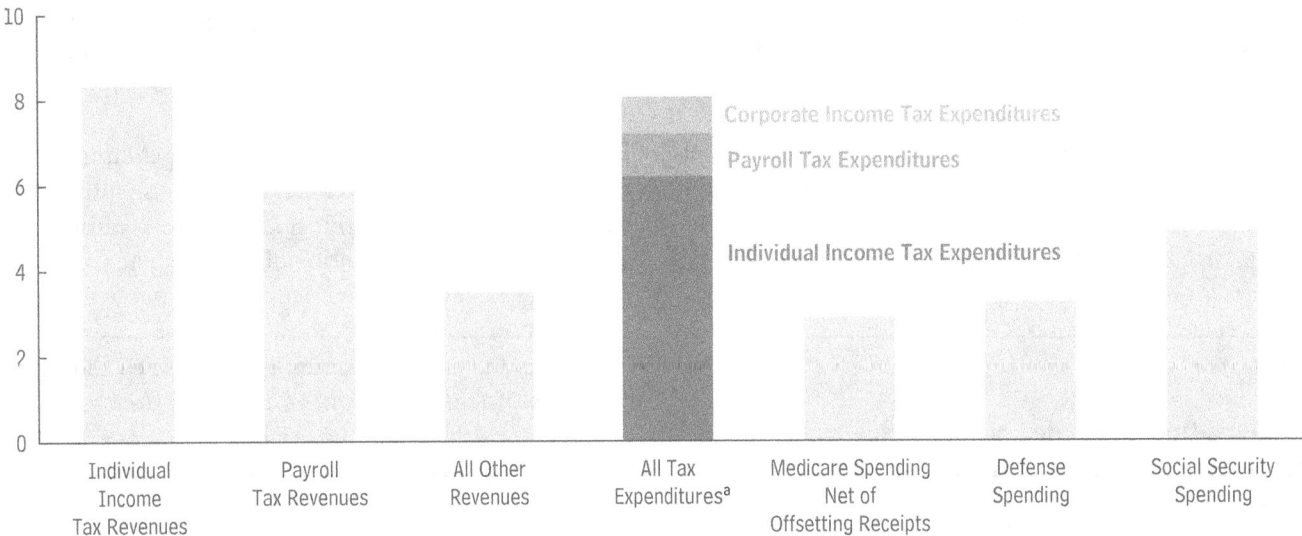

Source: Congressional Budget Office based on estimates by the staff of the Joint Committee on Taxation.

a. This total is the sum of the estimates for all of the separate tax expenditures and does not account for any interactions among them. However, CBO estimates that in 2015, the total of all tax expenditures roughly equals the sum of each considered separately. Furthermore, because estimates of tax expenditures are based on people's behavior with the tax expenditures in place, the estimates do not reflect the amount of revenue that would be raised if those provisions of the tax code were eliminated and taxpayers adjusted their activities in response to the changes.

requirements can receive the benefits. Because of their budgetary treatment, however, tax expenditures are much less transparent than spending on benefit programs.

The Magnitude of Tax Expenditures

Tax expenditures have a major impact on the federal budget. On the basis of the estimates prepared by JCT, CBO projects that the more than 200 tax expenditures in the individual and corporate income tax systems will total roughly $1.5 trillion in fiscal year 2015—or 8.1 percent of GDP—if their effects on payroll taxes as well as on income taxes are included.[13] That amount equals nearly half of all federal revenues projected for 2015 and exceeds projected spending on Social Security, defense, or Medicare (see Figure 4-3).

A simple total of the estimates for particular tax expenditures does not account for the interactions among them if they are considered together. For instance, the tax expenditure for all itemized deductions taken as a group is smaller than the sum of the separate tax expenditures for each deduction; the reason is that, if the entire group of

deductions did not exist, more taxpayers would claim the standard deduction instead of itemizing deductions than would be the case if any single deduction did not exist. However, the structure of tax brackets and marginal rates ensures that the opposite would be the case with income exclusions; that is, the tax expenditure for all exclusions considered together would be greater than the sum of the separate tax expenditures for each exclusion. Currently, those and other factors are approximately offsetting, so

---

13. Most estimates of tax expenditures include only their effects on individual and corporate income taxes. However, tax expenditures can also reduce the amount of income subject to payroll taxes. JCT has previously estimated the effect on payroll taxes of the provision that excludes employers' contributions for health insurance premiums from their workers' taxable income. See Joint Committee on Taxation, *Background Materials for Senate Committee on Finance Roundtable on Health Care Financing*, JCX-27-09 (May 2009), http://go.usa.gov/ZJcx. Tax expenditures that reduce the tax base for payroll taxes will eventually decrease spending for Social Security by reducing the earnings base on which Social Security benefits are calculated.

the total amount of tax expenditures roughly equals the sum of all of the individual tax expenditures.

However, the total amount of tax expenditures does not represent the increase in revenues that would occur if all tax expenditures were eliminated, because repealing a tax expenditure would change incentives and lead taxpayers to modify their behavior in ways that would diminish the revenue impact of the repeal. For example, if preferential tax rates on capital gains realizations were eliminated, taxpayers would reduce the amount of capital gains they realized; as a result, the amount of additional revenues that would be produced by eliminating the preferential rates would be smaller than the estimated size of the tax expenditure.

Economic and Distributional Effects of Tax Expenditures

Tax expenditures are generally designed to further societal goals. For example, those for health insurance costs, pension contributions, and mortgage interest payments may help to promote a healthier population, adequate financial resources for retirement and greater national saving, and stable communities of homeowners. But tax expenditures also have a broad range of effects that may not always further societal goals. They may lead to an inefficient allocation of economic resources by encouraging more consumption of the goods and services that receive preferential treatment, and they may subsidize an activity that would have taken place even without the tax incentives. Moreover, by providing benefits to particular activities, entities, or groups of people, tax expenditures increase the extent of federal involvement in the economy. Tax expenditures also reduce the amount of revenue that is collected for any given set of statutory tax rates— and therefore require higher rates to collect any particular amount of revenue. All else being equal, those higher tax rates lessen people's incentives to work and save, thus decreasing output and income.

Tax expenditures are distributed unevenly across the income scale. When measured in dollars, much more of the tax expenditures go to higher-income households than to lower-income households. As a percentage of people's income, tax expenditures are greater for the highest-income and lowest-income households than for households in the middle of the income distribution.[14]

The Largest Tax Expenditures

CBO estimates that the 11 largest tax expenditures will account for almost three-quarters of the total budgetary

effects of all tax expenditures in fiscal year 2015 and will total 6.6 percent of GDP over the period from 2016 to 2025.[15] Those 11 tax expenditures fall into four categories: exclusions from taxable income, itemized deductions, preferential tax rates, and tax credits.

Exclusions From Taxable Income. Exclusions of certain types of income from taxation account for the greatest share of total tax expenditures. The largest items in that category are employers' contributions for their employees' health care, health insurance premiums, and long-term-care insurance premiums; contributions to and earnings of pension funds (minus pension benefits that are included in taxable income); Medicare benefits (net of premiums paid); and profits earned abroad, which certain corporations may exclude from their taxable income until those profits are returned to the United States.

The exclusion of employers' health insurance contributions is the single largest tax expenditure in the individual income tax code; including effects on payroll taxes, it is projected to equal 1.6 percent of GDP over the 2016– 2025 period (see Figure 4-4). The exclusion of pension contributions and earnings has the next-largest impact, resulting in tax expenditures, including effects on payroll taxes, estimated to total 1.1 percent of GDP over the same period.[16] Over the coming decade, the tax expenditures for the deferral of corporate profits earned abroad and for the exclusion of Medicare benefits are each projected to equal 0.4 percent of GDP.

---

14. For a detailed analysis, see Congressional Budget Office, *The Distribution of Major Tax Expenditures in the Individual Income Tax System* (May 2013), www.cbo.gov/publication/43768.

15. Those 11 tax expenditures are the ones whose budgetary effects, according to JCT's estimates, will equal more than 0.25 percent of GDP over the 2014–2018 period. CBO combined the components of certain tax expenditures that JCT reported separately, such as tax expenditures for different types of charitable contributions. CBO also extrapolated JCT's estimates for the 2014–2018 period through 2025. (Those extrapolated estimates would not precisely match estimates produced by JCT.) See Joint Committee on Taxation, *Estimates of Federal Tax Expenditures for Fiscal Years 2014–2018*, JCX-97-14 (August 2014), http://go.usa.gov/zDb5.

16. That total includes amounts from defined benefit and defined contribution plans offered by employers; it does not include amounts from self-directed individual retirement arrangements or from Keogh plans that cover partners and sole proprietors, although contributions to and earnings in those plans also are excluded from taxable income.

Figure 4-4.

Budgetary Effects of the Largest Tax Expenditures From 2016 to 2025

Percentage of Gross Domestic Product

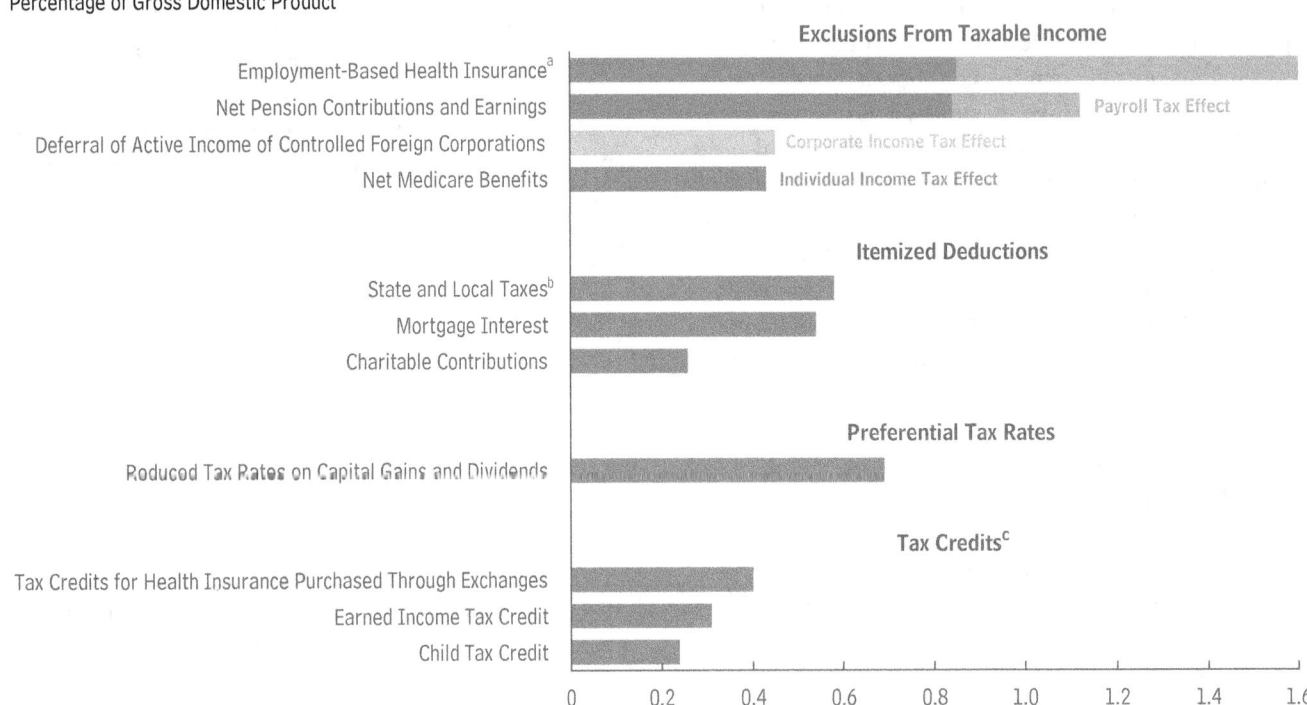

Source: Congressional Budget Office based on estimates by the staff of the Joint Committee on Taxation.

Note: These effects are calculated as the sum of the tax expenditures over the 2016–2025 period divided by the sum of gross domestic product over the same 10 years. Because estimates of tax expenditures are based on people's behavior with the tax expenditures in place, the estimates do not reflect the amount of revenue that would be raised if those provisions of the tax code were eliminated and taxpayers adjusted their activities in response to the changes.

a.   Includes employers' contributions for health care, health insurance premiums, and long-term-care insurance premiums.

b.   Consists of nonbusiness income, sales, real estate, and personal property taxes paid to state and local governments.

c.   Includes effect on outlays.

Itemized Deductions. Itemized deductions for certain types of payments allow taxpayers to further reduce their taxable income. The tax expenditures for deductions for state and local taxes (on nonbusiness income, sales, real estate, and personal property) are projected to equal 0.6 percent of GDP between 2016 and 2025. Those for interest paid on mortgages for owner-occupied residences and for charitable contributions are projected to equal 0.5 percent and 0.3 percent of GDP respectively over that period.

Preferential Tax Rates. Under the individual income tax, preferential tax rates apply to some forms of income, including dividends and long-term capital gains.[17] Tax expenditures for the preferential tax rates on dividends and long-term capital gains are projected to total 0.7 percent of GDP between 2016 and 2025.[18]

Tax Credits. Tax credits reduce eligible taxpayers' tax liability. Nonrefundable tax credits cannot reduce a

17. Not all analysts agree that those lower tax rates on investment income constitute tax expenditures. Although such tax preferences are tax expenditures relative to a pure income tax, which is the benchmark used by JCT and the Office of Management and Budget in calculating tax expenditures, they are not tax expenditures relative to a pure consumption tax, because investment income generally is excluded from taxation under a consumption tax.

18. Taxpayers with income over certain thresholds—$200,000 for single filers and $250,000 for married couples filing joint returns—face a surtax equal to 3.8 percent of their investment income (including capital gains and dividend income, as well as interest income and some passive business income). That surtax effectively reduces the preferential tax rate on dividends and capital gains. JCT treats the surtax as a negative tax expenditure—that is, as a deviation from the tax system that increases rather than decreases taxes—and it is not included in the figures presented here.

taxpayer's income tax liability to below zero, but refundable tax credits may provide direct payments to taxpayers who do not owe any income taxes.

The ACA provides refundable tax credits, called premium assistance credits, to help low- and moderate-income people purchase health insurance through exchanges (see Appendix B). Tax expenditures for those credits are projected to total 0.4 percent of GDP over the next decade.

The next-largest refundable credits are the earned income tax credit and the child tax credit. Both credits were significantly expanded in 2001 and again in later years, but expansions enacted since 2008 are scheduled to expire at the end of December 2017. Thus, under current law, the budgetary effect of those two credits will decline modestly after that. Including the refundable portion, the tax expenditures for the earned income tax credit are projected to be 0.3 percent of GDP between 2016 and 2025. Tax expenditures for the child tax credit, again including the refundable portion, are projected to be 0.2 percent of GDP over the same period.

Changes in CBO's Baseline Since August 2014

The Congressional Budget Office anticipates that in the absence of further legislation affecting spending and revenues, the budget deficit for fiscal year 2015 will total $468 billion. That amount is almost identical to the deficit that CBO projected in August 2014—when it released its previous set of baseline projections—and it is the result of changes to CBO's estimates of revenues and outlays that almost exactly offset each other (see Table A-1).[1] CBO currently expects that revenues this year will be $93 billion (about 3 percent) less and outlays will be $94 billion (or about 2½ percent) less than it previously projected.

CBO projects that over the 2015–2024 period the cumulative deficit would be $175 billion less than it projected in August—$7.0 trillion rather than $7.2 trillion—if current laws remained the same. Almost all of that reduction occurs in the projections for fiscal years 2016 through 2018; baseline deficits for other years are virtually unchanged. The cumulative projections of both revenues

---

1. Those projections were published in Congressional Budget Office, *An Update to the Budget and Economic Outlook: 2014 to 2024* (August 2014), www.cbo.gov/publication/45653. CBO constructs its baseline projections in accordance with provisions of the Balanced Budget and Emergency Deficit Control Act of 1985 and the Congressional Budget and Impoundment Control Act of 1974. To project revenues and mandatory spending, CBO assumes that current laws, with only a few exceptions, will remain unchanged throughout the 10-year projection period. To project discretionary spending, CBO assumes that annual appropriations through 2021 will adhere to the caps and automatic spending reductions established in the Budget Control Act of 2011 (Public Law 112-25), as amended, and that appropriations for 2022 through 2025 will increase from the 2021 amounts at the rate of inflation. CBO assumes that certain discretionary appropriations not constrained by the caps, such as those for overseas contingency operations, will increase in future years at the rate of inflation. The resulting baseline projections are not intended to be a prediction of future budgetary outcomes; rather, they serve as a benchmark against which to measure the potential effects of changes in laws governing taxes and spending.

and outlays are lower than those CBO published in August 2014. On net, about half of the differences arise from the enactment of new legislation.

Changes to Projections of Outlays

CBO has trimmed its estimate of outlays for 2015 by $94 billion, mainly because of technical updates—notably, larger-than-expected receipts to the U.S. Treasury from auctions of licenses for commercial use of the electromagnetic spectrum and the recording of receipts from the mortgage finance institutions Fannie Mae and Freddie Mac. In both cases, those collections are recorded in the budget as offsetting receipts, which are a credit against outlays.

CBO has reduced its projections of outlays for the 2015–2024 period by $590 billion (or 1.2 percent). Nearly half of that change is the result of revisions to its economic forecast.

Economic Changes

CBO's current economic forecast incorporates updated projections of gross domestic product (GDP), the unemployment rate, interest rates, inflation, and other factors that affect federal spending and revenues (see Chapter 2 for details). Those updates led the agency to reduce its estimates of outlays by $25 billion for 2015 and by $272 billion for the 2015–2024 period. That 10-year change is almost entirely the result of projections of lower spending for mandatory programs ($105 billion) and reduced net interest costs ($147 billion).

Mandatory Spending. Revisions to the economic forecast led CBO to reduce its projections of mandatory spending by $6 billion for 2015 and by $105 billion for the 2015–2024 period. The largest changes occurred in CBO's projections for Social Security and Medicare.

Table A-1.

Changes in CBO's Baseline Projections of the Deficit Since August 2014

Billions of Dollars

	2015	2016	2017	2018	2019	2020	2021	2022	2023	2024	Total 2015-2019	Total 2015-2024
Deficit in CBO's August 2014 Baseline	-469	-556	-530	-560	-661	-737	-820	-946	-957	-960	-2,777	-7,196
Changes to Revenue Projections												
Legislative Changes												
Individual income taxes	-31	6	4	3	2	*	*	*	*	*	-16	-16
Corporate income taxes	-50	12	7	4	3	1	*	-1	-1	-1	-24	-27
Payroll taxes	*	*	*	*	*	*	*	*	*	*	*	*
Other	*	*	*	*	*	*	*	*	*	*	*	*
Subtotal	-81	18	11	7	5	1	*	-1	-2	-2	-40	-44
Economic Changes												
Individual income taxes	12	9	-4	-15	-21	-25	-26	-25	-25	-25	-19	-146
Corporate income taxes	18	5	-3	-2	-2	-1	4	8	12	18	17	58
Payroll taxes	-1	-4	-8	-14	-18	-16	-21	-21	-21	-20	-45	-144
Other	1	1	-2	-4	5	3	*	-2	-2	-1	1	-1
Subtotal	29	11	-17	-34	-36	-39	-43	-40	-36	-29	-47	-234
Technical Changes												
Individual income taxes	-3	6	11	9	7	7	8	6	7	9	30	68
Corporate income taxes	-30	-1	-18	-18	-17	-17	-17	-17	-17	-18	-83	-169
Payroll taxes	-8	-3	-2	-1	-4	-12	-2	-4	-3	-2	-17	-40
Other	*	5	-1	3	2	1	1	*	-2	-4	9	4
Subtotal	-40	7	-11	-6	-11	-20	-9	-15	-16	-16	-61	-137
Total Revenue Changes	**-93**	**37**	**-17**	**-33**	**-43**	**-58**	**-52**	**-56**	**-53**	**-46**	**-149**	**-415**
Changes to Outlay Projections												
Legislative Changes												
Discretionary outlays	*	-9	-8	-13	-14	-16	-16	-16	-16	-16	-44	-125
Mandatory outlays	*	-2	-1	*	3	*	1	*	*	*	-1	-1
Net interest outlays (Debt service)	*	1	1	*	*	-1	-1	-2	-3	-3	1	-9
All Legislative Changes	1	-10	-9	-13	-12	-17	-17	-18	-19	-20	-44	-134
Economic Changes												
Mandatory outlays												
Social Security	-3	-11	-13	-11	-11	-11	-12	-12	-13	-14	-49	-110
Medicare	*	*	1	2	4	6	8	10	12	13	7	57
Unemployment compensation	-2	-2	-2	-3	-2	-2	-2	-2	-2	-1	-11	-19
Medicaid	*	-2	-2	-2	-2	-2	-2	-2	-2	-2	-8	-16
Other	*	-4	-5	-4	-2	-1	-1	*	*	*	-15	-16
Subtotal	-6	-18	-21	-18	-13	-9	-8	-5	-4	-3	-75	-105
Discretionary outlays	*	*	*	-1	*	*	*	*	*	*	-2	-3
Net interest outlays												
Effect of rates and inflation	-19	-6	-5	-2	-12	-19	-20	-21	-21	-21	-45	-147
Debt service	*	-1	-2	-3	-2	-2	-2	-2	-1	-1	-8	-17
Subtotal	-19	-8	-7	-4	-15	-21	-22	-23	-23	-23	-53	-164
All Economic Changes	-25	-26	-29	-22	-28	-31	-30	-28	-27	-26	-130	-272

Continued

Table A-1.   **Continued**

Changes in CBO's Baseline Projections of the Deficit Since August 2014

Billions of Dollars

	2015	2016	2017	2018	2019	2020	2021	2022	2023	2024	Total 2015-2019	Total 2015-2024
	Changes to Outlay Projections (Continued)											
Technical Changes												
Mandatory outlays												
Spectrum auctions	-30	10	1	-7	-5	-2	-2	-1	*	*	-31	-35
Fannie Mae and Freddie Mac	-29	*	1	1	1	1	*	*	*	1	-25	-23
Health insurance subsidies and related spending	-5	-13	-11	-2	-3	-6	-7	-8	-9	-8	-34	-71
Social Security	-1	-3	-6	-6	-7	-7	-8	-8	-9	-10	-23	-65
Medicaid	7	-4	-9	-9	-8	-7	-6	-6	-8	-10	-23	-60
Student loans	2	3	4	4	4	4	4	4	5	5	17	39
Other	4	*	4	2	5	5	4	8	7	9	15	48
Subtotal	-52	-5	-16	-18	-13	-12	-15	-10	-13	-14	-104	-168
Discretionary outlays	-13	-7	-4	-2	-1	*	1	1	*	*	-27	-25
Net interest outlays												
Debt service	*	1	1	1	1	1	1	2	2	2	5	12
Other	-6	-5	-2	1	2	3	2	1	*	2	-10	-3
Subtotal	-5	-4	-1	2	3	4	3	2	2	4	-6	9
All Technical Changes	-70	-16	-21	-17	-12	-8	-11	-7	-11	-9	-137	-184
Total Outlay Changes	**-94**	**-52**	**-58**	**-53**	**-52**	**-55**	**-58**	**-54**	**-57**	**-55**	**-310**	**-590**
	All Changes											
Total Effect on the Deficit[a]	**2**	**89**	**41**	**20**	**9**	**-3**	**6**	**-2**	**4**	**9**	**161**	**175**
Deficit in CBO's January 2015 Baseline	-468	-467	-489	-540	-652	-739	-814	-948	-953	-951	-2,615	-7,021
Memorandum:[a]												
Total Legislative Changes	-82	28	20	21	17	18	17	17	17	18	4	91
Total Economic Changes	54	37	12	-12	-8	-8	-13	-12	-9	-3	83	38
Total Technical Changes	30	24	10	11	1	-12	2	-8	-5	-6	75	46

Source: Congressional Budget Office.

Note: * = between -$500 million and $500 million.

a.   Negative numbers indicate an increase in the deficit; positive numbers indicate a decrease in the deficit.

Social Security. Because of changes in the economic forecast since August, CBO's projections of Social Security spending over the 2015–2024 period have declined by $110 billion (or 1 percent). The cost-of-living adjustment of 1.7 percent that Social Security beneficiaries received in January 2015 is 0.5 percentage points less than CBO had projected. CBO also anticipates a smaller cost-of-living adjustment in 2016 (0.9 percent compared with 1.9 percent in the August forecast). Those reductions are partially offset by an increase in CBO's projections for inflation over the 2016–2021 period. Taken together, those changes reduce the agency's estimates of

benefit payments for the period by $81 billion. A further reduction of $29 billion resulted from revisions to CBO's projections of growth in wages and salaries (which affect its projections of initial benefit amounts for new retirees).

Medicare. Under current law, payment rates for much of Medicare's fee-for-service sector (such as hospital care and services provided by physicians, home health agencies, and skilled nursing facilities) are updated automatically. Those updates are tied to changes in the prices of the labor, goods, and services that health care providers purchase, coupled with an adjustment for economywide gains in productivity (the ability to produce the same output using fewer inputs, such as hours of labor, than before) over a 10-year period. CBO's current projections of productivity growth are slightly lower than the agency forecast in August. Consequently, CBO now anticipates higher payment rates for Medicare services than it did in August—a change that increases its projections of outlays over the 2015–2024 period by $57 billion (or 0.8 percent).

Unemployment Compensation. CBO's forecast of the unemployment rate over the next 10 years was revised downward by an average of 0.2 percentage points for each year. As a result, projections of outlays for unemployment compensation have dropped by a total of $19 billion (or 4 percent) for 2015 through 2024.

Medicaid. Reductions in the prices projected for most medical services and in projected labor costs, combined with a drop in the anticipated unemployment rate, have reduced estimates of Medicaid spending—by about $16 billion (or 0.4 percent)—over the 2015–2024 period.

Net Interest. Since August, CBO has revised its projections of net interest costs because of changes in the agency's forecasts for interest rates and inflation as well as changes in CBO's projections of government borrowing that resulted from changes in the economic outlook (labeled in Table A-1 as debt service). Together, those revisions led CBO to reduce—by $164 billion—the amount it projects for net interest spending over the 2015–2024 period, mostly because of the revisions related to interest rates and inflation.

Specifically, CBO now expects that interest rates on most Treasury securities will be lower throughout the period. The agency also has markedly reduced (by about 1 percentage point) its estimate of inflation for 2015, which results in a lower projection of the cost of Treasury inflation-protected securities, but has slightly increased its estimate (by no more than 0.2 percentage points) of inflation over the 2016–2024 period. Overall, those and other changes to CBO's economic forecast since last August have led the agency to project net interest outlays that are $19 billion lower for 2015 and an additional $128 billion lower for the 2016–2024 period.

Furthermore, changes to CBO's economic projections have reduced the agency's calculation of the total deficit for the 2015–2024 period by $21 billion (the net effect

of updates to projections of revenues and outlays). Because of the reduced borrowing associated with lower deficits, CBO has decreased its projections of debt-service costs for the 2015–2024 period by $17 billion.

Legislative Changes
Laws enacted since August have led CBO to increase its estimate of outlays in 2015 by less than $1 billion and to reduce its 10-year projection by $134 billion (or 0.3 percent). Changes to projections of discretionary spending for activities that are not constrained by the annual funding caps established in the Budget Control Act of 2011 are responsible for almost all of that decrease.

Discretionary Spending. On net, legislative changes to discretionary programs led CBO to leave its estimates for 2015 outlays nearly unchanged but to cut $125 billion from its outlay projections for the 2015–2024 period. Because most discretionary spending is subject to the caps, the changes to spending projections in the baseline result mostly from changes in appropriations that are not constrained by the caps—those for overseas contingency operations, disaster relief, emergency requirements, and program integrity initiatives.[2]

In CBO's current baseline, the changes in discretionary spending that are attributable to legislation stem primarily from funding for overseas contingency operations (that is, military operations and related activities in Afghanistan and other countries). As a result of legislation enacted to date, such funding for 2015 is $18 billion less than the amount provided for 2014. Because projections of future appropriations for such operations are based on the assumption that they will equal current appropriations with an adjustment for inflation, the smaller amount provided for 2015 caused CBO to reduce its projection of discretionary outlays for the 2015–2024 period by about $200 billion.

In contrast, lawmakers provided $5.4 billion in emergency funding for responding to the outbreak of the Ebola virus (no emergency funding was provided for 2014), and funding in 2015 for disaster relief and program integrity initiatives is about $1 billion higher than it

---

2. Program integrity initiatives are aimed at reducing improper benefit payments in one or more of the following programs: Disability Insurance, Supplemental Security Income, Medicare, Medicaid, and the Children's Health Insurance Program. For more information on the discretionary caps, see Congressional Budget Office, *Final Sequestration Report for Fiscal Year 2015* (January 2015), www.cbo.gov/publication/49889.

was in 2014; extrapolating those amounts adds about $65 billion to the projection for discretionary outlays.

Mandatory Spending. Legislative activity since August has not substantially changed CBO's estimates of mandatory outlays either for the current year or for the 2015–2024 period.

Net Interest. All told, the changes that CBO made to its projections of revenues and outlays because of recently enacted legislation reduce its projection of the cumulative deficit for the 2015–2024 period by $82 billion (excluding interest costs). The resulting decrease in the estimate of federal borrowing led CBO to reduce its projection of outlays for interest payments on federal debt by $9 billion through 2024.

Technical Changes

As a result of technical updates to spending estimates for various programs and certain receipts, CBO has lowered its estimate of outlays in 2015 by $70 billion. Such changes have led CBO to reduce its projection of outlays for the 10-year period by $184 billion (or 0.4 percent), mostly because of lower projections of mandatory outlays.

Mandatory Spending. Technical revisions have reduced the amount of mandatory outlays projected for the current year by $52 billion, mostly because of receipts related to auctions of the electromagnetic spectrum and the recording of the Treasury's transactions with Fannie Mae and Freddie Mac. For the 2015–2024 period, technical updates involving several programs lowered the total projection for mandatory spending by $168 billion.

Spectrum Auctions. CBO estimates that receipts from auctions of licenses to use the electromagnetic spectrum will total $59 billion over the 2015–2024 period, which is $35 billion more than it projected in August 2014. (Those collections are classified as offsetting receipts and are shown in the budget as a reduction in outlays.) Most of the increase stems from bids for licenses already auctioned during this fiscal year. Those bids were much higher than expected: In all, on the basis of the bids that were placed at the time this report was completed, CBO estimates gross receipts of $45 billion from auctions held in 2015. After adjusting for bidding credits that will be awarded to certain firms, CBO estimates that the net proceeds over the next two years will be about $27 billion more than the agency had previously anticipated. Those results led CBO to boost its estimates of the net proceeds

from other auctions that may be held before the Federal Communications Commission's auction authority expires in 2022. The year-by-year change in CBO's projections also reflects updated information about the timing of future auctions and revised estimates of the federal spending that will be needed to make portions of the spectrum available for commercial use.

Fannie Mae and Freddie Mac. Because the government placed Fannie Mae and Freddie Mac into conservatorship in 2008 and now controls their operations, CBO considers their activities to be governmental. For the 10-year period after the current fiscal year, CBO projected subsidy costs of the entities' new activities using procedures that are similar to those specified in the Federal Credit Reform Act of 1990 for determining the costs of federal credit programs, but with adjustments to reflect the market risk associated with those activities. The Administration, in contrast, considers Fannie Mae and Freddie Mac to be outside the federal government for budgetary purposes and records cash transactions between those entities and the Treasury as federal outlays or receipts. (In CBO's view, those transactions should be considered intragovernmental.)

To provide CBO's best estimate of the amount that the Treasury ultimately will report as the federal deficit for 2015, CBO's current baseline includes an estimate of the cash receipts from the two entities to the Treasury for this year (that is, adopting the Administration's treatment for 2015 while retaining CBO's risk-adjusted projections of subsidy costs for later years). CBO estimates that payments from Fannie Mae and Freddie Mac to the Treasury will total $26 billion in 2015 (on the basis of the entities' most recent quarterly financial releases); those payments are recorded in the budget as offsets to outlays (offsetting receipts). By comparison, CBO's August 2014 baseline showed an estimated subsidy cost—that is, additional outlays—of about $3 billion for the entities' activities in 2015. All told, that difference—mostly conceptual in nature—reduces CBO's estimate of outlays in 2015 by $29 billion.

For 2016 through 2024, CBO's baseline follows the agency's customary approach of showing the estimated subsidy costs of mortgage guarantees provided and loans purchased by Fannie Mae and Freddie Mac. Those estimates are calculated on a fair-value basis, reflecting the market risk associated with the activities of the two institutions. For the 2016–2024 period, CBO now estimates that those subsidy costs will total $19 billion—about

$6 billion more than it projected in August, mostly because Fannie Mae and Freddie Mac's regulator announced that in January 2015 the two entities will begin making cash contributions to certain affordable-housing programs. Those programs, and the annual contributions from Fannie Mae and Freddie Mac, were authorized in the Housing and Economic Recovery Act of 2008 (Public Law 110-289).

Health Insurance Subsidies and Related Spending. CBO and the staff of the Joint Committee on Taxation have reduced their projections of outlays for exchange subsidies and related spending by $71 billion for the 2015–2024 period. (The subsidies are provided to eligible people to purchase health insurance through exchanges established under the Affordable Care Act, or ACA, or to assist them in paying out-of-pocket costs.) That reduction largely consists of a $39 billion decrease in cost-sharing subsidies, primarily stemming from higher actual and projected enrollment in insurance plans for which those subsidies are not available, and a $24 billion decrease in outlays for premium assistance tax credits, mainly resulting from lower estimated enrollment through the exchanges in every year.[3] The remainder of the reduction is accounted for by the Administration's reclassification of the risk corridor program from a mandatory to a discretionary program, along with other small revisions to projected outlays for risk adjustment and grants to states for establishing health insurance exchanges.[4] (See Appendix B for a more extensive discussion of the changes in CBO's baseline projections related to the ACA's insurance coverage provisions.)

---

3. People who enroll in health insurance plans through the exchanges are potentially eligible for at least one of two types of subsidies. Premium assistance tax credits cover a portion of eligible individuals' and families' health insurance premiums, and cost-sharing subsidies reduce out-of-pocket payments for low-income enrollees. Eligible low-income people must enroll in a "silver" plan (one that pays about 70 percent of the costs of covered benefits) to receive cost-sharing subsidies, but they are not required to enroll in a silver plan to receive premium assistance tax credits.

4. The risk corridor program reduces risk for health insurers by using a portion of some insurers' large profits to partially offset others' large losses. CBO's April 2014 baseline included net collections and payments for risk corridors as mandatory outlays and revenues. The risk corridors program is now recorded in the budget as a discretionary program; CBO estimates, as it did prior to the reclassification, that payments and collections will offset each other in each year, resulting in no net budgetary effect. CBO now projects that those offsetting transactions will total about $5 billion over the 2015–2017 period, a decrease of about $4 billion from the agency's previous projection.

Social Security. CBO has reduced its projections of outlays for Social Security for the 2015–2024 period by $65 billion (or 0.6 percent) on the basis of updated population projections and new information about participation in the Old-Age and Survivors Insurance program and the Disability Insurance program. Specifically, CBO has reduced its projections of the total number of people eligible to receive benefits. In addition, CBO now expects that a slightly smaller percentage of eligible people will collect benefits for the Old-Age and Survivors Insurance program than it projected in August. Also, on the basis of recent data regarding new awards, CBO expects that fewer people will be newly awarded benefits under the Disability Insurance program than it had previously projected.

Medicaid. CBO reduced its projections of spending for Medicaid over the 2015–2024 period by $60 billion (or about 1.3 percent) compared with its August 2014 estimates. That drop represents the net effect of several adjustments. The largest change is attributable to a reduction in spending growth for long-term services and supports. CBO lowered its estimate of spending for those services for the 2015–2024 period by $69 billion on the basis of an analysis of recent growth in such spending, which slowed from an estimated average annual rate of 6 percent between 1999 and 2009 to less than 2 percent over the past four years. CBO also lowered its projections of Medicaid spending as a result of new analysis indicating a lower expected per capita cost for some children who would enroll in Medicaid if funding for the Children's Health Insurance Program (CHIP) declined in 2016, as it does in CBO's baseline projections. CBO now estimates that Medicaid costs for those children would be lower than the program average, and it therefore has reduced its estimate of outlays by $31 billion over the 10-year projection period. Finally, CBO lowered its projection for spending by $19 billion because of certain technical adjustments and because actual spending in 2014 was less than anticipated in August.

Partially offsetting those reductions in projected spending was an update to CBO's estimate of the effects of the ACA. The agency now projects that a larger share of Medicaid enrollees will consist of people who will be newly eligible under the act. That change boosts spending projections because the federal government pays states a higher matching rate for those enrollees—between 90 percent and 100 percent—depending on the year. In addition, CBO now projects, a drop in funding for CHIP that starts in 2016 (as assumed in the baseline) would shift more children into Medicaid and fewer into coverage obtained through the exchanges or from employment-based insurance. Together those changes increase spending estimates by $59 billion for the 2015–2024 period (see Appendix B).

Student Loans. CBO increased its projection of outlays for federal student loans by $39 billion over the 2015–2024 period. That increase is primarily attributable to higher projections of participation in repayment plans that are based on a borrower's income. Under those plans, the government forgives the loans of borrowers who meet certain criteria, so they cost more than other repayment plans.

Other Mandatory Programs. Technical updates led CBO to boost its projections of outlays for several other mandatory programs, by $4 billion for 2015 and by $48 billion over the 2015–2024 period. CBO now projects that spending for the agricultural programs of the Commodity Credit Corporation will be $18 billion higher over the 2015–2024 period than it projected in the August baseline, primarily because of lower estimated crop prices and higher estimates of spending for livestock disaster assistance. In addition, CBO boosted its projections of Medicare outlays by $14 billion (because of higher projected outlays for Part C, known as Medicare Advantage, and for prescription drug coverage under Part D) and for federal civilian retirement benefits by $13 billion (stemming largely from updated projections of federal employee retirements and other technical adjustments) over the 2015–2024 period.

Discretionary Spending. Technical updates to CBO's projections of discretionary spending have the net effect of reducing its estimates of outlays by $13 billion for 2015 and by $25 billion for the 2015–2024 period (mostly in the first three years). The largest reductions in the 10-year period stem from higher projections of receipts (which reduce outlays) related to mortgage guarantees provided by the Federal Housing Administration and from lower projections of outlays for some categories of military spending, mainly for military personnel and for operations and maintenance.

Net Interest. As a result of technical updates to its spending and revenue projections, CBO's estimate of net interest outlays declined by $5 billion for 2015 but increased by $9 billion for the 2015–2024 period.

Excluding debt service, CBO's estimate of interest outlays decreased by $13 billion for the 2015–2017 period but increased by $10 billion over the 2018–2024 period. Those changes are mainly attributable to new information about the Treasury's auctions of securities: Since CBO issued its projections in August, the Treasury has issued a higher proportion of bills, or short-term debt, than CBO had anticipated, leading CBO to project lower interest costs for the near term and higher costs for later in the baseline period as interest rates are forecast to rise. All told, such changes reduce the projection for net interest outlays by $3 billion over the 2015–2024 period.

In the opposite direction, CBO projects that higher debt-service costs—mostly related to what is known as other means of financing—will add $12 billion to net interest outlays over the same period.[5]

Changes to Projections of Revenues

Since releasing its baseline projections in August, CBO has reduced its estimates of revenues by $93 billion for 2015 and by $415 billion for the 2015–2024 period. Recent enactment of the Tax Increase Prevention Act of 2014 (Division A of P.L. 113-295) explains most of the reduction for 2015. In later years, economic factors—mostly slightly lower projections of GDP—account for the bulk of the reductions in the revenue projections. Technical factors (those not related to legislative activity or to changes in the economic forecast) resulted in smaller reductions.

Economic Changes

Revisions to CBO's economic projections have caused the agency to increase its revenue estimates by $29 billion (or 0.9 percent) for 2015 and by $11 billion (or 0.3 percent) for 2016 but to decrease them by $274 billion (or 0.8 percent) for the period from 2017 through 2024. CBO raised its revenue projections for the first two years of the 10-year period mostly because it now anticipates higher corporate profits than it did last year, which results in projections of higher payments of corporate income taxes and, to a much lesser extent, of individual income taxes. (Those upward revisions for revenues for 2015 were more than offset by technical and legislative changes, as described below.) The projection of larger profits is made

---

5. *Other means of financing* refers to the borrowing needs of the Treasury that are not directly included in budget totals; those factors include changes in the government's cash balances and the cash flows of federal programs that provide loans and loan guarantees.

on the basis of recent information from the national income and product accounts of the Bureau of Economic Analysis, which indicate that profits in 2014 were larger than CBO projected last August.

A change in CBO's forecast of economic growth lowered revenue projections for the 2017–2024 period. CBO has slightly reduced its projection for the pace of economic growth over the 2016–2019 period: Real (inflation-adjusted) GDP is now projected to be about 1.1 percent lower, on average, over the 2017–2024 period than CBO anticipated in August, and nominal GDP—the main source of taxable income—is projected to be lower by 1.2 percent over the same period. (The projection for inflation as measured by the price indexes for GDP is little changed.)

Consequently, CBO also has lowered its projections for wages and salaries—the most highly taxed type of income specified in the economic forecast—by an average of 1.2 percent over the 2017–2024 period. That change in the forecast has led CBO to make a downward adjustment—of slightly more than $300 billion (or 1.1 percent)—in its projections of revenue from individual income and payroll taxes for that period.

CBO's projections of corporate profits overall are up slightly from its previous forecast, mostly because lower interest costs for businesses are projected to raise profits; that effect is only partially offset by the reduction in CBO's projections of economic activity generally.[6] As a result of those and other smaller effects of the new economic forecast, CBO's updated projections for corporate income taxes are slightly higher, on net, for the 2021–2024 period.

Technical Changes

CBO has reduced its projections of revenues by $40 billion (or 1.2 percent) for 2015 and by $137 billion (or 0.3 percent) for the 2015–2024 period for reasons that are unrelated to new legislation or to changes in the economic outlook. Those technical changes can be traced to new information from tax returns and about recent tax collections, new analysis of elements of the projections, and other factors.

---

6. The lower projected interest costs for businesses are also reflected in lower personal interest income, thereby reducing projected revenues from individual income taxes.

Of the projections for the different revenue sources, those for corporate income taxes have changed the most since August as a result of technical factors: Corporate income tax receipts are projected to be lower by $30 billion (or 7.6 percent) for 2015 and by $169 billion (or 3.8 percent) for the 10-year projection period. The largest effects arise from new information from corporate income tax returns and, to a lesser extent, from an updated projection of the growing reductions in the corporate tax base that are anticipated to result from corporations' following international tax avoidance strategies. Corporate inversion—in which a U.S. company merges with a foreign enterprise to become an affiliate of that foreign company—is one such strategy. CBO also incorporated an anticipated delay in the payment of corporate income taxes in 2015, with the effect of decreasing revenues in 2015 and increasing them equally in 2016. That change arises from rules that allow businesses to delay increasing their tax payments when their depreciation deductions drop significantly in a year, as occurs in 2015 under current law with the expiration at the end of 2014 of enhanced equipment-expensing provisions.

Legislative Changes

Legislation enacted since August 2014 has prompted CBO to reduce its revenue projections for 2015 by $81 billion (or 2.5 percent) but to raise them by $38 billion for the 2016–2024 period, resulting in a net $44 billion (or 0.1 percent) decrease for the 2015–2024 period.

Those changes result almost entirely from the Tax Increase Prevention Act of 2014, which extended about 50 expiring tax provisions for one year through 2014. Those provisions, which reduced the tax liabilities of individuals and businesses, include the tax credit for research and experimentation, certain eligibility rules for renewable energy facilities claiming energy tax credits, the deferral of certain active financing income of multinational corporations, and other provisions with smaller 10-year effects on revenues. The act will increase revenues over the 2016–2024 period largely because it retroactively extended (for 2014) enhanced expensing provisions that allowed businesses to take larger up-front deductions for investments in equipment or, for companies with relatively small investments in new equipment, to fully deduct those costs; that change will result in larger deductions being applied to the calculation of 2014 tax liabilities (when tax returns are filed in 2015), but it will lead to smaller deductions in later years.

Updated Estimates of the Insurance Coverage Provisions of the Affordable Care Act

In preparing the January 2015 baseline budget projections, the Congressional Budget Office and the staff of the Joint Committee on Taxation (JCT) have updated their estimates of the budgetary effects of the major provisions of the Affordable Care Act (ACA) that relate to health insurance coverage.[1] The new baseline estimates rely on analyses completed in the early part of December 2014 and incorporate information on enrollment made available by then and administrative actions issued through early November 2014. However, the estimates do not reflect CBO's updated economic projections (which were completed after the agency's analysis of insurance coverage was under way), the most recent data on enrollment through insurance exchanges, or any federal administrative actions or decisions by states about expanding Medicaid coverage that have occurred since that time. Hence, the updates are preliminary.

CBO and JCT currently estimate that the ACA's coverage provisions will result in net costs to the federal government of $76 billion in 2015 and $1,350 billion over the 2016–2025 period. Compared with the projection from last April, which spanned the 2015–2024 period, the current projection represents a downward revision in the net costs of those provisions of $101 billion over those 10 years, or a reduction of about 7 percent.[2] And compared with the projection made by CBO and JCT in March 2010, just before the ACA was enacted, the current estimate represents a downward revision in the net

costs of those provisions of $139 billion—or 20 percent—for the five-year period ending in 2019, the last year of the 10-year budget window used in that original estimate.

Those estimates address only the insurance coverage provisions of the ACA and do not reflect all of the act's budgetary effects. Because the provisions of the ACA that relate to health insurance coverage established entirely new programs or components of programs and because those provisions have mostly just begun to be implemented, CBO and JCT have produced separate estimates of the effects of the provisions as part of the baseline process. By contrast, because the provisions of the ACA that do not relate directly to health insurance coverage generally modified existing federal programs (such as Medicare) or made various changes to the tax code, determining what would have happened since the enactment of the ACA had the law not been in effect is becoming increasingly difficult. The incremental budgetary effects of those noncoverage provisions are embedded in CBO's baseline projections for those programs and tax revenues, respectively, but they cannot all be separately identified using the agency's normal procedures. As a result, CBO does not produce estimates of the budgetary effects of the ACA as a whole as part of the baseline process. Moreover,

---

1. As referred to in this report, the Affordable Care Act comprises the Patient Protection and Affordable Care Act (Public Law 111-148); the health care provisions of the Health Care and Education Reconciliation Act of 2010 (P.L. 111-152); and the effects of subsequent judicial decisions, statutory changes, and administrative actions. In addition to provisions dealing with health insurance coverage, that act included other provisions that made changes to the federal tax code, Medicare, Medicaid, and other programs.

2. For the most recent previous baseline, published in August 2014, CBO and JCT did not update their detailed estimates of the coverage provisions of the ACA for any years after 2014, except for a $600 million decline in outlays relative to the April 2014 baseline for grants to states for operating exchanges over the 2015–2017 period. Therefore, this appendix compares the current baseline projections with the detailed projections from April 2014. See Congressional Budget Office, "Updated Estimates of the Effects of the Insurance Coverage Provisions of the Affordable Care Act, April 2014" (April 2014), www.cbo.gov/publication/45231, which was released together with Congressional Budget Office, *Updated Budget Projections: 2014 to 2024* (April 2014), www.cbo.gov/publication/45229.

as the implementation of the provisions related to insurance coverage proceeds and historical data increasingly include the effects of those provisions, CBO and JCT will also cease to make separate projections of the effects of all of those provisions.

CBO typically revises its baseline budget projections after the Administration releases its proposed budget for the coming year (in part because that release includes data on federal spending that has occurred during the previous year). The revised projections that CBO will prepare this spring will include further updates to CBO and JCT's estimates of the insurance coverage provisions of the ACA, incorporating new information about health insurance coverage and the insurance exchanges that has become available, as well as the economic projections published in this report.

Insurance Coverage Provisions

Among the key elements of the ACA's insurance coverage provisions that are encompassed by the estimates discussed here are the following:

■ Many individuals and families are able to purchase subsidized health insurance through exchanges (often called marketplaces) operated by the federal government, by a state government, or through a partnership between the federal and state governments.

■ States are permitted but not required to expand eligibility for Medicaid, and the federal government pays a larger share of the costs for individuals who are newly eligible under the ACA than for those who were eligible previously.

■ The Children's Health Insurance Program (CHIP), which was previously funded through the end of fiscal year 2013, received funding under the ACA for fiscal years 2014 and 2015.

■ Most citizens of the United States and noncitizens who are lawfully present in the country must either obtain health insurance or pay a penalty for not doing so (under a provision known as the individual mandate).

■ Certain employers that decline to offer their employees health insurance coverage that meets specified standards will be assessed penalties.

■ A federal excise tax will be imposed on some health insurance plans with high premiums.

■ Most insurers offering policies either for purchase through the exchanges or directly to consumers outside of the exchanges must meet several requirements. In particular, they must accept all applicants regardless of health status, and they may vary premiums only by age, smoking status, and geographic location (and premiums charged for adults age 21 or older may not vary according to age by a ratio of more than 3 to 1).

■ Certain small employers that provide health insurance to their employees are eligible to receive a tax credit of up to 50 percent of the cost of that insurance.

The ACA also made other changes to rules governing health insurance coverage that are not listed here. Those other provisions address coverage in the nongroup, small-group, and large-group markets, in some cases including employment-based plans that are financed by employers, which are often called self-insured plans.

Budgetary Effects of the Insurance Coverage Provisions

CBO and JCT currently estimate that the ACA's coverage provisions will result in net costs to the federal government of $76 billion in 2015 and $1,350 billion over the 2016–2025 period. The estimated net costs in 2015 stem almost entirely from spending for subsidies that are provided through insurance exchanges and from an increase in spending for Medicaid (see Table B-1). For the 2016–2025 period, the projected net costs consist of the following:

■ Gross costs of $1,993 billion for subsidies for insurance obtained through the exchanges and related spending and revenues, for Medicaid and CHIP, and for tax credits for small employers, and

■ An offsetting amount of $643 billion in net receipts from penalty payments, additional revenues resulting from the excise tax on certain high-premium insurance plans, and the effects on income and payroll tax revenues and associated outlays arising from projected changes in coverage offered through employers.

Table B-1.

Direct Spending and Revenue Effects of the Insurance Coverage Provisions of the Affordable Care Act

Billions of Dollars, by Fiscal Year

	2015	2016	2017	2018	2019	2020	2021	2022	2023	2024	2025	Total, 2016-2025
Exchange Subsidies and Related Spending and Revenues[a]	32	66	87	99	103	106	111	117	120	123	127	1,058
Medicaid and CHIP Outlays[b]	47	64	70	76	84	91	97	102	107	112	117	920
Small-Employer Tax Credits[c]	2	1	1	1	1	1	2	2	2	2	2	15
Gross Cost of Coverage Provisions	81	131	159	176	188	198	209	220	229	237	245	1,993
Penalty Payments by Uninsured People	-2	-4	-4	-4	-4	-4	-5	-5	-5	-5	-6	-47
Penalty Payments by Employers[c]	0	-7	-11	-13	-15	-15	-17	-19	-20	-22	-23	-164
Excise Tax on High-Premium Insurance Plans[c]	0	0	0	-5	-10	-13	-16	-19	-24	-29	-34	-149
Other Effects on Revenues and Outlays[d]	-3	-11	-19	-24	-27	-29	-31	-33	-35	-36	-38	-284
Net Cost of Coverage Provisions	**76**	**109**	**124**	**130**	**132**	**137**	**141**	**144**	**144**	**145**	**145**	**1,350**
Memorandum:												
Changes in Mandatory Spending	92	135	163	177	190	202	213	224	233	241	249	2,026
Changes in Revenues[e]	16	26	39	47	58	64	73	80	88	97	104	677

Sources: Congressional Budget Office; staff of the Joint Committee on Taxation.

Notes: These numbers exclude effects on the deficit of provisions of the Affordable Care Act that are not related to insurance coverage and effects on discretionary spending of the coverage provisions.

Except as noted, positive numbers indicate an increase in the deficit, and negative numbers indicate a decrease in the deficit.

CHIP = Children's Health Insurance Program.

a. Includes spending for exchange grants to states and net spending and revenues for risk adjustment and reinsurance. The risk corridors program is now recorded in the budget as a discretionary program; CBO estimates that payments and collections will offset each other in each year, resulting in no net budgetary effect.

b. Under current law, states have the flexibility to make programmatic and other budgetary changes to Medicaid and CHIP. CBO estimates that state spending on Medicaid and CHIP over the 2016–2025 period will be about $63 billion higher because of the coverage provisions of the Affordable Care Act than it would be otherwise.

c. These effects on the deficit include the associated effects of changes in taxable compensation on revenues.

d. Consists mainly of the effects of changes in taxable compensation on revenues. CBO estimates that outlays for Social Security benefits will increase by about $8 billion over the 2016–2025 period and that the coverage provisions will have negligible effects on outlays for other federal programs.

e. Positive numbers indicate an increase in revenues.

CBO and JCT estimate that the net costs of the coverage provisions of the ACA will rise sharply as the effects of the act phase in from 2015 through 2017, continue to rise steadily through 2022, and then change little from 2022 through 2025. The annual net costs are estimated to level off at about $145 billion in the last years of the projection period.

The projected costs stop growing toward the end of the period in large part because of the nature of the rules for the indexing of exchange subsidies and the high-premium excise tax, which over time will slow the growth of gross costs and increase the growth of receipts. The ACA specifies that if total exchange subsidies exceed a certain threshold in any year after 2017—a condition that CBO and JCT expect may be satisfied in some years—people will be required to pay a larger share of premiums in the following year than would otherwise be the case, thus restraining the amount that the federal government pays in subsidies. In addition, CBO and JCT expect that premiums for health insurance will tend to increase more rapidly than the threshold for determining liability for the high-premium excise tax, so the tax will affect an increasing share of coverage offered through employers and thus generate rising revenues. In response, many employers are expected to avoid the tax by holding premiums below the threshold, but the resulting shift in compensation from nontaxable insurance benefits to taxable wages and salaries would subject an increasing share of employees' compensation to taxes. Those trends in exchange subsidies and in revenues related to the high-premium excise tax will continue beyond 2025, CBO and JCT anticipate, causing the net costs of the ACA's coverage provisions to decline in subsequent years.

Effects of the Insurance Coverage Provisions on the Number of People With and Without Insurance

By CBO and JCT's estimates, about 42 million non-elderly residents of the United States were uninsured in 2014, about 12 million fewer than would have been uninsured in the absence of the ACA.[3] In 2015, the agencies estimate, 36 million nonelderly people will be uninsured—about 19 million fewer than would have been uninsured in the absence of the ACA. From 2016 through 2025, the annual number of uninsured is expected to decrease to between 29 million and 31 million—that is, between 24 million and 27 million fewer than would have been uninsured in the law's absence (see Table B-2).

The 31 million people projected to be uninsured in 2025 represent roughly one out of every nine residents under age 65 (see Figure B-1). In that year, about 30 percent of those uninsured people are expected to be unauthorized immigrants and thus ineligible for exchange subsidies or for most Medicaid benefits; about 10 percent will be ineligible for Medicaid because they live in a state that will not have chosen to expand coverage; about 15 percent to 20 percent will be eligible for Medicaid but will choose not to enroll; and the remaining 40 percent to 45 percent will not purchase insurance to which they have access through an employer, through an exchange, or directly from an insurer.

---

3. CBO and JCT's estimate of the outcome relative to what would have happened in the absence of the ACA is different from the result of subtracting the number of people who were uninsured in 2013 from the number who were uninsured in 2014. The agencies' estimate accounts for effects of the coverage provisions since the law's enactment, whereas tallies in any given year after the enactment would incorporate the incremental change in that year from both the effects of the ACA and any underlying trends that would have occurred in the absence of the law.

The projected gains in insurance coverage relative to what would have occurred in the absence of the ACA are the net result of several changes in the extent and types of coverage. In 2018 and later years, between 24 million and 25 million people are projected to have coverage through the exchanges, and 14 million to 16 million more, on net, are projected to have coverage through Medicaid and CHIP than would have had it in the absence of the ACA. Partly offsetting those increases, however, are projected net decreases of 9 million to 10 million in the number of people with employment-based coverage and 4 million to 5 million in the number of people with coverage in the nongroup market outside the exchanges.

Enrollment in and Subsidies for Coverage Through Exchanges

Subsidies for insurance obtained through exchanges and related spending and revenues account for a little more than half of the gross costs of the coverage provisions of the ACA. Those amounts depend on the number of people who purchase insurance through the exchanges, the premiums charged for such insurance, and other factors.

Enrollment in Exchange Coverage

CBO and JCT's estimate of total exchange subsidies for each year is based on the agencies' projection of the average number of people who will enroll in that year. That average number for each year will be less than the total number of people who will have coverage at some point during the year because some people will be covered for only part of the year. Coverage through the exchanges varies over the course of a year because people who experience qualifying life events (such as a change in income or family size, the loss of employment-based insurance, the birth of a child, and several other situations) are allowed to purchase coverage later in the year and because some people leave their exchange-based coverage as they become eligible for insurance through other sources or stop paying the premiums. In 2014, for example, despite a peak in April of about 8 million people who had selected a plan through an insurance exchange, only about 6 million, on average, were covered through the exchanges over the course of the calendar year, according to CBO and JCT's estimates. That average is less than the total number of people covered through the exchanges during some part of 2014 particularly because of lower enrollment during the open-enrollment period early in the year and net attrition of enrollees later in the year.

Table B-2.

Effects of the Affordable Care Act on Health Insurance Coverage

Millions of Nonelderly People, by Calendar Year

	2015	2016	2017	2018	2019	2020	2021	2022	2023	2024	2025
Insurance Coverage Without the ACA[a]											
Medicaid and CHIP	35	34	33	33	34	34	34	35	35	35	35
Employment-based coverage	158	160	163	164	165	165	165	166	166	166	166
Nongroup and other coverage[b]	24	25	25	26	26	26	26	27	27	27	27
Uninsured[c]	55	55	55	55	56	56	56	57	57	57	57
Total	272	274	277	278	280	281	282	283	284	285	286
Change in Insurance Coverage Under the ACA											
Insurance exchanges	12	21	25	25	25	24	25	24	24	24	24
Medicaid and CHIP	11	13	13	14	15	16	16	16	16	16	16
Employment-based coverage[d]	-2	-7	-8	-9	-9	-9	-10	-9	-9	-9	-9
Nongroup and other coverage[h]	-3	-4	-4	-4	-4	-4	-4	-4	-5	-4	-4
Uninsured[c]	-19	-24	-26	-26	-26	-27	-27	-27	-27	-27	-27
Uninsured Under Current Law											
Number of uninsured nonelderly people[c]	36	31	30	30	29	29	29	30	30	30	31
Insured as a percentage of the nonelderly population											
Including all U.S. residents	87	89	89	89	90	90	90	89	89	89	89
Excluding unauthorized immigrants	89	91	92	92	92	92	92	92	92	92	92
Memorandum:											
Exchange Enrollees and Subsidies											
Number with access to unaffordable employment-based insurance[e]	*	*	1	1	1	1	1	1	1	1	1
Number of unsubsidized exchange enrollees[f]	3	5	6	6	6	6	7	6	7	7	7
Average exchange subsidy per subsidized enrollee (Dollars)	4,330	4,700	4,940	5,350	5,620	5,930	6,260	6,650	6,990	7,340	7,710

Sources: Congressional Budget Office; staff of the Joint Committee on Taxation.

Notes: Figures for the nonelderly population include residents of the 50 states and the District of Columbia who are younger than 65.

      ACA = Affordable Care Act; CHIP = Children's Health Insurance Program; * = between zero and 500,000.

a. Figures reflect average enrollment over the course of a year and include spouses and dependents covered under family policies; people reporting multiple sources of coverage are assigned a primary source.

b. "Other" includes Medicare; the changes under the ACA are almost entirely for nongroup coverage.

c. The uninsured population includes people who will be unauthorized immigrants and thus ineligible either for exchange subsidies or for most Medicaid benefits; people who will be ineligible for Medicaid because they live in a state that has chosen not to expand coverage; people who will be eligible for Medicaid but will choose not to enroll; and people who will not purchase insurance to which they have access through an employer, through an exchange, or directly from an insurer.

d. The change in employment-based coverage is the net result of projected increases and decreases in offers of health insurance from employers and changes in enrollment by workers and their families.

e. Under the ACA, health insurance coverage is considered affordable for a worker and related individuals if the worker would be required to pay no more than a specified share of his or her income (9.56 percent in 2015) for self-only coverage. If coverage is considered unaffordable, the worker and related individuals may receive subsidies through an exchange if other eligibility requirements are met.

f. Excludes coverage purchased directly from insurers outside of an exchange.

Figure B-1.

Effects of the Affordable Care Act on Health Insurance Coverage, 2025

Millions of Nonelderly People

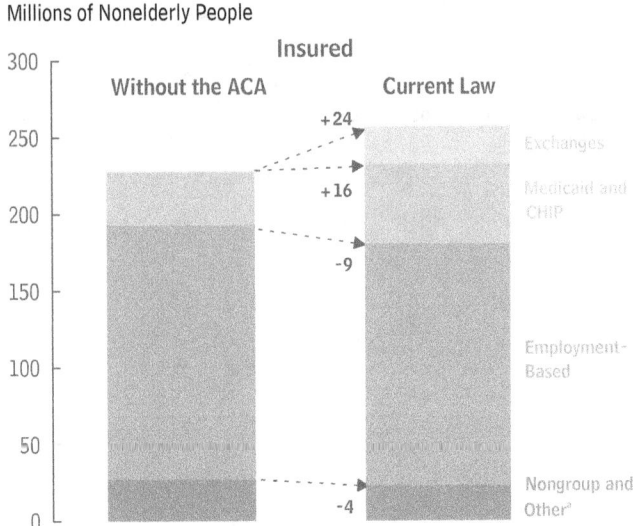

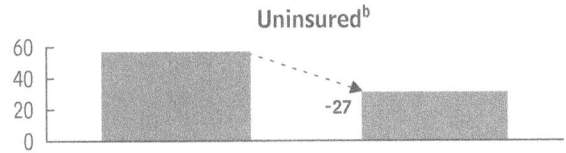

Sources: Congressional Budget Office; staff of the Joint Committee on Taxation.

Notes: The nonelderly population consists of residents of the 50 states and the District of Columbia who are younger than 65.

ACA = Affordable Care Act; CHIP = Children's Health Insurance Program.

a. "Other" includes Medicare; the changes under the ACA are almost entirely for nongroup coverage.

b. The uninsured population includes people who will be unauthorized immigrants and thus ineligible for exchange subsidies or for most Medicaid benefits; people who will be ineligible for Medicaid because they live in a state that will not have chosen to expand coverage; people who will be eligible for Medicaid but will choose not to enroll; and people who will not purchase insurance to which they have access through an employer, through an exchange, or directly from an insurer.

Over the course of calendar year 2015, an average of 12 million people are expected to be covered by insurance through the exchanges, but the actual number will not be known precisely until after the year has ended. (The total number enrolled at any particular time during the year might be higher.) Average annual enrollments are projected to increase to 21 million people in 2016 and then

to 24 million to 25 million people each year between 2017 and 2025. Roughly three-quarters of those enrollees are expected to receive subsidies for purchasing that insurance.

Premiums for Exchange Coverage

CBO and JCT currently estimate that the average cost of individual policies for the second-lowest-cost "silver" plan in the exchanges—that is, a plan that pays about 70 percent of the costs of covered benefits and represents the benchmark for determining exchange subsidies—is about $4,000 in calendar year 2015.[4] That estimate represents a national average, reflecting the agencies' projections of the age, sex, health status, and geographic distribution of those who will obtain coverage through the exchanges this year.

However, CBO and JCT expect to revise their estimates of premiums in the baseline projections to be published this spring. Those revisions will incorporate the economic projections that are included in this report, additional analysis of the available information about health care costs and insurance premiums, and revised estimates of the demographics of people receiving coverage through the exchanges. On the basis of the early stages of that analysis, CBO and JCT anticipate lowering their projections of premiums and thus the federal cost of exchange subsidies during the 2016–2025 period—though changes in other aspects of the coverage estimates and further analysis might lead to different conclusions.

Subsidies for Exchange Coverage

Exchange subsidies depend both on benchmark premiums for policies sold through the exchanges and on certain characteristics of enrollees, such as age, family size, and income. CBO and JCT estimate that, under current law, exchange subsidies and related spending and revenues will amount to a net cost of $32 billion in fiscal year 2015. That estimate is uncertain in part because the average number of people who will have such coverage during the fiscal year is not yet known and in part because detailed information on the demographics and income of the people who had such coverage last year is not yet available.

---

4. The size of the subsidy that someone will receive will be based in part on the premium of the second-lowest-cost silver plan offered through the exchange in which that person participates.

Over the 2016–2025 period, exchange subsidies and related spending and revenues are projected to result in a net cost of $1.1 trillion, distributed as follows:

- Outlays of $775 billion and a reduction in revenues of $134 billion for premium assistance tax credits (to cover a portion of eligible individuals' and families' health insurance premiums), which sum to $909 billion (see Table B-3);[5]

- Outlays of $147 billion for cost-sharing subsidies (which reduce out-of-pocket payments for low-income enrollees);

- Outlays of $1 billion in 2016 and 2017 for grants to states for operating exchanges; and

- Outlays of $181 billion and revenues of $180 billion related to payments and collections for risk adjustment and reinsurance (the projected outlays and revenues for those programs are exactly offsetting, with no net budgetary effect, when the amounts for 2015 are included).[6]

Subsidies in the exchanges are projected to average about $5,000 per subsidized enrollee from 2016 through 2018 and to reach almost $8,000 in 2025.[7]

The programs involving risk adjustment and reinsurance, along with another involving risk corridors, were established under the ACA to reduce the likelihood that particular health insurers will bear especially high costs to cover the expenses of a disproportionate share of less healthy enrollees. The programs, which took effect in 2014, generate payments by the federal government to insurers and collections by the federal government from insurers that reflect differences in the health status of each insurer's enrollees and the resulting costs to the insurers.

Payments and collections under the risk adjustment and reinsurance programs are recorded in the budget as mandatory outlays and revenues. Risk corridors are treated differently: The payments to insurers are recorded as discretionary spending, and the government's collections are recorded as offsets to discretionary spending. By CBO's projections, over the 2016–2025 period:

- Risk-adjustment payments and collections will both total $170 billion;

- Reinsurance payments will total $11 billion, and collections will total $10 billion (although the projected payments and collections are exactly offsetting when the amounts for 2015 are included); and

- Risk corridor payments and collections will both total $5 billion.[8]

Enrollment in Medicaid and CHIP and the Federal Cost of Such Coverage

In calendar year 2014, according to CBO and JCT's estimates, Medicaid enrollment increased by 6 million people who became newly eligible under the ACA, and Medicaid and CHIP enrollment increased by an additional 2 million people who were previously eligible and chose to enroll as a result of the ACA—for a total increase of 8 million people, on average, enrolled in Medicaid or CHIP compared with what would have occurred in the absence of the law. Over the coming years, the increase in the number of people enrolled in

---

5. The subsidies for health insurance premiums are structured as refundable tax credits; CBO and JCT treat the portions of such credits that exceed taxpayers' other income tax liabilities as outlays and the portions that reduce tax payments as reductions in revenues.

6. Because outlays are subject to sequestration in 2015, some of the revenues collected in 2015 will be spent in 2016.

7. The average exchange subsidy per subsidized enrollee includes both premium subsidies and cost-sharing subsidies and can therefore exceed the average benchmark premium in the exchanges.

8. Collections and payments for the risk adjustment, reinsurance, and risk corridor programs will occur after the close of a benefit year. Therefore, collections and payments for insurance provided in one year will occur in the next year. Under the reinsurance program, an additional $5 billion will be collected from health insurance plans and deposited into the general fund of the U.S. Treasury. That amount is the same as the sum appropriated for another program also established by the ACA, the Early Retiree Reinsurance Program, which was in operation before 2014 and which is not included here as part of the budgetary effects of the ACA's insurance coverage provisions. The risk corridors program does not extend throughout the projection period; instead, it covers insurance issued for calendar years 2014 to 2016, and corresponding payments and collections will occur during fiscal years 2015 to 2017. CBO expects that the payments and collections for that program will both total $1 billion in 2015, $1.5 billion in 2016, and $2.5 billion in 2017.

Table B-3.

Enrollment in, and Budgetary Effects of, Health Insurance Exchanges

	2015	2016	2017	2018	2019	2020	2021	2022	2023	2024	2025	Total, 2016-2025
Exchange Enrollment (Millions of nonelderly people, by calendar year)[a]												
Individually Purchased Coverage												
Subsidized	9	16	19	19	18	18	18	18	17	17	17	n.a.
Unsubsidized[b]	3	5	6	6	6	6	7	6	7	7	7	n.a.
Total	12	21	25	25	25	24	25	24	24	24	24	n.a.
Employment-Based Coverage Purchased Through SHOP Exchanges[b]	1	3	4	4	4	4	4	4	4	4	4	n.a.
Effects on Direct Spending and Revenues (Billions of dollars, by fiscal year)												
Changes in Mandatory Spending												
Outlays for premium credits	22	45	63	72	75	77	81	86	89	92	95	775
Cost-sharing subsidies	6	10	12	14	14	14	15	16	17	17	18	147
Exchange grants to states	1	1	*	0	0	0	0	0	0	0	0	1
Payments for risk adjustment and reinsurance[c]	16	16	17	15	17	19	19	20	20	19	19	181
Total, Exchange Subsidies and Related Spending	45	71	93	101	106	110	116	122	125	128	131	1,104
Changes in Revenues												
Reductions in revenues from premium credits	-5	-9	-12	-13	-14	-14	-14	-14	-14	-14	-14	-134
Collections for risk adjustment and reinsurance[c]	17	15	17	15	17	19	19	20	20	19	19	180
Total, Revenues	12	5	5	2	3	4	5	5	5	5	5	46
Net Increase in the Deficit From Exchange Subsidies and Related Spending and Revenues	32	66	87	99	103	106	111	117	120	123	127	1,058
Memorandum:												
Total Exchange Subsidies (Billions of dollars)[d]												
By fiscal year	32	64	87	99	103	106	111	117	120	123	127	1,057
By calendar year	38	75	92	102	104	106	113	118	121	124	128	1,084
Average Exchange Subsidy per Subsidized Enrollee (Dollars, by calendar year)	4,330	4,700	4,940	5,350	5,620	5,930	6,260	6,650	6,990	7,340	7,710	n.a.

Sources: Congressional Budget Office; staff of the Joint Committee on Taxation.

Note: SHOP = Small Business Health Options Program; n.a. = not applicable; * = between zero and $500 million.

a. Figures reflect average enrollment over the course of a year and include spouses and dependents covered under family policies. Figures for the nonelderly population include residents of the 50 states and the District of Columbia who are younger than 65.

b. Excludes coverage purchased directly from insurers outside of an exchange.

c. CBO's April 2014 baseline for direct spending and revenues also included the net collections and payments for risk corridors. The risk corridors program is included in CBO's January 2015 baseline as a discretionary program. CBO estimates that the payments and collections for the risk corridors program will each total $1 billion in fiscal year 2015, $1.5 billion in fiscal year 2016, and $2.5 billion in fiscal year 2017.

d. Total exchange subsidies include premium credit outlays, reductions in revenues from premium credits, and outlays for cost-sharing subsidies.

Medicaid or CHIP because of the ACA is expected to be even larger—about 11 million in 2015 and 13 million to 16 million in each year between 2016 and 2025 (see Table B-2 on page 119).

Several factors account for the increase over time in the number of additional people enrolled in Medicaid or CHIP because of the ACA. Some of those additional enrollees will be people who are eligible for Medicaid because of the ACA's expansion of coverage: CBO and JCT expect that, in future years, more states will expand eligibility for Medicaid, and more people in states that have already expanded eligibility will enroll in the program. Others of the additional enrollees will be people who would have been eligible for Medicaid or CHIP in the absence of the ACA but would not have enrolled: CBO and JCT expect that the ACA's individual mandate, increased outreach, and new opportunities for people deemed eligible for those programs to apply via the exchanges will increase enrollment among that group.[9]

As with enrollment through the exchanges, the numbers that CBO and JCT project for Medicaid and CHIP enrollment represent averages over the course of a year and differ from enrollment at any particular point during a year. Unlike exchange plans, for which enrollment opportunities are limited to an annual open-enrollment period and times at which people experience qualifying life events, people who are eligible for Medicaid or CHIP can enroll at any time during a year. People move into and out of those programs for many reasons, including changes in their need for health care, a change in their awareness of the availability of coverage, and changes in their financial circumstances.

The ACA's total effect on enrollment in Medicaid can never be precisely determined. In particular, the number of people who were previously eligible and who sign up for the program after 2013 because of the ACA can be estimated but not observed directly. However, the number of people who sign up who are newly eligible can eventually be determined because states that expand coverage under the ACA will report the number of enrollees who became eligible as a result of that expansion in order to receive the additional federal funding that is provided for such enrollees.

CBO and JCT estimate that the added costs to the federal government for Medicaid and CHIP resulting from the ACA will be $47 billion in 2015 and will grow to $76 billion in 2018 and $117 billion in 2025. For the 2016–2025 period as a whole, those costs are projected to total $920 billion (see Table B-1 on page 117).[10]

Tax Credits for Small Employers

Certain small employers are eligible to receive tax credits to defray the cost of providing health insurance to their employees. CBO and JCT project that those tax credits will total $2 billion in 2015 and $15 billion over the 2016–2025 period.

Penalty Payments and Excise Taxes

Under the ACA, some large employers who do not offer health insurance that meets certain standards will need to pay a penalty if they have full-time employees who receive a subsidy through an exchange. The standards specify thresholds for affordability and the share of the cost of covered benefits paid by the employer's insurance plan.[11] The requirement generally applies to employers with at least 50 full-time-equivalent (FTE) employees, but this year, employers with at least 50 but fewer than 100 FTE employees will be exempt from the requirement if they certify that they have not diminished health insurance coverage in certain ways or reduced their number

---

9. Under current law, CHIP is funded through 2015, and CBO's projection of annual spending for the program is expected to reach $10 billion in 2015. If the Congress does not provide additional funding for subsequent years, most state programs will terminate at some point during fiscal year 2016. However, under the rules governing baseline projections for expiring programs, CBO projects funding for CHIP after 2015 at an annualized amount of about $6 billion; the estimates of enrollment shown here are based on that projected amount of funding. Because such funding is substantially less than the funding provided through 2015, projected enrollment in CHIP in CBO's baseline declines after that year. (For details about the CHIP baseline, see Chapter 3.)

10. Under current law, states have the flexibility to make programmatic and other budgetary changes to Medicaid and CHIP. CBO estimates that state spending on Medicaid and CHIP over the 2016–2025 period will be about $63 billion higher because of the coverage provisions of the ACA than it would have been otherwise.

11. To meet the standards, the cost to the employee for self-only coverage must not exceed a specified share of income (which is 9.56 percent in 2015 and is indexed for inflation over time), and the plan must pay at least 60 percent of the cost of covered benefits.

of FTE employees to avoid the penalty. CBO and JCT estimate that payments of those penalties will total $164 billion over the 2016–2025 period.

In addition, most citizens of the United States and lawfully present noncitizens are required to obtain health insurance or pay a penalty. People who do not obtain coverage owe the greater of two amounts: (1) a flat dollar penalty per uninsured adult in a family, rising from $325 in 2015 to $695 in 2016 and indexed to inflation thereafter (the penalty for an uninsured child is half the amount for an uninsured adult, and an overall cap applies to family payments), or (2) a percentage of a household's adjusted gross income in excess of the income threshold for mandatory tax-filing—a share that will rise from 2.0 percent in 2015 to 2.5 percent in 2016 and subsequent years (also subject to a cap). CBO and JCT estimate that such payments from individuals will total $47 billion over the 2016–2025 period.

Among the roughly 36 million nonelderly residents that CBO and JCT estimate will be uninsured in 2015, the majority will be exempt from the penalty. Those who are exempt include unauthorized immigrants (who are prohibited from receiving exchange subsidies and almost all Medicaid benefits), people with income low enough that they do not file income tax returns, people who have income below 138 percent of federal poverty guidelines and are ineligible for Medicaid because their state did not expand the program, members of Indian tribes, people who are incarcerated, and people whose premiums exceed a specified share of their income (which is 8.05 percent in 2015 and is indexed for inflation over time).

According to CBO and JCT's estimates, federal revenues stemming from the excise tax on high-premium insurance plans will be $149 billion over the 2016–2025 period. Roughly one-quarter of that amount will stem from excise tax receipts, and three-quarters will come from the effects on revenues of changes in employees' taxable compensation. In particular, CBO and JCT anticipate that many employers and workers will shift to health plans with premiums that are below the specified thresholds to avoid paying the tax, resulting generally in higher taxable wages for affected workers.

Other Effects on Revenues and Outlays

Changes in insurance coverage under the ACA also affect federal tax revenues and outlays because fewer people will have employment-based health insurance and thus more of their income will take the form of taxable wages. CBO and JCT project that, as a result of the ACA, between 7 million and 10 million fewer people will have employment-based insurance coverage each year from 2016 through 2025 than would have been the case in the absence of the ACA. That difference is the net result of projected increases and decreases in offers of health insurance from employers and in decisions to enroll by active workers, early retirees (people under the age of 65 at retirement), and their families.

In 2019, for example, about 13 million people who would have enrolled in employment-based coverage in the absence of the ACA will not have an offer of such coverage under current law, CBO and JCT estimate; in addition, an estimated 3 million people who would have enrolled in employment-based coverage in the absence of the ACA will still have such an offer but will choose not to enroll in that coverage. Some of those 16 million people are expected to gain coverage through some other source; others will forgo health insurance. Those decreases in employment-based coverage will be partially offset, however. About 7 million people who would not have had employment-based coverage in the absence of the ACA are expected to receive such coverage under current law; they will either take up an offer of coverage they would have received anyway or take up a new offer. Some of those enrollees would have been uninsured in the absence of the ACA. On balance, an estimated 9 million fewer people will have employment-based insurance under current law than would have had it in the absence of the ACA.

Because of the net reduction in employment-based coverage, the share of workers' pay that takes the form of nontaxable benefits (such as payments toward health insurance premiums) will be smaller—and the share that takes the form of taxable wages will be larger—than would otherwise have been the case. That shift in compensation is projected to reduce deficits by a total of $292 billion over the 2016–2025 period by boosting federal tax receipts (and reducing outlays from certain refundable tax credits). Partially offsetting those added receipts will be an estimated $8 billion increase in Social Security benefits that will be paid because of the higher wages paid to workers. All told, CBO and JCT project, those changes will reduce federal budget deficits by $284 billion over the 2016–2025 period.

Changes in the Estimates Since April 2014

CBO and JCT currently project that the insurance coverage provisions of the ACA will have a smaller budgetary cost than they estimated in April 2014, when the agencies last published a detailed projection for those provisions. For the 2015–2024 period (the period covered by last April's estimates), CBO and JCT have lowered their estimate of the net costs, from $1,383 billion to $1,281 billion (see Table B-4).[12] That reduction of $101 billion (or 7 percent) largely comprises the following:

- A $68 billion reduction in the net cost of exchange subsidies and related spending and revenues;

- A $59 billion increase in federal spending for Medicaid and CHIP; and

- A $97 billion net increase in revenues (and decrease in outlays from certain refundable tax credits) arising from projected changes in coverage offered through employers.

In addition to those three sets of changes, which are discussed below, the revision also reflects an increase in net costs of $5 billion stemming from changes in estimated penalty payments and estimated collections from the excise tax on high-premium insurance plans.

Various factors, including new data and improvements in the agencies' modeling, account for the differences. Relevant updates of information included these: Average enrollment in the exchanges over the course of 2014 was slightly lower than anticipated; enrollment in "bronze" plans (which pay about 60 percent of the costs of covered benefits) during 2014 was higher than anticipated; and the estimated proportion of Medicaid enrollees who were newly eligible under the ACA was larger than expected.

Exchange Subsidies and Related Spending and Revenues

CBO and JCT now project that the government's net costs for exchange subsidies and related spending and revenues over the 2015–2024 period will be $964 billion, $68 billion (or 7 percent) below the previous projection:

- Premium assistance tax credits are projected to be $827 billion, about $28 billion (or 3 percent) less than in the previous projection, and

- Cost-sharing subsidies are projected to be $135 billion, about $39 billion (or 23 percent) less than in the previous projection.[13]

Premium Assistance Tax Credits. Lower estimated enrollment in coverage obtained through the exchanges in every year accounts for the majority of the $28 billion reduction in the estimated cost of premium assistance tax credits.

CBO and JCT have reduced their estimate of average enrollment over the course of 2015 by 1 million people, from 13 million to 12 million. That revision occurred for two reasons. First, attrition from exchange plans during calendar year 2014 was slightly greater than the agencies had previously anticipated. Second, enrollment between mid-November and mid-December for coverage in 2015 was slightly lower than the agencies had previously anticipated. (About 7 million people selected a plan during that period.)[14] CBO and JCT expect that many people will sign up near the end of the ongoing open-enrollment period, which lasts through mid-February, following a pattern similar to last year's. Even so, the agencies now view 12 million (rather than 13 million) as being closer to

---

12. See Congressional Budget Office, *Updated Estimates of the Effects of the Insurance Coverage Provisions of the Affordable Care Act, April 2014* (April 2014), www.cbo.gov/publication/45231.

13. In addition, the risk corridors program has been reclassified in the federal budget as discretionary rather than mandatory. As a result, collections and payments for that program are included in the discretionary portion of CBO's baseline estimates and are no longer included here as part of "exchange subsidies and related spending and revenues." Because CBO had previously estimated that collections and payments for the program would exactly offset each other, that reclassification has no effect on CBO and JCT's estimates of the net costs of the insurance coverage provisions of the ACA. However, the change reduces both mandatory outlays and revenues relative to previous projections.

14. About 6.4 million people enrolled through federally facilitated exchanges through December 19 (see Department of Health and Human Services, "Open Enrollment Week 5: December 13–December 19, 2014," *HHS Blog* [December 23, 2014], http://go.usa.gov/znbA), and another 0.6 million people enrolled through state-based exchanges through December 13 (see Department of Health and Human Services, Office of the Assistant Secretary for Planning and Evaluation, *Health Insurance Marketplace 2015 Open Enrollment Period: December Enrollment Report*, ASPE Issue Brief [December 2014], http://go.usa.gov/tVx4).

Table B-4.

Comparison of CBO and JCT's Current and Previous Estimates of the Effects of the Insurance Coverage Provisions of the Affordable Care Act

	April 2014 Baseline	January 2015 Baseline	Difference
	Change in Insurance Coverage Under the ACA in 2024 (Millions of nonelderly people, by calendar year)[a]		
Insurance Exchanges	25	24	-1
Medicaid and CHIP	13	16	3
Employment-Based Coverage[b]	-7	-9	-1
Nongroup and Other Coverage[c]	-5	-4	*
Uninsured[d]	-26	-27	-1
	Effects on the Cumulative Federal Deficit, 2015 to 2024[e] (Billions of dollars)		
Exchange Subsidies and Related Spending and Revenues[f]	1,032	964	-68
Medicaid and CHIP Outlays	792	851	59
Small-Employer Tax Credits[g]	15	14	**
Gross Cost of Coverage Provisions	1,839	1,829	-9
Penalty Payments by Uninsured People	-46	-43	3
Penalty Payments by Employers[g]	-139	-140	-1
Excise Tax on High-Premium Insurance Plans[g]	-120	-116	4
Other Effects on Revenues and Outlays[h]	-152	-249	-97
Net Cost of Coverage Provisions	**1,383**	**1,281**	**-101**

Sources: Congressional Budget Office; staff of the Joint Committee on Taxation.

Note: ACA = Affordable Care Act; CHIP = Children's Health Insurance Program; * = between zero and 500,000; ** = between -$500 million and zero.

a. Figures for the nonelderly population include residents of the 50 states and the District of Columbia who are younger than 65.

b. The change in employment-based coverage is the net result of projected increases and decreases in offers of health insurance from employers and changes in enrollment by workers and their families.

c. "Other" includes Medicare; the changes under the ACA are almost entirely for nongroup coverage.

d. The uninsured population includes people who will be unauthorized immigrants and thus ineligible either for exchange subsidies or for most Medicaid benefits; people who will be ineligible for Medicaid because they live in a state that has chosen not to expand coverage; people who will be eligible for Medicaid but will choose not to enroll; and people who will not purchase insurance to which they have access through an employer, through an exchange, or directly from an insurer.

e. Positive numbers indicate an increase in the deficit; negative numbers indicate a decrease in the deficit. These numbers exclude effects on the deficit of provisions of the ACA that are not related to insurance coverage and discretionary spending effects of the coverage provisions.

f. Includes spending for exchange grants to states and net spending and revenues for risk adjustment and reinsurance. The risk corridors program is now recorded in the budget as a discretionary program; CBO estimates that payments and collections will offset each other in each year, resulting in no net budgetary effect.

g. These effects on the deficit include the associated effects of changes in taxable compensation on revenues.

h. Consists mainly of the effects of changes in taxable compensation on revenues.

the middle of the distribution of possible outcomes for average enrollment during 2015 as a whole.

For 2016, CBO and JCT have also revised downward their estimate of average enrollment through exchanges, from 24 million to 21 million. The agencies still expect enrollment to grow rapidly over the next two years in response to increased outreach by state health agencies and others and to increased awareness of the individual mandate; however, that growth is now anticipated to occur a little more gradually than it was previously.

In addition, for most years after 2016, CBO and JCT currently estimate that enrollment through exchanges will be 1 million lower than previously thought. That reduction primarily reflects an increase in the number of children who are expected to receive coverage through Medicaid, as discussed below.

CBO and JCT have incorporated several improvements to the modeling of benchmark premiums for exchange plans to better reflect the premium structure observed in 2014 and 2015. Those revisions resulted in higher projected premiums for some people and lower projected premiums for others, yielding largely offsetting effects on total exchange enrollment and a slight increase (on net) in premium assistance tax credits.

Cost-Sharing Subsidies. Outlays for cost-sharing subsidies over the 2015–2024 period are currently projected to be $39 billion less than previously estimated, primarily because CBO and JCT now expect that more people will forgo those subsidies by choosing to enroll in a bronze plan instead of a silver plan. (Although eligible low-income individuals must enroll in a silver plan to receive cost-sharing subsidies, they are not required to enroll in a silver plan to receive premium assistance tax credits.)

The agencies had previously estimated that few people would forgo cost-sharing subsidies; however, data released since April 2014 show that 15 percent of people who chose a plan through an exchange during the open-enrollment period for 2014 and who qualified for a premium assistance tax credit chose a bronze plan.[15]

---

15. See Department of Health and Human Services, Office of the Assistant Secretary for Planning and Evaluation, *Health Insurance Marketplace: Summary Enrollment Report for the Initial Annual Open Enrollment Period*, ASPE Issue Brief (May 2014), p. 21, http://go.usa.gov/MwFF.

Those data suggest that a significant number of people are selecting plans that minimize their monthly premium payments, even if the amounts they ultimately pay for health care (including out-of-pocket payments) exceed what they would pay under silver plans. Over time, CBO and JCT expect, some enrollees will switch from bronze plans to silver plans because they incur large medical bills or become concerned (perhaps because of outreach efforts by insurers or others) about the possibility of incurring large out-of-pocket payments. Nonetheless, the agencies expect that some people purchasing coverage through exchanges solely to comply with the individual mandate will be focused on minimizing their premium payments and thus will continue to choose bronze plans. Therefore, CBO and JCT now estimate that, in years after 2015, 3 million people who would have been eligible for cost-sharing subsidies if enrolled in a silver plan will forgo those subsidies by signing up for a bronze plan.

Medicaid and CHIP Outlays

CBO and JCT now project that the federal cost of the additional enrollment in Medicaid and CHIP under the ACA over the 2015–2024 period will be $851 billion, $59 billion (7 percent) more than the April 2014 projection. Roughly half of the upward revision reflects an increase in the estimated share of people enrolling in Medicaid under the ACA who will be newly eligible because of the law (and a decrease in the share who would have been eligible but would not have enrolled in the absence of the law). The remainder of the upward revision can be attributed mostly to an increase in the number of children who are projected to enroll in Medicaid after 2015, when CHIP is no longer funded under current law.

The Composition of Enrollment in Medicaid. CBO and JCT now estimate that enrollment in Medicaid in 2014 among those eligible for the program because of the ACA's coverage expansion was higher than originally thought and that enrollment among those previously eligible for the program was lower. As a result, the agencies now project that newly eligible Medicaid enrollees will represent a larger share of the projected increment to Medicaid enrollment under the ACA in future years as well. For 2015 and beyond, the agencies currently expect that roughly 70 percent of the people who will receive Medicaid coverage because of the ACA will be newly eligible for the program, compared with 55 percent to 65 percent in the previous projection.

Federal costs per Medicaid enrollee are much higher for those who are newly eligible than for those who were previously eligible because the federal government pays a larger share of the costs for newly eligible enrollees (100 percent to 90 percent, depending on the year) than for other enrollees (an average of 57 percent). Therefore, the revision to the mix of enrollees resulted in a $29 billion increase in projected federal spending for Medicaid over the 2015–2024 period.

Enrollment of Children in CHIP and Medicaid. Under current law, states will receive no new budget authority for their CHIP programs in fiscal year 2016 and later. However, under the rules governing baseline projections for expiring programs, CBO projects funding for CHIP in each of those years of about $6 billion. That assumed funding level compares to total state allotments in 2014 of $9.7 billion. If CHIP is funded at the reduced $6 billion level, CBO and JCT expect that some children will lose coverage through CHIP and will instead receive coverage through Medicaid, obtain private coverage (through the exchanges or their parents' employers), or become uninsured. On the basis of information provided by the Medicaid and CHIP Payment and Advisory Commission regarding requirements in current law to provide Medicaid coverage to certain children if CHIP funding is reduced, CBO and JCT now estimate that more of those children (about 3 million by 2024) will receive coverage through Medicaid rather than through the exchanges and employment-based coverage than the agencies previously estimated.[16] As a result, the agencies project greater spending for Medicaid (and reductions in enrollment through the exchanges and employment-based coverage, with corresponding budgetary effects).

Other Effects on Revenues and Outlays
CBO and JCT now anticipate that the ACA's insurance coverage provisions will have other effects on revenues and outlays that will, on net, reduce the deficit by $97 billion more for the 2015–2024 period than was anticipated previously. That revision stems from improvements in estimating methodology and from a downward revision to the number of people who are projected to have employment-based coverage in most years.

---

16. Medicaid and CHIP Payment and Access Commission, *Report to Congress on Medicaid and CHIP* (June 2014), pp. 6 and 8, www.macpac.gov/reports.

The lower estimate of the number of people who will have employment-based coverage (about 1 million fewer in most years of the projection period than thought previously) derives largely from an increase in the number of children who are expected to receive coverage through Medicaid after 2015. Less employment-based coverage means that nontaxable compensation in the form of health benefits provided by employers will be less and taxable compensation in the form of wages and salaries will be greater, as total compensation is expected to remain roughly the same. And to the extent that wages and salaries do not increase as much as payments for health benefits are reduced, corporate profits—which are also taxable—would increase. Therefore, the decrease in the estimate of employment-based coverage implies higher federal revenues than projected previously.

Other methodological improvements also increased CBO and JCT's estimate of tax revenues stemming from projected changes in coverage through employers. For example, as previously discussed, the new projections include modeling improvements to benchmark premiums for exchange plans. Although those changes resulted in largely offsetting effects on the number of people projected to have employment-based health insurance, the average income of those projected to no longer obtain employment-based insurance under the ACA is now higher than previously estimated. As a result, the reduction in employment-based insurance under the ACA yields a larger increase in federal revenues than previously estimated.

Changes in the Estimates Since the Enactment of the ACA
CBO and JCT have updated their baseline estimates of the budgetary effects of the ACA's insurance coverage provisions many times since the law was enacted in March 2010. As time has passed, projected costs over the subsequent 10 years have risen because the period spanned by the estimates has changed: Each time the projection period changes, a less expensive early year is replaced by a more expensive later year. But when compared year by year, CBO and JCT's estimates of the net budgetary impact of the ACA's insurance coverage provisions have decreased, on balance, over the past five years (see Figure B-2).

In March 2010, CBO and JCT projected that the provisions of the ACA related to health insurance coverage

Figure B-2.

Comparison of CBO and JCT's Estimates of the Net Budgetary Effects of the Coverage Provisions of the Affordable Care Act

Billions of Dollars, by Fiscal Year

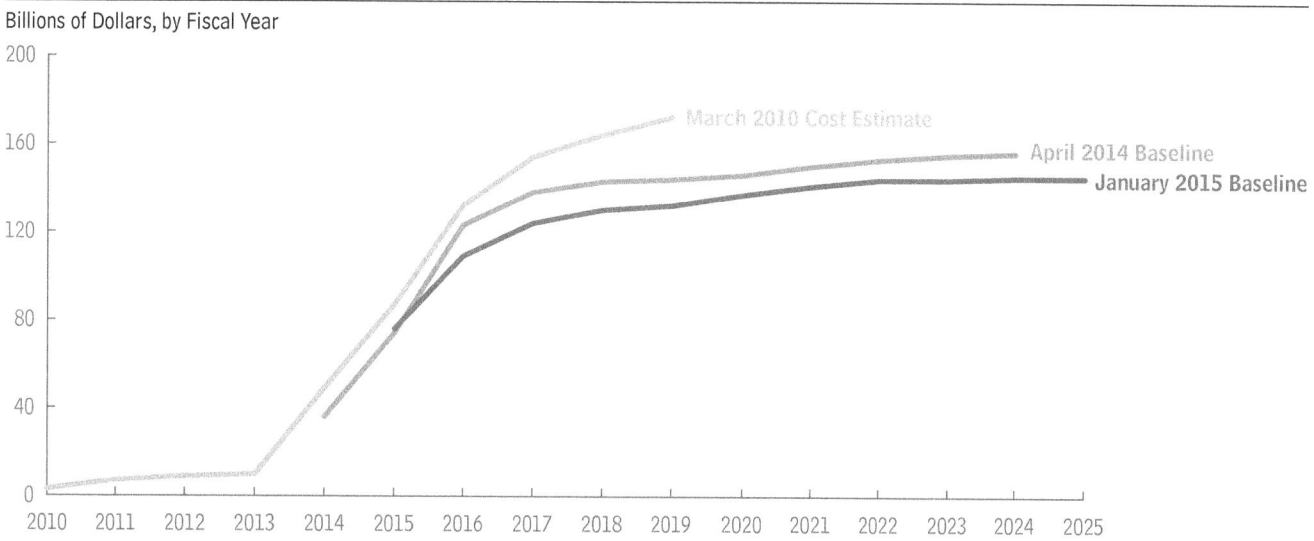

Sources: Congressional Budget Office; staff of the Joint Committee on Taxation.

Note: These numbers exclude effects on the deficit of provisions of the Affordable Care Act that are not related to insurance coverage and effects on discretionary spending of the coverage provisions.

would cost the federal government $710 billion during fiscal years 2015 through 2019 (the last year of the 10-year projection period used in that estimate). The newest projections indicate that those provisions will cost $571 billion over that same period, a reduction of 20 percent. For 2019, for example, CBO and JCT projected in March 2010 that the ACA's insurance coverage provisions would have a net federal cost of $172 billion; the current projections show a cost of $132 billion—a reduction of $40 billion, or 23 percent.

The downward revision since March 2010 to CBO and JCT's estimate of the net federal costs of the ACA's insurance coverage provisions (when measured on a year-by-year basis) is attributable to many factors: Changes in law, revisions to CBO's economic projections, the Supreme Court decision that made the expansion of eligibility for

Medicaid optional for states, administrative actions, new data, and numerous improvements in CBO and JCT's modeling have all affected the projections. Another notable influence on the downward revision to projected federal costs is the slowdown in the growth of health care costs that has been experienced by private insurers, as well as by the Medicare and Medicaid programs. Although views differ on how much of the slowdown is attributable to the recession and its aftermath and how much to other factors, the slower growth has been sufficiently broad and persistent to persuade the agencies to significantly lower their projections of federal health care spending. In particular, since early 2010, CBO and JCT have reduced their 2016 projections of both insurance premiums for policies purchased through the exchanges and Medicaid spending per beneficiary by between 10 percent and 15 percent.

How Changes in Economic Projections Might Affect Budget Projections

The federal budget is highly sensitive to economic conditions. Revenues depend on the amount of taxable income, including wages and salaries, other income received by individuals, and corporate profits. Those types of income generally rise or fall with overall economic activity, although not necessarily in proportion. Spending for many mandatory programs depends on inflation, either through explicit cost-of-living adjustments or in other ways. In addition, the U.S. Treasury regularly refinances portions of the government's outstanding debt—and issues more debt to finance new deficits—at market interest rates. Thus, the amount that the federal government spends for interest on its debt is directly tied to those rates.

To show how projections for the economy can affect projections of the federal budget, the Congressional Budget Office has constructed simplified "rules of thumb." The rules provide a rough sense of how differences in individual economic variables, taken in isolation, would affect the budget totals; they are not, however, substitutes for a full analysis of the implications of alternative economic forecasts.

The rules of thumb have been developed for three variables:

■ Growth of real (inflation-adjusted) gross domestic product (GDP),

■ Interest rates, and

■ Inflation.

All three rules of thumb reflect alternative assumptions about economic conditions beginning in January 2015.

CBO's rule of thumb for the growth of real GDP shows the effects of growth rates that are 0.1 percentage point lower each year than the rates that underlie the agency's baseline budget projections. (The budget projections are summarized in Chapter 1, and the economic projections are described in Chapter 2.) The rule of thumb for interest rates shows the effects of rates that are 1 percentage point higher each year than the rates used in the baseline; because inflation is held equal to its baseline projection in this rule of thumb, the results show the effects of higher real interest rates. Finally, the rule of thumb for inflation shows the effects of inflation that is 1 percentage point higher each year than projected in the baseline.

Each rule of thumb is roughly symmetrical. Thus, if instead economic growth was 0.1 percentage point higher than in CBO's baseline, or if interest rates or inflation were 1 percentage point lower, the effects would be about the same as those shown here, but with the opposite sign.[1]

CBO chose variations of 0.1 percentage point and 1 percentage point solely for simplicity. Those differences do not necessarily indicate the extent to which actual economic performance might differ from CBO's projections. For example, although the rule of thumb for real GDP growth shows the effects of a difference of 0.1 percentage point, the standard deviation of the 10-year average of growth rates for real GDP is 0.7 percentage points.[2] And

---

1. Interest rates on short-term Treasury securities could not be much lower in the near term. Those rates are currently near zero, and CBO does not project them to rise much until fiscal year 2016.

2. Standard deviation is a conventional measure of variability. In the case of real GDP growth, CBO calculated the extent to which actual growth over 10-year periods differed from the post–World War II average. The standard deviation is the size of the difference that was exceeded about one-third of the time.

although the rules of thumb for real interest rates and inflation show the effects of a difference of 1 percentage point, the standard deviations of the 10-year averages of real interest rates for 10-year Treasury notes and inflation are 1.5 and 2.1 percentage points, respectively.

Lower Real Growth

Stronger economic growth improves the budget's bottom line, and weaker growth worsens it. The first rule of thumb illustrates the effects of economic growth that is slightly weaker than expected. A change in the rate of real economic growth could affect inflation, unemployment, and interest rates; however, CBO's rule of thumb does not include the effects of changes in those variables.

CBO's baseline includes real GDP growth of between 2.7 percent and 3.0 percent for the next three calendar years and an average of 2.1 percent from 2018 to 2025. If 0.1 percentage point was subtracted from each of those rates, by 2025 GDP would be roughly 1 percent smaller than the amount underlying CBO's baseline.

Slower GDP growth would have several effects on the budget. If growth was 0.1 percentage point lower per year, it would result in less growth in taxable income and thus lower tax revenues—$2 billion less in 2015 and $59 billion less in 2025 (see Table C-1). With a smaller amount of revenues, the federal government would need to borrow more and thus would incur higher interest costs. Additional payments to service federal debt would be very small during the first few years of the projection period but larger in later years, reaching $11 billion by 2025. Mandatory spending, however, would be only slightly affected by a decline in economic growth of that magnitude: Medicare outlays would be somewhat lower, but that decrease would be partially offset by higher outlays for the refundable portions of the earned income and child tax credits.[3]

---

3. Medicare's payment rates for physicians' services are computed using a formula that compares annual spending with a target amount that partly reflects the growth of GDP. Slower GDP growth leads to a lower target and therefore to smaller Medicare payments to physicians. Tax credits reduce a taxpayer's income tax liability; if a refundable credit exceeds a taxpayer's other liability, all or a portion of the excess is refunded to the taxpayer and recorded as an outlay in the budget.

All told, if growth of real GDP each year was 0.1 percentage point lower than in CBO's baseline projections, annual deficits would be larger by amounts that would climb to $69 billion by 2025. The cumulative deficit for 2016 through 2025 would be $326 billion higher.

Higher Interest Rates

The second rule of thumb illustrates the sensitivity of the budget to changes in interest rates, which affect the flow of interest payments to and from the federal government. When the budget is in deficit, the Treasury must borrow additional funds from the public to cover the shortfall. Moreover, each year the Treasury refinances a substantial portion of the nation's outstanding debt at market interest rates. Those rates also help determine how much the Federal Reserve remits to the Treasury.

If interest rates on all types of Treasury securities were 1 percentage point higher each year through 2025 than projected in the baseline and all other economic variables were unchanged, the government's interest costs would be substantially larger. The difference would amount to only $12 billion in 2015 because most marketable government debt is in the form of securities that have maturities greater than one year. As the Treasury replaced maturing securities, however, the budgetary effects of higher interest rates would mount, climbing to an additional $198 billion in 2025 under this scenario (see Table C-1).

As part of its conduct of monetary policy, the Federal Reserve buys and sells Treasury securities and other securities, including, over the past few years, a large amount of mortgage-backed securities. The Federal Reserve also pays interest on reserves (deposits that banks hold at the central bank). The interest that the Federal Reserve earns on its portfolio of securities and the interest that it pays on reserves affect its remittances to the Treasury, which are counted as revenues. If all interest rates were 1 percentage point higher for the coming decade than CBO projects, the Federal Reserve's remittances would be lower for a number of years because higher interest payments on reserves would outstrip additional interest earnings on its portfolio. However, over time, the current holdings in the portfolio would mature and be replaced with higher-yielding investments; CBO projects that by 2023 the Federal Reserve's remittances would be higher if projected interest rates were higher. Overall, rates that were 1 percentage point higher than in CBO's baseline would

Table C-1.

How Selected Economic Changes Might Affect CBO's Baseline Budget Projections

Billions of Dollars

	2015	2016	2017	2018	2019	2020	2021	2022	2023	2024	2025	Total 2016-2020	Total 2016-2025
Growth Rate of Real GDP Is 0.1 Percentage Point Lower per Year													
Change in Revenues	-2	-5	-9	-14	-19	-24	-30	-36	-43	-50	-59	-71	-288
Change in Outlays													
Mandatory spending	*	*	*	*	*	*	*	-1	-1	-1	-1	*	-4
Debt service	*	*	*	1	2	2	4	5	7	9	11	5	41
Total	*	*	*	1	1	2	3	4	6	8	10	5	37
Change in the Deficit[a]	**-2**	**-5**	**-9**	**-14**	**-20**	**-26**	**-33**	**-41**	**-49**	**-59**	**-69**	**-75**	**-326**
Interest Rates Are 1 Percentage Point Higher per Year													
Change in Revenues	-23	-28	-24	-17	-15	-9	-6	-3	1	3	5	-93	-93
Change in Outlays													
Higher interest rates	12	40	66	92	112	131	146	161	175	188	198	440	1,307
Debt service	*	2	5	11	18	26	35	45	56	68	79	63	345
Total	12	42	71	103	130	157	181	206	230	256	277	503	1,653
Change in the Deficit[a]	**-35**	**-70**	**-95**	**-120**	**-145**	**-166**	**-187**	**-209**	**-230**	**-253**	**-272**	**-596**	**-1,745**
Inflation Is 1 Percentage Point Higher per Year													
Change in Revenues	-6	21	63	109	155	208	264	323	388	459	536	555	2,526
Change in Outlays													
Discretionary spending[b]	0	1	1	2	3	4	5	13	24	36	50	11	139
Mandatory spending	3	15	34	57	86	116	150	191	229	270	325	308	1,473
Higher interest rates[c]	17	54	83	112	135	157	175	194	210	228	241	540	1,589
Debt service	*	2	4	7	11	15	20	24	30	35	40	39	188
Total	20	72	122	178	235	292	350	422	493	569	656	899	3,389
Change in the Deficit[a]	**-27**	**-50**	**-60**	**-70**	**-80**	**-85**	**-86**	**-99**	**-104**	**-110**	**-120**	**-344**	**-863**
Memorandum:													
Deficit in CBO's January 2015 Baseline	-468	-467	-489	-540	-652	-739	-814	-948	-953	-951	-1,088	-2,887	-7,641

Source: Congressional Budget Office.

Note: GDP = gross domestic product; * = between -$500 million and $500 million.

a.   Negative numbers indicate an increase in the deficit.

b.   Most discretionary spending through 2021 is governed by caps established by the Budget Control Act of 2011; in CBO's baseline, that spending would not be affected by changes in projected inflation.

c.   The change in outlays attributable to higher interest rates in this scenario differs from the estimate in the scenario for interest rates because the principal of inflation-protected securities issued by the Treasury grows with inflation.

(holding all else equal) cause revenues to be $93 billion lower between 2016 and 2025.

The larger deficits generated by the increase in interest rates would require the Treasury to borrow more than is projected in the baseline. That extra borrowing would

raise the cost of servicing the debt by amounts that would reach $79 billion in 2025.

All told, if interest rates were 1 percentage point higher than projected in CBO's baseline, the deficit would worsen progressively over the projection period by amounts increasing from $35 billion in 2015 to $272 billion in 2025. The cumulative deficit would be $1.7 trillion higher over the 2016–2025 period.

Higher Inflation

The third rule of thumb shows the budgetary effects of inflation that is 1 percentage point higher than is projected in CBO's baseline—with no differences in other economic variables except for interest rates, as described below. Although higher inflation increases both revenues and outlays, the net effect would be substantially larger budget deficits.

Larger increases in prices generally lead to greater wages, profits, and other income, which in turn generate larger collections of individual income taxes, payroll taxes, and corporate income taxes. The parameters in the individual income tax system that affect most taxpayers—including the income thresholds for both the regular and alternative minimum tax brackets, the standard deduction, and personal exemptions—are indexed for inflation. Therefore, the share of taxpayers' income taxed at certain rates does not change very much when income is higher because of higher inflation, so tax collections tend to rise roughly proportionally with income under those circumstances. However, some parameters of the individual income tax system are not indexed for inflation: For example, the income thresholds for the surtax on investment income are fixed in nominal dollars, so if income was higher because of higher inflation, the surtax would apply to a larger share of taxpayers' income.

For the payroll tax, rates are mostly the same across income levels, and the maximum amount of earnings subject to the Social Security tax rises with average wages in the economy, which generally rise more when inflation is higher; therefore, higher inflation leads to an increase in revenues that is roughly proportional to the increase in earnings. Similarly, because the brackets under the corporate income tax are not indexed for inflation and nearly all corporate profits are taxed at the top rate, an increase in profits due to higher inflation generates a roughly proportional increase in corporate tax revenues.

Higher inflation also increases the cost of many mandatory spending programs. Benefits for many mandatory programs are automatically adjusted each year to reflect increases in prices. Specifically, benefits paid for Social Security, federal employees' retirement programs,

Supplemental Security Income, disability compensation for veterans, the Supplemental Nutrition Assistance Program, and child nutrition programs, among others, are adjusted (with a lag) for changes in the consumer price index or one of its components. Many of Medicare's payment rates also are adjusted annually for inflation. Spending for some other programs, such as Medicaid, is not formally indexed to price changes but tends to grow with inflation because the costs of providing benefits under those programs increase as prices rise. In addition, to the extent that initial benefit payments to participants in retirement and disability programs are linked to wages, increases in nominal wages resulting from higher inflation boost future outlays for those programs.

Higher inflation would raise CBO's baseline projections of future spending for discretionary programs, but only by a small amount. The Budget Control Act of 2011 (Public Law 112-25), as modified by subsequent legislation, imposes caps on most discretionary budget authority through 2021, and CBO's baseline incorporates the assumption that appropriations for most purposes will be equal to those caps. Higher inflation would not alter those caps and thus would have no effect on CBO's projections of those appropriations.

However, higher inflation would raise other projected appropriations for two reasons. First, the law specifies that the caps may be adjusted to accommodate appropriations for certain purposes. In 2015, those adjustments include $74 billion designated for overseas contingency operations, $6 billion in funding provided for disaster relief, $5 billion in emergency funding for responding to the outbreak of the Ebola virus, and $1.5 billion for initiatives aimed at enhancing program integrity by reducing improper payments from certain benefit programs. CBO's baseline extrapolates the funding provided for those purposes in future years on the basis of the 2015 amount with adjustments for inflation; if inflation was 1 percentage point higher, projected outlays from such funding would increase by $48 billion between 2016 and 2025. Second, CBO's baseline projections incorporate the assumption that the discretionary funding that is capped through 2021 will increase thereafter with inflation (from the amount of the cap in 2021); inflation that was 1 percentage point higher than in the baseline would boost projected outlays in those years by a total of $92 billion.

Although the caps on discretionary appropriations are not indexed for inflation, higher inflation would diminish the amount of goods that could be acquired and the benefits and services that could be provided under those fixed caps. If, over time, higher inflation led lawmakers to adjust the discretionary caps, the impact on spending would be greater and the net impact on the deficit would be more severe.

Inflation also has an impact on outlays for net interest because it affects interest rates. If inflation was 1 percentage point higher than CBO projects, for example, then interest rates would be 1 percentage point higher (all else being equal). As a result, new federal borrowing would incur higher interest costs, and outstanding inflation-indexed securities would be more costly for the federal government. In addition, higher interest rates would first reduce and then increase revenues from the Federal Reserve's remittances to the Treasury, as explained above.

If inflation each year was 1 percentage point higher than the rate underlying CBO's baseline, total revenues and outlays over the 10-year period would be about 6 percent and 7 percent greater, respectively, than in the baseline. Over the 2016–2025 period, the deficit would be $863 billion higher (see Table C-1).

The Effects of Automatic Stabilizers on the Federal Budget as of 2015

During recessions, federal tax liabilities and, therefore, federal revenues automatically shrink because of the reductions in the taxable income of individuals and corporations that accompany downturns in the economy's total output of goods and services. In addition, some federal outlays—payments of unemployment benefits, for example—automatically increase in a recession. Such reductions in tax collections and increases in outlays help bolster economic activity during downturns—thus they are known as automatic stabilizers—but they also temporarily boost budget deficits. By contrast, when real (inflation-adjusted) output—the nation's gross domestic product (GDP)—moves closer to the economy's maximum sustainable output (called potential GDP), revenues automatically rise and outlays automatically fall. Under those circumstances, automatic stabilizers provide less of a boost to economic activity. (In both cases, the effects of automatic stabilizers are additional to the effects of any legislated changes in tax and spending policies.)

The Congressional Budget Office uses statistical techniques to estimate the automatic effects of cyclical movements in real output and unemployment on federal revenues and outlays and, thus, on federal budget deficits. According to CBO's estimates, automatic stabilizers added significantly to the budget deficit—and thereby substantially strengthened economic activity relative to what it would have been otherwise—in fiscal years 2009 through 2014. On the basis of CBO's economic and budgetary projections under current law, the agency expects that automatic stabilizers will continue to add significantly to the budget deficit and to support economic activity in 2015 but to decline in size in 2016 and 2017 as the economy strengthens further. For the period from 2018 to 2025, CBO projects that GDP will fall slightly short of potential GDP, on average, which causes the automatic stabilizers to add small amounts to the projected budget deficit during those years. (See Chapter 2 for a discussion of CBO's economic projections for the next 10 years.)

How Large Were the Budgetary Effects of Automatic Stabilizers Last Year?

In fiscal year 2014, automatic stabilizers added $192 billion to the federal budget deficit, an amount equal to 1.1 percent of potential GDP, according to CBO's analysis (see Table D-1 and Table D-2).[1] That outcome marked the sixth consecutive year that automatic stabilizers added to the deficit by more than 1 percent of potential GDP—the longest such period over the past 50 years (see Figure D-1 on page 142). (The estimated sizes of the automatic stabilizers in different years are presented as percentages of potential rather than actual GDP because potential GDP excludes fluctuations that are attributable to the business cycle.)[2]

---

1. CBO's estimates of the automatic stabilizers reflect the assumption that discretionary spending and interest payments do not respond automatically to the business cycle. For a description of a methodology for estimating automatic stabilizers that is similar to CBO's methodology, see Darrel Cohen and Glenn Follette, "The Automatic Fiscal Stabilizers: Quietly Doing Their Thing," *Economic Policy Review*, Federal Reserve Bank of New York, vol. 6, no. 1 (April 2000), pp. 35–68, http://tinyurl.com/pcxcohz. See also Glenn Follette and Byron Lutz, *Fiscal Policy in the United States: Automatic Stabilizers, Discretionary Fiscal Policy Actions, and the Economy*, Finance and Economics Discussion Series Paper 2010–43 (Board of Governors of the Federal Reserve System, June 2010), http://tinyurl.com/nl6qc6e.

2. For CBO's previous estimates of the automatic stabilizers, see Congressional Budget Office, *The Budget and Economic Outlook: 2014 to 2024* (February 2014), Appendix E, www.cbo.gov/publication/45010. Revisions to estimates since that publication stem from the July 2014 annual revision of the national income and product accounts by the Bureau of Economic Analysis, changes to CBO's economic estimates and projections, and technical improvements in CBO's approach to estimating the automatic stabilizers.

Table D-1.

Deficit or Surplus With and Without CBO's Estimate of Automatic Stabilizers, and Related Estimates, in Billions of Dollars

	Deficit (-) or Surplus With Automatic Stabilizers	− Automatic Stabilizers	= Deficit (-) or Surplus Without Automatic Stabilizers	Revenues and Outlays Without Automatic Stabilizers		GDP Gap[a]	Unemployment Gap (Percent)[b]
				Revenues	Outlays		
1965	-1	4	-5	114	119	10	-0.7
1966	-4	11	-15	122	137	35	-1.7
1967	-9	11	-20	141	161	34	-2.0
1968	-25	10	-36	146	182	31	-2.0
1969	3	13	-10	178	188	36	-2.4
1970	-3	6	-9	191	200	12	-1.9
1971	-23	-4	-19	192	211	-10	-0.2
1972	-23	-2	-21	210	231	-2	-0.1
1973	-15	11	-26	222	248	39	-0.9
1974	-6	10	-16	257	273	24	-1.2
1975	-53	-20	-33	297	330	-63	1.2
1976	-74	-26	-48	317	365	-60	1.8
1977	-54	-15	-39	366	404	-37	1.1
1978	-59	-1	-58	400	458	-7	*
1979	-41	7	-48	458	506	9	-0.4
1980	-74	-21	-53	536	589	-68	0.6
1981	-79	-33	-46	624	670	-74	1.2
1982	-128	-78	-50	677	727	-210	3.0
1983	-208	-104	-104	673	777	-249	4.1
1984	-185	-34	-151	689	840	-92	1.8
1985	-212	-12	-200	740	940	-47	1.2
1986	-221	-9	-212	772	985	-34	1.0
1987	-150	-14	-136	866	1,001	-50	0.4
1988	-155	4	-159	907	1,066	5	-0.3
1989	-153	19	-172	976	1,148	47	-0.7
1990	-221	9	-230	1,026	1,256	16	-0.5
1991	-269	-57	-212	1,107	1,319	-177	0.8
1992	-290	-73	-217	1,152	1,369	-185	1.7
1993	-255	-67	-188	1,209	1,397	-174	1.5
1994	-203	-51	-153	1,301	1,454	-130	0.9
1995	-164	-40	-124	1,389	1,513	-122	0.3
1996	-107	-40	-68	1,490	1,558	-113	0.2
1997	-22	-3	-19	1,588	1,606	-16	*
1998	69	25	44	1,702	1,658	63	-0.5
1999	126	72	54	1,764	1,710	191	-0.7

Continued

Table D-1. Continued

Deficit or Surplus With and Without CBO's Estimate of Automatic Stabilizers, and Related Estimates, in Billions of Dollars

	Deficit (-) or Surplus With Automatic Stabilizers	− Automatic Stabilizers =	Deficit (-) or Surplus Without Automatic Stabilizers	Revenues and Outlays Without Automatic Stabilizers		GDP Gap[a]	Unemployment Gap (Percent)[b]
				Revenues	Outlays		
2000	236	115	121	1,923	1,802	295	-1.0
2001	128	57	71	1,944	1,873	101	-0.7
2002	-158	-44	-114	1,890	2,004	-139	0.7
2003	-378	-94	-284	1,862	2,146	-266	1.0
2004	-413	-55	-357	1,923	2,281	-132	0.6
2005	-318	-15	-303	2,164	2,467	-30	0.2
2006	-248	11	-259	2,399	2,658	19	-0.3
2007	-161	-7	-154	2,583	2,737	-58	-0.5
2008	-459	-70	-389	2,592	2,980	-249	0.3
2009	-1,413	-320	-1,093	2,365	3,458	-1,012	3.5
2010	-1,294	-373	-921	2,443	3,364	-944	4.6
2011	-1,300	-336	-964	2,550	3,514	-857	3.9
2012	-1,087	-272	-815	2,650	3,465	-713	3.0
2013	-680	-247	-432	2,968	3,400	-662	2.1
2014	-483	-192	-291	3,183	3,474	-522	1.0
2015	-468	-124	-343	3,303	3,646	-353	0.2
2016	-467	-61	-406	3,518	3,923	-164	0.1
2017	-489	-19	-470	3,606	4,075	-49	*
2018	-540	-13	-527	3,727	4,254	-40	*
2019	-652	-33	-620	3,893	4,513	-91	0.2
2020	-739	-43	-696	4,062	4,758	-108	0.2
2021	-814	-46	-768	4,242	5,010	-113	0.2
2022	-948	-47	-901	4,428	5,329	-117	0.2
2023	-953	-49	-904	4,631	5,536	-122	0.2
2024	-951	-51	-900	4,846	5,745	-127	0.2
2025	-1,088	-53	-1,034	5,073	6,108	-132	0.2

Sources: Congressional Budget Office; Office of Management and Budget.

Notes: Automatic stabilizers are automatic changes in revenues and outlays that are attributable to cyclical movements in real (inflation-adjusted) output and unemployment.

Shaded amounts are actual deficits or surpluses.

GDP = gross domestic product; * = between -0.05 percent and 0.05 percent.

a. The GDP gap equals actual or projected GDP minus CBO's estimate of potential GDP (the maximum sustainable output of the economy).

b. The unemployment gap equals the actual or projected rate of unemployment minus the underlying long-term rate of unemployment.

Table D-2.

Deficit or Surplus With and Without CBO's Estimate of Automatic Stabilizers, and Related Estimates, as a Percentage of Potential Gross Domestic Product

	Deficit (-) or Surplus With Automatic Stabilizers	− Automatic Stabilizers	= Deficit (-) or Surplus Without Automatic Stabilizers	Revenues and Outlays Without Automatic Stabilizers		GDP Gap[a]	Unemployment Gap (Percent)[b]
				Revenues	Outlays		
1965	-0.2	0.5	-0.7	16.3	17.0	1.5	-0.7
1966	-0.5	1.5	-1.9	16.4	18.3	4.7	-1.7
1967	-1.1	1.4	-2.5	17.5	20.0	4.3	-2.0
1968	-2.9	1.2	-4.1	16.8	20.9	3.6	-2.0
1969	0.3	1.4	-1.1	18.8	19.9	3.8	-2.4
1970	-0.3	0.6	-0.8	18.4	19.3	1.1	-1.9
1971	-2.0	-0.3	-1.7	17.0	18.7	-0.8	-0.2
1972	-1.9	-0.2	-1.7	17.2	18.9	-0.2	-0.1
1973	-1.1	0.9	-2.0	16.8	18.8	2.9	-0.9
1974	-0.4	0.7	-1.1	17.6	18.7	1.6	-1.2
1975	-3.2	-1.2	-2.0	17.7	19.7	-3.8	1.2
1976	-4.0	-1.4	-2.6	17.1	19.7	-3.2	1.8
1977	-2.6	-0.7	-1.9	17.7	19.6	-1.8	1.1
1978	-2.6	*	-2.6	17.5	20.1	-0.3	*
1979	-1.6	0.3	-1.9	17.9	19.8	0.3	-0.4
1980	-2.6	-0.7	-1.9	18.7	20.5	-2.4	0.6
1981	-2.5	-1.0	-1.4	19.4	20.9	-2.3	1.2
1982	-3.6	-2.2	-1.4	19.2	20.6	-6.0	3.0
1983	-5.5	-2.7	-2.7	17.8	20.5	-6.6	4.1
1984	-4.6	-0.8	-3.7	17.0	20.8	-2.3	1.8
1985	-4.9	-0.3	-4.6	17.1	21.8	-1.1	1.2
1986	-4.8	-0.2	-4.6	16.9	21.6	-0.7	1.0
1987	-3.1	-0.3	-2.8	17.9	20.7	-1.0	0.4
1988	-3.0	0.1	-3.1	17.6	20.7	0.1	-0.3
1989	-2.8	0.3	-3.1	17.7	20.8	0.8	-0.7
1990	-3.7	0.2	-3.9	17.4	21.3	0.3	-0.5
1991	-4.3	-0.9	-3.4	17.6	21.0	-2.8	0.8
1992	-4.4	-1.1	-3.3	17.4	20.7	-2.8	1.7
1993	-3.7	-1.0	-2.7	17.3	20.0	-2.5	1.5
1994	-2.8	-0.7	-2.1	17.8	19.8	-1.8	0.9
1995	-2.1	-0.5	-1.6	18.0	19.6	-1.6	0.3
1996	-1.3	-0.5	-0.8	18.4	19.3	-1.4	0.2
1997	-0.3	*	-0.2	18.7	18.9	-0.2	*
1998	0.8	0.3	0.5	19.1	18.6	0.7	-0.5
1999	1.3	0.8	0.6	18.9	18.4	2.1	-0.7

Continued

Table D-2.   Continued

Deficit or Surplus With and Without CBO's Estimate of Automatic Stabilizers, and Related Estimates, as a Percentage of Potential Gross Domestic Product

	Deficit (-) or Surplus With Automatic Stabilizers	− Automatic Stabilizers	= Deficit (-) or Surplus Without Automatic Stabilizers	Revenues and Outlays Without Automatic Stabilizers		GDP Gap[a]	Unemployment Gap (Percent)[b]
				Revenues	Outlays		
2000	2.4	1.2	1.2	19.5	18.3	3.0	-1.0
2001	1.2	0.5	0.7	18.6	17.9	1.0	-0.7
2002	-1.4	-0.4	-1.0	17.2	18.2	-1.3	0.7
2003	-3.3	-0.8	-2.4	16.1	18.5	-2.3	1.0
2004	-3.4	-0.5	-2.9	15.7	18.7	-1.1	0.6
2005	-2.5	-0.1	-2.3	16.7	19.1	-0.2	0.2
2006	-1.8	0.1	-1.9	17.6	19.5	0.1	-0.3
2007	-1.1	*	-1.1	18.0	19.0	-0.4	-0.5
2008	-3.1	-0.5	-2.6	17.3	19.9	-1.7	0.3
2009	-9.2	-2.1	-7.1	15.3	22.4	-6.6	3.5
2010	-8.2	-2.4	-5.9	15.5	21.4	-6.0	4.6
2011	-8.0	-2.1	-5.9	15.7	21.6	-5.3	3.9
2012	-6.5	-1.6	-4.9	15.8	20.7	-4.3	3.0
2013	-3.9	-1.4	-2.5	17.2	19.7	-3.8	2.1
2014	-2.7	-1.1	-1.6	17.9	19.5	-2.9	1.0
2015	-2.5	-0.7	-1.9	18.0	19.8	-1.9	0.2
2016	-2.5	-0.3	-2.1	18.5	20.7	-0.9	0.1
2017	-2.5	-0.1	-2.4	18.3	20.6	-0.2	*
2018	-2.6	-0.1	-2.6	18.1	20.7	-0.2	*
2019	-3.0	-0.2	-2.9	18.1	21.0	-0.4	0.2
2020	-3.3	-0.2	-3.1	18.1	21.2	-0.5	0.2
2021	-3.5	-0.2	-3.3	18.1	21.4	-0.5	0.2
2022	-3.9	-0.2	-3.7	18.2	21.9	-0.5	0.2
2023	-3.8	-0.2	-3.6	18.2	21.8	-0.5	0.2
2024	-3.6	-0.2	-3.4	18.3	21.7	-0.5	0.2
2025	-3.9	-0.2	-3.7	18.4	22.1	-0.5	0.2

Sources: Congressional Budget Office; Office of Management and Budget.

Notes: Automatic stabilizers are automatic changes in revenues and outlays that are attributable to cyclical movements in real (inflation-adjusted) output and unemployment.

Shaded amounts are actual deficits or surpluses.

GDP = gross domestic product; * = between -0.05 percent and 0.05 percent.

a. The GDP gap equals the difference between actual or projected GDP and CBO's estimate of potential GDP (the maximum sustainable output of the economy, expressed as a percentage of potential GDP).

b. The unemployment gap equals the actual or projected rate of unemployment minus the underlying long-term rate of unemployment.

Figure D-1.

Contribution of Automatic Stabilizers to Budget Deficits and Surpluses

Percentage of Potential Gross Domestic Product

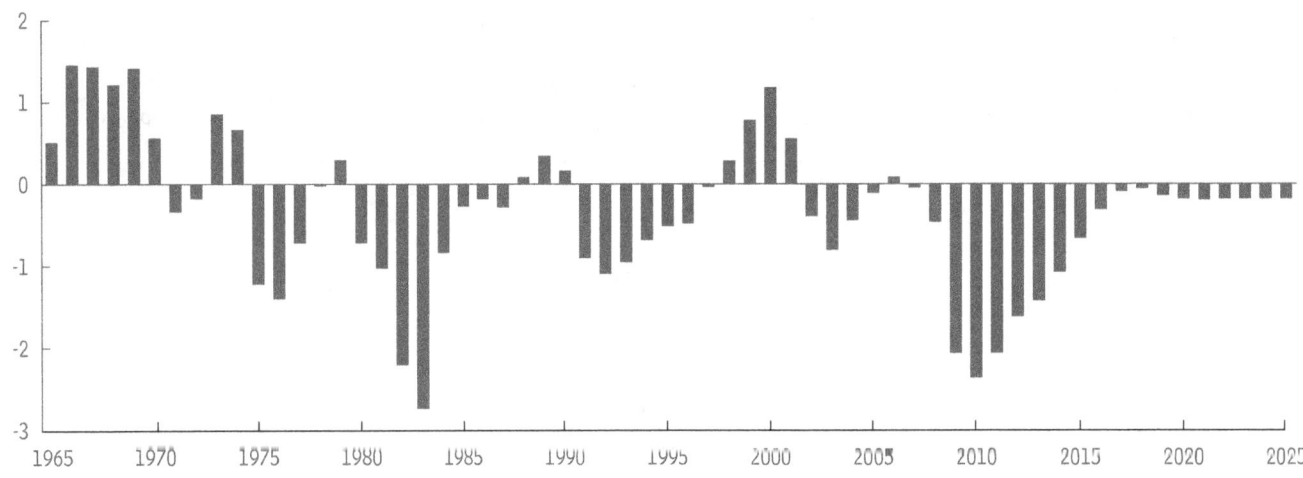

Sources: Congressional Budget Office; Office of Management and Budget.

Notes: Automatic stabilizers are automatic changes in revenues and outlays that are attributable to cyclical movements in real (inflation-adjusted) output and unemployment.

Potential gross domestic product is CBO's estimate of the maximum sustainable output of the economy.

How Large Will the Budgetary Effects of Automatic Stabilizers Be Over the Next Decade?

According to CBO's projections under current law, the contribution of automatic stabilizers to the federal budget deficit will fall to 0.7 percent of potential GDP in fiscal year 2015. That amount accounts for a bit more than a quarter of the estimated deficit this year, just a little below the average share between 2009 and 2014.

CBO expects that the budgetary effects of automatic stabilizers will be significant this year but smaller than in the six preceding years because of the continued—albeit diminishing—weakness in the economy. Specifically, CBO projects that the gap between actual and potential GDP will amount to about 2 percent of potential GDP in fiscal year 2015, compared with roughly 3 percent in 2014 and more than 5 percent, on average, for the period from 2009 through 2013.

The contribution of the automatic stabilizers to the budget deficit is projected to fall further in 2016 and 2017— to 0.3 percent and then to 0.1 percent of potential GDP—as the output gap continues to narrow. That contribution is then projected to remain at 0.1 percent of

potential GDP in 2018, before settling at 0.2 percent of potential GDP in 2019 and later years.[3] CBO projects that GDP will be one-half of a percent below potential GDP, on average, during the 2020–2025 period (although in any particular year the gap could be larger or smaller than one-half of a percent).[4] As a result, the automatic stabilizers are estimated to continue to add to budget deficits in those years.

How Large Will Budget Deficits Without Automatic Stabilizers Be Over the Next Decade?

The federal budget deficit or surplus with the effects of automatic stabilizers filtered out is an estimate of what the deficit or surplus would be if GDP was at its potential, the unemployment rate was at its underlying

---

3. The estimated budgetary impact of automatic stabilizers is smaller in 2017 and 2018 than in subsequent years because CBO projects that the GDP gap will temporarily be narrower than it will be, on average, in later years.

4. That difference is based on CBO's estimate that output has been that much lower than potential output, on average, over the period from 1961 to 2009. For further discussion, see Chapter 2.

Figure D-2.

Budget Deficits and Surpluses With and Without Automatic Stabilizers

The estimated deficit without automatic stabilizers has tended to increase during recessions and early in recoveries in part as a result of legislation enacted to boost the economy.

Percentage of Potential Gross Domestic Product

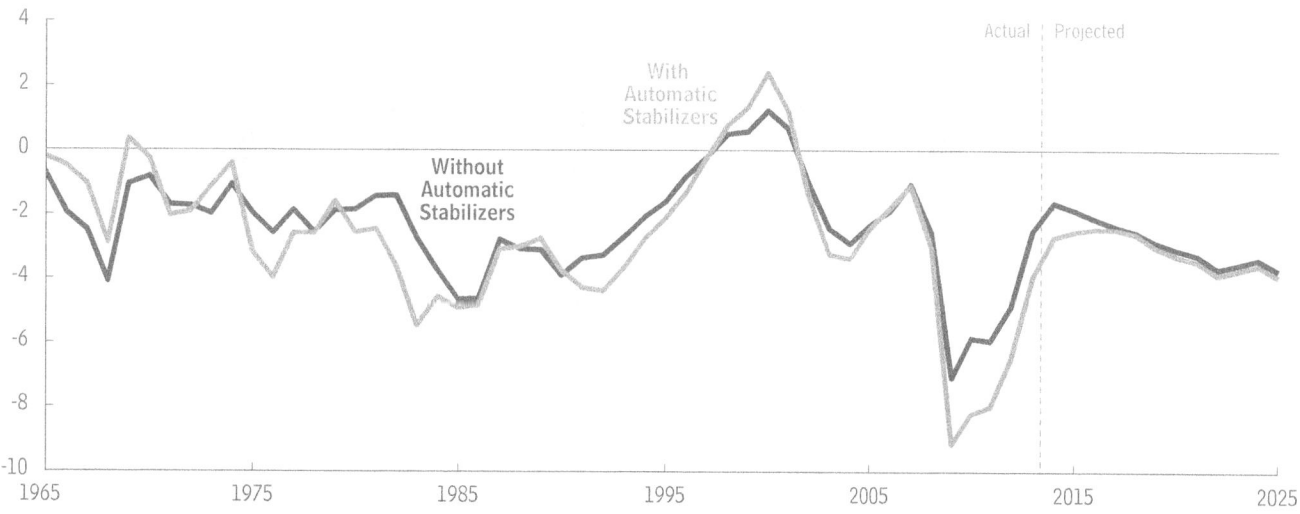

Sources: Congressional Budget Office; Office of Management and Budget.

Notes: Automatic stabilizers are automatic changes in revenues and outlays that are attributable to cyclical movements in real (inflation-adjusted) output and unemployment.

Potential gross domestic product is CBO's estimate of the maximum sustainable output of the economy.

long-term rate, and all other factors were unchanged. (The budget deficit without automatic stabilizers also has been called the cyclically adjusted or structural deficit.) That measure, when compared with the budget deficit with automatic stabilizers, is useful for analysts who wish to evaluate the extent to which changes in the budget deficit or surplus are caused by cyclical developments in the economy and thus are likely to prove temporary rather than enduring.

Under current law, CBO projects, the budget deficit without automatic stabilizers will equal 1.9 percent of potential GDP in fiscal year 2015, up from 1.6 percent in 2014, but still well below the values in the period from 2008 through 2013 (see Figure D-2). The increase between 2014 and 2015 results from a projected rise in outlays without automatic stabilizers relative to potential GDP. That rise can be attributed primarily to an increase in the estimated cost of the insurance coverage provisions of the Affordable Care Act that outweighs the declines relative to potential GDP that are anticipated for discretionary outlays and interest payments.

For the decade after 2015, CBO projects ongoing increases in the budget deficit without automatic stabilizers: By 2025, the projected budget deficit without automatic stabilizers equals 3.7 percent of potential GDP. (Small declines projected for 2023 and 2024 are the result of shifts in the timing of certain payments that occur when scheduled payment dates fall on weekends or holidays.) Essentially all of the anticipated increase in the deficit without automatic stabilizers between 2016 and 2025 under current law can be attributed to increases in mandatory spending without automatic stabilizers and in interest payments that are only partly offset by a decline in discretionary spending (all measured as a percentage of potential GDP).

Why Do Budget Deficits Appear Cyclical Even After the Estimated Effects of Automatic Stabilizers Are Filtered Out?

Despite adjustments to revenues and outlays for the estimated effects of the business cycle, the estimated deficit without automatic stabilizers exhibits movements that appear to be correlated with the business cycle. In particular, the estimated deficit without automatic stabilizers tends to increase during times of recession and early in a recovery.

That pattern probably reflects several factors. One factor is that estimates of the budgetary impact of automatic stabilizers may only partly remove the effects of certain changes (such as large fluctuations in the stock market) that have not had a sufficiently regular relationship to business cycles to be viewed as mostly cyclical. Another factor is that policymakers often choose to support a weak economy by cutting taxes or increasing government spending, both of which increase the deficit (or reduce

the surplus). Such responses to recessions and high unemployment require legislation, so their budgetary effects are not automatic, and they are not viewed as automatic stabilizers. During the past several years, for example, lawmakers have enacted the Tax Increase Prevention Act of 2014 (Public Law 113-295); the American Taxpayer Relief Act of 2012 (P.L. 112-240); the Tax Relief, Unemployment Insurance Reauthorization, and Job Creation Act of 2010 (P.L. 111-312); the American Recovery and Reinvestment Act of 2009 (P.L. 111-5); the Emergency Economic Stabilization Act of 2008 (P.L. 110-343); and the Housing and Economic Recovery Act of 2008 (P.L. 110-289).

Trust Funds

The federal government uses several accounting mechanisms to link earmarked receipts—money designated for a specific purpose—with corresponding expenditures. Those mechanisms include trust funds (such as the Social Security trust funds), special funds (such as the fund that the Department of Defense uses to finance its health care program for military retirees), and revolving funds (such as the Federal Employees' Group Life Insurance fund). When the receipts designated for those funds exceed the amounts needed for expenditures, the funds are credited with nonmarketable debt instruments known as Government Account Series (GAS) securities, which are issued by the Treasury. At the end of fiscal year 2014, there was $5.0 trillion in such securities outstanding, over 90 percent of which was held by trust funds.[1]

The federal budget has numerous trust funds, although most of the money credited to such funds goes to fewer than a dozen of them. By far the largest trust funds are the Social Security Old-Age and Survivors Insurance Trust Fund, Medicare's Hospital Insurance Trust Fund, and the funds dedicated to the government's retirement programs for its military and civilian personnel (see Table E-1).

Ordinarily, when a trust fund receives cash that is not needed immediately to pay benefits or cover other expenses, the Treasury issues GAS securities in that amount to the fund and then uses the extra income to reduce the amount of new federal borrowing that is necessary to finance the governmentwide deficit. In other words, in the absence of changes to other tax and spend-

ing policies, the government borrows less from the public than it would without that extra net income. The reverse happens when revenues for a trust fund program fall short of expenses.

The balance of a trust fund at any given time is a measure of the historical relationship between the related program's receipts and expenditures. That balance (in the form of government securities) is an asset for the individual program, such as Social Security, but a liability for the rest of the government. The resources required to redeem a trust fund's government securities—and thereby pay for benefits or other spending—in some future year must be generated through taxes, income from other government sources, or borrowing from the public in that year. Trust funds have an important legal meaning in that their balances are a measure of the amounts that the government has the legal authority to spend for certain purposes under current law, but they have little relevance in an economic or budgetary sense.

To assess how all federal activities, taken together, affect the economy and financial markets, it is useful to include the cash receipts and expenditures of trust funds in the budget totals along with the receipts and expenditures of other federal programs. Therefore, the Congressional Budget Office, the Office of Management and Budget, and other fiscal analysts generally focus on the total deficit in that "unified budget," which includes the transactions of trust funds.

According to CBO's current baseline projections, the balances held by federal trust funds will increase by $82 billion in fiscal year 2015. CBO projects that, in total, income credited to the trust funds will exceed outlays in each year from 2015 through 2020; however, in each year thereafter, spending from the trust funds is projected to exceed income by an increasing amount.

---

1. Debt issued in the form of government account securities is included in a measure of federal debt designated "gross debt." Because such debt is intragovernmental in nature, however, it is not included in the measure "debt held by the public." (For a discussion of different measures of federal debt, see Chapter 1.)

Table E-1.

Trust Fund Balances Projected in CBO's Baseline

Billions of Dollars

	Actual, 2014	2015	2016	2017	2018	2019	2020	2021	2022	2023	2024	2025
Social Security												
Old-Age and Survivors Insurance	2,713	2,763	2,802	2,826	2,828	2,806	2,755	2,676	2,566	2,422	2,239	2,012
Disability Insurance[a]	70	40	9	0	0	0	0	0	0	0	0	0
Subtotal	2,783	2,802	2,811	2,826	2,828	2,806	2,755	2,676	2,566	2,422	2,239	2,012
Medicare												
Hospital Insurance (Part A)	202	204	201	207	218	216	208	194	161	132	107	57
Supplementary Medical Insurance (Part B)	68	67	67	67	67	67	67	67	67	68	68	68
Subtotal	271	271	267	274	284	282	275	261	229	199	175	125
Military Retirement	483	533	592	670	759	850	947	1,052	1,159	1,278	1,411	1,547
Civilian Retirement[b]	876	895	910	927	943	959	976	992	1,008	1,024	1,041	1,057
Unemployment Insurance	29	37	41	44	45	45	48	53	57	60	62	65
Highway and Mass Transit[a]	15 [c]	1	0	0	0	0	0	0	0	0	0	0
Airport and Airway	13	12	11	11	12	12	13	15	17	19	21	24
Railroad Retirement (Treasury holdings)[d]	3	3	3	3	3	3	3	3	3	3	3	3
Other[e]	108	110	112	113	115	117	119	121	123	125	127	129
Total Trust Fund Balance	**4,581**	**4,662**	**4,747**	**4,869**	**4,989**	**5,074**	**5,136**	**5,173**	**5,161**	**5,130**	**5,078**	**4,963**
Memorandum:												
Railroad Retirement (Non-Treasury holdings)[d]	26	25	24	23	22	21	21	20	19	19	18	18

Source: Congressional Budget Office.

Note: These balances are for the end of the fiscal year and include only securities invested in Treasury holdings, unless otherwise noted.

a. In keeping with the rules in section 257 of the Deficit Control Act of 1985, CBO's baseline incorporates the assumption that scheduled payments will continue to be made in full after the balance of the trust fund has been exhausted, although there is no legal authority to make such payments. Because the manner by which those payments would continue would depend on future legislation, CBO shows zero rather than a cumulative negative balance in the trust fund after the exhaustion date.

b. Includes Civil Service Retirement, Foreign Service Retirement, and several smaller retirement trust funds.

c. Includes $4 billion in uninvested balances.

d. The Railroad Retirement and Survivors' Improvement Act of 2001 established the National Railroad Retirement Investment Trust, which is allowed to invest in non-Treasury securities, such as stocks and corporate bonds.

e. Consists primarily of trust funds for federal employees' health and life insurance, Superfund, and various insurance programs for veterans.

All told, CBO projects a cumulative net deficit of $219 billion over the 2016–2025 period (see Table E-2).

Some of the trust funds' income is in the form of intragovernmental transfers—which are projected to total $658 billion in 2015 and to reach nearly $1.1 trillion in 2025. Those transfers consist of interest credited to the trust funds; payments from general funds to cover most of the costs of Medicare's payments for outpatient services, prescription drugs, and some other services; the government's share of payments for federal employees' retirement; and certain other transfers of general funds.

Such transfers shift resources from one category of the budget to another, but they do not directly change the total deficit or the government's borrowing needs. With those intragovernmental transfers excluded and only income from sources outside of the government (such as payroll taxes and Medicare premiums) counted, the trust funds will add to federal deficits throughout the 2016–2025 period by amounts that grow from $596 billion in 2016 to $1.2 trillion in 2025, CBO projects.

Without legislative action to address shortfalls, balances in two trust funds are projected to be exhausted during

Table E-2.

Trust Fund Deficits or Surpluses Projected in CBO's Baseline

Billions of Dollars

	Actual, 2014	2015	2016	2017	2018	2019	2020	2021	2022	2023	2024	2025	Total 2016-2020	Total 2016-2025
Social Security														
Old-Age and Survivors Insurance	57	50	40	24	2	-22	-51	-79	-110	-145	-183	-227	-7	-750
Disability Insurance[a]	-31	-30	-30	-32	-34	-34	-35	-39	-42	-45	-49	-51	-165	-390
Subtotal	27	19	9	-7	-31	-57	-86	-118	-151	-189	-231	-278	-173	-1,141
Medicare														
Hospital Insurance (Part A)	-4	2	-3	7	10	-2	-7	-14	-33	-30	-25	-50	4	-147
Supplementary Medical Insurance (Part B)	1	-2	*	*	*	*	*	*	*	*	*	*	*	2
Subtotal	-3	*	-3	7	10	-2	-7	-14	-33	-29	-25	-50	5	-146
Military Retirement	62	50	59	78	89	91	97	105	107	119	133	136	414	1,013
Civilian Retirement[b]	138	19	16	17	16	16	16	16	16	16	17	17	81	163
Unemployment Insurance	6	7	4	3	1	0	3	6	3	3	2	3	11	29
Highway and Mass Transit[a]	9	-14	-14	-14	-14	-15	-16	-17	-18	-19	-20	-21	-73	-169
Airport and Airway	1	-1	*	*	*	1	1	1	2	2	3	3	2	13
Other[c]	4	2	2	1	1	2	2	2	2	2	2	2	8	19
Total Trust Fund Deficit (-) or Surplus	**244**	**82**	**72**	**85**	**73**	**36**	**10**	**-18**	**-72**	**-96**	**-121**	**-188**	**275**	**-219**
Intragovernmental Transfers to Trust Funds[d]	972	658	668	692	707	747	791	837	897	949	973	1,052	3,604	8,313
Net Budgetary Impact of Trust Fund Programs	**-728**	**-577**	**-596**	**-606**	**-635**	**-711**	**-781**	**-855**	**-969**	**-1,045**	**-1,094**	**-1,240**	**-3,329**	**-8,532**

Source: Congressional Budget Office.

Notes: Negative numbers indicate that the trust fund transactions add to total budget deficits.

   * = between -$500 million and $500 million.

a. CBO projects that the balance of this trust fund will be exhausted during the 2016–2025 period. However, in keeping with the rules in section 257 of the Deficit Control Act of 1985, CBO's baseline incorporates the assumption that scheduled payments will continue to be made in full after the balance of the trust fund has been exhausted, although there is no legal authority to make such payments. The manner by which those payments continue would depend on future legislation.

b. Includes Civil Service Retirement, Foreign Service Retirement, and several smaller retirement trust funds.

c. Consists primarily of trust funds for railroad workers' retirement, federal employees' health and life insurance, Superfund, and various insurance programs for veterans.

d. Includes interest paid to trust funds, payments from the Treasury's general fund to the Supplementary Medical Insurance Trust Fund, the government's share of payments for federal employees' retirement, lump-sum payments to the Civil Service and Military Retirement Trust Funds, taxes on Social Security benefits, and smaller miscellaneous payments.

that period: the Highway Trust Fund (early in fiscal year 2016) and Social Security's Disability Insurance Trust Fund (early in fiscal year 2017).

Social Security Trust Funds

Social Security provides benefits to retired workers, their families, and some survivors of deceased workers through the Old-Age and Survivors Insurance (OASI) program; it also provides benefits to some people with disabilities and their families through the Disability Insurance (DI) program. Those benefits are financed mainly through payroll taxes collected on workers' earnings, at a rate of 12.4 percent—6.2 percent of which is paid by the worker and 6.2 percent by the employer.

Table E-3.

Deficits, Surpluses, and Balances Projected in CBO's Baseline for the OASI, DI, and HI Trust Funds

Billions of Dollars

	Actual, 2014	2015	2016	2017	2018	2019	2020	2021	2022	2023	2024	2025	Total 2016-2020	Total 2016-2025
							OASI Trust Fund							
Beginning-of-Year Balance	2,656	2,713	2,763	2,802	2,826	2,828	2,806	2,755	2,676	2,566	2,422	2,239	n.a.	n.a.
Income (Excluding interest)	667	696	724	754	786	818	852	887	924	962	1,002	1,043	3,933	8,752
Expenditures	-706	-740	-775	-820	-875	-934	-997	-1,061	-1,127	-1,198	-1,272	-1,351	-4,401	-10,411
Noninterest Deficit	-39	-45	-51	-66	-90	-116	-145	-174	-203	-236	-270	-308	-468	-1,659
Interest received	96	94	90	90	92	94	94	95	94	91	87	81	461	909
Total Deficit (-) or Surplus	57	50	40	24	2	-22	-51	-79	-110	-145	-183	-227	-7	-750
End-of-Year Balance	**2,713**	**2,763**	**2,802**	**2,826**	**2,828**	**2,806**	**2,755**	**2,676**	**2,566**	**2,422**	**2,239**	**2,012**	**n.a.**	**n.a.**
							DI Trust Fund[a]							
Beginning-of-Year Balance	101	70	40	9	0	0	0	0	0	0	0	0	n.a.	n.a.
Income (Excluding interest)	110	115	119	124	129	134	139	145	151	157	163	169	646	1,430
Expenditures	-145	-148	-152	-157	-162	-168	-175	-183	-192	-202	-212	-221	-814	-1,824
Noninterest Deficit	-34	-33	-33	-33	-34	-34	-35	-39	-42	-45	-49	-51	-169	-394
Interest received	4	3	2	1	0	0	0	0	0	0	0	0	3	3
Total Deficit	-31	-30	-30	-32	-34	-34	-35	-39	-42	-45	-49	-51	-165	-390
End-of-Year Balance	**70**	**40**	**9**	**0**	**0**	**0**	**0**	**0**	**0**	**0**	**0**	**0**	**n.a.**	**n.a.**
							HI Trust Fund							
Beginning-of-Year Balance	206	202	204	201	207	218	216	208	194	161	132	107	n.a.	n.a.
Income (Excluding interest)	262	273	287	303	317	332	348	366	384	404	424	446	1,587	3,610
Expenditures	-275	-281	-300	-306	-316	-344	-365	-389	-426	-441	-455	-500	-1,632	-3,843
Noninterest Deficit (-) or Surplus	-13	-8	-13	-3	1	-12	-17	-23	-42	-37	-31	-55	-45	-232
Interest received	9	10	10	10	10	10	10	9	9	7	6	4	49	85
Total Deficit (-) or Surplus	-4	2	-3	7	10	-2	-7	-14	-33	-30	-25	-50	4	-147
End-of-Year Balance	**202**	**204**	**201**	**207**	**218**	**216**	**208**	**194**	**161**	**132**	**107**	**57**	**n.a.**	**n.a.**

Source: Congressional Budget Office.

Notes: Balances shown are invested in Treasury Government Account Series securities.

DI = Disability Insurance; HI = Hospital Insurance; OASI = Old-Age and Survivors Insurance; n.a. = not applicable.

a.   In keeping with the rules in section 257 of the Deficit Control Act of 1985, CBO's baseline incorporates the assumption that scheduled payments will continue to be made in full after the balance of the trust fund has been exhausted, although there is no legal authority to make such payments. Because the manner by which those payments would continue would depend on future legislation, CBO shows zero rather than a cumulative negative balance in the trust fund after the exhaustion date.

Old-Age and Survivors Insurance

The OASI trust fund is by far the largest of all federal trust funds, with $2.7 trillion in holdings of government account securities at the end of 2014. CBO projects that the fund's annual income, excluding interest on those securities, will amount to $696 billion in 2015 and increase to more than $1.0 trillion by 2025 (see Table E-3).[2] Annual expenditures from the fund are projected to be greater and to grow faster than noninterest income, rising from

$740 billion in 2015 to nearly $1.4 trillion in 2025. With expenditures growing by an average of about

---

2.   Although it is an employer, the federal government does not pay taxes. However, it makes an intragovernmental transfer from the general fund of the Treasury to the OASI and DI trust funds to cover the employer's share of the Social Security payroll tax for federal workers. That transfer is included in the income line in Table E-3.

Figure E-1.

Annual Deficits or Surpluses Projected in CBO's Baseline for the OASI, DI, and HI Trust Funds

Billions of Dollars

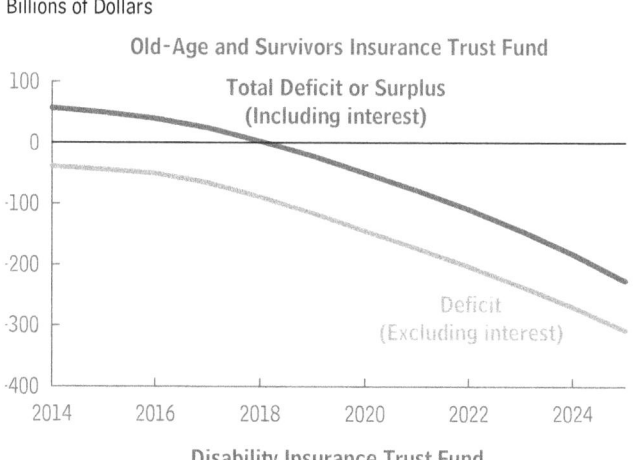

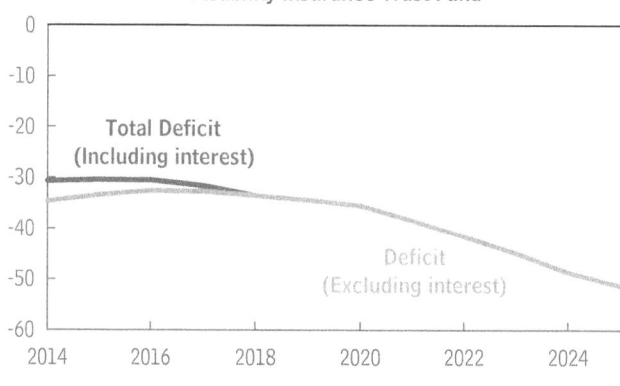

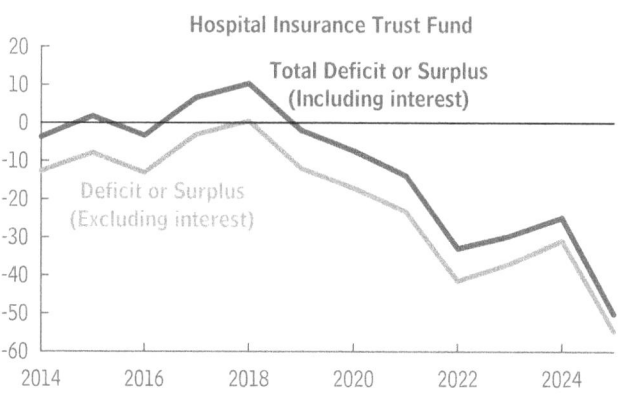

Source: Congressional Budget Office.

Note: DI = Disability Insurance; HI = Hospital Insurance; OASI = Old-Age and Survivors Insurance.

6 percent a year and noninterest income (mostly from payroll taxes) growing by an average of about 4 percent a year, the annual cash flows of the OASI program, excluding interest credited to the trust fund, will add to federal deficits in every year of the coming decade by amounts that will grow to $308 billion in 2025, CBO estimates.

With interest receipts included, the OASI trust fund will show a surplus in every year through 2018 but by amounts that will decline over that period. By 2019, even taking into account interest receipts, the trust fund is projected to start recording deficits that will reach $227 billion in 2025 (see Figure E-1).[3]

Disability Insurance

The DI trust fund is much smaller than the OASI fund, with a balance of $70 billion at the end of 2014. In its current baseline, CBO projects that, excluding interest, the yearly income of the DI fund will rise from $115 billion in 2015 to $169 billion in 2025 (see Table E-3). But, as with the OASI fund, annual expenditures from the DI fund are expected to be greater than noninterest income, rising steadily from $148 billion in 2015 to $221 billion in 2025. Thus, the annual cash flows of the DI program, excluding interest, will also add to federal deficits in each year of the projection period, by amounts that increase from $33 billion early in the period to $51 billion in 2025, CBO estimates. Even with interest receipts included, the DI trust fund is expected to run a yearly deficit throughout that period (see Figure E-1). In the absence of legislative action, the balance of the DI fund will be exhausted in 2017, CBO projects (the same year the agency projected in its August 2014 baseline).

Medicare Trust Funds

Cash flows for payments to hospitals and payments for other services covered by Medicare are accounted for in two trust funds. The Hospital Insurance (HI) Trust Fund accounts for payments made to hospitals and providers of post-acute care services under Part A of the Medicare program, and the Supplementary Medical Insurance (SMI) Trust Fund accounts for payments made for outpatient services, prescription drugs, and other services under Parts B and D of Medicare.[4]

Hospital Insurance Trust Fund

The HI fund is the larger of the two Medicare trust funds, with a balance of $202 billion at the end of 2014. The fund's income is derived largely from the Medicare

3. According to CBO's most recent projections, the balance of the OASI trust fund will be exhausted in calendar year 2032. See Congressional Budget Office, *The 2014 Long-Term Budget Outlook* (July 2014), www.cbo.gov/publication/45471.

4. Part C of Medicare (known as Medicare Advantage) specifies the rules under which private health care plans can assume responsibility for, and be compensated for, providing benefits covered under Parts A, B, and D.

payroll tax (2.9 percent of workers' earnings, divided equally between the worker and the employer); in 2014, those taxes accounted for 87 percent of the $262 billion in noninterest income credited to the HI trust fund.[5] Another 7 percent came from part of the income taxes on Social Security benefits collected from beneficiaries with relatively high income. The remaining 6 percent of non-interest income credited to the HI trust fund consisted largely of premiums paid by beneficiaries; amounts paid to providers and later recovered; fines, penalties and other amounts collected by the Health Care Fraud and Abuse Control program; and other transfers and appropriations. In addition, the trust fund is credited with interest on its balances; that interest amounted to $9 billion in 2014.

The fund's noninterest income is projected to increase from $273 billion in 2015 to $446 billion in 2025—an average annual increase of about 5 percent. But annual expenditures from the HI fund are projected to grow more rapidly—at an average annual rate of close to 6 percent, rising from $281 billion in 2015 to $500 billion in 2025. CBO expects expenditures to outstrip income, excluding interest, in all years through 2025 other than in 2018, producing annual deficits that are relatively small in the first half of the period but rise to $55 billion in 2025.[6] Including interest receipts, the trust fund is expected to run deficits in most years during the baseline period (see Table E-3 and Figure E-1). By 2025, CBO projects, the annual deficit (including interest receipts) will reach $50 billion and the fund's balance will be down to $57 billion. CBO has not projected the fund's balance beyond the 10-year period spanned by the baseline, but it is likely that such projections would show the fund continuing to incur deficits in subsequent years. CBO anticipates that, if current law remained in place, the fund's balance would probably be exhausted early in the decade after 2025.

---

5. Starting in 2013, an additional Medicare tax of 0.9 percent has been assessed on the amount of an individual's earnings over $200,000 (or $250,000 for married couples filing joint income tax returns). As it does with the Social Security payroll tax, the federal government makes an intragovernmental transfer from the general fund of the Treasury to the HI trust fund to cover the employer's share of the Medicare payroll tax for federal workers.

6. The small surplus in 2018 occurs because October 1, 2017, falls on a weekend. Therefore, payments to private Medicare plans for that month will be accelerated into fiscal year 2017, resulting in one fewer payment during fiscal year 2018. (The same type of shift occurs from 2017 to 2016, from 2023 to 2022, and from 2024 to 2023.)

Supplementary Medical Insurance Trust Fund

The SMI trust fund contains two separate accounts: one that pays for physicians' services and other health care provided on an outpatient basis under Part B of Medicare (Medical Insurance) and one that pays for prescription drug benefits under Part D. The funding mechanisms used for the two accounts differ slightly:

■ The Part B portion of the SMI fund is financed primarily through transfers from the general fund of the Treasury and through monthly premium payments from Medicare beneficiaries. The basic monthly premium for the SMI program is set to cover approximately 25 percent of the program's spending (with adjustments to maintain a contingency reserve to cover unexpected spikes in spending); an additional premium is assessed on beneficiaries with relatively high income. The amount transferred from the general fund equals about three times the amount expected to be collected from basic premiums minus the amount collected from the income-related premiums and fees from drug manufacturers.

■ The Part D portion of the SMI fund is financed mainly through transfers from the general fund, monthly premium payments from beneficiaries, and transfers from states (which are based on the number of people in a state who would have received prescription drug coverage under Medicaid in the absence of Part D). The basic monthly premium for Part D is set to cover 25.5 percent of the program's estimated spending, under the assumption that all participants would pay it. However, low-income people who receive subsidies available under Part D are not required to pay Part D premiums, so receipts are projected to cover less than 25.5 percent of the program's costs. Higher-income participants in Part D pay an income-related premium. The amount transferred from the general fund is set to cover total expected spending for benefits and administrative costs, net of the amounts transferred from states and collected from basic and income-related premiums.

Unlike the HI trust fund, the income to the SMI fund (other than interest) does not consist mainly of a specified set of revenues collected from the public. Rather, the amounts credited to those accounts from the general fund of the Treasury are automatically adjusted to cover the differences between program spending and specified revenues. (In 2014, for example, $245 billion was transferred from general funds to the SMI fund, accounting for about three-quarters of its income.) Thus, the balance in the SMI fund cannot be exhausted.

The SMI fund currently holds $68 billion in government account securities, and the amount of such holdings is projected to remain at about that level throughout the next decade.

Highway Trust Fund

The Highway Trust Fund comprises two accounts: the highway account, which funds construction of highways and highway safety programs, and the transit account, which funds mass transit programs. Revenues credited to those accounts are derived mostly from excise taxes on gasoline and certain other motor fuels, which account for more than 85 percent of all receipts to the trust fund.[7]

Almost all spending from the fund is controlled by limitations on obligations set in appropriation acts. Over the past eight years, spending has exceeded the fund's revenues by $64 billion. In addition, CBO expects spending to exceed revenues by $14 billion in 2015, reflecting outlays of $53 billion and revenues of $39 billion. To keep the Highway Trust Fund from delaying payments to state and local governments, starting in 2008, lawmakers have authorized a series of transfers to the fund. Including amounts transferred in accordance with the most recent authorization for highway and transit programs, those transfers have totaled more than $65 billion, mostly from the general fund of the Treasury.

For its baseline spending projections, CBO assumes that future limitations on obligations will be equal to amounts set for 2015, adjusted annually for inflation. Under those circumstances, and without further legislative action, the two accounts would be unable to meet all obligations in a timely manner at some point in 2015, and the fund's balance would be exhausted in early fiscal year 2016. The Department of Transportation has indicated that it needs $5 billion in cash—$4 billion in the highway account and $1 billion in the transit account—to make required payments. The most recent authorization for highway and transit programs expires on May 31, 2015.

Other Trust Funds

Among the remaining trust funds in the federal budget, the largest balances are held by various civilian employee retirement funds (a total of $876 billion at the end of 2014) and by the Military Retirement Trust Fund ($483 billion).[8] In its current baseline, CBO projects that the balances of those funds will increase steadily over the coming decade, reaching $1.1 trillion for the civilian funds and $1.5 trillion for the military retirement fund in 2025, more in total than the balance of the OASI trust fund (see Table E-1 on page 146). Unlike the Social Security and Medicare trust funds, these funds are projected to run surpluses throughout the coming decade, growing to more than $150 billion combined in 2025. The balances of the military retirement fund will grow at a rapid rate over the next 10 years because the Treasury is making additional payments to that fund to cover the initial unfunded liabilities that arose from the fund's creation.

---

7. The other revenues credited to the Highway Trust Fund come from excise taxes on trucks and trailers, on truck tires, and on the use of certain kinds of vehicles.

8. Those civilian retirement funds include the Civil Service Retirement Trust Fund, the Foreign Service Retirement Trust Fund, and several smaller retirement funds.

CBO's Economic Projections for 2015 to 2025

The tables in this appendix expand on the information in Chapter 2 by showing the Congressional Budget Office's economic projections for each year from 2015 to 2025 (by calendar year in Table F-1 and by fiscal year in Table F-2). For years after 2019, CBO did not attempt to forecast the frequency or size of fluctuations in the business cycle. Instead, the values shown in these tables for 2020 to 2025 reflect CBO's assessment of the effects in the medium term of economic and demographic trends, federal tax and spending policies under current law, the 2007–2009 recession, and the slow economic recovery since then.

Table F-1.

CBO's Economic Projections, by Calendar Year

	Estimated, 2014	2015	2016	2017	2018	2019	2020	2021	2022	2023	2024	2025
					Percentage Change From Year to Year							
Gross Domestic Product												
Real (Inflation-adjusted)	2.2	2.8	3.0	2.7	2.2	2.1	2.2	2.2	2.2	2.1	2.1	2.1
Nominal	3.9	4.5	4.6	4.6	4.3	4.1	4.3	4.3	4.2	4.2	4.2	4.2
Inflation												
PCE price index	1.4	1.1	1.9	1.9	2.0	2.0	2.0	2.0	2.0	2.0	2.0	2.0
Core PCE price index[a]	1.4	1.7	1.9	1.9	2.0	2.0	2.0	2.0	2.0	2.0	2.0	2.0
Consumer price index[b]	1.6 [c]	1.1	2.2	2.3	2.3	2.4	2.4	2.4	2.4	2.4	2.4	2.4
Core consumer price index[a]	1.7 [c]	2.0	2.2	2.3	2.3	2.3	2.3	2.3	2.3	2.3	2.3	2.3
GDP price index	1.6	1.6	1.6	1.9	2.0	2.0	2.0	2.0	2.0	2.0	2.0	2.0
Employment Cost Index[d]	2.0	2.7	3.0	3.5	3.6	3.6	3.5	3.5	3.4	3.4	3.3	3.3
					Calendar Year Average							
Unemployment Rate (Percent)	6.2 [c]	5.5	5.4	5.3	5.4	5.5	5.5	5.5	5.4	5.4	5.4	5.4
Payroll Employment (Monthly change, in thousands)[e]	234 [c]	184	148	111	70	68	75	77	79	80	80	80
Interest Rates (Percent)												
Three-month Treasury bills	* [c]	0.2	1.2	2.6	3.5	3.4	3.4	3.4	3.4	3.4	3.4	3.4
Ten-year Treasury notes	2.5 [c]	2.8	3.4	3.9	4.2	4.5	4.6	4.6	4.6	4.6	4.6	4.6
Tax Bases (Percentage of GDP)												
Wages and salaries	42.7	42.6	42.6	42.7	42.8	42.8	42.9	42.9	43.0	43.0	43.1	43.1
Domestic economic profits	9.9	10.0	9.7	9.4	9.0	8.6	8.4	8.2	8.0	7.9	7.8	7.8
Tax Bases (Billions of dollars)												
Wages and salaries	7,432	7,755	8,118	8,503	8,880	9,259	9,665	10,090	10,533	10,994	11,472	11,965
Domestic economic profits	1,716	1,825	1,843	1,867	1,875	1,865	1,889	1,924	1,962	2,016	2,086	2,161
Nominal GDP (Billions of dollars)	17,422	18,204	19,045	19,919	20,768	21,625	22,550	23,515	24,515	25,550	26,625	27,736

Sources: Congressional Budget Office; Bureau of Labor Statistics; Federal Reserve.

Note: GDP = gross domestic product; PCE = personal consumption expenditures; * = between zero and 0.05 percent.

a. Excludes prices for food and energy.

b. The consumer price index for all urban consumers.

c. Actual value for 2014.

d. The employment cost index for wages and salaries of workers in private industries.

e. Calculated as the monthly average of the fourth-quarter-to-fourth-quarter change in payroll employment.

Table F-2.

CBO's Economic Projections, by Fiscal Year

	Actual, 2014	2015	2016	2017	2018	2019	2020	2021	2022	2023	2024	2025
					Percentage Change From Year to Year							
Gross Domestic Product												
Real (Inflation-adjusted)	2.6	2.7	3.0	2.8	2.3	2.0	2.2	2.2	2.2	2.1	2.1	2.1
Nominal	4.1	4.4	4.5	4.6	4.3	4.1	4.3	4.3	4.3	4.2	4.2	4.2
Inflation												
PCE price index	1.3	1.1	1.7	1.9	2.0	2.0	2.0	2.0	2.0	2.0	2.0	2.0
Core PCE price index[a]	1.4	1.6	1.9	1.9	1.9	2.0	2.0	2.0	2.0	2.0	2.0	2.0
Consumer price index[b]	1.6	1.1	2.0	2.3	2.4	2.3	2.4	2.4	2.4	2.4	2.4	2.4
Core consumer price index[a]	1.7	1.9	2.2	2.2	2.3	2.3	2.3	2.3	2.3	2.3	2.3	2.3
GDP price index	1.5	1.7	1.5	1.8	2.0	2.0	2.0	2.0	2.0	2.0	2.0	2.0
Employment Cost Index[c]	1.9	2.7	2.9	3.4	3.6	3.6	3.6	3.5	3.4	3.4	3.3	3.3
					Fiscal Year Average							
Unemployment Rate (Percent)	6.5	5.6	5.4	5.4	5.3	5.4	5.5	5.5	5.5	5.4	5.4	5.4
Payroll Employment (Monthly change, in thousands)[d]	217	208	153	119	80	65	75	76	79	79	80	79
Interest Rates (Percent)												
Three-month Treasury bills	*	0.1	0.9	2.2	3.4	3.4	3.4	3.4	3.4	3.4	3.4	3.4
Ten-year Treasury notes	2.7	2.6	3.2	3.8	4.1	4.4	4.6	4.6	4.6	4.6	4.6	4.6
Tax Bases (Percentage of GDP)												
Wages and salaries	42.6	42.6	42.6	42.7	42.7	42.8	42.8	42.9	43.0	43.0	43.1	43.1
Domestic economic profits	9.8	10.1	9.8	9.4	9.1	8.7	8.4	8.2	8.0	7.9	7.8	7.8
Tax Bases (Billions of dollars)												
Wages and salaries	7,350	7,668	8,024	8,406	8,787	9,162	9,562	9,982	10,421	10,877	11,351	11,840
Domestic economic profits	1,684	1,827	1,842	1,861	1,878	1,863	1,880	1,916	1,951	2,001	2,068	2,142
Nominal GDP (Billions of dollars)	17,263	18,016	18,832	19,701	20,558	21,404	22,315	23,271	24,261	25,287	26,352	27,456

Sources: Congressional Budget Office; Bureau of Labor Statistics; Federal Reserve.

Note: GDP = gross domestic product; PCE = personal consumption expenditures; * = between zero and 0.05 percent.

a. Excludes prices for food and energy.

b. The consumer price index for all urban consumers.

c. The employment cost index for wages and salaries of workers in private industries.

d. Calculated as the monthly average of the fourth-quarter-to-fourth-quarter change in payroll employment.

Historical Budget Data

This appendix provides historical data on revenues, outlays, and the deficit or surplus—in forms consistent with the projections in Chapters 1, 3, and 4—for fiscal years 1965 to 2014. The data, which come from the Congressional Budget Office and the Office of Management and Budget, are shown both in nominal dollars and as a percentage of gross domestic product. Some of the numbers have been revised since August 2014, when these tables were previously published on CBO's website (www.cbo.gov/publication/45653).

Federal revenues, outlays, the deficit or surplus, and debt held by the public are shown in Table G-1. Revenues, outlays, and the deficit or surplus have both on-budget and off-budget components. Social Security's receipts and outlays were placed off-budget by the Balanced Budget and Emergency Deficit Control Act of 1985. For the sake of consistency, Table G-1 shows the budgetary components of Social Security as off-budget before that year. The Postal Service was classified as off-budget by the Omnibus Budget Reconciliation Act of 1989.

The major sources of federal revenues (including off-budget revenues) are presented in Table G-2 on page 160. Payroll taxes include payments by employers and employees for Social Security, Medicare, Railroad Retirement, and unemployment insurance, as well as pension contributions by federal workers. Excise taxes are levied on certain products and services, such as gasoline, alcoholic beverages, and air travel. Estate and gift taxes are levied on assets when they are transferred. Miscellaneous receipts consist of earnings of the Federal Reserve System and income from numerous fees and charges.

Total outlays for major categories of spending (including off-budget outlays) appear in Table G-3 on page 162. Spending controlled by the appropriation process is classified as discretionary. Spending governed by laws other than appropriation acts, such as laws that set eligibility requirements for certain programs, is considered mandatory. Offsetting receipts include the government's contributions to retirement programs for its employees, as well as fees, charges (such as Medicare premiums), and receipts from the use of federally controlled land and offshore territory. Net interest consists mostly of the government's interest payments on federal debt offset by its interest income.

Table G-4 on page 164 divides discretionary spending into its defense and nondefense components. Table G-5 on page 166 shows mandatory outlays for three major benefit programs—Social Security, Medicare, and Medicaid—and for other categories of mandatory spending. Income security programs provide benefits to recipients with limited income and assets; those programs include unemployment compensation, Supplemental Security Income, and the Supplemental Nutrition Assistance Program (formerly known as the Food Stamp program). Other federal retirement and disability programs provide benefits to federal civilian employees, members of the military, and veterans. The category of other mandatory programs includes the activities of the Commodity Credit Corporation, the Medicare-Eligible Retiree Health Care Fund, the subsidy costs of federal student loan programs, and the Children's Health Insurance Program.

Table G-1.

Revenues, Outlays, Deficits, Surpluses, and Debt Held by the Public Since 1965

	Revenues	Outlays	Deficit (-) or Surplus				Debt Held by the Public[a]
			On-Budget	Social Security	Postal Service	Total	
			In Billions of Dollars				
1965	116.8	118.2	-1.6	0.2	0	-1.4	260.8
1966	130.8	134.5	-3.1	-0.6	0	-3.7	263.7
1967	148.8	157.5	-12.6	4.0	0	-8.6	266.6
1968	153.0	178.1	-27.7	2.6	0	-25.2	289.5
1969	186.9	183.6	-0.5	3.7	0	3.2	278.1
1970	192.8	195.6	-8.7	5.9	0	-2.8	283.2
1971	187.1	210.2	-26.1	3.0	0	-23.0	303.0
1972	207.3	230.7	-26.1	3.1	-0.4	-23.4	322.4
1973	230.8	245.7	-15.2	0.5	-0.2	-14.9	340.9
1974	263.2	269.4	-7.2	1.8	-0.8	-6.1	343.7
1975	279.1	332.3	-54.1	2.0	-1.1	-53.2	394.7
1976	298.1	371.8	-69.4	-3.2	-1.1	-73.7	477.4
1977	355.6	409.2	-49.9	-3.9	0.2	-53.7	549.1
1978	399.6	458.7	-55.4	-4.3	0.5	-59.2	607.1
1979	463.3	504.0	-39.6	-2.0	0.9	-40.7	640.3
1980	517.1	590.9	-73.1	-1.1	0.4	-73.8	711.9
1981	599.3	678.2	-73.9	-5.0	-0.1	-79.0	789.4
1982	617.8	745.7	-120.6	-7.9	0.6	-128.0	924.6
1983	600.6	808.4	-207.7	0.2	-0.3	-207.8	1,137.3
1984	666.4	851.8	-185.3	0.3	-0.4	-185.4	1,307.0
1985	734.0	946.3	-221.5	9.4	-0.1	-212.3	1,507.3
1986	769.2	990.4	-237.9	16.7	*	-221.2	1,740.6
1987	854.3	1,004.0	-168.4	19.6	-0.9	-149.7	1,889.8
1988	909.2	1,064.4	-192.3	38.8	-1.7	-155.2	2,051.6
1989	991.1	1,143.7	-205.4	52.4	0.3	-152.6	2,190.7
1990	1,032.0	1,253.0	-277.6	58.2	-1.6	-221.0	2,411.6
1991	1,055.0	1,324.2	-321.4	53.5	-1.3	-269.2	2,689.0
1992	1,091.2	1,381.5	-340.4	50.7	-0.7	-290.3	2,999.7
1993	1,154.3	1,409.4	-300.4	46.8	-1.4	-255.1	3,248.4
1994	1,258.6	1,461.8	-258.8	56.8	-1.1	-203.2	3,433.1
1995	1,351.8	1,515.7	-226.4	60.4	2.0	-164.0	3,604.4
1996	1,453.1	1,560.5	-174.0	66.4	0.2	-107.4	3,734.1
1997	1,579.2	1,601.1	-103.2	81.3	*	-21.9	3,772.3
1998	1,721.7	1,652.5	-29.9	99.4	-0.2	69.3	3,721.1
1999	1,827.5	1,701.8	1.9	124.7	-1.0	125.6	3,632.4
2000	2,025.2	1,789.0	86.4	151.8	-2.0	236.2	3,409.8
2001	1,991.1	1,862.8	-32.4	163.0	-2.3	128.2	3,319.6
2002	1,853.1	2,010.9	-317.4	159.0	0.7	-157.8	3,540.4
2003	1,782.3	2,159.9	-538.4	155.6	5.2	-377.6	3,913.4
2004	1,880.1	2,292.8	-568.0	151.1	4.1	-412.7	4,295.5
2005	2,153.6	2,472.0	-493.6	173.5	1.8	-318.3	4,592.2
2006	2,406.9	2,655.1	-434.5	185.2	1.1	-248.2	4,829.0
2007	2,568.0	2,728.7	-342.2	186.5	-5.1	-160.7	5,035.1
2008	2,524.0	2,982.5	-641.8	185.7	-2.4	-458.6	5,803.1
2009	2,105.0	3,517.7	-1,549.7	137.3	-0.3	-1,412.7	7,544.7
2010	2,162.7	3,457.1	-1,371.4	81.7	-4.7	-1,294.4	9,018.9
2011	2,303.5	3,603.1	-1,366.8	68.0	-0.8	-1,299.6	10,128.2
2012	2,450.0	3,537.0	-1,148.9	64.6	-2.7	-1,087.0	11,281.1
2013	2,775.1	3,454.6	-719.0	37.6	1.9	-679.5	11,982.6
2014	3,020.8	3,504.2	-512.8	32.0	-2.5	-483.3	12,779.4

Continued

Table G-1.   Continued

Revenues, Outlays, Deficits, Surpluses, and Debt Held by the Public Since 1965

	Revenues	Outlays	Deficit (-) or Surplus				Debt Held by the Public[a]
			On-Budget	Social Security	Postal Service	Total	
As a Percentage of Gross Domestic Product							
1965	16.4	16.6	-0.2	**	0	-0.2	36.7
1966	16.7	17.2	-0.4	-0.1	0	-0.5	33.7
1967	17.8	18.8	-1.5	0.5	0	-1.0	31.8
1968	17.0	19.8	-3.1	0.3	0	-2.8	32.2
1969	19.0	18.7	-0.1	0.4	0	0.3	28.3
1970	18.4	18.7	-0.8	0.6	0	-0.3	27.0
1971	16.7	18.8	-2.3	0.3	0	-2.1	27.1
1972	17.0	18.9	-2.1	0.3	**	-1.9	26.4
1973	17.0	18.1	-1.1	**	**	-1.1	25.1
1974	17.7	18.1	-0.5	0.1	-0.1	-0.4	23.1
1975	17.3	20.6	-3.4	0.1	-0.1	-3.3	24.5
1976	16.6	20.8	-3.9	-0.2	-0.1	-4.1	26.7
1977	17.5	20.2	-2.5	-0.2	**	-2.6	27.1
1978	17.5	20.1	-2.4	-0.2	**	-2.6	26.6
1979	18.0	19.6	-1.5	-0.1	**	-1.6	24.9
1980	18.5	21.1	-2.6	**	**	-2.6	25.5
1981	19.1	21.6	-2.4	-0.2	**	-2.5	25.2
1982	18.6	22.5	-3.6	-0.2	**	-3.9	27.9
1983	17.0	22.8	-5.9	**	**	-5.9	32.1
1984	16.9	21.5	-4.7	**	**	-4.7	33.1
1985	17.2	22.2	-5.2	0.2	**	-5.0	35.3
1986	17.0	21.8	-5.2	0.4	**	-4.9	38.4
1987	17.9	21.0	-3.5	0.4	**	-3.1	39.5
1988	17.6	20.6	-3.7	0.8	**	-3.0	39.8
1989	17.8	20.5	-3.7	0.9	**	-2.7	39.3
1990	17.4	21.2	-4.7	1.0	**	-3.7	40.8
1991	17.3	21.7	-5.3	0.9	**	-4.4	44.0
1992	17.0	21.5	-5.3	0.8	**	-4.5	46.6
1993	17.0	20.7	-4.4	0.7	**	-3.8	47.8
1994	17.5	20.3	-3.6	0.8	**	-2.8	47.7
1995	17.8	20.0	-3.0	0.8	**	-2.2	47.5
1996	18.2	19.6	-2.2	0.8	**	-1.3	46.8
1997	18.6	18.9	-1.2	1.0	**	-0.3	44.5
1998	19.2	18.5	-0.3	1.1	**	0.8	41.6
1999	19.2	17.9	**	1.3	**	1.3	38.2
2000	20.0	17.6	0.9	1.5	**	2.3	33.6
2001	18.8	17.6	-0.3	1.5	**	1.2	31.4
2002	17.0	18.5	-2.9	1.5	**	-1.5	32.6
2003	15.7	19.1	-4.8	1.4	**	-3.3	34.5
2004	15.6	19.0	-4.7	1.3	**	-3.4	35.5
2005	16.7	19.2	-3.8	1.3	**	-2.5	35.6
2006	17.6	19.4	-3.2	1.4	**	-1.8	35.3
2007	17.9	19.1	-2.4	1.3	**	-1.1	35.2
2008	17.1	20.2	-4.4	1.3	**	-3.1	39.3
2009	14.6	24.4	-10.8	1.0	**	-9.8	52.3
2010	14.6	23.4	-9.3	0.6	**	-8.7	60.9
2011	15.0	23.4	-8.9	0.4	**	-8.5	65.9
2012	15.3	22.1	-7.2	0.4	**	-6.8	70.4
2013	16.7	20.8	-4.3	0.2	**	-4.1	72.3
2014	17.5	20.3	-3.0	0.2	**	-2.8	74.1

Sources: Congressional Budget Office; Office of Management and Budget.

Note: * = between -$500 million and $500 million; ** = between -0.05 and 0.05 percent.

a.   End of year.

Table G-2.

Revenues, by Major Source, Since 1965

	Individual Income Taxes	Payroll Taxes	Corporate Income Taxes	Excise Taxes	Estate and Gift Taxes	Customs Duties	Miscellaneous Receipts	Total
				In Billions of Dollars				
1965	48.8	22.2	25.5	14.6	2.7	1.4	1.6	116.8
1966	55.4	25.5	30.1	13.1	3.1	1.8	1.9	130.8
1967	61.5	32.6	34.0	13.7	3.0	1.9	2.1	148.8
1968	68.7	33.9	28.7	14.1	3.1	2.0	2.5	153.0
1969	87.2	39.0	36.7	15.2	3.5	2.3	2.9	186.9
1970	90.4	44.4	32.8	15.7	3.6	2.4	3.4	192.8
1971	86.2	47.3	26.8	16.6	3.7	2.6	3.9	187.1
1972	94.7	52.6	32.2	15.5	5.4	3.3	3.6	207.3
1973	103.2	63.1	36.2	16.3	4.9	3.2	3.9	230.8
1974	119.0	75.1	38.6	16.8	5.0	3.3	5.4	263.2
1975	122.4	84.5	40.6	16.6	4.6	3.7	6.7	279.1
1976	131.6	90.8	41.4	17.0	5.2	4.1	8.0	298.1
1977	157.6	106.5	54.9	17.5	7.3	5.2	6.5	355.6
1978	181.0	121.0	60.0	18.4	5.3	6.6	7.4	399.6
1979	217.8	138.9	65.7	18.7	5.4	7.4	9.3	463.3
1980	244.1	157.8	64.6	24.3	6.4	7.2	12.7	517.1
1981	285.9	182.7	61.1	40.8	6.8	8.1	13.8	599.3
1982	297.7	201.5	49.2	36.3	8.0	8.9	16.2	617.8
1983	288.9	209.0	37.0	35.3	6.1	8.7	15.6	600.6
1984	298.4	239.4	56.9	37.4	6.0	11.4	17.0	666.4
1985	334.5	265.2	61.3	36.0	6.4	12.1	18.5	734.0
1986	349.0	283.9	63.1	32.9	7.0	13.3	19.9	769.2
1987	392.6	303.3	83.9	32.5	7.5	15.1	19.5	854.3
1988	401.2	334.3	94.5	35.2	7.6	16.2	20.2	909.2
1989	445.7	359.4	103.3	34.4	8.7	16.3	23.2	991.1
1990	466.9	380.0	93.5	35.3	11.5	16.7	28.0	1,032.0
1991	467.8	396.0	98.1	42.4	11.1	15.9	23.6	1,055.0
1992	476.0	413.7	100.3	45.6	11.1	17.4	27.2	1,091.2
1993	509.7	428.3	117.5	48.1	12.6	18.8	19.4	1,154.3
1994	543.1	461.5	140.4	55.2	15.2	20.1	23.1	1,258.6
1995	590.2	484.5	157.0	57.5	14.8	19.3	28.5	1,351.8
1996	656.4	509.4	171.8	54.0	17.2	18.7	25.5	1,453.1
1997	737.5	539.4	182.3	56.9	19.8	17.9	25.4	1,579.2
1998	828.6	571.8	188.7	57.7	24.1	18.3	32.6	1,721.7
1999	879.5	611.8	184.7	70.4	27.8	18.3	34.9	1,827.5
2000	1,004.5	652.9	207.3	68.9	29.0	19.9	42.8	2,025.2
2001	994.3	694.0	151.1	66.2	28.4	19.4	37.7	1,991.1
2002	858.3	700.8	148.0	67.0	26.5	18.6	33.9	1,853.1
2003	793.7	713.0	131.8	67.5	22.0	19.9	34.5	1,782.3
2004	809.0	733.4	189.4	69.9	24.8	21.1	32.6	1,880.1
2005	927.2	794.1	278.3	73.1	24.8	23.4	32.7	2,153.6
2006	1,043.9	837.8	353.9	74.0	27.9	24.8	44.6	2,406.9
2007	1,163.5	869.6	370.2	65.1	26.0	26.0	47.5	2,568.0
2008	1,145.7	900.2	304.3	67.3	28.8	27.6	50.0	2,524.0
2009	915.3	890.9	138.2	62.5	23.5	22.5	52.1	2,105.0
2010	898.5	864.8	191.4	66.9	18.9	25.3	96.8	2,162.7
2011	1,091.5	818.8	181.1	72.4	7.4	29.5	102.8	2,303.5
2012	1,132.2	845.3	242.3	79.1	14.0	30.3	106.8	2,450.0
2013	1,316.4	947.8	273.5	84.0	18.9	31.8	102.6	2,775.1
2014	1,394.6	1,023.9	320.7	93.4	19.3	33.9	135.0	3,020.8

Continued

Table G-2.   Continued

Revenues, by Major Source, Since 1965

	Individual Income Taxes	Payroll Taxes	Corporate Income Taxes	Excise Taxes	Estate and Gift Taxes	Customs Duties	Miscellaneous Receipts	Total
	As a Percentage of Gross Domestic Product							
1965	6.9	3.1	3.6	2.1	0.4	0.2	0.2	16.4
1966	7.1	3.3	3.8	1.7	0.4	0.2	0.2	16.7
1967	7.3	3.9	4.1	1.6	0.4	0.2	0.3	17.8
1968	7.6	3.8	3.2	1.6	0.3	0.2	0.3	17.0
1969	8.9	4.0	3.7	1.6	0.4	0.2	0.3	19.0
1970	8.6	4.2	3.1	1.5	0.3	0.2	0.3	18.4
1971	7.7	4.2	2.4	1.5	0.3	0.2	0.3	16.7
1972	7.8	4.3	2.6	1.3	0.4	0.3	0.3	17.0
1973	7.6	4.7	2.7	1.2	0.4	0.2	0.3	17.0
1974	8.0	5.1	2.6	1.1	0.3	0.2	0.4	17.7
1975	7.6	5.2	2.5	1.0	0.3	0.2	0.4	17.3
1976	7.4	5.1	2.3	0.9	0.3	0.2	0.4	16.6
1977	7.8	5.3	2.7	0.9	0.4	0.3	0.3	17.5
1978	7.9	5.3	2.6	0.8	0.2	0.3	0.3	17.5
1979	8.5	5.4	2.6	0.7	0.2	0.3	0.4	18.0
1980	8.7	5.6	2.3	0.9	0.2	0.3	0.5	18.5
1981	9.1	5.8	1.9	1.3	0.2	0.3	0.4	19.1
1982	9.0	6.1	1.5	1.1	0.2	0.3	0.5	18.6
1983	8.2	5.9	1.0	1.0	0.2	0.2	0.4	17.0
1984	7.5	6.1	1.4	0.9	0.2	0.3	0.4	16.9
1985	7.8	6.2	1.4	0.8	0.2	0.3	0.4	17.2
1986	7.7	6.3	1.4	0.7	0.2	0.3	0.4	17.0
1987	8.2	6.3	1.8	0.7	0.2	0.3	0.4	17.9
1988	7.8	6.5	1.8	0.7	0.1	0.3	0.4	17.6
1989	8.0	6.5	1.9	0.6	0.2	0.3	0.4	17.8
1990	7.9	6.4	1.6	0.6	0.2	0.3	0.5	17.4
1991	7.7	6.5	1.6	0.7	0.2	0.3	0.4	17.3
1992	7.4	6.4	1.6	0.7	0.2	0.3	0.4	17.0
1993	7.5	6.3	1.7	0.7	0.2	0.3	0.3	17.0
1994	7.5	6.4	2.0	0.8	0.2	0.3	0.3	17.5
1995	7.8	6.4	2.1	0.8	0.2	0.3	0.4	17.8
1996	8.2	6.4	2.2	0.7	0.2	0.2	0.3	18.2
1997	8.7	6.4	2.1	0.7	0.2	0.2	0.3	18.6
1998	9.3	6.4	2.1	0.6	0.3	0.2	0.4	19.2
1999	9.2	6.4	1.9	0.7	0.3	0.2	0.4	19.2
2000	9.9	6.4	2.0	0.7	0.3	0.2	0.4	20.0
2001	9.4	6.6	1.4	0.6	0.3	0.2	0.4	18.8
2002	7.9	6.4	1.4	0.6	0.2	0.2	0.3	17.0
2003	7.0	6.3	1.2	0.6	0.2	0.2	0.3	15.7
2004	6.7	6.1	1.6	0.6	0.2	0.2	0.3	15.6
2005	7.2	6.2	2.2	0.6	0.2	0.2	0.3	16.7
2006	7.6	6.1	2.6	0.5	0.2	0.2	0.3	17.6
2007	8.1	6.1	2.6	0.5	0.2	0.2	0.3	17.9
2008	7.8	6.1	2.1	0.5	0.2	0.2	0.3	17.1
2009	6.4	6.2	1.0	0.4	0.2	0.2	0.4	14.6
2010	6.1	5.8	1.3	0.5	0.1	0.2	0.7	14.6
2011	7.1	5.3	1.2	0.5	*	0.2	0.7	15.0
2012	7.1	5.3	1.5	0.5	0.1	0.2	0.7	15.3
2013	7.9	5.7	1.6	0.5	0.1	0.2	0.6	16.7
2014	8.1	5.9	1.9	0.5	0.1	0.2	0.8	17.5

Sources: Congressional Budget Office; Office of Management and Budget.

Note: * = between zero and 0.05 percent.

Table G-3.

Outlays, by Major Category, Since 1965

| | | Mandatory | | | |
	Discretionary	Programmatic Outlays[a]	Offsetting Receipts	Net Interest	Total
		In Billions of Dollars			
1965	77.8	39.7	-7.9	8.6	118.2
1966	90.1	43.4	-8.4	9.4	134.5
1967	106.5	50.9	-10.2	10.3	157.5
1968	118.0	59.7	-10.6	11.1	178.1
1969	117.3	64.6	-11.0	12.7	183.6
1970	120.3	72.5	-11.5	14.4	195.6
1971	122.5	86.9	-14.1	14.8	210.2
1972	128.5	100.8	-14.1	15.5	230.7
1973	130.4	116.0	-18.0	17.3	245.7
1974	138.2	130.9	-21.2	21.4	269.4
1975	158.0	169.4	-18.3	23.2	332.3
1976	175.6	189.1	-19.6	26.7	371.8
1977	197.1	203.7	-21.5	29.9	409.2
1978	218.7	227.4	-22.8	35.5	458.7
1979	240.0	247.0	-25.6	42.6	504.0
1980	276.3	291.2	-29.2	52.5	590.9
1981	307.9	339.4	-37.9	68.8	678.2
1982	326.0	370.8	-36.0	85.0	745.7
1983	353.3	410.6	-45.3	89.8	808.4
1984	379.4	405.5	-44.2	111.1	851.8
1985	415.8	448.2	-47.1	129.5	946.3
1986	438.5	461.7	-45.9	136.0	990.4
1987	444.2	474.2	-52.9	138.6	1,004.0
1988	464.4	505.0	-56.8	151.8	1,064.4
1989	488.8	546.1	-60.1	169.0	1,143.7
1990	500.6	625.6	-57.5	184.3	1,253.0
1991	533.3	702.0	-105.5	194.4	1,324.2
1992	533.8	717.7	-69.3	199.3	1,381.5
1993	539.8	736.8	-65.9	198.7	1,409.4
1994	541.3	786.0	-68.5	202.9	1,461.8
1995	544.8	817.5	-78.7	232.1	1,515.7
1996	532.7	857.6	-70.9	241.1	1,560.5
1997	547.0	895.5	-85.4	244.0	1,601.1
1998	552.0	942.9	-83.5	241.1	1,652.5
1999	572.1	979.4	-79.4	229.8	1,701.8
2000	614.6	1,032.4	-81.0	222.9	1,789.0
2001	649.0	1,096.8	-89.2	206.2	1,862.8
2002	734.0	1,196.3	-90.3	170.9	2,010.9
2003	824.3	1,283.4	-100.9	153.1	2,159.9
2004	895.1	1,346.4	-108.9	160.2	2,292.8
2005	968.5	1,448.1	-128.7	184.0	2,472.0
2006	1,016.6	1,556.1	-144.3	226.6	2,655.1
2007	1,041.6	1,627.9	-177.9	237.1	2,728.7
2008	1,134.9	1,780.3	-185.4	252.8	2,982.5
2009	1,237.5	2,287.8	-194.6	186.9	3,517.7
2010	1,347.2	2,110.2	-196.5	196.2	3,457.1
2011	1,347.1	2,234.9	-209.0	230.0	3,603.1
2012	1,286.1	2,258.8	-228.3	220.4	3,537.0
2013	1,202.1	2,336.4	-304.8	220.9	3,454.6
2014	1,178.7	2,372.6	-276.3	229.2	3,504.2

Continued

Outlays, by Major Category, Since 1965

	Discretionary	Mandatory		Net Interest	Total
		Programmatic Outlays[a]	Offsetting Receipts		
As a Percentage of Gross Domestic Product					
1965	10.9	5.6	-1.1	1.2	16.6
1966	11.5	5.5	-1.1	1.2	17.2
1967	12.7	6.1	-1.2	1.2	18.8
1968	13.1	6.6	-1.2	1.2	19.8
1969	11.9	6.6	-1.1	1.3	18.7
1970	11.5	6.9	-1.1	1.4	18.7
1971	10.9	7.8	-1.3	1.3	18.8
1972	10.5	8.3	-1.2	1.3	18.9
1973	9.6	8.6	-1.3	1.3	18.1
1974	9.3	8.8	-1.4	1.4	18.1
1975	9.8	10.5	-1.1	1.4	20.6
1976	9.8	10.6	-1.1	1.5	20.8
1977	9.7	10.0	-1.1	1.5	20.2
1978	9.6	10.0	-1.0	1.6	20.1
1979	9.3	9.6	-1.0	1.7	19.6
1980	9.9	10.4	-1.0	1.9	21.1
1981	9.8	10.8	-1.2	2.2	21.6
1982	9.8	11.2	-1.1	2.6	22.5
1983	10.0	11.6	-1.3	2.5	22.8
1984	9.6	10.3	-1.1	2.8	21.5
1985	9.7	10.5	-1.1	3.0	22.2
1986	9.7	10.2	-1.0	3.0	21.8
1987	9.3	9.9	-1.1	2.9	21.0
1988	9.0	9.8	-1.1	2.9	20.6
1989	8.8	9.8	-1.1	3.0	20.5
1990	8.5	10.6	-1.0	3.1	21.2
1991	8.7	11.5	-1.7	3.2	21.7
1992	8.3	11.2	-1.1	3.1	21.5
1993	7.9	10.8	-1.0	2.9	20.7
1994	7.5	10.9	-1.0	2.8	20.3
1995	7.2	10.8	-1.0	3.1	20.0
1996	6.7	10.7	-0.9	3.0	19.6
1997	6.4	10.6	-1.0	2.9	18.9
1998	6.2	10.5	-0.9	2.7	18.5
1999	6.0	10.3	-0.8	2.4	17.9
2000	6.1	10.2	-0.8	2.2	17.6
2001	6.1	10.4	-0.8	2.0	17.6
2002	6.7	11.0	-0.8	1.6	18.5
2003	7.3	11.3	-0.9	1.4	19.1
2004	7.4	11.1	-0.9	1.3	19.0
2005	7.5	11.2	-1.0	1.4	19.2
2006	7.4	11.4	-1.1	1.7	19.4
2007	7.3	11.4	-1.2	1.7	19.1
2008	7.7	12.1	-1.3	1.7	20.2
2009	8.6	15.9	-1.4	1.3	24.4
2010	9.1	14.3	-1.3	1.3	23.4
2011	8.8	14.5	-1.4	1.5	23.4
2012	8.0	14.1	-1.4	1.4	22.1
2013	7.3	14.1	-1.8	1.3	20.8
2014	6.8	13.8	-1.6	1.3	20.3

Sources: Congressional Budget Office; Office of Management and Budget.

a. Excludes offsetting receipts.

Table G-4.

Discretionary Outlays Since 1965

	Defense	Nondefense	Total
		In Billions of Dollars	
1965	51.0	26.8	77.8
1966	59.0	31.1	90.1
1967	72.0	34.5	106.5
1968	82.2	35.8	118.0
1969	82.7	34.6	117.3
1970	81.9	38.4	120.3
1971	79.0	43.5	122.5
1972	79.3	49.2	128.5
1973	77.1	53.3	130.4
1974	80.7	57.5	138.2
1975	87.6	70.4	158.0
1976	89.9	85.7	175.6
1977	97.5	99.6	197.1
1978	104.6	114.1	218.7
1979	116.8	123.2	240.0
1980	134.6	141.7	276.3
1981	158.0	149.9	307.9
1982	185.9	140.0	326.0
1983	209.9	143.4	353.3
1984	228.0	151.4	379.4
1985	253.1	162.7	415.8
1986	273.8	164.7	438.5
1987	282.5	161.6	444.2
1988	290.9	173.5	464.4
1989	304.0	184.8	488.8
1990	300.1	200.4	500.6
1991	319.7	213.6	533.3
1992	302.6	231.2	533.8
1993	292.4	247.3	539.8
1994	282.3	259.1	541.3
1995	273.6	271.2	544.8
1996	266.0	266.8	532.7
1997	271.7	275.4	547.0
1998	270.3	281.7	552.0
1999	275.5	296.7	572.1
2000	295.0	319.7	614.6
2001	306.1	343.0	649.0
2002	349.0	385.0	734.0
2003	404.9	419.4	824.3
2004	454.1	441.0	895.1
2005	493.6	474.9	968.5
2006	520.0	496.7	1,016.6
2007	547.9	493.7	1,041.6
2008	612.4	522.5	1,134.9
2009	656.7	580.8	1,237.5
2010	688.9	658.3	1,347.2
2011	699.4	647.7	1,347.1
2012	670.5	615.6	1,286.1
2013	625.8	576.4	1,202.1
2014	595.8	582.9	1,178.7

Continued

Table G-4.   Continued

Discretionary Outlays Since 1965

	Defense	Nondefense	Total
	As a Percentage of Gross Domestic Product		
1965	7.2	3.8	10.9
1966	7.5	4.0	11.5
1967	8.6	4.1	12.7
1968	9.1	4.0	13.1
1969	8.4	3.5	11.9
1970	7.8	3.7	11.5
1971	7.1	3.9	10.9
1972	6.5	4.0	10.5
1973	5.7	3.9	9.6
1974	5.4	3.9	9.3
1975	5.4	4.4	9.8
1976	5.0	4.8	9.8
1977	4.8	4.9	9.7
1978	4.6	5.0	9.6
1979	4.5	4.8	9.3
1980	4.8	5.1	9.9
1981	5.0	4.8	9.8
1982	5.6	4.2	9.8
1983	5.9	4.1	10.0
1984	5.8	3.8	9.6
1985	5.9	3.8	9.7
1986	6.0	3.6	9.7
1987	5.9	3.4	9.3
1988	5.6	3.4	9.0
1989	5.5	3.3	8.8
1990	5.1	3.4	8.5
1991	5.2	3.5	8.7
1992	4.7	3.6	8.3
1993	4.3	3.6	7.9
1994	3.9	3.6	7.5
1995	3.6	3.6	7.2
1996	3.3	3.3	6.7
1997	3.2	3.2	6.4
1998	3.0	3.1	6.2
1999	2.9	3.1	6.0
2000	2.9	3.2	6.1
2001	2.9	3.2	6.1
2002	3.2	3.5	6.7
2003	3.6	3.7	7.3
2004	3.8	3.6	7.4
2005	3.8	3.7	7.5
2006	3.8	3.6	7.4
2007	3.8	3.4	7.3
2008	4.2	3.5	7.7
2009	4.6	4.0	8.6
2010	4.7	4.4	9.1
2011	4.5	4.2	8.8
2012	4.2	3.8	8.0
2013	3.8	3.5	7.3
2014	3.5	3.4	6.8

Sources: Congressional Budget Office; Office of Management and Budget.

Table G-5.

Mandatory Outlays Since 1965

	Social Security	Medicare[a]	Medicaid	Income Security[b]	Other Retirement and Disability	Other Programs	Offsetting Receipts	Total	Memorandum: Major Health Care Programs (Net)[c]
					In Billions of Dollars				
1965	17.1	0	0.3	5.4	7.9	9.0	-7.9	31.8	0.3
1966	20.3	0	0.8	5.1	8.4	8.8	-8.4	35.0	0.8
1967	21.3	3.2	1.2	5.1	9.3	10.9	-10.2	40.7	3.7
1968	23.3	5.1	1.8	5.9	10.1	13.4	-10.6	49.1	6.2
1969	26.7	6.3	2.3	6.5	11.1	11.8	-11.0	53.6	7.7
1970	29.6	6.8	2.7	8.2	12.4	12.8	-11.5	61.0	8.6
1971	35.1	7.5	3.4	13.4	14.5	13.0	-14.1	72.8	9.6
1972	39.4	8.4	4.6	16.4	16.2	15.8	-14.1	86.7	11.6
1973	48.2	9.0	4.6	14.5	18.5	21.3	-18.0	98.0	12.2
1974	55.0	10.7	5.8	17.4	20.9	21.1	-21.2	109.7	14.8
1975	63.6	14.1	6.8	28.9	26.4	29.6	-18.3	151.1	19.1
1976	72.7	16.9	8.6	37.6	27.7	25.6	-19.6	169.5	23.6
1977	83.7	20.8	9.9	34.6	31.2	23.6	-21.5	182.2	28.5
1978	92.4	24.3	10.7	32.1	33.9	34.0	-22.8	204.6	32.5
1979	102.6	28.2	12.4	32.2	38.7	32.9	-25.6	221.4	37.9
1980	117.1	34.0	14.0	44.3	44.4	37.5	-29.2	262.1	45.0
1981	137.9	41.3	16.8	49.9	50.8	42.6	-37.9	301.6	54.8
1982	153.9	49.2	17.4	53.2	55.0	42.1	-36.0	334.8	62.7
1983	168.5	55.5	19.0	64.0	58.0	45.5	-45.3	365.2	70.2
1984	176.1	61.1	20.1	51.7	59.8	36.7	-44.2	361.3	76.1
1985	186.4	69.7	22.7	52.3	61.0	56.2	-47.1	401.1	86.7
1986	196.5	74.2	25.0	54.2	63.4	48.4	-45.9	415.8	93.4
1987	205.1	79.9	27.4	55.0	66.5	40.2	-52.9	421.2	100.8
1988	216.8	85.7	30.5	57.3	71.1	43.7	-56.8	448.2	107.4
1989	230.4	93.2	34.6	62.9	57.3	67.6	-60.1	485.9	117.3
1990	246.5	107.0	41.1	68.7	60.0	102.2	-57.5	568.1	136.9
1991	266.8	114.2	52.5	86.9	64.4	117.1	-105.5	596.5	154.6
1992	285.2	129.4	67.8	110.8	66.5	58.0	-69.3	648.4	184.0
1993	302.0	143.2	75.8	117.1	68.3	30.4	-65.9	670.9	203.7
1994	316.9	159.6	82.0	116.1	72.3	39.1	-68.5	717.5	223.9
1995	333.3	177.1	89.1	116.6	75.2	26.2	-78.7	738.8	246.0
1996	347.1	191.3	92.0	121.6	77.3	28.4	-70.9	786.7	263.3
1997	362.3	207.9	95.6	122.5	80.5	26.8	-85.4	810.1	283.0
1998	376.1	211.0	101.2	122.1	82.5	49.8	-83.5	859.3	291.5
1999	387.0	209.3	108.0	129.0	85.3	60.8	-79.4	900.0	296.3
2000	406.0	216.0	117.9	133.9	87.8	70.6	-81.0	951.4	313.3
2001	429.4	237.9	129.4	143.1	92.7	64.4	-89.2	1,007.6	347.1
2002	452.1	253.7	147.5	180.3	96.1	66.6	-90.3	1,106.0	378.9
2003	470.5	274.2	160.7	196.2	99.8	82.1	-100.9	1,182.5	410.8
2004	491.5	297.0	176.2	190.6	103.6	87.4	-108.9	1,237.5	445.7
2005	518.7	335.1	181.7	196.9	109.7	105.9	-128.7	1,319.4	481.2
2006	543.9	376.8	180.6	200.0	113.1	141.6	-144.3	1,411.8	511.0
2007	581.4	436.1	190.6	203.1	122.4	94.2	-177.9	1,450.0	567.4
2008	612.1	456.0	201.4	260.7	128.9	121.3	-185.4	1,594.9	594.1
2009	677.7	499.9	250.9	350.2	137.7	371.4	-194.6	2,093.2	683.6
2010	700.8	520.5	272.8	437.3	138.4	40.5	-196.5	1,913.7	727.1
2011	724.9	559.6	275.0	404.1	144.2	127.2	-209.0	2,026.0	763.5
2012	767.7	551.2	250.5	353.6	143.5	192.2	-228.3	2,030.5	725.8
2013	807.8	585.2	265.4	339.5	152.5	185.9	-304.8	2,031.6	767.6
2014	844.9	599.9	301.5	311.1	163.9	151.3	-276.3	2,096.3	831.1

Continued

Table G-5.

Mandatory Outlays Since 1965

Continued

	Social Security	Medicare[a]	Medicaid	Income Security[b]	Other Retirement and Disability	Other Programs	Offsetting Receipts	Total	Memorandum: Major Health Care Programs (Net)[c]
				As a Percentage of Gross Domestic Product					
1965	2.4	0	*	0.8	1.1	1.3	-1.1	4.5	*
1966	2.6	0	0.1	0.7	1.1	1.1	-1.1	4.5	0.1
1967	2.5	0.4	0.1	0.6	1.1	1.3	-1.2	4.9	0.4
1968	2.6	0.6	0.2	0.7	1.1	1.5	-1.2	5.5	0.7
1969	2.7	0.6	0.2	0.7	1.1	1.2	-1.1	5.5	0.8
1970	2.8	0.6	0.3	0.8	1.2	1.2	-1.1	5.8	0.8
1971	3.1	0.7	0.3	1.2	1.3	1.2	-1.3	6.5	0.9
1972	3.2	0.7	0.4	1.3	1.3	1.3	-1.2	7.1	1.0
1973	3.6	0.7	0.3	1.1	1.4	1.6	-1.3	7.2	0.9
1974	3.7	0.7	0.4	1.2	1.4	1.4	-1.4	7.4	1.0
1975	3.9	0.9	0.4	1.8	1.6	1.8	-1.1	9.4	1.2
1976	4.1	0.9	0.5	2.1	1.5	1.4	-1.1	9.5	1.3
1977	4.1	1.0	0.5	1.7	1.5	1.2	-1.1	9.0	1.4
1978	4.1	1.1	0.5	1.4	1.5	1.5	-1.0	9.0	1.4
1979	4.0	1.1	0.5	1.3	1.5	1.3	-1.0	8.6	1.5
1980	4.2	1.2	0.5	1.6	1.6	1.3	-1.0	9.4	1.6
1981	4.4	1.3	0.5	1.6	1.6	1.4	-1.2	9.6	1.7
1982	4.6	1.5	0.5	1.6	1.7	1.3	-1.1	10.1	1.9
1983	4.8	1.6	0.5	1.8	1.6	1.3	-1.3	10.3	2.0
1984	4.5	1.5	0.5	1.3	1.5	0.9	-1.1	9.1	1.9
1985	4.4	1.6	0.5	1.2	1.4	1.3	-1.1	9.4	2.0
1986	4.3	1.6	0.6	1.2	1.4	1.1	-1.0	9.2	2.1
1987	4.3	1.7	0.6	1.2	1.4	0.8	-1.1	8.8	2.1
1988	4.2	1.7	0.6	1.1	1.4	0.8	-1.1	8.7	2.1
1989	4.1	1.7	0.6	1.1	1.0	1.2	-1.1	8.7	2.1
1990	4.2	1.8	0.7	1.2	1.0	1.7	-1.0	9.6	2.3
1991	4.4	1.9	0.9	1.4	1.1	1.9	-1.7	9.8	2.5
1992	4.4	2.0	1.1	1.7	1.0	0.9	-1.1	10.1	2.9
1993	4.4	2.1	1.1	1.7	1.0	0.4	-1.0	9.9	3.0
1994	4.4	2.2	1.1	1.6	1.0	0.5	-1.0	10.0	3.1
1995	4.4	2.3	1.2	1.5	1.0	0.3	-1.0	9.7	3.2
1996	4.4	2.4	1.2	1.5	1.0	0.4	-0.9	9.9	3.3
1997	4.3	2.5	1.1	1.4	0.9	0.3	-1.0	9.5	3.3
1998	4.2	2.4	1.1	1.4	0.9	0.6	-0.9	9.6	3.3
1999	4.1	2.2	1.1	1.4	0.9	0.6	-0.8	9.5	3.1
2000	4.0	2.1	1.2	1.3	0.9	0.7	-0.8	9.4	3.1
2001	4.1	2.3	1.2	1.4	0.9	0.6	-0.8	9.5	3.3
2002	4.2	2.3	1.4	1.7	0.9	0.6	-0.8	10.2	3.5
2003	4.2	2.4	1.4	1.7	0.9	0.7	-0.9	10.4	3.6
2004	4.1	2.5	1.5	1.6	0.9	0.7	-0.9	10.2	3.7
2005	4.0	2.6	1.4	1.5	0.9	0.8	-1.0	10.2	3.7
2006	4.0	2.8	1.3	1.5	0.8	1.0	-1.1	10.3	3.7
2007	4.1	3.0	1.3	1.4	0.9	0.7	-1.2	10.1	4.0
2008	4.1	3.1	1.4	1.8	0.9	0.8	-1.3	10.8	4.0
2009	4.7	3.5	1.7	2.4	1.0	2.6	-1.4	14.5	4.7
2010	4.7	3.5	1.8	3.0	0.9	0.3	-1.3	12.9	4.9
2011	4.7	3.6	1.8	2.6	0.9	0.8	-1.4	13.2	5.0
2012	4.8	3.4	1.6	2.2	0.9	1.2	-1.4	12.7	4.5
2013	4.9	3.5	1.6	2.0	0.9	1.1	-1.8	12.3	4.6
2014	4.9	3.5	1.7	1.8	1.0	0.9	-1.6	12.2	4.8

Sources: Congressional Budget Office; Office of Management and Budget.

Note: * = between zero and 0.05 percent.

a. Excludes offsetting receipts.

b. Includes unemployment compensation, Supplemental Security Income, the refundable portion of the earned income and child tax credits, the Supplemental Nutrition Assistance Program, family support, child nutrition, and foster care.

c. Spending on Medicare (net of offsetting receipts), Medicaid, the Children's Health Insurance Program, and subsidies for health insurance purchased through exchanges and related spending.

List of Tables and Figures

Tables

Figures

About This Document

This volume is one of a series of reports on the state of the budget and the economy that the Congressional Budget Office issues each year. It satisfies the requirement of section 202(e) of the Congressional Budget Act of 1974 for CBO to submit to the Committees on the Budget periodic reports about fiscal policy and to provide baseline projections of the federal budget. In keeping with CBO's mandate to provide objective, impartial analysis, this report makes no recommendations.

CBO's Panel of Economic Advisers commented on an early version of the economic forecast underlying this report. Members of the panel are Rosanne Altshuler, Alan J. Auerbach, Markus K. Brunnermeier, Mary C. Daly, Steven J. Davis, Roger W. Ferguson Jr., Claudia Goldin, Robert E. Hall, Jan Hatzius, Simon Johnson, Anil Kashyap, Lawrence Katz, Donald Kohn, N. Gregory Mankiw, Adam S. Posen, James Poterba, Joel Prakken, Valerie A. Ramey, Carmen M. Reinhart, Brian Sack, Robert Shimer, Justin Wolfers, and Mark Zandi. John Fernald and Erica Groshen attended the panel's meeting as guests. Although CBO's outside advisers provided considerable assistance, they are not responsible for the contents of this report.

The CBO staff members who contributed to this report—by preparing the economic, revenue, and spending projections; writing the report; reviewing, editing, and publishing it; compiling the supplemental materials posted along with it on CBO's website (www.cbo.gov/publication/49892); and providing other support—are listed on the following pages.

Douglas W. Elmendorf
Director

January 2015

Economic Projections

The economic projections were prepared by the Macroeconomic Analysis Division, with contributions from analysts in other divisions. That work was supervised by Wendy Edelberg, Kim Kowalewski, Robert Arnold, and Benjamin Page.

Alexander Arnon	Housing, research assistance
Lauren Bresnahan	Inflation
Gabriel Ehrlich	Interest rates, monetary policy, house prices
Daniel Fried	Net exports, exchange rates, energy prices
Edward Gamber	Current quarter analysis
Ronald Gecan	Energy prices
Mark Lasky	Business investment, housing
Leah Loversky	Motor vehicle sector, model and data management
Joshua Montes	Labor markets
Frank Russek	Federal, state, and local government spending and revenues
Robert Shackleton	Potential output, productivity
Christopher Williams	Consumer spending, incomes
Shiqi Zheng	Research assistance

Revenue Projections

The revenue projections were prepared by the Tax Analysis Division, supervised by David Weiner, Mark Booth, Edward Harris, and Janet Holtzblatt. In addition, the staff of the Joint Committee on Taxation provided valuable assistance.

Paul Burnham	Retirement income
Nathaniel Frentz	Federal Reserve System earnings, customs duties, miscellaneous fees and fines
Jennifer Gravelle	International taxation, depreciation
Pamela Greene	Corporate income taxes
Robert McClelland	Capital gains realizations
Shannon Mok	Estate and gift taxes, refundable tax credits
Kevin Perese	Tax modeling, Federal Reserve System earnings
Molly Saunders-Scott	International taxation, business taxation
Kurt Seibert	Payroll taxes, depreciation, tax modeling
Joshua Shakin	Individual income taxes, refundable tax credits
Logan Timmerhoff	Excise taxes
Marvin Ward	Tax modeling

Spending Projections

The spending projections were prepared by the Budget Analysis Division, with contributions from analysts in other divisions; that work was supervised by Peter Fontaine, Theresa Gullo, Holly Harvey, Janet Airis, Tom Bradley, Kim Cawley, Chad Chirico, Jeffrey Holland, Sarah Jennings, and Sam Papenfuss of the Budget Analysis Division, as well as by Jessica Banthin of the Health, Retirement, and Long-Term Analysis Division and Damien Moore of the Financial Analysis Division.

Defense, International Affairs, and Veterans' Affairs

Kent Christensen	Defense (projections, working capital funds, operation and maintenance, procurement, scorekeeping)
Sunita D'Monte	International affairs
Ann Futrell	Veterans' health care, international food assistance
Raymond Hall	Defense (research and development, stockpile sales, atomic energy, other programs)
William Ma	Veterans' readjustment benefits, reservists' education benefits
David Newman	Defense (military construction and family housing, military activities in Afghanistan), veterans' housing
Dawn Sauter Regan	Defense (military personnel)
Matthew Schmit	Military retirement, military health care
Jason Wheelock	Defense (operation and maintenance, procurement, compensation for radiation exposure and energy employees' occupational illness, other defense programs)
Dwayne Wright	Veterans' compensation and pensions

Health

Julia Christensen	Food and Drug Administration, prescription drugs
Kate Fritzsche	Health insurance exchanges, other programs
Daniel Hoople	Medicaid, Children's Health Insurance Program
Lori Housman	Medicare
Paul Jacobs	Health insurance coverage
Sean Lyons	Health insurance coverage
Paul Masi	Medicare, Federal Employees Health Benefits program
Sarah Masi	Health insurance exchanges, other programs
Jamease Miles	Medicare, Public Health Service
Alexandra Minicozzi	Health insurance coverage
Eamon Molloy	Health insurance coverage
Andrea Noda	Medicaid prescription drugs, long-term care, Public Health Service
Romain Parsad	Health insurance coverage

Health (Continued)

Allison Percy	Health insurance coverage
Lisa Ramirez-Branum	Medicaid, health insurance coverage, Health Resources and Services Administration
Lara Robillard	Medicare
Erica Socker	Medicare
Robert Stewart	Medicaid, Children's Health Insurance Program, Indian Health Service
Sam Trachtman	Health insurance coverage
Ellen Werble	Prescription drugs, Public Health Service
Zoe Williams	Medicare
Rebecca Yip	Medicare Part D, prescription drugs, Public Health Service

Income Security and Education

Christina Hawley Anthony	Unemployment insurance, training programs, Administration on Aging, Smithsonian Institution, arts and humanities
Sheila Dacey	Old-Age and Survivors Insurance, Social Security trust funds, Pension Benefit Guaranty Corporation
Elizabeth Cove Delisle	Housing assistance
Kathleen FitzGerald	Supplemental Nutrition Assistance Program and other nutrition programs
Jennifer Gray	Social Services Block Grant, Child and Family Services, child nutrition and other nutrition programs
Justin Humphrey	Elementary and secondary education, Pell grants, student loans
Deborah Kalcevic	Student loans, higher education
David Rafferty	Temporary Assistance for Needy Families, Child Support Enforcement, foster care, child care programs, Low Income Home Energy Assistance Program, refugee assistance
Emily Stern	Disability Insurance, Supplemental Security Income

Natural and Physical Resources

Marin Burnett	Administration of justice, science and space exploration, recreational resources
Megan Carroll	Energy, air transportation

Natural and Physical Resources (Continued)

Martin von Gnechten	Community and regional development, Federal Emergency Management Agency, Bureau of Indian Affairs, credit unions
Mark Grabowicz	Administration of justice, Postal Service
Kathleen Gramp	Energy, Outer Continental Shelf receipts, spectrum auction receipts, Orderly Liquidation Fund
David Hull	Agriculture
Jeff LaFave	Conservation and land management, other natural resources
James Langley	Agriculture
Susanne Mehlman	Pollution control and abatement, Federal Housing Administration and other housing credit programs
Matthew Pickford	General government, legislative branch
Sarah Puro	Highways, mass transit, Amtrak, water transportation
Aurora Swanson	Water resources, Fannie Mae and Freddie Mac
Susan Willie	Commerce, Small Business Administration, Universal Service Fund, agricultural trade and credit

Other Areas and Functions

Janet Airis	Appropriation bill (Legislative Branch)
Shane Beaulieu	Computer support
Barry Blom	Federal pay, monthly Treasury data
Joanna Capps	Appropriation bills (Labor, Health and Human Services, and Education; State and Foreign Operations)
Gabriel Ehrlich	Fannie Mae and Freddie Mac, Federal Housing Administration
Mary Froehlich	Computer support
Avi Lerner	Troubled Asset Relief Program, automatic budget enforcement and sequestration, interest on the public debt, other interest, Federal Deposit Insurance Corporation
Amber Marcellino	Federal civilian retirement, historical data
Virginia Myers	Appropriation bills (Commerce, Justice, and Science; Financial Services and General Government)
Jeffrey Perry	Fannie Mae and Freddie Mac, Federal Housing Administration
Dan Ready	Various federal retirement programs, national income and product accounts, federal pay

THE BUDGET AND ECONOMIC OUTLOOK: 2015 TO 2025 **177**

Other Areas and Functions (Continued)

Mitchell Remy	Fannie Mae and Freddie Mac, Federal Housing Administration
Mark Sanford	Appropriation bills (Agriculture and Food and Drug Administration; Defense)
Esther Steinbock	Appropriation bills (Transportation and Housing and Urban Development; Military Construction and Veterans Affairs; Energy and Water Development)
J'nell Blanco Suchy	Authorization bills
Patrice Watson	Database system administrator
Adam Wilson	Appropriation bills (Homeland Security; Interior)

Writing

Christina Hawley Anthony wrote the summary. Barry Blom wrote Chapter 1, with assistance from Mark Booth and Jeffrey Holland. Daniel Fried and Charles Whalen wrote Chapter 2. Christina Hawley Anthony, Megan Carroll, Avi Lerner, and Amber Marcellino wrote Chapter 3. Mark Booth, Pamela Greene, Joshua Shakin, and David Weiner wrote Chapter 4. Amber Marcellino wrote Appendix A, with assistance from Nathaniel Frentz. Sarah Masi and Kate Fritzsche wrote Appendix B, with assistance from Jessica Banthin, Holly Harvey, and Chad Chirico. Dan Ready wrote Appendix C, with assistance from Nathaniel Frentz. Frank Russek wrote Appendix D; Jeffrey Holland wrote Appendix E. Shiqi Zheng compiled Appendix F, and Amber Marcellino compiled Appendix G.

Review, Editing, and Publishing

Jeffrey Kling and Robert Sunshine reviewed the report. The editing and publishing were handled by CBO's editing and publishing group, supervised by John Skeen, and the agency's web team, supervised by Deborah Kilroe.

Christine Bogusz, Kate Kelly, Loretta Lettner, Bo Peery, Benjamin Plotinsky, Jeanine Rees, and John Skeen edited the report; Leigh Angres, Maureen Costantino, and Jeanine Rees prepared it for publication; and Robert Dean, Annette Kalicki, Adam Russell, and Simone Thomas published it on CBO's website.

Sarah Puro coordinated the preparation of tables of baseline projections for selected programs, and Leah Loversky and Logan Timmerhoff compiled supplemental economic and tax data—all posted with this report on the agency's website. Jeanine Rees and Simone Thomas coordinated the presentation of those materials.

www.ingramcontent.com/pod-product-compliance
Lightning Source LLC
Chambersburg PA
CBHW080808180526
45168CB00006B/2369